THE DESIGN OF THE UNIX® OPERATING SYSTEM

Maurice J. Bach

Prentice/Hall International, Inc.

Published by Prentice-Hall, Inc.
A division of Simon & Schuster
Englewood Cliffs, New Jersey 07632

Prentice-Hall Software Series
Brian W. Kernighan, Advisor

UNIX® is a registered trademark of AT&T.
DEC, PDP, and VAX are trademarks of Digital Equipment Corp.
Series 32000 is a trademark of National Semiconductor Corp.
®Ada is a registered trademark of the U.S. Government (Ada Joint Program Office).
UNIVAC is a trademark of Sperry Corp.
This document was set on an AUTOLOGIC, Inc. APS-5 phototypesetter driven by the
TROFF formatter operating under the UNIX system on an AT&T 3B20 computer.

Printed in the United States of America

10 9 8 7 6 5

ISBN 0-13-201757-1 025

Prentice-Hall International (UK) Limited, *London*
Prentice-Hall of Australia Pty. Limited, *Sydney*
Prentice-Hall Canada Inc., *Toronto*
Prentice-Hall Hispanoamericana, S.A., *Mexico*
Prentice-Hall of India Private Limited, *New Delhi*
Prentice-Hall of Japan, Inc., *Tokyo*
Prentice-Hall of Southeast Asia Pte. Ltd., *Singapore*
Editora Prentice-Hall do Brasil, Ltda., *Rio de Janeiro*
Prentice-Hall, Inc., *Englewood Cliffs, New Jersey*

To my parents, for their patience and devotion,
to my daughters, Sarah and Rachel, for their laughter,
to my son, Joseph, who arrived after the first printing,
and to my wife, Debby, for her love and understanding.

CONTENTS

PREFACE xi

CHAPTER 1 GENERAL OVERVIEW OF THE SYSTEM 1

   1.1 HISTORY 1

   1.2 SYSTEM STRUCTURE 4

   1.3 USER PERSPECTIVE 6

   1.4 OPERATING SYSTEM SERVICES 14

   1.5 ASSUMPTIONS ABOUT HARDWARE 15

   1.6 SUMMARY 18

CHAPTER 2 INTRODUCTION TO THE KERNEL 19

    2.1 ARCHITECTURE OF THE UNIX OPERATING
       SYSTEM 19

    2.2 INTRODUCTION TO SYSTEM CONCEPTS 22

    2.3 KERNEL DATA STRUCTURES 34

    2.4 SYSTEM ADMINISTRATION 34

    2.5 SUMMARY AND PREVIEW 36

    2.6 EXERCISES 37

CHAPTER 3 THE BUFFER CACHE 38

    3.1 BUFFER HEADERS 39

    3.2 STRUCTURE OF THE BUFFER POOL 40

    3.3 SCENARIOS FOR RETRIEVAL OF A BUFFER 42

    3.4 READING AND WRITING DISK BLOCKS 53

    3.5 ADVANTAGES AND DISADVANTAGES OF THE BUFFER
       CACHE 56

    3.6 SUMMARY 57

    3.7 EXERCISES 58

CHAPTER 4 INTERNAL REPRESENTATION OF FILES 60

    4.1 INODES 61

    4.2 STRUCTURE OF A REGULAR FILE 67

    4.3 DIRECTORIES 73

    4.4 CONVERSION OF A PATH NAME TO AN INODE . . . 74

    4.5 SUPER BLOCK 76

    4.6 INODE ASSIGNMENT TO A NEW FILE 77

    4.7 ALLOCATION OF DISK BLOCKS 84

    4.8 OTHER FILE TYPES 88

    4.9 SUMMARY 88

    4.10 EXERCISES 89

CHAPTER 5 SYSTEM CALLS FOR THE FILE SYSTEM 91

    5.1 OPEN 92

    5.2 READ 96

    5.3 WRITE 101

    5.4 FILE AND RECORD LOCKING 103

    5.5 ADJUSTING THE POSITION OF FILE I/O — LSEEK . . 103

    5.6 CLOSE 103

    5.7 FILE CREATION 105

    5.8 CREATION OF SPECIAL FILES 107

    5.9 CHANGE DIRECTORY AND CHANGE ROOT 109

    5.10 CHANGE OWNER AND CHANGE MODE 110

    5.11 STAT AND FSTAT 110

    5.12 PIPES 111

    5.13 DUP 117

    5.14 MOUNTING AND UNMOUNTING FILE SYSTEMS . . 119

    5.15 LINK 128

    5.16 UNLINK 132

    5.17 FILE SYSTEM ABSTRACTIONS 138

    5.18 FILE SYSTEM MAINTENANCE 139

    5.19 SUMMARY 140

    5.20 EXERCISES 140

CHAPTER 6 THE STRUCTURE OF PROCESSES 146

    6.1 PROCESS STATES AND TRANSITIONS 147

    6.2 LAYOUT OF SYSTEM MEMORY 151

    6.3 THE CONTEXT OF A PROCESS 159

    6.4 SAVING THE CONTEXT OF A PROCESS 162

    6.5 MANIPULATION OF THE PROCESS ADDRESS
         SPACE 171

    6.6 SLEEP 182

6.7 SUMMARY 188

6.8 EXERCISES 189

CHAPTER 7 PROCESS CONTROL 191

7.1 PROCESS CREATION 192

7.2 SIGNALS 200

7.3 PROCESS TERMINATION 212

7.4 AWAITING PROCESS TERMINATION 213

7.5 INVOKING OTHER PROGRAMS 217

7.6 THE USER ID OF A PROCESS 227

7.7 CHANGING THE SIZE OF A PROCESS 229

7.8 THE SHELL 232

7.9 SYSTEM BOOT AND THE INIT PROCESS 235

7.10 SUMMARY 238

7.11 EXERCISES 239

CHAPTER 8 PROCESS SCHEDULING AND TIME 247

8.1 PROCESS SCHEDULING 248

8.2 SYSTEM CALLS FOR TIME 258

8.3 CLOCK 260

8.4 SUMMARY 268

8.5 EXERCISES 268

CHAPTER 9 MEMORY MANAGEMENT POLICIES 271

9.1 SWAPPING 272

9.2 DEMAND PAGING 285

9.3 A HYBRID SYSTEM WITH SWAPPING AND DEMAND
    PAGING 307

9.4 SUMMARY 307

9.5 EXERCISES 308

CHAPTER 10 THE I/O SUBSYSTEM 312

    10.1 DRIVER INTERFACES   313

    10.2 DISK DRIVERS   325

    10.3 TERMINAL DRIVERS 329

    10.4 STREAMS   344

    10.5 SUMMARY 351

    10.6 EXERCISES   352

CHAPTER 11 INTERPROCESS COMMUNICATION   355

    11.1 PROCESS TRACING   356

    11.2 SYSTEM V IPC   359

    11.3 NETWORK COMMUNICATIONS 382

    11.4 SOCKETS   383

    11.5 SUMMARY 388

    11.6 EXERCISES   389

CHAPTER 12 MULTIPROCESSOR SYSTEMS 391

    12.1 PROBLEM OF MULTIPROCESSOR SYSTEMS   392

    12.2 SOLUTION WITH MASTER AND SLAVE
          PROCESSORS 393

    12.3 SOLUTION WITH SEMAPHORES 395

    12.4 THE TUNIS SYSTEM   410

    12.5 PERFORMANCE LIMITATIONS 410

    12.6 EXERCISES   410

CHAPTER 13 DISTRIBUTED UNIX SYSTEMS   412

    13.1 SATELLITE PROCESSORS   414

    13.2 THE NEWCASTLE CONNECTION   422

    13.3 TRANSPARENT DISTRIBUTED FILE SYSTEMS   . . . 426

    13.4 A TRANSPARENT DISTRIBUTED MODEL WITHOUT STUB
          PROCESSES   429

13.5 SUMMARY 430

13.6 EXERCISES   431

APPENDIX − SYSTEM CALLS 434

BIBLIOGRAPHY 454

INDEX 458

PREFACE

The UNIX system was first described in a 1974 paper in the Communications of the ACM [Thompson 74] by Ken Thompson and Dennis Ritchie. Since that time, it has become increasingly widespread and popular throughout the computer industry where more and more vendors are offering support for it on their machines. It is especially popular in universities where it is frequently used for operating systems research and case studies.

Many books and papers have described parts of the system, among them, two special issues of the Bell System Technical Journal in 1978 [BSTJ 78] and 1984 [BLTJ 84]. Many books describe the user level interface, particularly how to use electronic mail, how to prepare documents, or how to use the command interpreter called the shell; some books such as *The UNIX Programming Environment* [Kernighan 84] and *Advanced UNIX Programming* [Rochkind 85] describe the programming interface. This book describes the internal algorithms and structures that form the basis of the operating system (called the kernel) and their relationship to the programmer interface. It is thus applicable to several environments. First, it can be used as a textbook for an operating systems course at either the advanced undergraduate or first-year graduate level. It is most beneficial to reference the system source code when using the book, but the book can be read independently, too. Second, system programmers can use the book as a reference to gain better understanding of how the kernel works and to compare algorithms used in the UNIX system to algorithms used in other operating systems.

Finally, programmers on UNIX systems can gain a deeper understanding of how their programs interact with the system and thereby code more-efficient, sophisticated programs.

The material and organization for the book grew out of a course that I prepared and taught at AT&T Bell Laboratories during 1983 and 1984. While the course centered on reading the source code for the system, I found that understanding the code was easier once the concepts of the algorithms had been mastered. I have attempted to keep the descriptions of algorithms in this book as simple as possible, reflecting in a small way the simplicity and elegance of the system it describes. Thus, the book is not a line-by-line rendition of the system written in English; it is a description of the general flow of the various algorithms, and most important, a description of how they interact with each other. Algorithms are presented in a C-like pseudo-code to aid the reader in understanding the natural language description, and their names correspond to the procedure names in the kernel. Figures depict the relationship between various data structures as the system manipulates them. In later chapters, small C programs illustrate many system concepts as they manifest themselves to users. In the interests of space and clarity, these examples do not usually check for error conditions, something that should always be done when writing programs. I have run them on System V; except for programs that exercise features specific to System V, they should run on other versions of the system, too.

Many exercises originally prepared for the course have been included at the end of each chapter, and they are a key part of the book. Some exercises are straightforward, designed to illustrate concepts brought out in the text. Others are more difficult, designed to help the reader understand the system at a deeper level. Finally, some are exploratory in nature, designed for investigation as a research problem. Difficult exercises are marked with asterisks.

The system description is based on UNIX System V Release 2 supported by AT&T, with some new features from Release 3. This is the system with which I am most familiar, but I have tried to portray interesting contributions of other variations to the operating system, particularly those of Berkeley Software Distribution (BSD). I have avoided issues that assume particular hardware characteristics, trying to cover the kernel-hardware interface in general terms and ignoring particular machine idiosyncrasies. Where machine-specific issues are important to understand implementation of the kernel, however, I delve into the relevant detail. At the very least, examination of these topics will highlight the parts of the operating system that are the most machine dependent.

The reader must have programming experience with a high-level language and, preferably, with an assembly language as a prerequisite for understanding this book. It is recommended that the reader have experience working with the UNIX system and that the reader knows the C language [Kernighan 78]. However, I have attempted to write this book in such a way that the reader should still be able to absorb the material without such background. The appendix contains a simplified description of the system calls, sufficient to understand the presentation in the book, but not a complete reference manual.

The book is organized as follows. Chapter 1 is the introduction, giving a brief, general description of system features as perceived by the user and describing the system structure. Chapter 2 describes the general outline of the kernel architecture and presents some basic concepts. The remainder of the book follows the outline presented by the system architecture, describing the various components in a building block fashion. It can be divided into three parts: the file system, process control, and advanced topics. The file system is presented first, because its concepts are easier than those for process control. Thus, Chapter 3 describes the system buffer cache mechanism that is the foundation of the file system. Chapter 4 describes the data structures and algorithms used internally by the file system. These algorithms use the algorithms explained in Chapter 3 and take care of the internal bookkeeping needed for managing user files. Chapter 5 describes the system calls that provide the user interface to the file system; they use the algorithms in Chapter 4 to access user files.

Chapter 6 turns to the control of processes. It defines the context of a process and investigates the internal kernel primitives that manipulate the process context. In particular, it considers the system call interface, interrupt handling, and the context switch. Chapter 7 presents the system calls that control the process context. Chapter 8 deals with process scheduling, and Chapter 9 covers memory management, including swapping and paging systems.

Chapter 10 outlines general driver interfaces, with specific discussion of disk drivers and terminal drivers. Although devices are logically part of the file system, their discussion is deferred until here because of issues in process control that arise in terminal drivers. This chapter also acts as a bridge to the more advanced topics presented in the rest of the book. Chapter 11 covers interprocess communication and networking, including System V messages, shared memory and semaphores, and BSD sockets. Chapter 12 explains tightly coupled multiprocessor UNIX systems, and Chapter 13 investigates loosely coupled distributed systems.

The material in the first nine chapters could be covered in a one-semester course on operating systems, and the material in the remaining chapters could be covered in advanced seminars with various projects being done in parallel.

A few caveats must be made at this time. No attempt has been made to describe system performance in absolute terms, nor is there any attempt to suggest configuration parameters for a system installation. Such data is likely to vary according to machine type, hardware configuration, system version and implementation, and application mix. Similarly, I have made a conscious effort to avoid predicting future development of UNIX operating system features. Discussion of advanced topics does not imply a commitment by AT&T to provide particular features, nor should it even imply that particular areas are under investigation.

It is my pleasure to acknowledge the assistance of many friends and colleagues who encouraged me while I wrote this book and provided constructive criticism of the manuscript. My deepest appreciation goes to Ian Johnstone, who suggested that I write this book, gave me early encouragement, and reviewed the earliest draft of the first chapters. Ian taught me many tricks of the trade, and I will always be indebted to him. Doris Ryan also had a hand in encouraging me from the very beginning, and I will always appreciate her kindness and thoughtfulness. Dennis Ritchie freely answered numerous questions on the historical and technical background of the system. Many people gave freely of their time and energy to review drafts of the manuscript, and this book owes a lot to their detailed comments. They are Debby Bach, Doug Bayer, Lenny Brandwein, Steve Buroff, Tom Butler, Ron Gomes, Mesut Gunduc, Laura Israel, Dean Jagels, Keith Kelleman, Brian Kernighan, Bob Martin, Bob Mitze, Dave Nowitz, Michael Poppers, Marilyn Safran, Curt Schimmel, Zvi Spitz, Tom Vaden, Bill Weber, Larry Wehr, and Bob Zarrow. Mary Fruhstuck provided help in preparing the manuscript for typesetting. I would like to thank my management for their continued support throughout this project and my colleagues, for providing such a stimulating atmosphere and wonderful work environment at AT&T Bell Laboratories. John Wait and the staff at Prentice-Hall provided much valuable assitance and advice to get the book into its final form. Last, but not least, my wife, Debby, gave me lots of emotional support, without which I could never have succeeded.

1

GENERAL OVERVIEW
OF THE SYSTEM

The UNIX system has become quite popular since its inception in 1969, running on machines of varying processing power from microprocessors to mainframes and providing a common execution environment across them. The system is divided into two parts. The first part consists of programs and services that have made the UNIX system environment so popular; it is the part readily apparent to users, including such programs as the shell, mail, text processing packages, and source code control systems. The second part consists of the operating system that supports these programs and services. This book gives a detailed description of the operating system. It concentrates on a description of UNIX System V produced by AT&T but considers interesting features provided by other versions too. It examines the major data structures and algorithms used in the operating system that ultimately provide users with the standard user interface.

This chapter provides an introduction to the UNIX system. It reviews its history and outlines the overall system structure. The next chapter gives a more detailed introduction to the operating system.

1.1 HISTORY

In 1965, Bell Telephone Laboratories joined an effort with the General Electric Company and Project MAC of the Massachusetts Institute of Technology to

1

develop a new operating system called Multics [Organick 72]. The goals of the Multics system were to provide simultaneous computer access to a large community of users, to supply ample computation power and data storage, and to allow users to share their data easily, if desired. Many people who later took part in the early development of the UNIX system participated in the Multics work at Bell Laboratories. Although a primitive version of the Multics system was running on a GE 645 computer by 1969, it did not provide the general service computing for which it was intended, nor was it clear when its development goals would be met. Consequently, Bell Laboratories ended its participation in the project.

With the end of their work on the Multics project, members of the Computing Science Research Center at Bell Laboratories were left without a "convenient interactive computing service" [Ritchie 84a]. In an attempt to improve their programming environment, Ken Thompson, Dennis Ritchie, and others sketched a paper design of a file system that later evolved into an early version of the UNIX file system. Thompson wrote programs that simulated the behavior of the proposed file system and of programs in a demand-paging environment, and he even encoded a simple kernel for the GE 645 computer. At the same time, he wrote a game program, "Space Travel," in Fortran for a GECOS system (the Honeywell 635), but the program was unsatisfactory because it was difficult to control the "space ship" and the program was expensive to run. Thompson later found a little-used PDP-7 computer that provided good graphic display and cheap executing power. Programming "Space Travel" for the PDP-7 enabled Thompson to learn about the machine, but its environment for program development required cross-assembly of the program on the GECOS machine and carrying paper tape for input to the PDP-7. To create a better development environment, Thompson and Ritchie implemented their system design on the PDP-7, including an early version of the UNIX file system, the process subsystem, and a small set of utility programs. Eventually, the new system no longer needed the GECOS system as a development environment but could support itself. The new system was given the name UNIX, a pun on the name Multics coined by another member of the Computing Science Research Center, Brian Kernighan.

Although this early version of the UNIX system held much promise, it could not realize its potential until it was used in a real project. Thus, while providing a text processing system for the patent department at Bell Laboratories, the UNIX system was moved to a PDP-11 in 1971. The system was characterized by its small size: 16K bytes for the system, 8K bytes for user programs, a disk of 512K bytes, and a limit of 64K bytes per file. After its early success, Thompson set out to implement a Fortran compiler for the new system, but instead came up with the language B, influenced by BCPL [Richards 69]. B was an interpretive language with the performance drawbacks implied by such languages, so Ritchie developed it into one he called C, allowing generation of machine code, declaration of data types, and definition of data structures. In 1973, the operating system was rewritten in C, an unheard of step at the time, but one that was to have tremendous impact on its acceptance among outside users. The number of installations at Bell

Laboratories grew to about 25, and a UNIX Systems Group was formed to provide internal support.

At this time, AT&T could not market computer products because of a 1956 Consent Decree it had signed with the Federal government, but it provided the UNIX system to universities who requested it for educational purposes. AT&T neither advertised, marketed, nor supported the system, in adherence to the terms of the Consent Decree. Nevertheless, the system's popularity steadily increased. In 1974, Thompson and Ritchie published a paper describing the UNIX system in the Communications of the ACM [Thompson 74], giving further impetus to its acceptance. By 1977, the number of UNIX system sites had grown to about 500, of which 125 were in universities. UNIX systems became popular in the operating telephone companies, providing a good environment for program development, network transaction operations services, and real-time services (via MERT [Lycklama 78a]). Licenses of UNIX systems were provided to commercial institutions as well as universities. In 1977, Interactive Systems Corporation became the first Value Added Reseller (VAR)[1] of a UNIX system, enhancing it for use in office automation environments. 1977 also marked the year that the UNIX system was first "ported" to a non-PDP machine (that is, made to run on another machine with few or no changes), the Interdata 8/32.

With the growing popularity of microprocessors, other companies ported the UNIX system to new machines, but its simplicity and clarity tempted many developers to enhance it in their own way, resulting in several variants of the basic system. In the period from 1977 to 1982, Bell Laboratories combined several AT&T variants into a single system, known commercially as UNIX System III. Bell Laboratories later added several features to UNIX System III, calling the new product UNIX System V,[2] and AT&T announced official support for System V in January 1983. However, people at the University of California at Berkeley had developed a variant to the UNIX system, the most recent version of which is called 4.3 BSD for VAX machines, providing some new, interesting features. This book will concentrate on the description of UNIX System V and will occasionally talk about features provided in the BSD system.

By the beginning of 1984, there were about 100,000 UNIX system installations in the world, running on machines with a wide range of computing power from microprocessors to mainframes and on machines across different manufacturers' product lines. No other operating system can make that claim. Several reasons have been suggested for the popularity and success of the UNIX system.

---

1. Value Added Resellers add specific applications to a computer system to satisfy a particular market. They market the applications rather than the operating system upon which they run.

2. What happened to System IV? An internal version of the system evolved into System V.

- The system is written in a high-level language, making it easy to read, understand, change, and move to other machines. Ritchie estimates that the first system in C was 20 to 40 percent larger and slower because it was not written in assembly language, but the advantages of using a higher-level language far outweigh the disadvantages (see page 1965 of [Ritchie 78b]).
- It has a simple user interface that has the power to provide the services that users want.
- It provides primitives that permit complex programs to be built from simpler programs.
- It uses a hierarchical file system that allows easy maintenance and efficient implementation.
- It uses a consistent format for files, the byte stream, making application programs easier to write.
- It provides a simple, consistent interface to peripheral devices.
- It is a multi-user, multiprocess system; each user can execute several processes simultaneously.
- It hides the machine architecture from the user, making it easier to write programs that run on different hardware implementations.

The philosophy of simplicity and consistency underscores the UNIX system and accounts for many of the reasons cited above.

Although the operating system and many of the command programs are written in C, UNIX systems support other languages, including Fortran, Basic, Pascal, Ada, Cobol, Lisp, and Prolog. The UNIX system can support any language that has a compiler or interpreter and a system interface that maps user requests for operating system services to the standard set of requests used on UNIX systems.

1.2 SYSTEM STRUCTURE

Figure 1.1 depicts the high-level architecture of the UNIX system. The hardware at the center of the diagram provides the operating system with basic services that will be described in Section 1.5. The operating system interacts directly[3] with the hardware, providing common services to programs and insulating them from hardware idiosyncrasies. Viewing the system as a set of layers, the operating system is commonly called the *system kernel*, or just the kernel, emphasizing its

---

3. In some implementations of the UNIX system, the operating system interacts with a native operating system that, in turn, interacts with the underlying hardware and provides necessary services to the system. Such configurations allow installations to run other operating systems and their applications in parallel to the UNIX system. The classic example of such a configuration is the MERT system [Lycklama 78a]. More recent configurations include implementations for IBM System/370 computers [Felton 84] and for UNIVAC 1100 Series computers [Bodenstab 84].

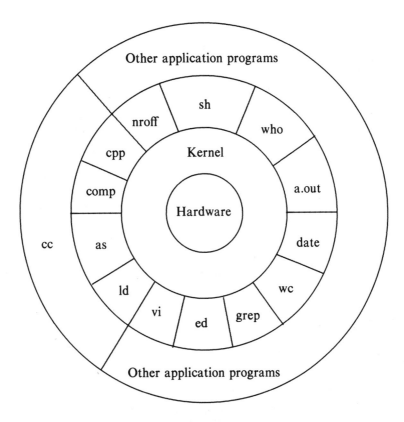

Figure 1.1. Architecture of UNIX Systems

isolation from user programs. Because programs are independent of the underlying hardware, it is easy to move them between UNIX systems running on different hardware if the programs do not make assumptions about the underlying hardware. For instance, programs that assume the size of a machine word are more difficult to move to other machines than programs that do not make this assumption.

Programs such as the shell and editors (*ed* and *vi*) shown in the outer layers interact with the kernel by invoking a well defined set of *system calls*. The system calls instruct the kernel to do various operations for the calling program and exchange data between the kernel and the program. Several programs shown in the figure are in standard system configurations and are known as *commands*, but private user programs may also exist in this layer as indicated by the program whose name is *a.out*, the standard name for executable files produced by the C compiler. Other application programs can build on top of lower-level programs, hence the existence of the outermost layer in the figure. For example, the standard C compiler, *cc*, is in the outermost layer of the figure: it invokes a C preprocessor, two-pass compiler, assembler, and loader (link-editor), all separate lower-level programs. Although the figure depicts a two-level hierarchy of application programs, users can extend the hierarchy to whatever levels are appropriate. Indeed, the style of programming favored by the UNIX system encourages the combination of existing programs to accomplish a task.

Many application subsystems and programs that provide a high-level view of the system such as the shell, editors, SCCS (Source Code Control System), and document preparation packages, have gradually become synonymous with the name "UNIX system." However, they all use lower-level services ultimately provided by the kernel, and they avail themselves of these services via the set of system calls. There are about 64 system calls in System V, of which fewer than 32 are used frequently. They have simple options that make them easy to use but provide the user with a lot of power. The set of system calls and the internal algorithms that implement them form the body of the kernel, and the study of the UNIX operating system presented in this book reduces to a detailed study and analysis of the system calls and their interaction with one another. In short, the kernel provides the services upon which all application programs in the UNIX system rely, and it defines those services. This book will frequently use the terms "UNIX system," "kernel," or "system," but the intent is to refer to the kernel of the UNIX operating system and should be clear in context.

1.3 USER PERSPECTIVE

This section briefly reviews high-level features of the UNIX system such as the file system, the processing environment, and building block primitives (for example, *pipes*). Later chapters will explore kernel support of these features in detail.

1.3.1 The File System

The UNIX file system is characterized by

- a hierarchical structure,
- consistent treatment of file data,
- the ability to create and delete files,
- dynamic growth of files,
- the protection of file data,
- the treatment of peripheral devices (such as terminals and tape units) as files.

The file system is organized as a tree with a single root node called *root* (written "/"); every non-leaf node of the file system structure is a *directory* of files, and files at the leaf nodes of the tree are either directories, *regular files*, or *special* device files. The name of a file is given by a *path name* that describes how to locate the file in the file system hierarchy. A path name is a sequence of component names separated by slash characters; a component is a sequence of characters that

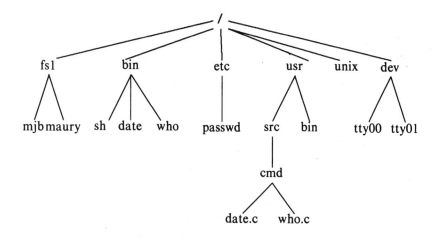

Figure 1.2. Sample File System Tree

designates a file name that is uniquely contained in the previous (directory) component. A full path name starts with a slash character and specifies a file that can be found by starting at the file system root and traversing the file tree, following the branches that lead to successive component names of the path name. Thus, the path names "/etc/passwd", "/bin/who", and "/usr/src/cmd/who.c" designate files in the tree shown in Figure 1.2, but "/bin/passwd" and "/usr/src/date.c" do not. A path name does not have to start from root but can be designated relative to the *current directory* of an executing process, by omitting the initial slash in the path name. Thus, starting from directory "/dev", the path name "tty01" designates the file whose full path name is "/dev/tty01".

Programs in the UNIX system have no knowledge of the internal format in which the kernel stores file data, treating the data as an unformatted stream of bytes. Programs may interpret the byte stream as they wish, but the interpretation has no bearing on how the operating system stores the data. Thus, the syntax of accessing the data in a file is defined by the system and is identical for all programs, but the semantics of the data are imposed by the program. For example, the text formatting program *troff* expects to find "new-line" characters at the end of each line of text, and the system accounting program *acctcom* expects to find fixed length records. Both programs use the same system services to access the data in the file as a byte stream, and internally, they parse the stream into a suitable format. If either program discovers that the format is incorrect, it is responsible for taking the appropriate action.

Directories are like regular files in this respect; the system treats the data in a directory as a byte stream, but the data contains the names of the files in the directory in a predictable format so that the operating system and programs such as *ls* (list the names and attributes of files) can discover the files in a directory.

Permission to access a file is controlled by *access permissions* associated with the file. Access permissions can be set independently to control read, write, and execute permission for three classes of users: the file owner, a file group, and everyone else. Users may create files if directory access permissions allow it. The newly created files are leaf nodes of the file system directory structure.

To the user, the UNIX system treats devices as if they were files. Devices, designated by special device files, occupy node positions in the file system directory structure. Programs access devices with the same syntax they use when accessing regular files; the semantics of reading and writing devices are to a large degree the same as reading and writing regular files. Devices are protected in the same way that regular files are protected: by proper setting of their (file) access permissions. Because device names look like the names of regular files and because the same operations work for devices and regular files, most programs do not have to know internally the types of files they manipulate.

For example, consider the C program in Figure 1.3, which makes a new copy of an existing file. Suppose the name of the executable version of the program is *copy*. A user at a terminal invokes the program by typing

    copy oldfile newfile

where *oldfile* is the name of the existing file and *newfile* is the name of the new file. The system invokes *main*, supplying *argc* as the number of parameters in the list *argv*, and initializing each member of the array *argv* to point to a user-supplied parameter. In the example above, *argc* is 3, *argv[0]* points to the character string *copy* (the program name is conventionally the 0th parameter), *argv[1]* points to the character string *oldfile*, and *argv[2]* points to the character string *newfile*. The program then checks that it has been invoked with the proper number of parameters. If so, it invokes the *open* system call "read-only" for the file *oldfile*, and if the system call succeeds, invokes the *creat* system call to create *newfile*. The permission modes on the newly created file will be 0666 (octal), allowing all users access to the file for reading and writing. All system calls return −1 on failure; if the *open* or *creat* calls fail, the program prints a message and calls the *exit* system call with return status 1, terminating its execution and indicating that something went wrong.

The *open* and *creat* system calls return an integer called a *file descriptor*, which the program uses for subsequent references to the files. The program then calls the subroutine *copy*, which goes into a loop, invoking the *read* system call to read a buffer's worth of characters from the existing file, and invoking the *write* system call to write the data to the new file. The *read* system call returns the number of bytes read, returning 0 when it reaches the end of file. The program finishes the loop when it encounters the end of file, or when there is some error on the *read* system call (it does not check for *write* errors). Then it returns from *copy* and *exits* with return status 0, indicating that the program completed successfully.

```
#include  <fcntl.h>
char buffer[2048];
int version = 1;        /* Chapter 2 explains this */

main(argc, argv)
      int argc;
      char *argv[];
{
      int fdold, fdnew;

      if (argc != 3)
      {
            printf("need 2 arguments for copy program\n");
            exit(1);
      }
      fdold = open(argv[1], O_RDONLY);   /* open source file read only */
      if (fdold == -1)
      {
            printf("cannot open file %s\n", argv[1]);
            exit(1);
      }
      fdnew = creat(argv[2], 0666);   /* create target file rw for all */
      if (fdnew == -1)
      {
            printf("cannot create file %s\n", argv[2]);
            exit(1);
      }
      copy(fdold, fdnew);
      exit(0);
}

copy(old, new)
      int old, new;
{
      int count;

      while ((count = read(old, buffer, sizeof(buffer))) > 0)
            write(new, buffer, count);
}
```

Figure 1.3. Program to Copy a File

The program copies any files supplied to it as arguments, provided it has permission to *open* the existing file and permission to create the new file. The file can be a file of printable characters, such as the source code for the program, or it can contain unprintable characters, even the program itself. Thus, the two invocations

    copy copy.c newcopy.c
    copy copy newcopy

both work. The old file can also be a directory. For instance,

    copy . dircontents

copies the contents of the current directory, denoted by the name ".", to a regular file, "dircontents"; the data in the new file is identical, byte for byte, to the contents of the directory, but the file is a regular file. (The system call *mknod* creates a new directory.) Finally, either file can be a device special file. For example,

    copy /dev/tty terminalread

reads the characters typed at the terminal (the special file *ldev/tty* is the user's terminal) and copies them to the file *terminalread*, terminating only when the user types the character control-d. Similarly,

    copy /dev/tty /dev/tty

reads characters typed at the terminal and copies them back.

1.3.2 Processing Environment

A *program* is an executable file, and a *process* is an instance of the program in execution. Many processes can execute simultaneously on UNIX systems (this feature is sometimes called multiprogramming or multitasking) with no logical limit to their number, and many instances of a program (such as *copy*) can exist simultaneously in the system. Various system calls allow processes to create new processes, terminate processes, synchronize stages of process execution, and control reaction to various events. Subject to their use of system calls, processes execute independently of each other.

    For example, a process executing the program in Figure 1.4 executes the *fork* system call to create a new process. The new process, called the *child* process, gets a 0 return value from *fork* and invokes *execl* to execute the program *copy* (the program in Figure 1.3). The *execl* call overlays the address space of the child process with the file "copy", assumed to be in the current directory, and runs the program with the user-supplied parameters. If the *execl* call succeeds, it never returns because the process executes in a new address space, as will be seen in Chapter 7. Meanwhile, the process that had invoked *fork* (the parent) receives a non-0 return from the call, calls *wait*, suspending its execution until *copy* finishes, prints the message "copy done," and *exits* (every program *exits* at the end of its *main* function, as arranged by standard C program libraries that are linked during the compilation process). For example, if the name of the executable program is *run*, and a user invokes the program by

```
main(argc, argv)
     int argc;
     char *argv[];
{

     /* assume 2 args:  source file and target file */
     if (fork() == 0)
          execl("copy", "copy", argv[1], argv[2], 0);
     wait((int *) 0);
     printf("copy done\n");
}
```

Figure 1.4. Program that Creates a New Process to Copy Files

      run oldfile newfile

the process copies "oldfile" to "newfile" and prints out the message. Although this program adds little to the "copy" program, it exhibits four major system calls used for process control: *fork*, *exec*, *wait*, and, discreetly, *exit*.

Generally, the system calls allow users to write programs that do sophisticated operations, and as a result, the kernel of the UNIX system does not contain many functions that are part of the "kernel" in other systems. Such functions, including compilers and editors, are user-level programs in the UNIX system. The prime example of such a program is the *shell*, the command interpreter program that users typically execute after logging into the system. The shell interprets the first word of a *command line* as a *command* name: for many commands, the shell *forks* and the child process *execs* the command associated with the name, treating the remaining words on the command line as parameters to the command.

The shell allows three types of commands. First, a command can be an executable file that contains object code produced by compilation of source code (a C program for example). Second, a command can be an executable file that contains a sequence of shell command lines. Finally, a command can be an internal shell command (instead of an executable file). The internal commands make the shell a programming language in addition to a command interpreter and include commands for looping (*for-in-do-done* and *while-do-done*), commands for conditional execution (*if-then-else-fi*), a "case" statement command, a command to change the current directory of a process (*cd*), and several others. The shell syntax allows for pattern matching and parameter processing. Users execute commands without having to know their types.

The shell searches for commands in a given sequence of directories, changeable by user request per invocation of the shell. The shell usually executes a command synchronously, waiting for the command to terminate before reading the next command line. However, it also allows asynchronous execution, where it reads the next command line and executes it without waiting for the prior command to terminate. Commands executed asynchronously are said to execute in the *background*. For example, typing the command

who

causes the system to execute the program stored in the file */bin/who*,[4] which prints a list of people who are currently logged in to the system. While *who* executes, the shell waits for it to finish and then prompts the user for another command. By typing

who &

the system executes the program *who* in the background, and the shell is ready to accept another command immediately.

Every process executing in the UNIX system has an execution environment that includes a current directory. The current directory of a process is the start directory used for all path names that do not begin with the slash character. The user may execute the shell command *cd*, change directory, to move around the file system tree and change the current directory. The command line

cd /usr/src/uts

changes the shell's current directory to the directory "/usr/src/uts". The command line

cd ../..

changes the shell's current directory to the directory that is two nodes "closer" to the root node: the component ".." refers to the *parent directory* of the current directory.

Because the shell is a user program and not part of the kernel, it is easy to modify it and tailor it to a particular environment. For instance, users can use the C shell to provide a history mechanism and avoid retyping recently used commands, instead of the Bourne shell (named after its inventor, Steve Bourne), provided as part of the standard System V release. Or some users may be granted use only of a restricted shell, providing a scaled down version of the regular shell. The system can execute the various shells simultaneously. Users have the capability to execute many processes simultaneously, and processes can create other processes dynamically and synchronize their execution, if desired. These features provide users with a powerful execution environment. Although much of the power of the shell derives from its capabilities as a programming language and from its capabilities for pattern matching of arguments, this section concentrates on the process environment provided by the system via the shell. Other important shell

---

4. The directory "/bin" contains many useful commands and is usually included in the sequence of directories the shell searches.

features are beyond the scope of this book (see [Bourne 78] for a detailed description of the shell).

1.3.3 Building Block Primitives

As described earlier, the philosophy of the UNIX system is to provide operating system primitives that enable users to write small, modular programs that can be used as building blocks to build more complex programs. One such primitive visible to shell users is the capability to *redirect I/O*. Processes conventionally have access to three files: they read from their *standard input* file, write to their *standard output* file, and write error messages to their *standard error* file. Processes executing at a terminal typically use the terminal for these three files, but each may be "redirected" independently. For instance, the command line

     ls

lists all files in the current directory on the standard output, but the command line

     ls > output

redirects the standard output to the file called "output" in the current directory, using the *creat* system call mentioned above. Similarly, the command line

     mail mjb < letter

*open*s the file "letter" for its standard intput and *mail*s its contents to the user named "mjb." Processes can redirect input and output simultaneously, as in

     nroff −mm < doc1 > doc1.out 2> errors

where the text formatter *nroff* reads the input file *doc1*, redirects its standard output to the file *doc1.out*, and redirects error messages to the file *errors* (the notation "2>" means to redirect the output for file descriptor 2, conventionally the standard error). The programs *ls*, *mail*, and *nroff* do not know what file their standard input, standard output, or standard error will be; the shell recognizes the symbols "<", ">", and "2>" and sets up the standard input, standard output, and standard error appropriately before executing the processes.

The second building block primitive is the *pipe*, a mechanism that allows a stream of data to be passed between reader and writer processes. Processes can redirect their standard output to a pipe to be read by other processes that have redirected their standard input to come from the pipe. The data that the first processes write into the pipe is the input for the second processes. The second processes could also redirect their output, and so on, depending on programming need. Again, the processes need not know what type of file their standard output is; they work regardless of whether their standard output is a regular file, a pipe, or a device. When using the smaller programs as building blocks for a larger, more complex program, the programmer uses the pipe primitive and redirection of I/O to integrate the piece parts. Indeed, the system tacitly encourages such programming style so that new programs can work with existing programs.

For example, the program *grep* searches a set of files (parameters to grep) for a given pattern:

grep main a.c b.c c.c

searches the three files a.c, b.c, and c.c for lines containing the string "main" and prints the lines that it finds onto standard output. Sample output may be:

a.c: main(argc, argv)
c.c: /* here is the main loop in the program */
c.c: main()

The program *wc* with the option −l counts the number of lines in the standard input file. The command line

grep main a.c b.c c.c | wc −l

counts the number of lines in the files that contain the string "main"; the output from *grep* is "piped" directly into the *wc* command. For the previous sample output from *grep*, the output from the piped command is

3

The use of pipes frequently makes it unnecessary to create temporary files.

1.4 OPERATING SYSTEM SERVICES

Figure 1.1 depicts the kernel layer immediately below the layer of user application programs. The kernel performs various primitive operations on behalf of user processes to support the user interface described above. Among the services provided by the kernel are

- Controlling the execution of processes by allowing their creation, termination or suspension, and communication
- Scheduling processes fairly for execution on the CPU. Processes share the CPU in a *time-shared* manner: the CPU[5] executes a process, the kernel suspends it when its time quantum elapses, and the kernel schedules another process to execute. The kernel later reschedules the suspended process.
- Allocating main memory for an executing process. The kernel allows processes to share portions of their address space under certain conditions, but protects the private address space of a process from outside tampering. If the system runs low on free memory, the kernel frees memory by writing a process

---

5. Chapter 12 will consider multiprocessor systems; until then, assume a single processor model.

temporarily to secondary memory, called a *swap* device. If the kernel writes entire processes to a swap device, the implementation of the UNIX system is called a *swapping* system; if it writes pages of memory to a swap device, it is called a *paging* system.

- Allocating secondary memory for efficient storage and retrieval of user data. This service constitutes the file system. The kernel allocates secondary storage for user files, reclaims unused storage, structures the file system in a well understood manner, and protects user files from illegal access.
- Allowing processes controlled access to peripheral devices such as terminals, tape drives, disk drives, and network devices.

The kernel provides its services transparently. For example, it recognizes that a given file is a regular file or a device, but hides the distinction from user processes. Similarly, it formats data in a file for internal storage, but hides the internal format from user processes, returning an unformatted byte stream. Finally, it offers necessary services so that user-level processes can support the services they must provide, while omitting services that can be implemented at the user level. For example, the kernel supports the services that the shell needs to act as a command interpreter: It allows the shell to read terminal input, to spawn processes dynamically, to synchronize process execution, to create pipes, and to redirect I/O. Users can construct private versions of the shell to tailor their environments to their specifications without affecting other users. These programs use the same kernel services as the standard shell.

1.5 ASSUMPTIONS ABOUT HARDWARE

The execution of user processes on UNIX systems is divided into two levels: user and kernel. When a process executes a system call, the *execution mode* of the process changes from *user mode* to *kernel mode*: the operating system executes and attempts to service the user request, returning an error code if it fails. Even if the user makes no explicit requests for operating system services, the operating system still does bookkeeping operations that relate to the user process, handling interrupts, scheduling processes, managing memory, and so on. Many machine architectures (and their operating systems) support more levels than the two outlined here, but the two modes, user and kernel, are sufficient for UNIX systems.

The differences between the two modes are

- Processes in user mode can access their own instructions and data but not kernel instructions and data (or those of other processes). Processes in kernel mode, however, can access kernel and user addresses. For example, the virtual address space of a process may be divided between addresses that are accessible only in kernel mode and addresses that are accessible in either mode.
- Some machine instructions are privileged and result in an error when executed in user mode. For example, a machine may contain an instruction that manipulates the processor status register; processes executing in user mode

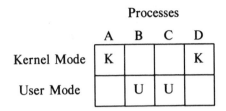

Figure 1.5. Multiple Processes and Modes of Execution

   should not have this capability.

   Put simply, the hardware views the world in terms of kernel mode and user mode and does not distinguish among the many users executing programs in those modes. The operating system keeps internal records to distinguish the many processes executing on the system. Figure 1.5 shows the distinction: the kernel distinguishes between processes A, B, C, and D on the horizontal axis, and the hardware distinguishes the mode of execution on the vertical axis.

   Although the system executes in one of two modes, the kernel runs on behalf of a user process. The kernel is not a separate set of processes that run in parallel to user processes, but it is part of each user process. The ensuing text will frequently refer to "the kernel" allocating resources or "the kernel" doing various operations, but what is meant is that a process executing in kernel mode allocates the resources or does the various operations. For example, the shell reads user terminal input via a system call: The kernel, executing on behalf of the shell process, controls the operation of the terminal and returns the typed characters to the shell. The shell then executes in user mode, interprets the character stream typed by the user, and does the specified set of actions, which may require invocation of other system calls.

1.5.1 Interrupts and Exceptions

The UNIX system allows devices such as I/O peripherals or the system clock to interrupt the CPU asynchronously. On receipt of the interrupt, the kernel saves its current *context* (a frozen image of what the process was doing), determines the cause of the interrupt, and services the interrupt. After the kernel services the interrupt, it restores its interrupted context and proceeds as if nothing had happened. The hardware usually prioritizes devices according to the order that interrupts should be handled: When the kernel services an interrupt, it *blocks* out lower priority interrupts but services higher priority interrupts.

   An exception condition refers to unexpected events caused by a process, such as addressing illegal memory, executing privileged instructions, dividing by zero, and so on. They are distinct from interrupts, which are caused by events that are external to a process. Exceptions happen "in the middle" of the execution of an instruction, and the system attempts to restart the instruction after handling the exception; interrupts are considered to happen between the execution of two instructions, and the system continues with the next instruction after servicing the interrupt. The UNIX system uses one mechanism to handle interrupts and exception conditions.

1.5.2 Processor Execution Levels

The kernel must sometimes prevent the occurrence of interrupts during critical activity, which could result in corrupt data if interrupts were allowed. For instance, the kernel may not want to receive a disk interrupt while manipulating linked lists, because handling the interrupt could corrupt the pointers, as will be seen in the next chapter. Computers typically have a set of privileged instructions that set the processor execution level in the processor status word. Setting the processor execution level to certain values masks off interrupts from that level and lower levels, allowing only higher-level interrupts. Figure 1.6 shows a sample set of execution levels. If the kernel masks out disk interrupts, all interrupts except for clock interrupts and machine error interrupts are prevented. If it masks out software interrupts, all other interrupts may occur.

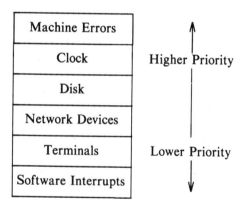

Figure 1.6. Typical Interrupt Levels

1.5.3 Memory Management

The kernel permanently resides in main memory as does the currently executing process (or parts of it, at least). When compiling a program, the compiler generates a set of addresses in the program that represent addresses of variables and data structures or the addresses of instructions such as functions. The compiler generates the addresses for a *virtual machine* as if no other program will execute simultaneously on the physical machine.

When the program is to run on the machine, the kernel allocates space in main memory for it, but the *virtual addresses* generated by the compiler need not be identical to the physical addresses that they occupy in the machine. The kernel coordinates with the machine hardware to set up a *virtual to physical* address translation that maps the compiler-generated addresses to the physical machine addresses. The mapping depends on the capabilities of the machine hardware, and the parts of UNIX systems that deal with them are therefore machine dependent. For example, some machines have special hardware to support demand paging. Chapters 6 and 9 will discuss issues of memory management and how they relate to hardware in more detail.

1.6 SUMMARY

This chapter has described the overall structure of the UNIX system, the relationship between processes running in user mode versus kernel mode, and the assumptions the kernel makes about the hardware. Processes execute in user mode or kernel mode, where they avail themselves of system services using a well-defined set of system calls. The system design encourages programmers to write small programs that do only a few operations but do them well, and then to combine the programs using *pipe*s and I/O redirection to do more sophisticated processing.

The system calls allow processes to do operations that are otherwise forbidden to them. In addition to servicing system calls, the kernel does general bookkeeping for the user community, controlling process scheduling, managing the storage and protection of processes in main memory, fielding interrupts, managing files and devices, and taking care of system error conditions. The UNIX system kernel purposely omits many functions that are part of other operating systems, providing a small set of system calls that allow processes to do necessary functions at user level. The next chapter gives a more detailed introduction to the kernel, describing its architecture and some basic concepts used in its implementation.

2

INTRODUCTION TO THE KERNEL

The last chapter gave a high-level perspective of the UNIX system environment. This chapter focuses on the kernel, providing an overview of its architecture and outlining basic concepts and structures essential for understanding the rest of the book.

2.1 ARCHITECTURE OF THE UNIX OPERATING SYSTEM

It has been noted (see page 239 of [Christian 83]) that the UNIX system supports the illusions that the file system has "places" and that processes have "life." The two entities, files and processes, are the two central concepts in the UNIX system model. Figure 2.1 gives a block diagram of the kernel, showing various modules and their relationships to each other. In particular, it shows the file subsystem on the left and the process control subsystem on the right, the two major components of the kernel. The diagram serves as a useful logical view of the kernel, although in practice the kernel deviates from the model because some modules interact with the internal operations of others.

Figure 2.1 shows three levels: user, kernel, and hardware. The system call and library interface represent the border between user programs and the kernel depicted in Figure 1.1. System calls look like ordinary function calls in C programs, and libraries map these function calls to the primitives needed to enter

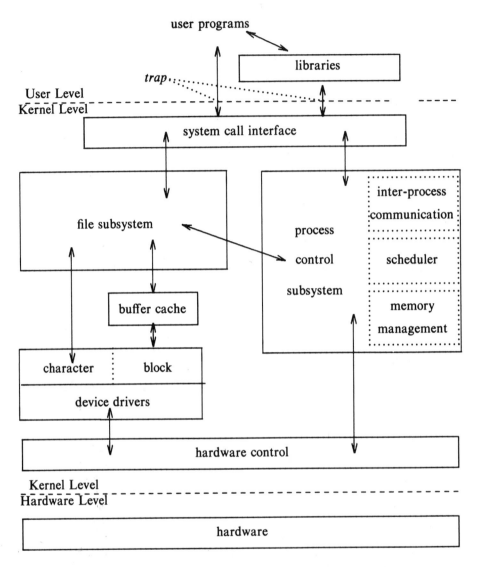

Figure 2.1. Block Diagram of the System Kernel

the operating system, as covered in more detail in Chapter 6. Assembly language programs may invoke system calls directly without a system call library, however. Programs frequently use other libraries such as the standard I/O library to provide a more sophisticated use of the system calls. The libraries are linked with the programs at compile time and are thus part of the user program for purposes of this discussion. An example later on will illustrate these points.

The figure partitions the set of system calls into those that interact with the file subsystem and those that interact with the process control subsystem. The file subsystem manages files, allocating file space, administering free space, controlling access to files, and retrieving data for users. Processes interact with the file subsystem via a specific set of system calls, such as *open* (to open a file for reading or writing), *close*, *read*, *write*, *stat* (query the attributes of a file), *chown* (change the record of who owns the file), and *chmod* (change the access permissions of a file). These and others will be examined in Chapter 5.

The file subsystem accesses file data using a buffering mechanism that regulates data flow between the kernel and secondary storage devices. The buffering mechanism interacts with block I/O device drivers to initiate data transfer to and from the kernel. Device drivers are the kernel modules that control the operation of peripheral devices. Block I/O devices are random access storage devices; alternatively, their device drivers make them appear to be random access storage devices to the rest of the system. For example, a tape driver may allow the kernel to treat a tape unit as a random access storage device. The file subsystem also interacts directly with "raw" I/O device drivers without the intervention of a buffering mechanism. Raw devices, sometimes called character devices, include all devices that are not block devices.

The process control subsystem is responsible for process synchronization, interprocess communication, memory management, and process scheduling. The file subsystem and the process control subsystem interact when loading a file into memory for execution, as will be seen in Chapter 7: the process subsystem reads executable files into memory before executing them.

Some of the system calls for controlling processes are *fork* (create a new process), *exec* (overlay the image of a program onto the running process), *exit* (finish executing a process), *wait* (synchronize process execution with the *exit* of a previously *fork*ed process), *brk* (control the size of memory allocated to a process), and *signal* (control process response to extraordinary events). Chapter 7 will examine these system calls and others.

The memory management module controls the allocation of memory. If at any time the system does not have enough physical memory for all processes, the kernel moves them between main memory and secondary memory so that all processes get a fair chance to execute. Chapter 9 will describe two policies for managing memory: swapping and demand paging. The swapper process is sometimes called the scheduler, because it "schedules" the allocation of memory for processes and influences the operation of the CPU scheduler. However, this text will refer to it as the swapper to avoid confusion with the CPU scheduler.

The *scheduler* module allocates the CPU to processes. It schedules them to run in turn until they voluntarily relinquish the CPU while awaiting a resource or until the kernel preempts them when their recent run time exceeds a time quantum. The scheduler then chooses the highest priority eligible process to run; the original process will run again when it is the highest priority eligible process available.

There are several forms of interprocess communication, ranging from asynchronous signaling of events to synchronous transmission of messages between processes.

Finally, the hardware control is responsible for handling interrupts and for communicating with the machine. Devices such as disks or terminals may interrupt the CPU while a process is executing. If so, the kernel may resume execution of the interrupted process after servicing the interrupt: Interrupts are *not* serviced by special processes but by special functions in the kernel, called in the context of the currently running process.

2.2 INTRODUCTION TO SYSTEM CONCEPTS

This section gives an overview of some major kernel data structures and describes the function of modules shown in Figure 2.1 in more detail.

2.2.1 An Overview of the File Subsystem

The internal representation of a file is given by an *inode*, which contains a description of the disk layout of the file data and other information such as the file owner, access permissions, and access times. The term inode is a contraction of the term *index node* and is commonly used in literature on the UNIX system. Every file has one inode, but it may have several names, all of which map into the inode. Each name is called a *link*. When a process refers to a file by name, the kernel parses the file name one component at a time, checks that the process has permission to search the directories in the path, and eventually retrieves the inode for the file. For example, if a process calls

open("/fs2/mjb/rje/sourcefile", 1);

the kernel retrieves the inode for "/fs2/mjb/rje/sourcefile". When a process creates a new file, the kernel assigns it an unused inode. Inodes are stored in the file system, as will be seen shortly, but the kernel reads them into an in-core[1] inode table when manipulating files.

The kernel contains two other data structures, the *file table* and the *user file descriptor table*. The file table is a global kernel structure, but the user file descriptor table is allocated per process. When a process *open*s or *creat*s a file, the kernel allocates an entry from each table, corresponding to the file's inode. Entries in the three structures — user file descriptor table, file table, and inode table — maintain the state of the file and the user's access to it. The file table keeps track of the byte offset in the file where the user's next *read* or *write* will start, and the

---

1. The term *core* refers to primary memory of a machine, not to hardware technology.

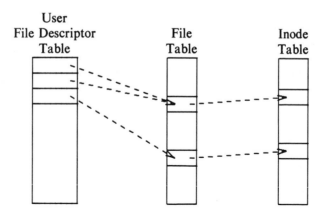

Figure 2.2. File Descriptors, File Table, and Inode Table

access rights allowed to the *open*ing process. The user file descriptor table identifies all open files for a process. Figure 2.2 shows the tables and their relationship to each other. The kernel returns a *file descriptor* for the *open* and *creat* system calls, which is an index into the user file descriptor table. When executing *read* and *write* system calls, the kernel uses the file descriptor to access the user file descriptor table, follows pointers to the file table and inode table entries, and, from the inode, finds the data in the file. Chapters 4 and 5 describe these data structures in great detail. For now, suffice it to say that use of three tables allows various degrees of sharing access to a file.

The UNIX system keeps regular files and directories on block devices such as tapes or disks. Because of the difference in access time between the two, few, if any, UNIX system installations use tapes for their file systems. In coming years, diskless work stations will be common, where files are located on a remote system and accessed via a network (see Chapter 13). For simplicity, however, the ensuing text assumes the use of disks. An installation may have several physical disk units, each containing one or more *file systems*. Partitioning a disk into several file systems makes it easier for administrators to manage the data stored there. The kernel deals on a logical level with file systems rather than with disks, treating each one as a *logical device* identified by a logical *device number*. The conversion between logical device (file system) addresses and physical device (disk) addresses is done by the disk driver. This book will use the term device to mean a logical device unless explicitly stated otherwise.

A file system consists of a sequence of logical blocks, each containing 512, 1024, 2048, or any convenient multiple of 512 bytes, depending on the system implementation. The size of a logical block is homogeneous within a file system but may vary between different file systems in a system configuration. Using large logical blocks increases the effective data transfer rate between disk and memory, because the kernel can transfer more data per disk operation and therefore make fewer time-consuming operations. For example, reading 1K bytes from a disk in one read operation is faster than reading 512 bytes twice. However, if a logical block is too large, effective storage capacity may drop, as will be shown in Chapter 5. For simplicity, this book will use the term "block" to mean a logical block, and it will assume that a logical block contains 1K bytes of data unless explicitly stated otherwise.

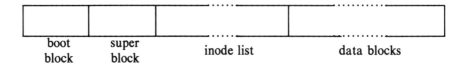

Figure 2.3. File System Layout

A file system has the following structure (Figure 2.3).

- The *boot block* occupies the beginning of a file system, typically the first sector, and may contain the *bootstrap* code that is read into the machine to *boot*, or initialize, the operating system. Although only one boot block is needed to boot the system, every file system has a (possibly empty) boot block.
- The *super block* describes the state of a file system — how large it is, how many files it can store, where to find free space on the file system, and other information.
- The *inode list* is a list of inodes that follows the super block in the file system. Administrators specify the size of the inode list when configuring a file system. The kernel references inodes by index into the inode list. One inode is the *root inode* of the file system: it is the inode by which the directory structure of the file system is accessible after execution of the *mount* system call (Section 5.14).
- The data blocks start at the end of the inode list and contain file data and administrative data. An allocated data block can belong to one and only one file in the file system.

2.2.2 Processes

This section examines the process subsystem more closely. It describes the structure of a process and some process data structures used for memory management. Then it gives a preliminary view of the process state diagram and considers various issues involved in some state transitions.

A process is the execution of a program and consists of a pattern of bytes that the CPU interprets as machine instructions (called "text"), data, and stack. Many processes appear to execute simultaneously as the kernel schedules them for execution, and several processes may be instances of one program. A process executes by following a strict sequence of instructions that is self-contained and does not jump to that of another process; it reads and writes its data and stack sections, but it cannot read or write the data and stack of other processes. Processes communicate with other processes and with the rest of the world via system calls.

In practical terms, a process on a UNIX system is the entity that is created by the *fork* system call. Every process except *process 0* is created when another process executes the *fork* system call. The process that invoked the *fork* system call is the *parent* process, and the newly created process is the *child* process. Every process has one parent process, but a process can have many child processes. The kernel identifies each process by its process number, called the *process ID* (PID). Process 0 is a special process that is created "by hand" when the system boots; after *fork*ing a child process (process 1), process 0 becomes the *swapper* process. Process 1, known as *init,* is the ancestor of every other process in the system and enjoys a special relationship with them, as explained in Chapter 7.

A user compiles the source code of a program to create an executable file, which consists of several parts:

- a set of "headers" that describe the attributes of the file,
- the program text,
- a machine language representation of data that has initial values when the program starts execution, and an indication of how much space the kernel should allocate for uninitialized data, called bss^2 (the kernel initializes it to 0 at run time),
- other sections, such as symbol table information.

For the program in Figure 1.3, the text of the executable file is the generated code for the functions *main* and *copy*, the initialized data is the variable *version* (put into the program just so that it should have some initialized data), and the uninitialized data is the array *buffer*. System V versions of the C compiler create a separate text section by default but support an option that allows inclusion of program instructions in the data section, used in older versions of the system.

The kernel loads an executable file into memory during an *exec* system call, and the loaded process consists of at least three parts, called *region*s: text, data, and the stack. The text and data regions correspond to the text and data-bss sections of the executable file, but the stack region is automatically created and its size is dynamically adjusted by the kernel at run time. The stack consists of logical *stack frames* that are *push*ed when calling a function and *pop*ped when returning; a special register called the *stack pointer* indicates the current stack depth. A stack

---

2. The name bss comes from an assembly pseudo-operator on the IBM 7090 machine, which stood for "block started by symbol."

frame contains the parameters to a function, its local variables, and the data necessary to recover the previous stack frame, including the value of the program counter and stack pointer at the time of the function call. The program code contains instruction sequences that manage stack growth, and the kernel allocates space for the stack, as needed. In the program in Figure 1.3, parameters *argc* and *argv* and variables *fdold* and *fdnew* in the function *main* appear on the stack when *main* is called (once in every program, by convention), and parameters *old* and *new* and the variable *count* in the function *copy* appear on the stack whenever *copy* is called.

Because a process in the UNIX system can execute in two modes, kernel or user, it uses a separate stack for each mode. The user stack contains the arguments, local variables, and other data for functions executing in user mode. The left side of Figure 2.4 shows the user stack for a process when it makes the *write* system call in the *copy* program. The process startup procedure (included in a library) had called the function *main* with two parameters, pushing frame 1 onto the user stack; frame 1 contains space for the two local variables of *main*. *Main* then called *copy* with two parameters, *old* and *new*, and pushed frame 2 onto the user stack; frame 2 contains space for the local variable *count*. Finally, the process invoked the system call *write* by invoking the library function *write*. Each system call has an entry point in a system call library; the system call library is encoded in assembly language and contains special *trap* instructions, which, when executed, cause an "interrupt" that results in a hardware switch to kernel mode. A process calls the library entry point for a particular system call just as it calls any function, creating a stack frame for the library function. When the process executes the special instruction, it switches mode to the kernel, executes kernel code, and uses the kernel stack.

The kernel stack contains the stack frames for functions executing in kernel mode. The function and data entries on the kernel stack refer to functions and data in the kernel, not the user program, but its construction is the same as that of the user stack. The kernel stack of a process is null when the process executes in user mode. The right side of Figure 2.4 depicts the kernel stack representation for a process executing the *write* system call in the *copy* program. The names of the algorithms are described during the detailed discussion of the *write* system call in later chapters.

Every process has an entry in the kernel *process table*, and each process is allocated a *u area*[3] that contains private data manipulated only by the kernel. The process table contains (or points to) a *per process region table*, whose entries point to entries in a *region* table. A region is a contiguous area of a process's address

---

3. The *u* in *u area* stands for "user." Another name for the *u area* is *u block*; this book will always refer to it as the *u area*.

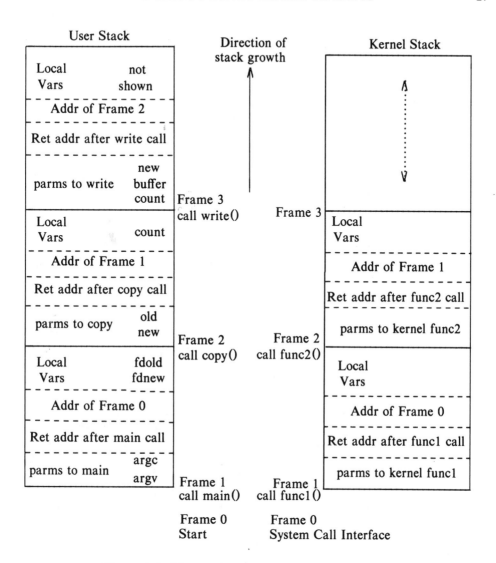

Figure 2.4. User and Kernel Stack for Copy Program

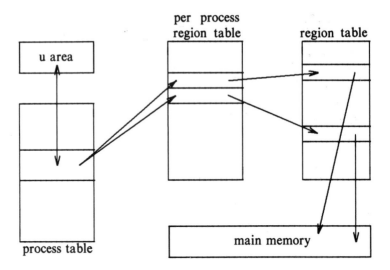

Figure 2.5. Data Structures for Processes

space, such as text, data, and stack. Region table entries describe the attributes of the region, such as whether it contains text or data, whether it is shared or private, and where the "data" of the region is located in memory. The extra level of indirection (from the per process region table to the region table) allows independent processes to share regions. When a process invokes the *exec* system call, the kernel allocates regions for its text, data, and stack after freeing the old regions the process had been using. When a process invokes *fork*, the kernel duplicates the address space of the old process, allowing processes to share regions when possible and making a physical copy otherwise. When a process invokes *exit*, the kernel frees the regions the process had used. Figure 2.5 shows the relevant data structures of a running process: The process table points to a per process region table with pointers to the region table entries for the text, data, and stack regions of the process.

The process table entry and the *u area* contain control and status information about the process. The *u area* is an extension of the process table entry, and Chapter 6 will examine the distinction between the two tables. Fields in the process table discussed in the following chapters are

- a state field,
- identifiers indicating the user who owns the process (user IDs, or UIDs),
- an event descriptor set when a process is suspended (in the *sleep* state).

The *u area* contains information describing the process that needs to be accessible only when the process is executing. The important fields are

- a pointer to the process table slot of the currently executing process,
- parameters of the current system call, return values and error codes,
- file descriptors for all open files,
- internal I/O parameters,
- current directory and current root (see Chapter 5),
- process and file size limits.

The kernel can directly access fields of the *u area* of the executing process but not of the *u area* of other processes. Internally, the kernel references the structure variable *u* to access the *u area* of the currently running process, and when another process executes, the kernel rearranges its virtual address space so that the structure *u* refers to the *u area* of the new process. The implementation gives the kernel an easy way to identify the current process by following the pointer from the *u area* to its process table entry.

2.2.2.1 Context of a process

The *context* of a process is its state, as defined by its text, the values of its global user variables and data structures, the values of machine registers it uses, the values stored in its process table slot and *u area*, and the contents of its user and kernel stacks. The text of the operating system and its global data structures are shared by all processes but do not constitute part of the context of a process.

When executing a process, the system is said to be executing in the context of the process. When the kernel decides that it should execute another process, it does a *context switch*, so that the system executes in the context of the other process. The kernel allows a context switch only under specific conditions, as will be seen. When doing a context switch, the kernel saves enough information so that it can later switch back to the first process and resume its execution. Similarly, when moving from user to kernel mode, the kernel saves enough information so that it can later return to user mode and continue execution from where it left off. Moving between user and kernel mode is a change in mode, not a context switch. Recalling Figure 1.5, the kernel does a context switch when it changes context from process A to process B; it changes execution mode from user to kernel or from kernel to user, still executing in the context of one process, such as process A.

The kernel services interrupts in the context of the interrupted process even though it may not have caused the interrupt. The interrupted process may have been executing in user mode or in kernel mode. The kernel saves enough information so that it can later resume execution of the interrupted process and services the interrupt in kernel mode. The kernel does not spawn or schedule a special process to handle interrupts.

2.2.2.2 Process states

The lifetime of a process can be divided into a set of *states*, each with certain characteristics that describe the process. Chapter 6 will describe all process states, but it is essential to understand the following states now:

1. The process is currently executing in user mode.
2. The process is currently executing in kernel mode.
3. The process is not executing, but it is ready to run as soon as the scheduler chooses it. Many processes may be in this state, and the scheduling algorithm determines which one will execute next.
4. The process is *sleeping*. A process puts itself to sleep when it can no longer continue executing, such as when it is waiting for I/O to complete.

Because a processor can execute only one process at a time, at most one process may be in states 1 and 2. The two states correspond to the two modes of execution, user and kernel.

2.2.2.3 State transitions

The process states described above give a static view of a process, but processes move continuously between the states according to well-defined rules. A *state transition* diagram is a directed graph whose *nodes* represent the states a process can enter and whose *edges* represent the events that cause a process to move from one state to another. State transitions are legal between two states if there exists an edge from the first state to the second. Several transitions may emanate from a state, but a process will follow one and only one transition depending on the system event that occurs. Figure 2.6 shows the state transition diagram for the process states defined above.

Several processes can execute simultaneously in a time-shared manner, as stated earlier, and they may all run simultaneously in kernel mode. If they were allowed to run in kernel mode without constraint, they could corrupt global kernel data structures. By prohibiting arbitrary context switches and controlling the occurrence of interrupts, the kernel protects its consistency.

The kernel allows a context switch only when a process moves from the state "kernel running" to the state "asleep in memory." Processes running in kernel mode cannot be preempted by other processes; therefore the kernel is sometimes said to be *non-preemptive*, although the system does preempt processes that are in user mode. The kernel maintains consistency of its data structures because it is non-preemptive, thereby solving the *mutual exclusion* problem — making sure that critical sections of code are executed by at most one process at a time.

For instance, consider the sample code in Figure 2.7 to put a data structure, whose address is in the pointer *bp1*, onto a doubly linked list after the structure whose address is in *bp*. If the system allowed a context switch while the kernel executed the code fragment, the following situation could occur. Suppose the

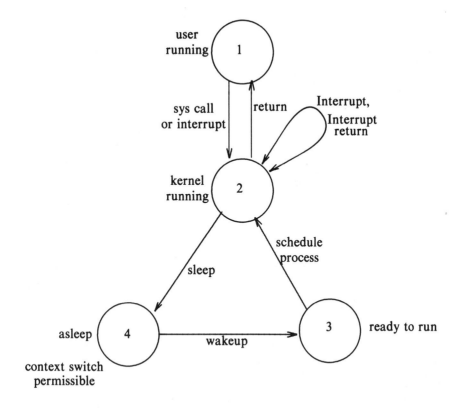

Figure 2.6. Process States and Transitions

kernel executes the code until the comment and then does a context switch. The doubly linked list is in an inconsistent state: the structure *bp1* is half on and half off the linked list. If a process were to follow the forward pointers, it would find *bp1* on the linked list, but if it were to follow the back pointers, it would not find *bp1* (Figure 2.8). If other processes were to manipulate the pointers on the linked list before the original process ran again, the structure of the doubly linked list could be permanently destroyed. The UNIX system prevents such situations by disallowing context switches when a process executes in kernel mode. If a process goes to sleep, thereby permitting a context switch, kernel algorithms are encoded to make sure that system data structures are in a safe, consistent state.

A related problem that can cause inconsistency in kernel data is the handling of interrupts, which can change kernel state information. For example, if the kernel was executing the code in Figure 2.7 and received an interrupt when it reached the

```
struct queue {


} *bp, *bp1;
bp1->forp = bp->forp;
bp1->backp = bp;
bp->forp = bp1;
/* consider possible context switch here */
bp1->forp->backp = bp1;
```

Figure 2.7. Sample Code Creating Doubly Linked List

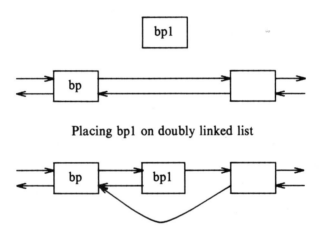

Placing bp1 on doubly linked list

Figure 2.8. Incorrect Linked List because of Context Switch

comment, the interrupt handler could corrupt the links if it manipulates the pointers, as illustrated earlier. To solve this problem, the system could prevent all interrupts while executing in kernel mode, but that would delay servicing of the interrupt, possibly hurting system throughput. Instead, the kernel raises the processor execution level to prevent interrupts when entering *critical* regions of code. A section of code is critical if execution of arbitrary interrupt handlers could result in consistency problems. For example, if a disk interrupt handler manipulates the buffer queues in the figure, the section of code where the kernel manipulates the buffer queues is a critical region of code with respect to the disk interrupt handler. Critical regions are small and infrequent so that system throughput is largely unaffected by their existence. Other operating systems solve this problem by preventing all interrupts when executing in system states or by using elaborate locking schemes to ensure consistency. Chapter 12 will return to this issue for multiprocessor systems, where the solution outlined here is insufficient.

To review, the kernel protects its consistency by allowing a context switch only when a process puts itself to sleep and by preventing one process from changing the state of another process. It also raises the processor execution level around critical regions of code to prevent interrupts that could otherwise cause inconsistencies. The process scheduler periodically preempts processes executing in user mode so that processes cannot monopolize use of the CPU.

2.2.2.4 Sleep and wakeup

A process executing in kernel mode has great autonomy in deciding what it is going to do in reaction to system events. Processes can communicate with each other and "suggest" various alternatives, but they make the final decision by themselves. As will be seen, there is a set of rules that processes obey when confronted with various circumstances, but each process ultimately follows these rules under its own initiative. For instance, when a process must temporarily suspend its execution ("go to sleep"), it does so of its own free will. Consequently, an interrupt handler cannot go to sleep, because if it could, the interrupted process would be put to sleep by default.

Processes go to sleep because they are awaiting the occurrence of some event, such as waiting for I/O completion from a peripheral device, waiting for a process to exit, waiting for system resources to become available, and so on. Processes are said to *sleep on an event*, meaning that they are in the sleep state until the event occurs, at which time they wake up and enter the state "ready to run." Many processes can simultaneously sleep on an event; when an event occurs, *all* processes sleeping on the event wake up because the event condition is no longer true. When a process wakes up, it follows the state transition from the "sleep" state to the "ready-to-run" state, where it is eligible for later scheduling; it does *not* execute immediately. Sleeping processes do not consume CPU resources: The kernel does not constantly check to see that a process is still sleeping but waits for the event to occur and awakens the process then.

For example, a process executing in kernel mode must sometimes lock a data structure in case it goes to sleep at a later stage; processes attempting to manipulate the locked structure must check the lock and sleep if another process owns the lock. The kernel implements such locks in the following manner:

```
while (condition is true)
      sleep (event: the condition becomes false);
   set condition true;
```

It unlocks the lock and awakens all processes asleep on the lock in the following manner:

set condition false;
wakeup (event: the condition is false);

Figure 2.9 depicts a scenario where three processes, A, B, and C, contend for a locked buffer. The sleep condition is that the buffer is locked. The processes execute one at a time, find the buffer locked, and sleep on the event that the buffer becomes unlocked. Eventually, the buffer is unlocked, and all processes wake up and enter the state "ready to run." The kernel eventually chooses one process, say B, to execute. Process B executes the "while" loop, finds that the buffer is unlocked, sets the buffer lock, and proceeds. If process B later goes to sleep again before unlocking the buffer (waiting for completion of an I/O operation, for example), the kernel can schedule other processes to run. If it chooses process A, process A executes the "while" loop, finds that the buffer is locked, and goes to sleep again; process C may do the same thing. Eventually, process B awakens and unlocks the buffer, allowing either process A or C to gain access to the buffer. Thus, the "while-sleep" loop insures that at most one process can gain access to a resource.

Chapter 6 will present the algorithms for sleep and wakeup in greater detail. In the meantime, they should be considered "atomic": A process enters the sleep state instantaneously and stays there until it wakes up. After it goes to sleep, the kernel schedules another process to run and switches context to it.

2.3 KERNEL DATA STRUCTURES

Most kernel data structures occupy fixed-size tables rather than dynamically allocated space. The advantage of this approach is that the kernel code is simple, but it limits the number of entries for a data structure to the number that was originally configured when generating the system: If, during operation of the system, the kernel should run out of entries for a data structure, it cannot allocate space for new entries dynamically but must report an error to the requesting user. If, on the other hand, the kernel is configured so that it it is unlikely to run out of table space, the extra table space may be wasted because it cannot be used for other purposes. Nevertheless, the simplicity of the kernel algorithms has generally been considered more important than the need to squeeze out every last byte of main memory. Algorithms typically use simple loops to find free table entries, a method that is easier to understand and sometimes more efficient than more complicated allocation schemes.

2.4 SYSTEM ADMINISTRATION

Administrative processes are loosely classified as those processes that do various functions for the general welfare of the user community. Such functions include disk formatting, creation of new file systems, repair of damaged file systems, kernel debugging, and others. Conceptually, there is no difference between administrative

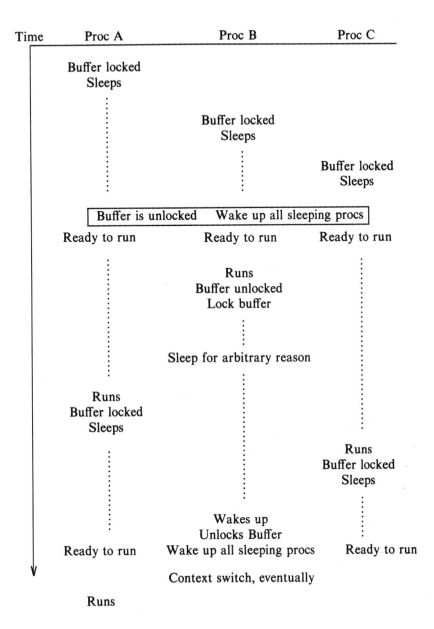

Figure 2.9. Multiple Processes Sleeping on a Lock

processes and user processes: They use the same set of system calls available to the general community. They are distinguished from general user processes only in the rights and privileges they are allowed. For example, file permission modes may allow administrative processes to manipulate files otherwise off-limits to general users. Internally, the kernel distinguishes a special user called the *superuser*, endowing it with special privileges, as will be seen. A user may become a superuser by going through a login-password sequence or by executing special programs. Other uses of superuser privileges will be studied in later chapters. In short, the kernel does not recognize a separate class of administrative processes.

2.5 SUMMARY AND PREVIEW

This chapter has described the architecture of the kernel; its two major components are the file subsystem and the process subsystem. The file subsystem controls the storage and retrieval of data in user files. Files are organized into file systems, which are treated as logical devices; a physical device such as a disk can contain several logical devices (file systems). Each file system has a super block that describes the structure and contents of the file system, and each file in a file system is described by an inode that gives the attributes of the file. System calls that manipulate files do so via inodes.

Processes exist in various states and move between them according to well-defined transition rules. In particular, processes executing in kernel mode can suspend their execution and enter the sleep state, but no process can put another process to sleep. The kernel is non-preemptive, meaning that a process executing in kernel mode will continue to execute until it enters the sleep state or until it returns to execute in user mode. The kernel maintains the consistency of its data structures by enforcing the policy of non-preemption and by blocking interrupts when executing critical regions of code.

The remainder of this text describes the subsystems shown in Figure 2.1 and their interactions in detail, starting with the file subsystem and continuing with the process subsystem. The next chapter covers the buffer cache and describes buffer allocation algorithms, used in the algorithms presented in Chapters 4, 5, and 7. Chapter 4 examines internal algorithms of the file system, including the manipulation of inodes, the structure of files, and the conversion of path names to inodes. Chapter 5 explains the system calls that use the algorithms in Chapter 4 to access the file system, such as *open*, *close*, *read*, and *write*. Chapter 6 deals with the basic ideas of the context of a process and its address space, and Chapter 7 covers system calls that deal with process management and use the algorithms in Chapter 6. Chapter 8 examines process scheduling, and Chapter 9 discusses memory management algorithms. Chapter 10 covers device drivers, postponed to this point so that the relationship between the terminal driver and process management can be explained. Chapter 11 presents several forms of interprocess communication. Finally, the last two chapters cover advanced topics, including multiprocessor systems and distributed systems.

2.6 EXERCISES

1. Consider the following sequence of commands:

   grep main a.c b.c c.c > grepout &
   wc −l < grepout &
   rm grepout &

   The ampersand ("&") at the end of each command line informs the shell to run the command in the background, and it can execute each command line in parallel. Why is this not equivalent to the following command line?

   grep main a.c b.c c.c | wc −l

2. Consider the sample kernel code in Figure 2.7. Suppose a context switch happens when the code reaches the comment, and suppose another process removes a buffer from the linked list by executing the following code:

   ```
   remove(qp)
        struct queue *qp;
   {

        qp−>forp−>backp = qp−>backp;
        qp−>backp−>forp = qp−>forp;
        qp−>forp = qp−>backp = NULL;
   }
   ```

   Consider three cases:
   — The process removes the structure *bp1* from the linked list.
   — The process removes the structure that currently follows *bp1* on the linked list.
   — The process removes the structure that originally followed *bp1* before *bp* was half placed on the linked list.

   What is the status of the linked list after the original process completes executing the code after the comment?

3. What should happen if the kernel attempts to awaken all processes sleeping on an event, but no processes are asleep on the event at the time of the wakeup?

3

THE BUFFER
CACHE

As mentioned in the previous chapter, the kernel maintains files on mass storage
devices such as disks, and it allows processes to store new information or to recall
previously stored information. When a process wants to access data from a file, the
kernel brings the data into main memory where the process can examine it, alter it,
and request that the data be saved in the file system again. For example, recall the
copy program in Figure 1.3: The kernel reads the data from the first file into
memory, and then writes the data into the second file. Just as it must bring file
data into memory, the kernel must also bring auxiliary data into memory to
manipulate it. For instance, the super block of a file system describes the free
space available on the file system, among other things. The kernel reads the super
block into memory to access its data and writes it back to the file system when it
wishes to save its data. Similarly, the inode describes the layout of a file. The
kernel reads an inode into memory when it wants to access data in a file and writes
the inode back to the file system when it wants to update the file layout. It
manipulates this auxiliary data without the explicit knowledge or request of running
processes.

   The kernel could read and write directly to and from the disk for all file system
accesses, but system response time and throughput would be poor because of the
slow disk transfer rate. The kernel therefore attempts to minimize the frequency of
disk access by keeping a pool of internal data buffers, called the buffer cache,[1]

which contains the data in recently used disk blocks.

Figure 2.1 showed the position of the buffer cache module in the kernel architecture between the file subsystem and (block) device drivers. When reading data from the disk, the kernel attempts to read from the buffer cache. If the data is already in the cache, the kernel does not have to read from the disk. If the data is not in the cache, the kernel reads the data from the disk and caches it, using an algorithm that tries to save as much good data in the cache as possible. Similarly, data being written to disk is cached so that it will be there if the kernel later tries to read it. The kernel also attempts to minimize the frequency of disk write operations by determining whether the data must really be stored on disk or whether it is transient data that will soon be overwritten. Higher-level kernel algorithms instruct the buffer cache module to pre-cache data or to delay-write data to maximize the caching effect. This chapter describes the algorithms the kernel uses to manipulate buffers in the buffer cache.

3.1 BUFFER HEADERS

During system initialization, the kernel allocates space for a number of buffers, configurable according to memory size and system performance constraints. A buffer consists of two parts: a memory array that contains data from the disk and a *buffer header* that identifies the buffer. Because there is a one to one mapping of buffer headers to data arrays, the ensuing text will frequently refer to both parts as a "buffer," and the context should make clear which part is being discussed.

The data in a buffer corresponds to the data in a logical disk block on a file system, and the kernel identifies the buffer contents by examining identifier fields in the buffer header. The buffer is the in-memory copy of the disk block; the contents of the disk block map into the buffer, but the mapping is temporary until the kernel decides to map another disk block into the buffer. A disk block can never map into more than one buffer at a time. If two buffers were to contain data for one disk block, the kernel would not know which buffer contained the current data and could write incorrect data back to disk. For example, suppose a disk block maps into two buffers, A and B. If the kernel writes data first into buffer A and then into buffer B, the disk block should contain the contents of buffer B if all write operations completely fill the buffer. However, if the kernel reverses the order when it copies the buffers to disk, the disk block will contain incorrect data.

The buffer header (Figure 3.1) contains a *device number* field and a *block number* field that specify the file system and block number of the data on disk and uniquely identify the buffer. The device number is the logical file system number

---

1. The buffer cache is a software structure that should not be confused with hardware caches that speed memory references.

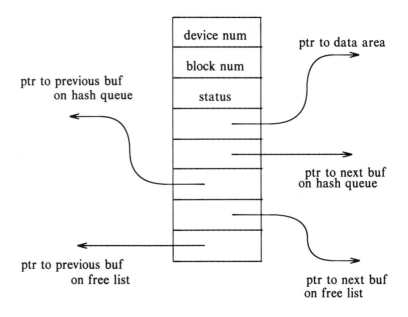

Figure 3.1. Buffer Header

(see Section 2.2.1), not a physical device (disk) unit number. The buffer header also contains a pointer to a data array for the buffer, whose size must be at least as big as the size of a disk block, and a status field that summarizes the current status of the buffer. The status of a buffer is a combination of the following conditions:

- The buffer is currently locked (the terms "locked" and "busy" will be used interchangeably, as will "free" and "unlocked"),
- The buffer contains valid data,
- The kernel must write the buffer contents to disk before reassigning the buffer; this condition is known as "delayed-write,"
- The kernel is currently reading or writing the contents of the buffer to disk,
- A process is currently waiting for the buffer to become free.

The buffer header also contains two sets of pointers, used by the buffer allocation algorithms to maintain the overall structure of the buffer pool, as explained in the next section.

3.2 STRUCTURE OF THE BUFFER POOL

The kernel caches data in the buffer pool according to a *least recently used* algorithm: after it allocates a buffer to a disk block, it cannot use the buffer for

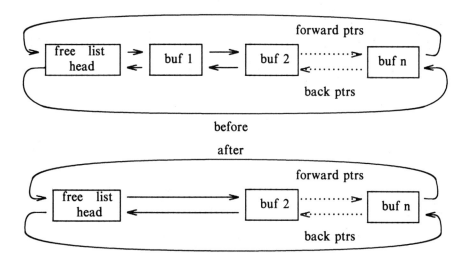

Figure 3.2. Free List of Buffers

another block until all other buffers have been used more recently. The kernel maintains a *free list* of buffers that preserves the least recently used order. The free list is a doubly linked circular list of buffers with a dummy buffer header that marks its beginning and end (Figure 3.2). Every buffer is put on the free list when the system is booted. The kernel takes a buffer from the head of the free list when it wants *any* free buffer, but it can take a buffer from the middle of the free list if it identifies a particular block in the buffer pool. In both cases, it removes the buffer from the free list. When the kernel returns a buffer to the buffer pool, it usually attaches the buffer to the tail of the free list, occasionally to the head of the free list (for error cases), but never to the middle. As the kernel removes buffers from the free list, a buffer with valid data moves closer and closer to head of the free list (Figure 3.2). Hence, the buffers that are closer to the head of the free list have not been used as recently as those that are further from the head of the free list.

When the kernel accesses a disk block, it searches for a buffer with the appropriate device-block number combination. Rather than search the entire buffer pool, it organizes the buffers into separate queues, *hashed* as a function of the device and block number. The kernel links the buffers on a hash queue into a circular, doubly linked list, similar to the structure of the free list. The number of buffers on a hash queue varies during the lifetime of the system, as will be seen. The kernel must use a hashing function that distributes the buffers uniformly across the set of hash queues, yet the hash function must be simple so that performance does not suffer. System administrators configure the number of hash queues when generating the operating system.

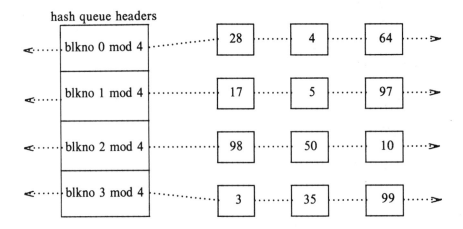

Figure 3.3. Buffers on the Hash Queues

Figure 3.3 shows buffers on their hash queues: the headers of the hash queues are on the left side of the figure, and the squares on each row are buffers on a hash queue. Thus, squares marked 28, 4, and 64 represent buffers on the hash queue for "blkno 0 mod 4" (block number 0 modulo 4). The dotted lines between the buffers represent the forward and back pointers for the hash queue; for simplicity, later figures in this chapter will not show these pointers, but their existence is implicit. Similarly, the figure identifies blocks only by their block number, and it uses a hash function dependent only on a block number; however, implementations use the device number, too.

Each buffer always exists on a hash queue, but there is no significance to its position on the queue. As stated above, no two buffers may simultaneously contain the contents of the same disk block; therefore, every disk block in the buffer pool exists on one and only one hash queue and only once on that queue. However, a buffer may be on the free list as well if its status is free. Because a buffer may be simultaneously on a hash queue and on the free list, the kernel has two ways to find it: It searches the hash queue if it is looking for a particular buffer, and it removes a buffer from the free list if it is looking for *any* free buffer. The next section will show how the kernel finds particular disk blocks in the buffer cache, and how it manipulates buffers on the hash queues and on the free list. To summarize, a buffer is always on a hash queue, but it may or may not be on the free list.

3.3 SCENARIOS FOR RETRIEVAL OF A BUFFER

As seen in Figure 2.1, high-level kernel algorithms in the file subsystem invoke the algorithms for managing the buffer cache. The high-level algorithms determine the logical device number and block number that they wish to access when they attempt to retrieve a block. For example, if a process wants to read data from a file, the kernel determines which file system contains the file and which block in the file system contains the data, as will be seen in Chapter 4. When about to read data from a particular disk block, the kernel checks whether the block is in the buffer pool and, if it is not there, assigns it a free buffer. When about to write data to a particular disk block, the kernel checks whether the block is in the buffer pool, and if not, assigns a free buffer for that block. The algorithms for reading and writing disk blocks use the algorithm *getblk* (Figure 3.4) to allocate buffers from the pool.

This section describes five typical scenarios the kernel may follow in *getblk* to allocate a buffer for a disk block.

1. The kernel finds the block on its hash queue, and its buffer is free.
2. The kernel cannot find the block on the hash queue, so it allocates a buffer from the free list.
3. The kernel cannot find the block on the hash queue and, in attempting to allocate a buffer from the free list (as in scenario 2), finds a buffer on the free list that has been marked "delayed write." The kernel must write the "delayed write" buffer to disk and allocate another buffer.
4. The kernel cannot find the block on the hash queue, and the free list of buffers is empty.
5. The kernel finds the block on the hash queue, but its buffer is currently busy.

Let us now discuss each scenario in greater detail.

When searching for a block in the buffer pool by its device-block number combination, the kernel finds the hash queue that should contain the block. It searches the hash queue, following the linked list of buffers until (in the first scenario) it finds the buffer whose device and block number match those for which it is searching. The kernel checks that the buffer is free and, if so, marks the buffer "busy" so that other processes[2] cannot access it. The kernel then removes the buffer from the free list, because a buffer cannot be both busy and on the free list. If other processes attempt to access the block while the buffer is busy, they sleep until the buffer is released, as will be seen. Figure 3.5 depicts the first scenario, where the kernel searches for block 4 on the hash queue marked "blkno 0 mod 4." Finding the buffer, the kernel removes it from the free list, leaving blocks 5 and 28 adjacent on the free list.

---

2. Recall from the last chapter that all kernel operations are done in the context of a process that is executing in kernel mode. Thus, the term "other processes" means that they are also executing in kernel mode. This term will be used when describing the interaction of several processes executing in kernel mode; if there is no interprocess interaction, the term "kernel" will be used.

```
algorithm getblk
input:   file system number
         block number
output: locked buffer that can now be used for block
{
       while (buffer not found)
       {
             if (block in hash queue)
             {
                    if (buffer busy)        /* scenario 5 */
                    {
                          sleep (event buffer becomes free);
                          continue;        /* back to while loop */
                    }
                    mark buffer busy;        /* scenario 1 */
                    remove buffer from free list;
                    return buffer;
             }
             else      /* block not on hash queue */
             {
                    if (there are no buffers on free list)        /* scenario 4 */
                    {
                          sleep (event any buffer becomes free);
                          continue;        /* back to while loop */
                    }
                    remove buffer from free list;
                    if (buffer marked for delayed write) {        /* scenario 3 */
                          asynchronous write buffer to disk;
                          continue;        /* back to while loop */
                    }
                    /* scenario 2 -- found a free buffer */
                    remove buffer from old hash queue;
                    put buffer onto new hash queue;
                    return buffer;
             }
       }
}
```

Figure 3.4. Algorithm for Buffer Allocation

hash queue headers

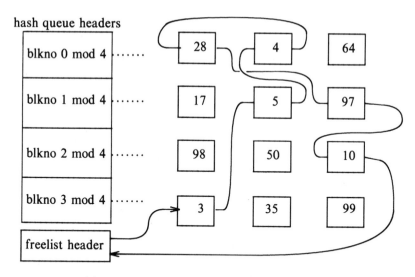

(a) Search for Block 4 on First Hash Queue

hash queue headers

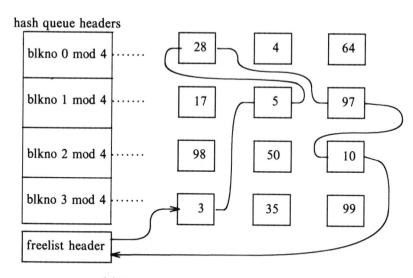

(b) Remove Block 4 from Free List

Figure 3.5. Scenario 1 in Finding a Buffer: Buffer on Hash Queue

```
algorithm brelse
input:   locked buffer
output: none
{
        wakeup all procs: event, waiting for any buffer to become free;
        wakeup all procs: event, waiting for this buffer to become free;
        raise processor execution level to block interrupts;
        if (buffer contents valid and buffer not old)
              enqueue buffer at end of free list
        else
              enqueue buffer at beginning of free list
        lower processor execution level to allow interrupts;
        unlock(buffer);
}
```

Figure 3.6. Algorithm for Releasing a Buffer

Before continuing to the other scenarios, let us consider what happens to a buffer after it is allocated. The kernel may read data from the disk to the buffer and manipulate it or write data to the buffer and possibly to the disk. The kernel leaves the buffer marked busy; no other process can access it and change its contents while it is busy, thus preserving the integrity of the data in the buffer. When the kernel finishes using the buffer, it releases the buffer according to algorithm *brelse* (Figure 3.6). It wakes up processes that had fallen asleep because the buffer was busy and processes that had fallen asleep because no buffers remained on the free list. In both cases, release of a buffer means that the buffer is available for use by the sleeping processes, although the first process that gets the buffer locks it and prevents the other processes from getting it (recall Section 2.2.2.4). The kernel places the buffer at the end of the free list, unless an I/O error occurred or unless it specifically marked the buffer "old," as will be seen later in this chapter; in the latter cases, it places the buffer at the beginning of the free list. The buffer is now free for another process to claim it.

Just as the kernel invokes algorithm *brelse* when a process has no more need for a buffer, it also invokes the algorithm when handling a disk interrupt to release buffers used for asynchronous I/O to and from the disk, as will be seen in Section 3.4. The kernel raises the processor execution level to prevent disk interrupts while manipulating the free list, thereby preventing corruption of the buffer pointers that could result from a nested call to *brelse*. Similar bad effects could happen if an interrupt handler invoked *brelse* while a process was executing *getblk*, so the kernel raises the processor execution level at strategic places in *getblk*, too. The exercises explore these cases in greater detail.

In the second scenario in algorithm *getblk*, the kernel searches the hash queue that should contain the block but fails to find it there. Since the block cannot be on another hash queue because it cannot "hash" elsewhere, it is not in the buffer

hash queue headers

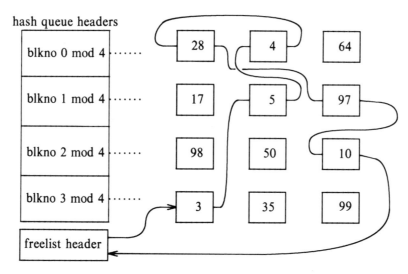

(a) Search for Block 18 - Not in Cache

hash queue headers

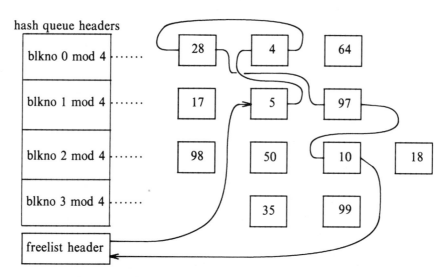

(b) Remove First Block from Free List, Assign to 18

Figure 3.7. Second Scenario for Buffer Allocation

cache. So the kernel removes the first buffer from the free list instead; that buffer had been allocated to another disk block and is also on a hash queue. If the buffer has not been marked for a delayed write (as will be described later), the kernel marks the buffer busy, removes it from the hash queue where it currently resides, reassigns the buffer header's device and block number to that of the disk block for which the process is searching, and places the buffer on the correct hash queue. The kernel uses the buffer but has no record that the buffer formerly contained data for another disk block. A process searching for the old disk block will not find it in the pool and will have to allocate a new buffer for it from the free list, exactly as outlined here. When the kernel finishes with the buffer, it releases it as described above. In Figure 3.7, for example, the kernel searches for block 18 but does not find it on the hash queue marked "blkno 2 mod 4." It therefore removes the first buffer from the free list (block 3), assigns it to block 18, and places it on the appropriate hash queue.

In the third scenario in algorithm *getblk*, the kernel also has to allocate a buffer from the free list. However, it discovers that the buffer it removes from the free list has been marked for "delayed write," so it must write the contents of the buffer to disk before using the buffer. The kernel starts an asynchronous write to disk and tries to allocate another buffer from the free list. When the asynchronous write completes, the kernel releases the buffer and places it at the head of the free list. The buffer had started at the end of the free list and had traveled to the head of the free list. If, after the asynchronous write, the kernel were to place the buffer at the end of the free list, the buffer would get a free trip through the free list, working against the least recently used algorithm. For example, in Figure 3.8, the kernel cannot find block 18, but when it attempts to allocate the first two buffers (one at a time) on the free list, it finds them marked for delayed write. The kernel removes them from the free list, starts write operations to disk for the blocks, and allocates the third buffer on the free list, block 4. It reassigns the buffer's device and block number fields appropriately and places the buffer, now marked block 18, on its new hash queue.

In the fourth scenario (Figure 3.9), the kernel, acting for process A, cannot find the disk block on its hash queue, so it attempts to allocate a new buffer from the free list, as in the second scenario. However, no buffers are available on the free list, so process A goes to sleep until another process executes algorithm *brelse*, freeing a buffer. When the kernel schedules process A, it must search the hash queue again for the block. It cannot allocate a buffer immediately from the free list, because it is possible that several processes were waiting for a free buffer and that one of them allocated a newly freed buffer for the target block sought by process A. Thus, searching for the block again insures that only one buffer contains the disk block. Figure 3.10 depicts the contention between two processes for a free buffer.

The final scenario (Figure 3.11) is complicated, because it involves complex relationships between several processes. Suppose the kernel, acting for process A, searches for a disk block and allocates a buffer but goes to sleep before freeing the

hash queue headers

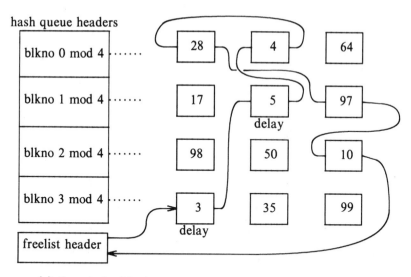

(a) Search for Block 18, Delayed Write Blocks on Free List

hash queue headers

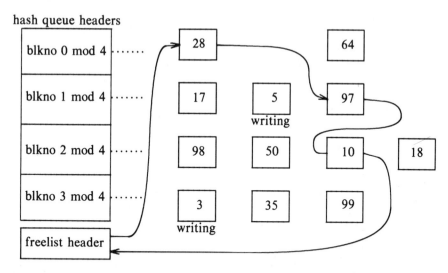

(b) Writing Blocks 3, 5, Reassign 4 to 18

Figure 3.8. Third Scenario for Buffer Allocation

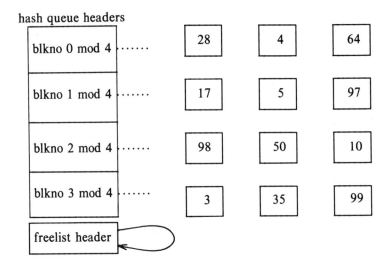

hash queue headers

blkno 0 mod 4 ······	28	4	64
blkno 1 mod 4 ······	17	5	97
blkno 2 mod 4 ······	98	50	10
blkno 3 mod 4 ······	3	35	99

freelist header

Search for Block 18, Empty Free List

Figure 3.9. Fourth Scenario for Allocating Buffer

buffer. For example, if process A attempts to read a disk block and allocates a buffer as in scenario 2, then it will sleep while it waits for the I/O transmission from disk to complete. While process A sleeps, suppose the kernel schedules a second process, B, which tries to access the disk block whose buffer was just locked by process A. Process B (going through scenario 5) will find the locked block on the hash queue. Since it is illegal to use a locked buffer and it is illegal to allocate a second buffer for a disk block, process B marks the buffer "in demand" and then sleeps and waits for process A to release the buffer.

Process A will eventually release the buffer and notice that the buffer is in demand. It awakens all processes sleeping on the event "the buffer becomes free," including process B. When the kernel again schedules process B, process B must verify that the buffer is free. Another process, C, may have been waiting for the same buffer, and the kernel may have scheduled C to run before process B; process C may have gone to sleep leaving the buffer locked. Hence, process B must check that the block is indeed free.

Process B must also verify that the buffer contains the disk block that it originally requested, because process C may have allocated the buffer to another block, as in scenario 2. When process B executes, it may find that it had been waiting for the wrong buffer, so it must search for the block again: If it were to allocate a buffer automatically from the free list, it would miss the possibility that another process just allocated a buffer for the block.

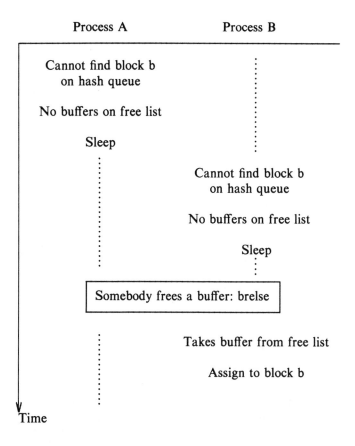

Figure 3.10. Race for Free Buffer

In the end, process B will find its block, possibly allocating a new buffer from the free list as in the second scenario. In Figure 3.11, for example, a process searching for block 99 finds it on its hash queue, but the block is marked busy. The process sleeps until the block becomes free and then restarts the algorithm from the beginning. Figure 3.12 depicts the contention for a locked buffer.

The algorithm for buffer allocation must be safe; processes must not sleep forever, and they must eventually get a buffer. The kernel guarantees that all processes waiting for buffers will wake up, because it allocates buffers during the execution of system calls and frees them before returning.[3] Processes in user mode

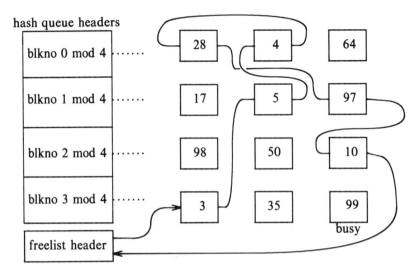

Search for Block 99, Block Busy

Figure 3.11. Fifth Scenario for Buffer Allocation

do not control the allocation of kernel buffers directly, so they cannot purposely "hog" buffers. The kernel loses control over a buffer only when it waits for the completion of I/O between the buffer and the disk. It is conceivable that a disk drive is corrupt so that it cannot interrupt the CPU, preventing the kernel from ever releasing the buffer. The disk driver must monitor the hardware for such cases and return an error to the kernel for a bad disk job. In short, the kernel can guarantee that processes sleeping for a buffer will wake up eventually.

It is also possible to imagine cases where a process is starved out of accessing a buffer. In the fourth scenario, for example, if several processes sleep while waiting for a buffer to become free, the kernel does not guarantee that they get a buffer in the order that they requested one. A process could sleep and wake up when a buffer becomes free, only to go to sleep again because another process got control of the buffer first. Theoretically, this could go on forever, but practically, it is not a problem because of the many buffers that are typically configured in the system.

---

3. The *mount* system call is an exception, because it allocates a buffer until a later *umount* call. This exception is not critical, because the total number of buffers far exceeds the number of active mounted file systems.

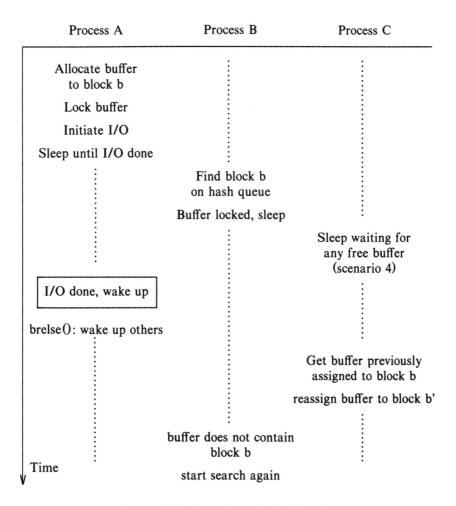

Figure 3.12. Race for a Locked Buffer

3.4 READING AND WRITING DISK BLOCKS

Now that the buffer allocation algorithm has been covered, the procedures for reading and writing disk blocks should be easy to understand. To read a disk block (Figure 3.13), a process uses algorithm *getblk* to search for it in the buffer cache. If it is in the cache, the kernel can return it immediately without physically reading the block from the disk. If it is not in the cache, the kernel calls the disk driver to "schedule" a read request and goes to sleep awaiting the event that the I/O completes. The disk driver notifies the disk controller hardware that it wants to read data, and the disk controller later transmits the data to the buffer. Finally,

```
algorithm bread      /* block read */
input:   file system block number
output: buffer containing data
{
        get buffer for block (algorithm getblk);
        if (buffer data valid)
            return buffer;
        initiate disk read;
        sleep(event disk read complete);
        return(buffer);
}
```

Figure 3.13. Algorithm for Reading a Disk Block

the disk controller interrupts the processor when the I/O is complete, and the disk interrupt handler awakens the sleeping process; the contents of the disk block are now in the buffer. The modules that requested the particular block now have the data; when they no longer need the buffer they release it so that other processes can access it.

Chapter 5 shows how higher-level kernel modules (such as the file subsystem) may anticipate the need for a second disk block when a process reads a file sequentially. The modules request the second I/O asynchronously in the hope that the data will be in memory when needed, improving performance. To do this, the kernel executes the block read-ahead algorithm *breada* (Figure 3.14): The kernel checks if the first block is in the cache and, if it is not there, invokes the disk driver to read that block. If the second block is not in the buffer cache, the kernel instructs the disk driver to read it asynchronously. Then the process goes to sleep awaiting the event that the I/O is complete on the first block. When it awakens, it returns the buffer for the first block, and does not care when the I/O for the second block completes. When the I/O for the second block does complete, the disk controller interrupts the system; the interrupt handler recognizes that the I/O was asynchronous and releases the buffer (algorithm *brelse*). If it would not release the buffer, the buffer would remain locked and, therefore, inaccessible to all processes. It is impossible to unlock the buffer beforehand, because I/O to the buffer was active, and hence the buffer contents were not valid. Later, if the process wants to read the second block, it should find it in the buffer cache, the I/O having completed in the meantime. If, at the beginning of *breada*, the first block was in the buffer cache, the kernel immediately checks if the second block is in the cache and proceeds as just described.

The algorithm for writing the contents of a buffer to a disk block is similar (Figure 3.15). The kernel informs the disk driver that it has a buffer whose contents should be output, and the disk driver schedules the block for I/O. If the write is synchronous, the calling process goes to sleep awaiting I/O completion and

```
algorithm breada        /* block read and read ahead */
input:  (1) file system block number for immediate read
        (2) file system block number for asynchronous read
output: buffer containing data for immediate read
{
        if (first block not in cache)
        {
                get buffer for first block (algorithm getblk);
                if (buffer data not valid)
                        initiate disk read;
        }
        if (second block not in cache)
        {
                get buffer for second block (algorithm getblk);
                if (buffer data valid)
                        release buffer (algorithm brelse);
                else
                        initiate disk read;
        }
        if (first block was originally in cache)
        {
                read first block (algorithm bread);
                return buffer;
        }
        sleep(event first buffer contains valid data);
        return buffer;
}
```

Figure 3.14. Algorithm for Block Read Ahead

releases the buffer when it awakens. If the write is asynchronous, the kernel starts the disk write but does not wait for the write to complete. The kernel will release the buffer when the I/O completes.

There are occasions, described in the next two chapters, when the kernel does not write data immediately to disk. If it does a "delayed write," it marks the buffer accordingly, releases the buffer using algorithm *brelse*, and continues without scheduling I/O. The kernel writes the block to disk before another process can reallocate the buffer to another block, as described in scenario 3 of *getblk*. In the meantime, the kernel hopes that a process accesses the block before the buffer must be written to disk; if that process subsequently changes the contents of the buffer, the kernel saves an extra disk operation.

A delayed write is different from an *asynchronous write*. When doing an asynchronous write, the kernel starts the disk operation immediately but does not wait for its completion. For a "delayed write," the kernel puts off the physical write to disk as long as possible; then, recalling the third scenario in algorithm

```
algorithm bwrite      /* block write */
input:   buffer
output: none
{
        initiate disk write;
        if (I/O synchronous)
        {
                sleep(event I/O complete);
                release buffer (algorithm brelse);
        }
        else if (buffer marked for delayed write)
                mark buffer to put at head of free list;
}
```

Figure 3.15. Algorithm for Writing a Disk Block

getblk, it marks the buffer "old" and writes the block to disk asynchronously. The disk controller later interrupts the system and releases the buffer, using algorithm *brelse*; the buffer ends up on the head of the free list, because it was "old." Because of the two asynchronous I/O operations — block read ahead and delayed write — the kernel can invoke *brelse* from an interrupt handler. Hence, it must prevent interrupts in any procedure that manipulates the buffer free list, because *brelse* places buffers on the free list.

3.5 ADVANTAGES AND DISADVANTAGES OF THE BUFFER CACHE

Use of the buffer cache has several advantages and, unfortunately, some disadvantages.

- The use of buffers allows uniform disk access, because the kernel does not need to know the reason for the I/O. Instead, it copies data to and from buffers, regardless of whether the data is part of a file, an inode, or a super block. The buffering of disk I/O makes the code more modular, since the parts of the kernel that do the I/O with the disk have one interface for all purposes. In short, system design is simpler.
- The system places no data alignment restrictions on user processes doing I/O, because the kernel aligns data internally. Hardware implementations frequently require a particular alignment of data for disk I/O, such as aligning the data on a two-byte boundary or on a four-byte boundary in memory. Without a buffer mechanism, programmers would have to make sure that their data buffers were correctly aligned. Many programmer errors would result, and programs would not be portable to UNIX systems running on machines with stricter address alignment properties. By copying data from user buffers to system buffers (and vice versa), the kernel eliminates the need for special alignment of user buffers,

making user programs simpler and more portable.

- Use of the buffer cache can reduce the amount of disk traffic, thereby increasing overall system throughput and decreasing response time. Processes reading from the file system may find data blocks in the cache and avoid the need for disk I/O. The kernel frequently uses "delayed write" to avoid unnecessary disk writes, leaving the block in the buffer cache and hoping for a cache hit on the block. Obviously, the chances of a cache hit are greater for systems with many buffers. However, the number of buffers a system can profitably configure is constrained by the amount of memory that should be kept available for executing processes: if too much memory is used for buffers, the system may slow down because of excessive process swapping or paging.

- The buffer algorithms help insure file system integrity, because they maintain a common, single image of disk blocks contained in the cache. If two processes simultaneously attempt to manipulate one disk block, the buffer algorithms (*getblk* for example) serialize their access, preventing data corruption.

- Reduction of disk traffic is important for good throughput and response time, but the cache strategy also introduces several disadvantages. Since the kernel does not immediately write data to the disk for a delayed write, the system is vulnerable to crashes that leave disk data in an incorrect state. Although recent system implementations have reduced the damage caused by catastrophic events, the basic problem remains: A user issuing a write system call is never sure when the data finally makes its way to disk.[4]

- Use of the buffer cache requires an extra data copy when reading and writing to and from user processes. A process writing data copies the data into the kernel, and the kernel copies the data to disk; a process reading data has the data read from disk into the kernel and from the kernel to the user process. When transmitting large amounts of data, the extra copy slows down performance, but when transmitting small amounts of data, it improves performance because the kernel buffers the data (using algorithms *getblk* and delayed write) until it is economical to transmit to or from the disk.

3.6 SUMMARY

This chapter has presented the structure of the buffer cache and the various methods by which the kernel locates blocks in the cache. The buffer algorithms combine several simple ideas to provide a sophisticated caching mechanism. The kernel uses the least-recently-used replacement algorithm to keep blocks in the

---

4. The standard I/O package available to C language programs includes an *fflush* call. This function call flushes data from buffers in the user address space (part of the package) into the kernel. However, the user still does not know when the kernel writes the data to the disk.

buffer cache, assuming that blocks that were recently accessed are likely to be accessed again soon. The order that the buffers appear on the free list specifies the order in which they were last used. Other buffer replacement algorithms, such as first-in-first-out or least-frequently-used, are either more complicated to implement or result in lower cache hit ratios. The hash function and hash queues enable the kernel to find particular blocks quickly, and use of doubly linked lists makes it easy to remove buffers from the lists.

The kernel identifies the block it needs by supplying a logical device number and block number. The algorithm *getblk* searches the buffer cache for a block and, if the buffer is present and free, locks the buffer and returns it. If the buffer is locked, the requesting process sleeps until it becomes free. The locking mechanism ensures that only one process at a time manipulates a buffer. If the block is not in the cache, the kernel reassigns a free buffer to the block, locks it and returns it. The algorithm *bread* allocates a buffer for a block and reads the data into the buffer, if necessary. The algorithm *bwrite* copies data into a previously allocated buffer. If, in execution of certain higher-level algorithms, the kernel determines that it is not necessary to copy the data immediately to disk, it marks the buffer "delayed write" to avoid unnecessary I/O. Unfortunately, the "delayed write" scheme means that a process is never sure when the data is physically on disk. If the kernel writes data synchronously to disk, it invokes the disk driver to write the block to the file system and waits for an I/O completion interrupt.

The kernel uses the buffer cache in many ways. It transmits data between application programs and the file system via the buffer cache, and it transmits auxiliary system data such as inodes between higher-level kernel algorithms and the file system. It also uses the buffer cache when reading programs into memory for execution. The following chapters will describe many algorithms that use the procedures described in this chapter. Other algorithms that cache inodes and pages of memory also use techniques similar to those described for the buffer cache.

3.7 EXERCISES

1. Consider the hash function in Figure 3.3. The best hash function is one that distributes the blocks uniformly over the set of hash queues. What would be an optimal hashing function? Should a hash function use the logical device number in its calculations?

2. In the algorithm *getblk*, if the kernel removes a buffer from the free list, it must raise the processor priority level to block out interrupts before checking the free list. Why?

* 3. In algorithm *getblk*, the kernel must raise the processor priority level to block out interrupts before checking if a block is busy. (This is not shown in the text.) Why?

4. In algorithm *brelse*, the kernel enqueues the buffer at the head of the free list if the buffer contents are invalid. If the contents are invalid, should the buffer appear on a hash queue?

5. Suppose the kernel does a delayed write of a block. What happens when another process takes that block from its hash queue? From the free list?

* 6. If several processes contend for a buffer, the kernel guarantees that none of them sleep forever, but it does not guarantee that a process will not be starved out from use of a buffer. Redesign *getblk* so that a process is guaranteed eventual use of a buffer.

7. Redesign the algorithms for *getblk* and *brelse* such that the kernel does not follow a least-recently-used scheme but a first-in-first-out scheme. Repeat this problem using a least-frequently-used scheme.

8. Describe a scenario where the buffer data is already valid in algorithm *bread*.

* 9. Describe the various scenarios that can happen in algorithm *breada*. What happens on the next invocation of *bread* or *breada* when the current read-ahead block will be read? In algorithm *breada*, if the first or second block are not in the cache, the later test to see if the buffer data is valid implies that the block could be in the buffer pool. How is this possible?

10. Describe an algorithm that asks for and receives any free buffer from the buffer pool. Compare this algorithm to *getblk*.

11. Various system calls such as *umount* and *sync* (Chapter 5) require the kernel to flush to disk all buffers that are "delayed write" for a particular file system. Describe an algorithm that implements a buffer flush. What happens to the order of buffers on the free list as a result of the flush operation? How can the kernel be sure that no other process sneaks in and writes a buffer with delayed write to the file system while the flushing process sleeps waiting for an I/O completion?

12. Define system response time as the average time it takes to complete a system call. Define system throughput as the number of processes the system can execute in a given time period. Describe how the buffer cache can help response time. Does it necessarily help system throughput?

4

INTERNAL
REPRESENTATION OF FILES

As observed in Chapter 2, every file on a UNIX system has a unique inode. The inode contains the information necessary for a process to access a file, such as file ownership, access rights, file size, and location of the file's data in the file system. Processes access files by a well defined set of system calls and specify a file by a character string that is the path name. Each path name uniquely specifies a file, and the kernel converts the path name to the file's inode.

This chapter describes the internal structure of files in the UNIX system, and the next chapter describes the system call interface to files. Section 4.1 examines the inode and how the kernel manipulates it, and Section 4.2 examines the internal structure of regular files and how the kernel reads and writes their data. Section 4.3 investigates the structure of directories, the files that allow the kernel to organize the file system as a hierarchy of files, and Section 4.4 presents the algorithm for converting user file names to inodes. Section 4.5 gives the structure of the super block, and Sections 4.6 and 4.7 present the algorithms for assignment of disk inodes and disk blocks to files. Finally, Section 4.8 talks about other file types in the system, namely, pipes and device files.

The algorithms described in this chapter occupy the layer above the buffer cache algorithms explained in the last chapter (Figure 4.1). The algorithm *iget* returns a previously identified inode, possibly reading it from disk via the buffer cache, and the algorithm *iput* releases the inode. The algorithm *bmap* sets kernel parameters for accessing a file. The algorithm *namei* converts a user-level path

Lower Level File System Algorithms

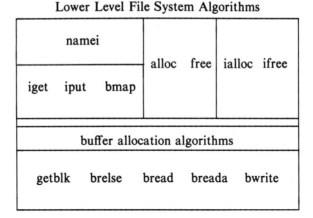

Figure 4.1. File System Algorithms

name to an inode, using the algorithms *iget*, *iput*, and *bmap*. Algorithms *alloc* and *free* allocate and free disk blocks for files, and algorithms *ialloc* and *ifree* assign and free inodes for files.

4.1 INODES

4.1.1 Definition

Inodes exist in a static form on disk, and the kernel reads them into an in-core inode to manipulate them. Disk inodes consist of the following fields:

- File owner identifier. Ownership is divided between an individual owner and a "group" owner and defines the set of users who have access rights to a file. The superuser has access rights to all files in the system.
- File type. Files may be of type regular, directory, character or block special, or FIFO (pipes).
- File access permissions. The system protects files according to three classes: the owner and the group owner of the file, and other users; each class has access rights to read, write and execute the file, which can be set individually. Because directories cannot be executed, execution permission for a directory gives the right to search the directory for a file name.
- File access times, giving the time the file was last modified, when it was last accessed, and when the inode was last modified.

- Number of links to the file, representing the number of names the file has in the directory hierarchy. Chapter 5 explains file links in detail.
- Table of contents for the disk addresses of data in a file. Although users treat the data in a file as a logical stream of bytes, the kernel saves the data in discontiguous disk blocks. The inode identifies the disk blocks that contain the file's data.
- File size. Data in a file is addressable by the number of bytes from the beginning of the file, starting from byte offset 0, and the file size is 1 greater than the highest byte offset of data in the file. For example, if a user creates a file and writes only 1 byte of data at byte offset 1000 in the file, the size of the file is 1001 bytes.

The inode does not specify the path name(s) that access the file.

```
owner mjb

group os

type regular file

perms rwxr-xr-x

accessed Oct 23 1984 1:45 P.M.

modified Oct 22 1984 10:30 A.M.

inode Oct 23 1984 1:30 P.M.

size 6030 bytes

disk addresses
```

Figure 4.2. Sample Disk Inode

Figure 4.2 shows the disk inode of a sample file. This inode is that of a regular file owned by "mjb," which contains 6030 bytes. The system permits "mjb" to read, write, or execute the file; members of the group "os" and all other users can only read or execute the file, not write it. The last time anyone read the file was on October 23, 1984, at 1:45 in the afternoon, and the last time anyone wrote the file was on October 22, 1984, at 10:30 in the morning. The inode was last changed on October 23, 1984, at 1:30 in the afternoon, although the data in the file was not written at that time. The kernel encodes the above information in the inode. Note the distinction between writing the contents of an inode to disk and writing the contents of a file to disk. The contents of a file change only when *writing* it. The contents of an inode change when changing the contents of a file or when changing its owner, permission, or link settings. Changing the contents of a file automatically implies a change to the inode, but changing the inode does not imply that the contents of the file change.

The in-core copy of the inode contains the following fields in addition to the fields of the disk inode: ·

- The status of the in-core inode, indicating whether
  - the inode is locked,
  - a process is waiting for the inode to become unlocked,
  - the in-core representation of the inode differs from the disk copy as a result of a change to the data in the inode,
  - the in-core representation of the file differs from the disk copy as a result of a change to the file data,
  - the file is a mount point (Section 5.15).
- The logical device number of the file system that contains the file.
- The inode number. Since inodes are stored in a linear array on disk (recall Section 2.2.1), the kernel identifies the number of a disk inode by its position in the array. The disk inode does not need this field.
- Pointers to other in-core inodes. The kernel links inodes on hash queues and on a free list in the same way that it links buffers on buffer hash queues and on the buffer free list. A hash queue is identified according to the inode's logical device number and inode number. The kernel can contain at most one in-core copy of a disk inode, but inodes can be simultaneously on a hash queue and on the free list.
- A reference count, indicating the number of instances of the file that are active (such as when *open*ed).

Many fields in the in-core inode are analogous to fields in the buffer header, and the management of inodes is similar to the management of buffers. The inode lock, when set, prevents other processes from accessing the inode; other processes set a flag in the inode when attempting to access it to indicate that they should be awakened when the lock is released. The kernel sets other flags to indicate discrepancies between the disk inode and the in-core copy. When the kernel needs to record changes to the file or to the inode, it writes the in-core copy of the inode to disk after examining these flags.

The most striking difference between an in-core inode and a buffer header is the in-core reference count, which counts the number of active instances of the file. An inode is active when a process allocates it, such as when *open*ing a file. An inode is on the free list only if its reference count is 0, meaning that the kernel can reallocate the in-core inode to another disk inode. The free list of inodes thus serves as a cache of inactive inodes: If a process attempts to access a file whose inode is not currently in the in-core inode pool, the kernel reallocates an in-core inode from the free list for its use. On the other hand, a buffer has no reference count; it is on the free list if and only if it is unlocked.

```
algorithm iget
input:  file system inode number
output: locked inode
{
     while (not done)
     {
          if (inode in inode cache)
          {
               if (inode locked)
               {
                    sleep (event inode becomes unlocked);
                    continue;       /* loop back to while */
               }
               /* special processing for mount points (Chapter 5) */
               if (inode on inode free list)
                    remove from free list;
               increment inode reference count;
               return (inode);
          }

          /* inode not in inode cache */
          if (no inodes on free list)
               return(error);
          remove new inode from free list;
          reset inode number and file system;
          remove inode from old hash queue, place on new one;
          read inode from disk (algorithm bread);
          initialize inode (e.g. reference count to 1);
          return(inode);
     }
}
```

Figure 4.3. Algorithm for Allocation of In-Core Inodes

4.1.2 Accessing Inodes

The kernel identifies particular inodes by their file system and inode number and allocates in-core inodes at the request of higher-level algorithms. The algorithm *iget* allocates an in-core copy of an inode (Figure 4.3); it is almost identical to the algorithm *getblk* for finding a disk block in the buffer cache. The kernel maps the device number and inode number into a hash queue and searches the queue for the inode. If it cannot find the inode, it allocates one from the free list and locks it. The kernel then prepares to read the disk copy of the newly accessed inode into the in-core copy. It already knows the inode number and logical device and computes the logical disk block that contains the inode according to how many disk inodes fit into a disk block. The computation follows the formula

block num = ((inode number − 1) / number of inodes per block) +
$$\text{start block of inode list}$$

where the division operation returns the integer part of the quotient. For example, assuming that block 2 is the beginning of the inode list and that there are 8 inodes per block, then inode number 8 is in disk block 2, and inode number 9 is in disk block 3. If there are 16 inodes in a disk block, then inode numbers 8 and 9 are in disk block 2, and inode number 17 is the first inode in disk block 3.

When the kernel knows the device and disk block number, it reads the block using the algorithm *bread* (Chapter 2), then uses the following formula to compute the byte offset of the inode in the block:

((inode number − 1) modulo (number of inodes per block)) * size of disk inode

For example, if each disk inode occupies 64 bytes and there are 8 inodes per disk block, then inode number 8 starts at byte offset 448 in the disk block. The kernel removes the in-core inode from the free list, places it on the correct hash queue, and sets its in-core reference count to 1. It copies the file type, owner fields, permission settings, link count, file size, and the table of contents from the disk inode to the in-core inode, and returns a locked inode.

The kernel manipulates the inode lock and reference count independently. The lock is set during execution of a system call to prevent other processes from accessing the inode while it is in use (and possibly inconsistent). The kernel releases the lock at the conclusion of the system call: an inode is never locked across system calls. The kernel increments the reference count for every active reference to a file. For example, Section 5.1 will show that it increments the inode reference count when a process *open*s a file. It decrements the reference count only when the reference becomes inactive, for example, when a process *close*s a file. The reference count thus remains set across multiple system calls. The lock is free between system calls to allow processes to share simultaneous access to a file; the reference count remains set between system calls to prevent the kernel from reallocating an active in-core inode. Thus, the kernel can lock and unlock an allocated inode independent of the value of the reference count. System calls other than *open* allocate and release inodes, as will be seen in Chapter 5.

Returning to algorithm *iget*, if the kernel attempts to take an inode from the free list but finds the free list empty, it reports an error. This is different from the philosophy the kernel follows for disk buffers, where a process sleeps until a buffer becomes free: Processes have control over the allocation of inodes at user level via execution of *open* and *close* system calls, and consequently the kernel cannot guarantee when an inode will become available. Therefore, a process that goes to sleep waiting for a free inode to become available may never wake up. Rather than leave such a process "hanging," the kernel fails the system call. However, processes do not have such control over buffers: Because a process cannot keep a buffer locked across system calls, the kernel can guarantee that a buffer will become free soon, and a process therefore sleeps until one is available.

The preceding paragraphs cover the case where the kernel allocated an inode that was not in the inode cache. If the inode is in the cache, the process (A) would find it on its hash queue and check if the inode was currently locked by another process (B). If the inode is locked, process A sleeps, setting a flag in the in-core inode to indicate that it is waiting for the inode to become free. When process B later unlocks the inode, it awakens all processes (including process A) waiting for the inode to become free. When process A is finally able to use the inode, it locks the inode so that other processes cannot allocate it. If the reference count was previously 0, the inode also appears on the free list, so the kernel removes it from there: the inode is no longer free. The kernel increments the inode reference count and returns a locked inode.

To summarize, the *iget* algorithm is used toward the beginning of system calls when a process first accesses a file. The algorithm returns a locked inode structure with reference count 1 greater than it had previously been. The in-core inode contains up-to-date information on the state of the file. The kernel unlocks the inode before returning from the system call so that other system calls can access the inode if they wish. Chapter 5 treats these cases in greater detail.

```
algorithm iput                /* release (put) access to in-core inode */
input:   pointer to in-core inode
output: none
{
      lock inode if not already locked;
      decrement inode reference count;
      if (reference count == 0)
      {
            if (inode link count == 0)
            {
                  free disk blocks for file (algorithm free, section 4.7);
                  set file type to 0;
                  free inode (algorithm ifree, section 4.6);
            }
            if (file accessed or inode changed or file changed)
                  update disk inode;
            put inode on free list;
      }
      release inode lock;
}
```

Figure 4.4. Releasing an Inode

4.1.3 Releasing Inodes

When the kernel releases an inode (algorithm *iput*, Figure 4.4), it decrements its in-core reference count. If the count drops to 0, the kernel writes the inode to disk if the in-core copy differs from the disk copy. They differ if the file data has changed, if the file access time has changed, or if the file owner or access permissions have changed. The kernel places the inode on the free list of inodes, effectively caching the inode in case it is needed again soon. The kernel may also release all data blocks associated with the file and free the inode if the number of links to the file is 0.

4.2 STRUCTURE OF A REGULAR FILE

As mentioned above, the inode contains the table of contents to locate a file's data on disk. Since each block on a disk is addressable by number, the table of contents consists of a set of disk block numbers. If the data in a file were stored in a contiguous section of the disk (that is, the file occupied a linear sequence of disk blocks), then storing the start block address and the file size in the inode would suffice to access all the data in the file. However, such an allocation strategy would not allow for simple expansion and contraction of files in the file system without running the risk of fragmenting free storage area on the disk. Furthermore, the kernel would have to allocate and reserve contiguous space in the file system before allowing operations that would increase the file size.

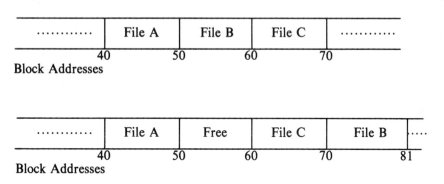

Figure 4.5. Allocation of Contiguous Files and Fragmentation of Free Space

For example, suppose a user creates three files, A, B and C, each consisting of 10 disk blocks of storage, and suppose the system allocated storage for the three files contiguously. If the user then wishes to add 5 blocks of data to the middle file, B, the kernel would have to copy file B to a place in the file system that had room for 15 blocks of storage. Aside from the expense of such an operation, the disk blocks previously occupied by file B's data would be unusable except for files smaller than 10 blocks (Figure 4.5). The kernel could minimize fragmentation of storage space by periodically running garbage collection procedures to compact available storage, but that would place an added drain on processing power.

For greater flexibility, the kernel allocates file space one block at a time and allows the data in a file to be spread throughout the file system. But this allocation scheme complicates the task of locating the data. The table of contents could consist of a list of block numbers such that the blocks contain the data belonging to the file, but simple calculations show that a linear list of file blocks in the inode is difficult to manage. If a logical block contains 1K bytes, then a file consisting of 10K bytes would require an index of 10 block numbers, but a file containing 100K bytes would require an index of 100 block numbers. Either the size of the inode would vary according to the size of the file, or a relatively low limit would have to be placed on the size of a file.

To keep the inode structure small yet still allow large files, the table of contents of disk blocks conforms to that shown in Figure 4.6. The System V UNIX system runs with 13 entries in the inode table of contents, but the principles are independent of the number of entries. The blocks marked "direct" in the figure contain the numbers of disk blocks that contain real data. The block marked "single indirect" refers to a block that contains a list of direct block numbers. To access the data via the indirect block, the kernel must read the indirect block, find the appropriate direct block entry, and then read the direct block to find the data. The block marked "double indirect" contains a list of indirect block numbers, and the block marked "triple indirect" contains a list of double indirect block numbers.

In principle, the method could be extended to support "quadruple indirect blocks," "quintuple indirect blocks," and so on, but the current structure has sufficed in practice. Assume that a logical block on the file system holds 1K bytes and that a block number is addressable by a 32 bit (4 byte) integer. Then a block can hold up to 256 block numbers. The maximum number of bytes that could be held in a file is calculated (Figure 4.7) at well over 16 gigabytes, using 10 direct blocks and 1 indirect, 1 double indirect, and 1 triple indirect block in the inode. Given that the file size field in the inode is 32 bits, the size of a file is effectively limited to 4 gigabytes (2^{32}).

Processes access data in a file by byte offset. They work in terms of byte counts and view a file as a stream of bytes starting at byte address 0 and going up to the size of the file. The kernel converts the user view of bytes into a view of blocks: The file starts at logical block 0 and continues to a logical block number corresponding to the file size. The kernel accesses the inode and converts the logical file block into the appropriate disk block. Figure 4.8 gives the algorithm *bmap* for converting a file byte offset into a physical disk block.

Consider the block layout for the file in Figure 4.9 and assume that a disk block contains 1024 bytes. If a process wants to access byte offset 9000, the kernel calculates that the byte is in direct block 8 in the file (counting from 0). It then accesses block number 367; the 808th byte in that block (starting from 0) is byte

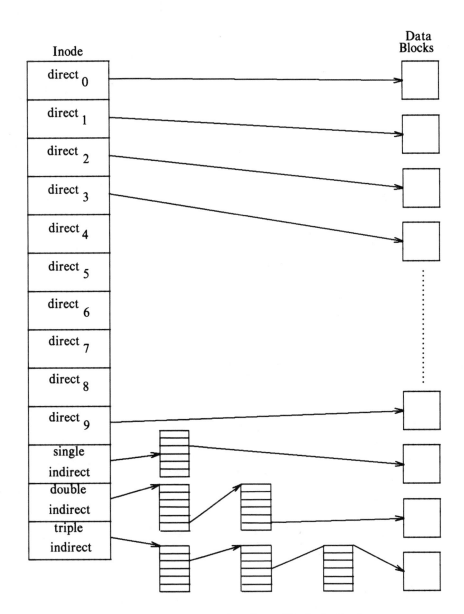

Figure 4.6. Direct and Indirect Blocks in Inode

10 direct blocks with 1K bytes each =	10K bytes
1 indirect block with 256 direct blocks =	256K bytes
1 double indirect block with 256 indirect blocks =	64M bytes
1 triple indirect block with 256 double indirect blocks =	16G bytes

Figure 4.7. Byte Capacity of a File — 1K Bytes Per Block

```
algorithm bmap      /* block map of logical file byte offset to file system block */
input:  (1) inode
        (2) byte offset
output: (1) block number in file system
        (2) byte offset into block
        (3) bytes of I/O in block
        (4) read ahead block number
{
        calculate logical block number in file from byte offset;
        calculate start byte in block for I/O;          /* output 2 */
        calculate number of bytes to copy to user;      /* output 3 */
        check if read—ahead applicable, mark inode;     /* output 4 */
        determine level of indirection;
        while (not at necessary level of indirection)
        {
                calculate index into inode or indirect block from
                        logical block number in file;
                get disk block number from inode or indirect block;
                release buffer from previous disk read, if any (algorithm brelse);
                if (no more levels of indirection)
                        return (block number);
                read indirect disk block (algorithm bread);
                adjust logical block number in file according to level of indirection;
        }
}
```

Figure 4.8. Conversion of Byte Offset to Block Number in File System

9000 in the file. If a process wants to access byte offset 350,000 in the file, it must access a double indirect block, number 9156 in the figure. Since an indirect block has room for 256 block numbers, the first byte accessed via the double indirect block is byte number 272,384 (256K + 10K); byte number 350,000 in a file is therefore byte number 77,616 of the double indirect block. Since each single indirect block accesses 256K bytes, byte number 350,000 must be in the 0th single indirect block of the double indirect block — block number 331. Since each direct block in a single indirect block contains 1K bytes, byte number 77,616 of a single

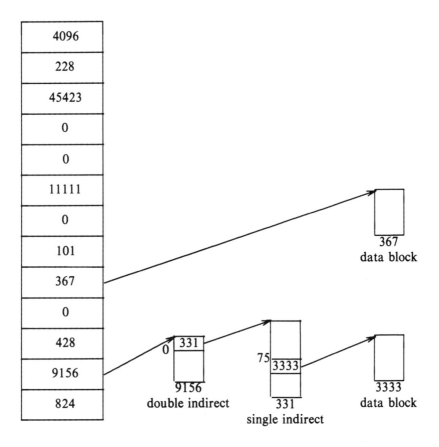

Figure 4.9. Block Layout of a Sample File and its Inode

indirect block is in the 75th direct block in the single indirect block — block number 3333. Finally, byte number 350,000 in the file is at byte number 816 in block 3333.

Examining Figure 4.9 more closely, several block entries in the inode are 0, meaning that the logical block entries contain no data. This happens if no process ever wrote data into the file at any byte offsets corresponding to those blocks and hence the block numbers remain at their initial value, 0. No disk space is wasted for such blocks. Processes can cause such a block layout in a file by using the *lseek* and *write* system calls, as described in the next chapter. The next chapter also describes how the kernel takes care of *read* system calls that access such blocks.

The conversion of a large byte offset, particularly one that is referenced via the triple indirect block, is an arduous procedure that could require the kernel to access three disk blocks in addition to the inode and data block. Even if the kernel finds the blocks in the buffer cache, the operation is still expensive, because the kernel must make multiple requests of the buffer cache and may have to sleep awaiting locked buffers. How effective is the algorithm in practice? That depends on how the system is used and whether the user community and job mix are such that the kernel accesses large files or small files more frequently. It has been observed [Mullender 84], however, that most files on UNIX systems contain less than 10K bytes, and many contain less than 1K bytes![1] Since 10K bytes of a file are stored in direct blocks, most file data can be accessed with one disk access. So in spite of the fact that accessing large files is an expensive operation, accessing common-sized files is fast.

Two extensions to the inode structure just described attempt to take advantage of file size characteristics. A major principle in the 4.2 BSD file system implementation [McKusick 84] is that the more data the kernel can access on the disk in a single operation, the faster file access becomes. That argues for having larger logical disk blocks, and the Berkeley implementation allows logical disk blocks of 4K or 8K bytes. But having larger block sizes on disk increases block fragmentation, leaving large portions of disk space unused. For instance, if the logical block size is 8K bytes, then a file of size 12K bytes uses 1 complete block and half of a second block. The other half of the second block (4K bytes) is wasted; no other file can use the space for data storage. If the sizes of files are such that the number of bytes in the last block of a file is uniformly distributed, then the average wasted space is half a block per file; the amount of wasted disk space can be as high as 45% for a file system with logical blocks of size 4K bytes [McKusick 84]. The Berkeley implementation remedies the situation by allocating a block *fragment* to contain the last data in a file. One disk block can contain fragments belonging to several files. An exercise in Chapter 5 explores some details of the implementation.

The second extension to the classic inode structure described here is to store file data in the inode (see [Mullender 84]). By expanding the inode to occupy an entire disk block, a small portion of the block can be used for the inode structures and the remainder of the block can store the entire file, in many cases, or the end of a file otherwise. The main advantage is that only one disk access is necessary to get the inode and its data if the file fits in the inode block.

---

1. For a sample of 19,978 files, Mullender and Tannenbaum say that approximately 85% of the files were smaller than 8K bytes and that 48% were smaller than 1K bytes. Although these percentages will vary from one installation to the next, they are representative of many UNIX systems.

4.3 DIRECTORIES

Recall from Chapter 1 that directories are the files that give the file system its hierarchical structure; they play an important role in conversion of a file name to an inode number. A directory is a file whose data is a sequence of entries, each consisting of an inode number and the name of a file contained in the directory. A path name is a null terminated character string divided into separate components by the slash ("/") character. Each component except the last must be the name of a directory, but the last component may be a non-directory file. UNIX System V restricts component names to a maximum of 14 characters; with a 2 byte entry for the inode number, the size of a directory entry is 16 bytes.

Byte Offset in Directory	Inode Number (2 bytes)	File Names
0	83	.
16	2	..
32	1798	init
48	1276	fsck
64	85	clri
80	1268	motd
96	1799	mount
112	88	mknod
128	2114	passwd
144	1717	umount
160	1851	checklist
176	92	fsdb1b
192	84	config
208	1432	getty
224	0	crash
240	95	mkfs
256	188	inittab

Figure 4.10. Directory Layout for /etc

Figure 4.10 depicts the layout of the directory "etc". Every directory contains the file names dot and dot-dot ("." and "..") whose inode numbers are those of the directory and its parent directory, respectively. The inode number of "." in "/etc" is located at offset 0 in the file, and its value is 83. The inode number of ".." is located at offset 16, and its value is 2. Directory entries may be empty, indicated by an inode number of 0. For instance, the entry at address 224 in "/etc" is empty, although it once contained an entry for a file named "crash". The program *mkfs* initializes a file system so that "." and ".." of the root directory have the root inode number of the file system.

The kernel stores data for a directory just as it stores data for an ordinary file, using the inode structure and levels of direct and indirect blocks. Processes may read directories in the same way they read regular files, but the kernel reserves exclusive right to write a directory, thus insuring its correct structure. The access permissions of a directory have the following meaning: read permission on a directory allows a process to read a directory; write permission allows a process to create new directory entries or remove old ones (via the *creat*, *mknod*, *link*, and *unlink* system calls), thereby altering the contents of the directory; execute permission allows a process to search the directory for a file name (it is meaningless to execute a directory). Exercise 4.6 explores the difference between reading and searching a directory.

4.4 CONVERSION OF A PATH NAME TO AN INODE

The initial access to a file is by its path name, as in the *open*, *chdir* (change directory), or *link* system calls. Because the kernel works internally with inodes rather than with path names, it converts the path names to inodes to access files. The algorithm *namei* parses the path name one component at a time, converting each component into an inode based on its name and the directory being searched, and eventually returns the inode of the input path name (Figure 4.11).

Recall from Chapter 2 that every process is associated with (resides in) a current directory; the *u area* contains a pointer to the current directory inode. The current directory of the first process in the system, process 0, is the root directory. The current directory of every other process starts out as the current directory of its parent process at the time it was created (see Section 5.10). Processes change their current directory by executing the *chdir* (change directory) system call. All path name searches start from the current directory of the process unless the path name starts with the slash character, signifying that the search should start from the root directory. In either case, the kernel can easily find the inode where the path name search starts: The current directory is stored in the process *u area*, and the system root inode is stored in a global variable.[2]

Namei uses intermediate inodes as it parses a path name; call them working inodes. The inode where the search starts is the first working inode. During each iteration of the *namei* loop, the kernel makes sure that the working inode is indeed that of a directory. Otherwise, the system would violate the assertion that non-directory files can only be leaf nodes of the file system tree. The process must also have permission to search the directory (read permission is insufficient). The user ID of the process must match the owner or group ID of the file, and execute

---

2. A process can execute the *chroot* system call to change its notion of the file system root. The changed root is stored in the *u area*.

```
algorithm namei          /* convert path name to inode */
input:   path name
output: locked inode
{
        if (path name starts from root)
                working inode = root inode (algorithm iget);
        else
                working inode = current directory inode (algorithm iget);

        while (there is more path name)
        {
                read next path name component from input;
                verify that working inode is of directory, access permissions OK;
                if (working inode is of root and component is "..")
                        continue;        /* loop back to while */
                read directory (working inode) by repeated use of algorithms
                        bmap, bread and brelse;
                if (component matches an entry in directory (working inode))
                {
                        get inode number for matched component;
                        release working inode (algorithm iput);
                        working inode = inode of matched component (algorithm iget);
                }
                else        /* component not in directory */
                        return (no inode);
        }
        return (working inode);
}
```

Figure 4.11. Algorithm for Conversion of a Path Name to an Inode

permission must be granted, or the file must allow search to all users. Otherwise the search fails.

The kernel does a linear search of the directory file associated with the working inode, trying to match the path name component to a directory entry name. Starting at byte offset 0, it converts the byte offset in the directory to the appropriate disk block according to algorithm *bmap* and reads the block using algorithm *bread*. It searches the block for the path name component, treating the contents of the block as a sequence of directory entries. If it finds a match, it records the inode number of the matched directory entry, releases the block (algorithm *brelse*) and the old working inode (algorithm *iput*), and allocates the inode of the matched component (algorithm *iget*). The new inode becomes the working inode. If the kernel does not match the path name with any names in the block, it releases the block, adjusts the byte offset by the number of bytes in a block, converts the new offset to a disk block number (algorithm *bmap*), and reads the next block. The kernel repeats the procedure until it matches the path name component with a directory entry name, or until it reaches the end of the directory.

For example, suppose a process wants to open the file "/etc/passwd". When the kernel starts parsing the file name, it encounters "/" and gets the system root inode. Making root its current working inode, the kernel gathers in the string "etc". After checking that the current inode is that of a directory ("/") and that the process has the necessary permissions to search it, the kernel searches root for a file whose name is "etc": It accesses the data in the root directory block by block and searches each block one entry at a time until it locates an entry for "etc". On finding the entry, the kernel releases the inode for root (algorithm *iput*) and allocates the inode for "etc" (algorithm *iget*) according to the inode number of the entry just found. After ascertaining that "etc" is a directory and that it has the requisite search permissions, the kernel searches "etc" block by block for a directory structure entry for the file "passwd". Referring to Figure 4.10, it would find the entry for "passwd" as the ninth entry of the directory. On finding it, the kernel releases the inode for "etc", allocates the inode for "passwd", and — since the path name is exhausted — returns that inode.

It is natural to question the efficiency of a linear search of a directory for a path name component. Ritchie points out (see page 1968 of [Ritchie 78b]) that a linear search is efficient because it is bounded by the size of the directory. Furthermore, early UNIX system implementations did not run on machines with large memory space, so there was heavy emphasis on simple algorithms such as linear search schemes. More complicated search schemes could require a different, more complex, directory structure, and would probably run more slowly on small directories than the linear search scheme.

4.5 SUPER BLOCK

So far, this chapter has described the structure of a file, assuming that the inode was previously bound to a file and that the disk blocks containing the data were already assigned. The next sections cover how the kernel assigns inodes and disk blocks. To understand those algorithms, let us examine the structure of the super block.

The super block consists of the following fields:

- the size of the file system,
- the number of free blocks in the file system,
- a list of free blocks available on the file system,
- the index of the next free block in the free block list,
- the size of the inode list,
- the number of free inodes in the file system,
- a list of free inodes in the file system,
- the index of the next free inode in the free inode list,

- lock fields for the free block and free inode lists,
- a flag indicating that the super block has been modified.

The remainder of this chapter will explain the use of the arrays, indices and locks. The kernel periodically writes the super block to disk if it had been modified so that it is consistent with the data in the file system.

4.6 INODE ASSIGNMENT TO A NEW FILE

The kernel uses algorithm *iget* to allocate a known inode, one whose (file system and) inode number was previously determined. In algorithm *namei* for instance, the kernel determines the inode number by matching a path name component to a name in a directory. Another algorithm, *ialloc*, assigns a disk inode to a newly created file.

The file system contains a linear list of inodes, as mentioned in Chapter 2. An inode is free if its type field is zero. When a process needs a new inode, the kernel could theoretically search the inode list for a free inode. However, such a search would be expensive, requiring at least one read operation (possibly from disk) for every inode. To improve performance, the file system super block contains an array to cache the numbers of free inodes in the file system.

Figure 4.12 shows the algorithm *ialloc* for assigning new inodes. For reasons cited later, the kernel first verifies that no other processes have locked access to the super block free inode list. If the list of inode numbers in the super block is not empty, the kernel assigns the next inode number, allocates a free in-core inode for the newly assigned disk inode using algorithm *iget* (reading the inode from disk if necessary), copies the disk inode to the in-core copy, initializes the fields in the inode, and returns the locked inode. It updates the disk inode to indicate that the inode is now in use: A non-zero file type field indicates that the disk inode is assigned. In the simplest case, the kernel has a good inode, but race conditions exist that necessitate more checking, as will be explained shortly. Loosely defined, a race condition arises when several processes alter common data structures such that the resulting computations depend on the order in which the processes executed, even though all processes obeyed the locking protocol. For example, it is implied here that a process could get a used inode. A race condition is related to the mutual exclusion problem defined in Chapter 2, except that locking schemes solve the mutual exclusion problem there but may not, by themselves, solve all race conditions.

If the super block list of free inodes is empty, the kernel searches the disk and places as many free inode numbers as possible into the super block. The kernel reads the inode list on disk, block by block, and fills the super block list of inode numbers to capacity, remembering the highest-numbered inode that it finds. Call that inode the "remembered" inode; it is the last one saved in the super block. The next time the kernel searches the disk for free inodes, it uses the remembered inode as its starting point, thereby assuring that it wastes no time reading disk blocks

```
algorithm ialloc        /* allocate inode */
input:   file system
output: locked inode
{
      while (not done)
      {
            if (super block locked)
            {
                  sleep (event super block becomes free);
                  continue;         /* while loop */
            }
            if (inode list in super block is empty)
            {
                  lock super block;
                  get remembered inode for free inode search;
                  search disk for free inodes until super block full,
                        or no more free inodes (algorithms bread and brelse);
                  unlock super block;
                  wake up (event super block becomes free);
                  if (no free inodes found on disk)
                        return (no inode);
                  set remembered inode for next free inode search;
            }
            /* there are inodes in super block inode list */
            get inode number from super block inode list;
            get inode (algorithm iget);
            if (inode not free after all)          /* !!! */
            {
                  write inode to disk;
                  release inode (algorithm iput);
                  continue;         /* while loop */
            }
            /* inode is free */
            initialize inode;
            write inode to disk;
            decrement file system free inode count;
            return (inode);
      }
}
```

Figure 4.12. Algorithm for Assigning New Inodes

where no free inodes should exist. After gathering a fresh set of free inode numbers, it starts the inode assignment algorithm from the beginning. Whenever the kernel assigns a disk inode, it decrements the free inode count recorded in the super block.

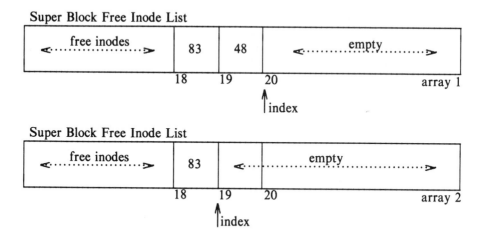

(a) Assigning Free Inode from Middle of List

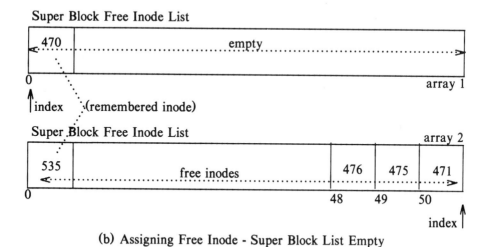

(b) Assigning Free Inode - Super Block List Empty

Figure 4.13. Two Arrays of Free Inode Numbers

Consider the two pairs of arrays of free inode numbers in Figure 4.13. If the list of free inodes in the super block looks like the first array in Figure 4.13(a) when the kernel assigns an inode, it decrements the index for the next valid inode number to 18 and takes inode number 48. If the list of free inodes in the super block looks like the first array in Figure 4.13(b), it will notice that the array is empty and search the disk for free inodes, starting from inode number 470, the remembered inode. When the kernel fills the super block free list to capacity, it remembers the last inode as the start point for the next search of the disk. The kernel assigns an inode it just took from the disk (number 471 in the figure) and continues whatever it was doing.

```
algorithm ifree          /* inode free */
input:   file system inode number
output: none
{
        increment file system free inode count;
        if (super block locked)
              return;
        if (inode list full)
        {
              if (inode number less than remembered inode for search)
                    set remembered inode for search ▬ input inode number;
        }
        else
              store inode number in inode list;
        return;
}
```

Figure 4.14. Algorithm for Freeing Inode

The algorithm for freeing an inode is much simpler. After incrementing the total number of available inodes in the file system, the kernel checks the lock on the super block. If locked, it avoids race conditions by returning immediately: The inode number is not put into the super block, but it can be found on disk and is available for reassignment. If the list is not locked, the kernel checks if it has room for more inode numbers and, if it does, places the inode number in the list and returns. If the list is full, the kernel may not save the newly freed inode there: It compares the number of the freed inode with that of the remembered inode. If the freed inode number is less than the remembered inode number, it "remembers" the newly freed inode number, discarding the old remembered inode number from the super block. The inode is not lost, because the kernel can find it by searching the inode list on disk. The kernel maintains the super block list such that the last inode it dispenses from the list is the remembered inode. Ideally, there should never be free inodes whose inode number is less than the remembered inode number, but

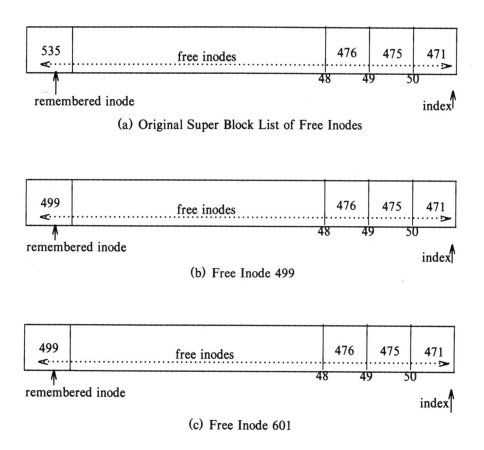

Figure 4.15. Placing Free Inode Numbers into the Super Block

exceptions are possible.

Consider two examples of freeing inodes. If the super block list of free inodes has room for more free inode numbers as in Figure 4.13(a), the kernel places the inode number on the list, increments the index to the next free inode, and proceeds. But if the list of free inodes is full as in Figure 4.15, the kernel compares the inode number it has freed to the remembered inode number that will start the next disk search. Starting with the free inode list in Figure 4.15(a), if the kernel frees inode 499, it makes 499 the remembered inode and evicts number 535 from the free list. If the kernel then frees inode number 601, it does not change the contents of the free list. When it later uses up the inodes in the super block free list, it will search the disk for free inodes starting from inode number 499, and find inodes 535 and 601 again.

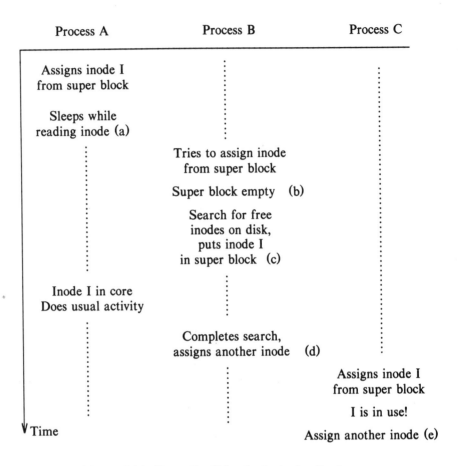

Figure 4.16. Race Condition in Assigning Inodes

The preceding paragraph described the simple cases of the algorithms. Now consider the case where the kernel assigns a new inode and then allocates an in-core copy for the inode. The algorithm implies that the kernel could find that the inode had already been assigned. Although rare, the following scenario shows such a case (refer to Figures 4.16 and 4.17). Consider three processes, A, B, and C, and suppose that the kernel, acting on behalf of process A,[3] assigns inode I but goes to sleep before it copies the disk inode into the in-core copy. Algorithms *iget* (invoked

---

3. As in the last chapter, the term "process" here will mean "the kernel, acting on behalf of a process."

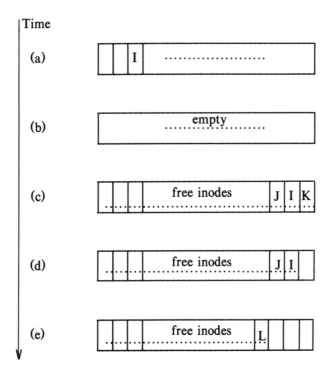

Figure 4.17. Race Condition in Assigning Inodes (continued)

by *ialloc*) and *bread* (invoked by *iget*) give process A ample opportunity to go to sleep. While process A is asleep, suppose process B attempts to assign a new inode but discovers that the super block list of free inodes is empty. Process B searches the disk for free inodes, and suppose it starts its search for free inodes at an inode number lower than that of the inode that A is assigning. It is possible for process B to find inode I free on the disk since process A is still asleep, and the kernel does not know that the inode is about to be assigned. Process B, not realizing the danger, completes its search of the disk, fills up the super block with (supposedly) free inodes, assigns an inode, and departs from the scene. However, inode I is in the super block free list of inode numbers. When process A wakes up, it completes the assignment of inode I. Now suppose process C later requests an inode and happens to pick inode I from the super block free list. When it gets the in-core copy of the inode, it will find its file type set, implying that the inode was already assigned. The kernel checks for this condition and, finding that the inode has been assigned, tries to assign a new one. Writing the updated inode to disk immediately after its assignment in *ialloc* makes the chance of the race smaller, because the file type field will mark the inode in use.

Locking the super block list of inodes while reading in a new set from disk prevents other race conditions. If the super block list were not locked, a process could find it empty and try to populate it from disk, occasionally sleeping while waiting for I/O completion. Suppose a second process also tried to assign a new inode and found the list empty. It, too, would try to populate the list from disk. At best, the two processes are duplicating their efforts and wasting CPU power. At worst, race conditions of the type described in the previous paragraph would be more frequent. Similarly, if a process freeing an inode did not check that the list is locked, it could overwrite inode numbers already in the free list while another process was populating it from disk. Again, the race conditions described above would be more frequent. Although the kernel handles them satisfactorily, system performance would suffer. Use of the lock on the super block free list prevents such race conditions.

4.7 ALLOCATION OF DISK BLOCKS

When a process writes data to a file, the kernel must allocate disk blocks from the file system for direct data blocks and, sometimes, for indirect blocks. The file system super block contains an array that is used to cache the numbers of free disk blocks in the file system. The utility program *mkfs* (make file system) organizes the data blocks of a file system in a linked list, such that each link of the list is a disk block that contains an array of free disk block numbers, and one array entry is the number of the next block of the linked list. Figure 4.18 shows an example of the linked list, where the first block is the super block free list and later blocks on the linked list contain more free block numbers.

When the kernel wants to allocate a block from a file system (algorithm *alloc*, Figure 4.19), it allocates the next available block in the super block list. Once allocated, the block cannot be reallocated until it becomes free. If the allocated block is the last available block in the super block cache, the kernel treats it as a pointer to a block that contains a list of free blocks. It reads the block, populates the super block array with the new list of block numbers, and then proceeds to use the original block number. It allocates a buffer for the block and clears the buffer's data (zeros it). The disk block has now been assigned, and the kernel has a buffer to work with. If the file system contains no free blocks, the calling process receives an error.

If a process *writes* a lot of data to a file, it repeatedly asks the system for blocks to store the data, but the kernel assigns only one block at a time. The program *mkfs* tries to organize the original linked list of free block numbers so that block numbers dispensed to a file are near each other. This helps performance, because it reduces disk seek time and latency when a process reads a file sequentially. Figure 4.18 depicts block numbers in a regular pattern, presumably based on the disk rotation speed. Unfortunately, the order of block numbers on the free block linked lists breaks down with heavy use as processes *write* files and remove them, because block numbers enter and leave the free list at random. The kernel makes no

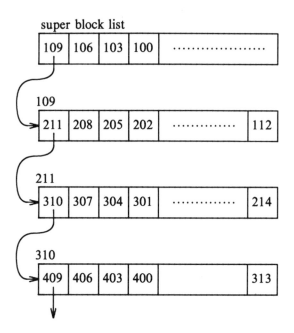

Figure 4.18. Linked List of Free Disk Block Numbers

attempt to sort block numbers on the free list.

The algorithm *free* for freeing a block is the reverse of the one for allocating a block. If the super block list is not full, the block number of the newly freed block is placed on the super block list. If, however, the super block list is full, the newly freed block becomes a link block; the kernel writes the super block list into the block and writes the block to disk. It then places the block number of the newly freed block in the super block list: That block number is the only member of the list.

Figure 4.20 shows a sequence of *alloc* and *free* operations, starting with one entry on the super block free list. The kernel frees block 949 and places the block number on the free list. It then allocates a block and removes block number 949 from the free list. Finally, it allocates a block and removes block number 109 from the free list. Because the super block free list is now empty, the kernel replenishes the list by copying in the contents of block 109, the next link on the linked list. Figure 4.20(d) shows the full super block list and the next link block, block 211.

The algorithms for assigning and freeing inodes and disk blocks are similar in that the kernel uses the super block as a cache containing indices of free resources, block numbers, and inode numbers. It maintains a linked list of block numbers such that every free block number in the file system appears in some element of the linked list, but it maintains no such list of free inodes. There are three reasons for

```
algorithm alloc     /* file system block allocation */
input:   file system number
output: buffer for new block
{
        while (super block locked)
                sleep (event super block not locked);
        remove block from super block free list;
        if (removed last block from free list)
        {
                lock super block;
                read block just taken from free list (algorithm bread);
                copy block numbers in block into super block;
                release block buffer (algorithm brelse);
                unlock super block;
                wake up processes (event super block not locked);
        }
        get buffer for block removed from super block list (algorithm getblk);
        zero buffer contents;
        decrement total count of free blocks;
        mark super block modified;
        return buffer;
}
```

Figure 4.19. Algorithm for Allocating Disk Block

the different treatment.

1. The kernel can determine whether an inode is free by inspection: If the file type field is clear, the inode is free. The kernel needs no other mechanism to describe free inodes. However, it cannot determine whether a block is free just by looking at it. It could not distinguish between a bit pattern that indicates the block is free and data that happened to have that bit pattern. Hence, the kernel requires an external method to identify free blocks, and traditional implementations have used a linked list.
2. Disk blocks lend themselves to the use of linked lists: A disk block easily holds large lists of free block numbers. But inodes have no convenient place for bulk storage of large lists of free inode numbers.
3. Users tend to consume disk block resources more quickly than they consume inodes, so the apparent lag in performance when searching the disk for free inodes is not as critical as it would be for searching for free disk blocks.

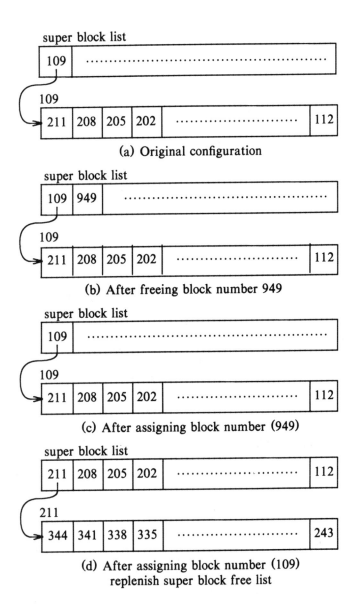

Figure 4.20. Requesting and Freeing Disk Blocks

4.8 OTHER FILE TYPES

The UNIX system supports two other file types: pipes and special files. A pipe, sometimes called a *fifo* (for "first-in-first-out"), differs from a regular file in that its data is transient: Once data is read from a pipe, it cannot be read again. Also, the data is read in the order that it was written to the pipe, and the system allows no deviation from that order. The kernel stores data in a pipe the same way it stores data in an ordinary file, except that it uses only the direct blocks, not the indirect blocks. The next chapter will examine the implementation of pipes.

The last file types in the UNIX system are special files, including block device special files and character device special files. Both types specify devices, and therefore the file inodes do not reference any data. Instead, the inode contains two numbers known as the major and minor device numbers. The major number indicates a device type such as terminal or disk, and the minor number indicates the unit number of the device. Chapter 10 examines special devices in detail.

4.9 SUMMARY

The inode is the data structure that describes the attributes of a file, including the layout of its data on disk. There are two versions of the inode: the disk copy that stores the inode information when the file is not in use and the in-core copy that records information about active files. Algorithms *ialloc* and *ifree* control assignment of a disk inode to a file during the *creat*, *mknod*, *pipe*, and *unlink* system calls (next chapter), and the algorithms *iget* and *iput* control the allocation of in-core inodes when a process accesses a file. Algorithm *bmap* locates the disk blocks of a file, according to a previously supplied byte offset in the file. Directories are files that correlate file name components to inode numbers. Algorithm *namei* converts file names manipulated by processes to inodes, used internally by the kernel. Finally, the kernel controls assignment of new disk blocks to a file using algorithms *alloc* and *free*.

The data structures discussed in this chapter consist of linked lists, hash queues, and linear arrays, and the algorithms that manipulate the data structures are therefore simple. Complications arise due to race conditions caused by the interaction of the algorithms, and the text has indicated some of these timing problems. Nevertheless, the algorithms are not elaborate and illustrate the simplicity of the system design.

The structures and algorithms explained here are internal to the kernel and are not visible to the user. Referring to the overall system architecture (Figure 2.1), the algorithms described in this chapter occupy the lower half of the file subsystem. The next chapter examines the system calls that provide the user interface to the file system, and it describes the upper half of the file subsystem that invokes the internal algorithms described here.

4.10 EXERCISES

1. The C language convention counts array indices from 0. Why do inode numbers start from 1 and not 0?

2. If a process sleeps in algorithm *iget* when it finds the inode locked in the cache, why must it start the loop again from the beginning after waking up?

3. Describe an algorithm that takes an in-core inode as input and updates the corresponding disk inode.

4. The algorithms *iget* and *iput* do not require the processor execution level to be raised to block out interrupts. What does this imply?

5. How efficiently can the loop for indirect blocks in *bmap* be encoded?

```
mkdir junk
for i in 1 2 3 4 5
do
echo hello > junk/$i
done
ls −ld junk
ls −l junk
chmod −r junk
ls −ld junk
ls junk
ls −l junk
cd junk
pwd
ls −l
echo *
cd ..
chmod +r junk
chmod −x junk
ls junk
ls −l junk
cd junk
chmod +x junk
```

Figure 4.21. Difference between Read and Search Permission on Directories

6. Execute the shell command script in Figure 4.21. It creates a directory "junk" and creates five files in the directory. After doing some control *ls* commands, the *chmod* command turns off read permission for the directory. What happens when the various *ls* commands are executed now? What happens after changing directory into "junk"? After restoring read permission but removing execute (search) permission from "junk", repeat the experiment. What happens? What is happening in the kernel to cause this behavior?

7. Given the current structure of a directory entry on a System V system, what is the maximum number of files a file system can contain?

8. UNIX System V allows a maximum of 14 characters for a path name component. *Namei* truncates extra characters in a component. How should the file system and respective algorithms be redesigned to allow arbitrary length component names?

9. Suppose a user has a private version of the UNIX system but changes it so that a path name component can consist of 30 characters; the private version of the operating system stores the directory entries the same way that the standard operating system does, except that the directory entries are 32 bytes long instead of 16. If the user mounts the private file system on a standard system, what would happen in algorithm *namei* when a process accesses a file on the private file system?

* 10. Consider the algorithm *namei* for converting a path name into an inode. As the search progresses, the kernel checks that the current working inode is that of a directory. Is it possible for another process to remove (*unlink*) the directory? How can the kernel prevent this? The next chapter will come back to this problem.

* 11. Design a directory structure that improves the efficiency of searching for path names by avoiding the linear search. Consider two techniques: hashing and *n*-ary trees.

* 12. Design a scheme that reduces the number of directory searches for file names by caching frequently used names.

* 13. Ideally, a file system should never contain a free inode whose inode number is less than the "remembered" inode used by *ialloc*. How is it possible for this assertion to be false?

14. The super block is a disk block and contains other information besides the free block list, as described in this chapter. Therefore, the super block free list cannot contain as many free block numbers as can be potentially stored in a disk block on the linked list of free disk blocks. What is the optimal number of free block numbers that should be stored in a block on the linked list?

* 15. Discuss a system implementation that keeps track of free disk blocks with a bit map instead of a linked list of blocks. What are the advantages and disadvantages of this scheme?

5

SYSTEM CALLS
FOR THE FILE SYSTEM

The last chapter described the internal data structures for the file system and the algorithms that manipulate them. This chapter deals with system calls for the file system, using the concepts explored in the previous chapter. It starts with system calls for accessing existing files, such as *open*, *read*, *write*, *lseek*, and *close*, then presents system calls to create new files, namely, *creat* and *mknod*, and then examines the system calls that manipulate the inode or that maneuver through the file system: *chdir*, *chroot*, *chown*, *chmod*, *stat*, and *fstat*. It investigates more advanced system calls: *pipe* and *dup* are important for the implementation of pipes in the shell; *mount* and *umount* extend the file system tree visible to users; *link* and *unlink* change the structure of the file system hierarchy. Then, it presents the notion of file system abstractions, allowing the support of various file systems as long as they conform to standard interfaces. The last section in the chapter covers file system maintenance. The chapter introduces three kernel data structures: the file table, with one entry allocated for every opened file in the system, the user file descriptor table, with one entry allocated for every file descriptor known to a process, and the mount table, containing information for every active file system.

Figure 5.1 shows the relationship between the system calls and the algorithms described previously. It classifies the system calls into several categories, although some system calls appear in more than one category:

File System Calls

Return File Desc	Use of namei	Assign inodes	File Attributes	File I/O	File Sys Structure	Tree Manipulation
open creat dup pipe close	open stat creat link chdir unlink chroot mknod chown mount chmod umount	creat mknod link unlink	chown chmod stat	read write lseek	mount umount	chdir chown

Lower Level File System Algorithms		
namei		
iget iput	ialloc ifree	alloc free bmap

buffer allocation algorithms
getblk   brelse   bread   breada   bwrite

Figure 5.1. File System Calls and Relation to Other Algorithms

- System calls that return file descriptors for use in other system calls;
- System calls that use the *namei* algorithm to parse a path name;
- System calls that assign and free inodes, using algorithms *ialloc* and *ifree*;
- System calls that set or change the attributes of a file;
- System calls that do I/O to and from a process, using algorithms *alloc*, *free*, and the buffer allocation algorithms;
- System calls that change the structure of the file system;
- System calls that allow a process to change its view of the file system tree.

5.1 OPEN

The *open* system call is the first step a process must take to access the data in a file. The syntax for the *open* system call is

  fd = open(pathname, flags, modes);

where *pathname* is a file name, *flags* indicate the type of open (such as for reading or writing), and *modes* give the file permissions if the file is being created. The *open* system call returns an integer[1] called the user *file descriptor*. Other file operations, such as reading, writing, seeking, duplicating the file descriptor, setting file I/O parameters, determining file status, and closing the file, use the file descriptor that the *open* system call returns.

The kernel searches the file system for the file name parameter using algorithm *namei* (see Figure 5.2). It checks permissions for opening the file after it finds the in-core inode and allocates an entry in the file table for the open file. The file table entry contains a pointer to the inode of the open file and a field that indicates the byte offset in the file where the kernel expects the next *read* or *write* to begin. The kernel initializes the offset to 0 during the *open* call, meaning that the initial *read* or *write* starts at the beginning of a file by default. Alternatively, a process can *open* a file in *write-append* mode, in which case the kernel initializes the offset to the size of the file. The kernel allocates an entry in a private table in the process *u area*, called the user file descriptor table, and notes the index of this entry. The index is the file descriptor that is returned to the user. The entry in the user file table points to the entry in the global file table.

```
algorithm open
inputs:  file name
         type of open
         file permissions (for creation type of open)
output: file descriptor
{
        convert file name to inode (algorithm namei);
        if (file does not exist or not permitted access)
                return(error);
        allocate file table entry for inode, initialize count, offset;
        allocate user file descriptor entry, set pointer to file table entry;
        if (type of open specifies truncate file)
                free all file blocks (algorithm free);
        unlock(inode);                /* locked above in namei */
        return(user file descriptor);
}
```

Figure 5.2. Algorithm for Opening a File

Suppose a process executes the following code, opening the file "/etc/passwd" twice, once read-only and once write-only, and the file "local" once, for reading and writing.[2]

---

1. All system calls return the value −1 if they fail. The return value −1 will not be explicitly mentioned when discussing the syntax of the system calls.

2. The definition of the *open* system call specifies three parameters (the third is used for the *create* mode of open), but programmers usually use only the first two. The C compiler does not check that the number of parameters is correct. System implementations typically pass the first two parameters and a third "garbage" parameter (whatever happens to be on the stack) to the kernel. The kernel

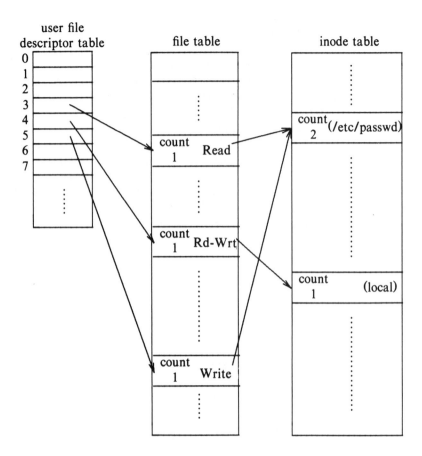

Figure 5.3. Data Structures after Open

fd1 = open("/etc/passwd", O_RDONLY);
fd2 = open("local", O_RDWR);
fd3 = open("/etc/passwd", O_WRONLY);

Figure 5.3 shows the relationship between the inode table, file table, and user file descriptor data structures. Each *open* returns a file descriptor to the process, and the corresponding entry in the user file descriptor table points to a unique entry in

does not check the third parameter unless the second parameter indicates that it must, allowing programmers to encode only two parameters.

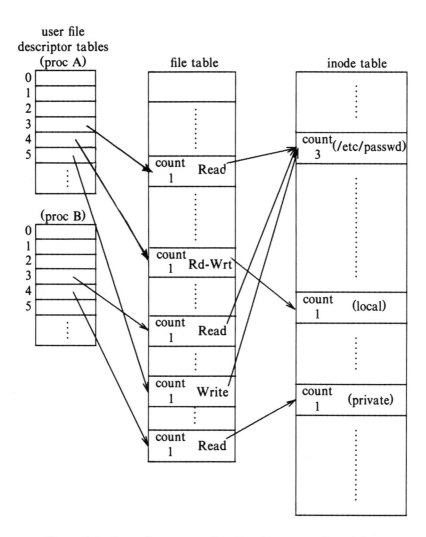

Figure 5.4. Data Structures after Two Processes Open Files

the kernel file table even though one file ("/etc/passwd") is opened twice. The file table entries of all instances of an open file point to one entry in the in-core inode table. The process can *read* or *write* the file "/etc/passwd" but only through file descriptors 3 and 5 in the figure. The kernel notes the capability to read or write the file in the file table entry allocated during the *open* call. Suppose a second process executes the following code.

```
fd1 = open("/etc/passwd", O_RDONLY);
fd2 = open("private", O_RDONLY);
```

Figure 5.4 shows the relationship between the appropriate data structures while both processes (and no others) have the files open. Again, each *open* call results in allocation of a unique entry in the user file descriptor table and in the kernel file table, but the kernel contains at most one entry per file in the in-core inode table.

The user file descriptor table entry could conceivably contain the file offset for the position of the next I/O operation and point directly to the in-core inode entry for the file, eliminating the need for a separate kernel file table. The examples above show a one-to-one relationship between user file descriptor entries and kernel file table entries. Thompson notes, however, that he implemented the file table as a separate structure to allow sharing of the offset pointer between several user file descriptors (see page 1943 of [Thompson 78]). The *dup* and *fork* system calls, explained in Sections 5.13 and 7.1, manipulate the data structures to allow such sharing.

The first three user file descriptors (0, 1, and 2) are called the *standard input*, *standard output*, and *standard error* file descriptors. Processes on UNIX systems conventionally use the standard input descriptor to read input data, the standard output descriptor to write output data, and the standard error descriptor to write error data (messages). Nothing in the operating system assumes that these file descriptors are special. A group of users could adopt the convention that file descriptors 4, 6, and 11 are special file descriptors, but counting from 0 (in C) is much more natural. Adoption of the convention by all user programs makes it easy for them to communicate via *pipes*, as will be seen in Chapter 7. Normally, the control terminal (see Chapter 10) serves as standard input, standard output and standard error.

5.2 READ

The syntax of the *read* system call is

```
number = read(fd, buffer, count)
```

where *fd* is the file descriptor returned by *open*, *buffer* is the address of a data structure in the user process that will contain the read data on successful completion of the call, *count* is the number of bytes the user wants to read, and *number* is the number of bytes actually read. Figure 5.5 depicts the algorithm *read* for reading a regular file. The kernel gets the file table entry that corresponds to

```
algorithm read
input:   user file descriptor
         address of buffer in user process
         number of bytes to read
output: count of bytes copied into user space
{
        get file table entry from user file descriptor;
        check file accessibility;
        set parameters in u area for user address, byte count, I/O to user;
        get inode from file table;
        lock inode;
        set byte offset in u area from file table offset;
        while (count not satisfied)
        {
                convert file offset to disk block (algorithm bmap);
                calculate offset into block, number of bytes to read;
                if (number of bytes to read is 0)
                        /* trying to read end of file */
                        break;                /* out of loop */
                read block (algorithm breada if with read ahead, algorithm
                                bread otherwise);
                copy data from system buffer to user address;
                update u area fields for file byte offset, read count,
                                address to write into user space;
                release buffer;            /* locked in bread */
        }
        unlock inode;
        update file table offset for next read;
        return(total number of bytes read);
}
```

Figure 5.5. Algorithm for Reading a File

the user file descriptor, following the pointer in Figure 5.3. It now sets several I/O parameters in the *u area* (Figure 5.6), eliminating the need to pass them as function parameters. Specifically, it sets the I/O mode to indicate that a read is being done, a flag to indicate that the I/O will go to user address space, a count field to indicate the number of bytes to read, the target address of the user data buffer, and finally, an offset field (from the file table) to indicate the byte offset into the file where the I/O should begin. After the kernel sets the I/O parameters in the *u area*, it follows the pointer from the file table entry to the inode, locking the inode before it reads the file.

The algorithm now goes into a loop until the *read* is satisfied. The kernel converts the file byte offset into a block number, using algorithm *bmap*, and it notes the byte offset in the block where the I/O should begin and how many bytes

mode	indicates read or write
count	count of bytes to read or write
offset	byte offset in file
address	target address to copy data, in user or kernel memory
flag	indicates if address is in user or kernel memory

Figure 5.6. I/O Parameters Saved in U Area

in the block it should read. After reading the block into a buffer, possibly using block read ahead (algorithms *bread* and *breada*) as will be described, it copies the data from the block to the target address in the user process. It updates the I/O parameters in the *u area* according to the number of bytes it read, incrementing the file byte offset and the address in the user process where the next data should be delivered, and decrementing the count of bytes it needs to read to satisfy the user read request. If the user request is not satisfied, the kernel repeats the entire cycle, converting the file byte offset to a block number, reading the block from disk to a system buffer, copying data from the buffer to the user process, releasing the buffer, and updating I/O parameters in the *u area*. The cycle completes either when the kernel completely satisfies the user request, when the file contains no more data, or if the kernel encounters an error in reading the data from disk or in copying the data to user space. The kernel updates the offset in the file table according to the number of bytes it actually read; consequently, successive *read*s of a file deliver the file data in sequence. The *lseek* system call (Section 5.6) adjusts the value of the file table offset and changes the order in which a process *read*s or *write*s a file.

```
#include  <fcntl.h>
main()
{
        int fd;
        char lilbuf[20], bigbuf[1024];

        fd = open("/etc/passwd", O_RDONLY);
        read(fd, lilbuf, 20);
        read(fd, bigbuf, 1024);
        read(fd, lilbuf, 20);
}
```

Figure 5.7. Sample Program for Reading a File

Consider the program in Figure 5.7. The *open* returns a file descriptor that the user assigns to the variable *fd* and uses in the subsequent *read* calls. In the *read* system call, the kernel verifies that the file descriptor parameter is legal, and that the process had previously *open*ed the file for reading. It stores the values *lilbuf*, 20, and 0 in the *u area*, corresponding to the address of the user buffer, the byte count, and the starting byte offset in the file. It calculates that byte offset 0 is in the 0th block of the file and retrieves the entry for the 0th block in the inode. Assuming such a block exists, the kernel reads the entire block of 1024 bytes into a buffer but copies only 20 bytes to the user address *lilbuf*. It increments the *u area* byte offset to 20 and decrements the count of data to read to 0. Since the *read* has been satisfied, the kernel resets the file table offset to 20, so that subsequent *read*s on the file descriptor will begin at byte 20 in the file, and the system call returns the number of bytes actually read, 20.

For the second *read* call, the kernel again verifies that the descriptor is legal and that the process had *open*ed the file for reading, because it has no way of knowing that the user *read* request is for the same file that was determined to be legal during the last *read*. It stores in the *u area* the user address *bigbuf*, the number of bytes the process wants to read, 1024, and the starting offset in the file, 20, taken from the file table. It converts the file byte offset to the correct disk block, as above, and reads the block. If the time between *read* calls is small, chances are good that the block will be in the buffer cache. But the kernel cannot satisfy the *read* request entirely from the buffer, because only 1004 out of the 1024 bytes for this request are in the buffer. So it copies the last 1004 bytes from the buffer into the user data structure *bigbuf* and updates the parameters in the *u area* to indicate that the next iteration of the read loop starts at byte 1024 in the file, that the data should be copied to byte position 1004 in *bigbuf*, and that the number of bytes to to satisfy the *read* request is 20.

The kernel now cycles to the beginning of the loop in the *read* algorithm. It converts byte offset 1024 to logical block offset 1, looks up the second direct block number in the inode, and finds the correct disk block to read. It reads the block from the buffer cache, reading the block from disk if it is not in the cache. Finally, it copies 20 bytes from the buffer to the correct address in the user process. Before leaving the system call, the kernel sets the offset field in the file table entry to 1044, the byte offset that should be accessed next. For the last *read* call in the example, the kernel proceeds as in the first *read* call, except that it starts reading at byte 1044 in the file, finding that value in the offset field in the file table entry for the descriptor.

The example shows how advantageous it is for I/O requests to start on file system block boundaries and to be multiples of the block size. Doing so allows the kernel to avoid an extra iteration in the *read* algorithm loop, with the consequent expense of accessing the inode to find the correct block number for the data and competing with other processes for access to the buffer pool. The standard I/O library was written to hide knowledge of the kernel buffer size from users; its use avoids the performance penalties inherent in processes that nibble at the file system inefficiently (see exercise 5.4).

As the kernel goes through the *read* loop, it determines whether a file is subject to read-ahead: if a process *read*s two blocks sequentially, the kernel assumes that all subsequent *read*s will be sequential until proven otherwise. During each iteration through the loop, the kernel saves the next logical block number in the in-core inode and, during the next iteration, compares the current logical block number to the value previously saved. If they are equal, the kernel calculates the physical block number for read-ahead and saves its value in the *u area* for use in the *breada* algorithm. Of course, if a process does not *read* to the end of a block, the kernel does not invoke read-ahead for the next block.

Recall from Figure 4.9 that it is possible for some block numbers in an inode or in indirect blocks to have the value 0, even though later blocks have nonzero value. If a process attempts to *read* data from such a block, the kernel satisfies the request by allocating an arbitrary buffer in the *read* loop, clearing its contents to 0, and copying it to the user address. This case is different from the case where a process encounters the end of a file, meaning that no data was ever written to any location beyond the current point. When encountering end of file, the kernel returns no data to the process (see exercise 5.1).

When a process invokes the *read* system call, the kernel locks the inode for the duration of the call. Afterwards, it could go to sleep reading a buffer associated with data or with indirect blocks of the inode. If another process were allowed to change the file while the first process was sleeping, *read* could return inconsistent data. For example, a process may *read* several blocks of a file; if it slept while reading the first block and a second process were to *write* the other blocks, the returned data would contain a mixture of old and new data. Hence, the inode is left locked for the duration of the *read* call, affording the process a consistent view of the file as it existed at the start of the call.

The kernel can preempt a *read*ing process between system calls in user mode and schedule other processes to run. Since the inode is unlocked at the end of a system call, nothing prevents other processes from accessing the file and changing its contents. It would be unfair for the system to keep an inode locked from the time a process *open*ed the file until it *close*d the file, because one process could keep a file open and thus prevent other processes from ever accessing it. If the file was "/etc/passwd", used by the login process to check a user's password, then one malicious (or, perhaps, just errant) user could prevent all other users from logging in. To avoid such problems, the kernel unlocks the inode at the end of each system call that uses it. If another process changes the file between the two *read* system calls by the first process, the first process may *read* unexpected data, but the kernel data structures are consistent.

For example, suppose the kernel executes the two processes in Figure 5.8 concurrently. Assuming both processes complete their *open* calls before either one starts its *read* or *write* calls, the kernel could execute the *read* and *write* calls in any of six sequences: *read1, read2, write1, write2,* or *read1, write1, read2, write2,* or *read1, write1, write2, read2,* and so on. The data that process A *read*s depends on the order that the system executes the system calls of the two processes; the system does not guarantee that the data in the file remains the same after *open*ing the file. Use of the *file and record locking* feature (Section 5.4) allows a process to

```
#include  <fcntl.h>
/* process A */
main()
{
     int fd;
     char buf[512];
     fd = open("/etc/passwd", O_RDONLY);
     read(fd, buf, sizeof(buf));       /* read1 */
     read(fd, buf, sizeof(buf));       /* read2 */
}

/* process B */
main()
{
     int fd, i;
     char buf[512];
     for (i = 0;  i < sizeof(buf);  i++)
          buf[i] = 'a';
     fd = open("/etc/passwd", O_WRONLY);
     write(fd, buf, sizeof(buf));       /* write1 */
     write(fd, buf, sizeof(buf));       /* write2 */
}
```

Figure 5.8. A Reader and a Writer Process

guarantee file consistency while it has a file *open*.

Finally, the program in Figure 5.9 shows how a process can *open* a file more than once and *read* it via different file descriptors. The kernel manipulates the file table offsets associated with the two file descriptors independently, and hence, the arrays *buf1* and *buf2* should be identical when the process completes, assuming no other process *write*s "/etc/passwd" in the meantime.

5.3 WRITE

The syntax for the *write* system call is

number = write(fd, buffer, count);

where the meaning of the variables *fd*, *buffer*, *count*, and *number* are the same as they are for the *read* system call. The algorithm for *writ*ing a regular file is similar to that for *read*ing a regular file. However, if the file does not contain a block that corresponds to the byte offset to be written, the kernel allocates a new block using algorithm *alloc* and assigns the block number to the correct position in the inode's table of contents. If the byte offset is that of an indirect block, the kernel may

```
#include  <fcntl.h>
main()
{
        int fd1, fd2;
        char buf1[512], buf2[512];

        fd1 = open("/etc/passwd", O_RDONLY);
        fd2 = open("/etc/passwd", O_RDONLY);
        read(fd1, buf1, sizeof(buf1));
        read(fd2, buf2, sizeof(buf2));
}
```

Figure 5.9. Reading a File via Two File Descriptors

have to allocate several blocks for use as indirect blocks and data blocks. The inode is locked for the duration of the *write*, because the kernel may change the inode when allocating new blocks; allowing other processes access to the file could corrupt the inode if several processes allocate blocks simultaneously for the same byte offsets. When the write is complete, the kernel updates the file size entry in the inode if the file has grown larger.

For example, suppose a process writes byte number 10,240 to a file, the highest-numbered byte yet written to the file. When accessing the byte in the file using algorithm *bmap*, the kernel will find not only that the file does not contain a block for that byte but also that it does not contain the necessary indirect block. It assigns a disk block for the indirect block and writes the block number in the in-core inode. Then it assigns a disk block for the data block and writes its block number into the first position in the newly assigned indirect block.

The kernel goes through an internal loop, as in the *read* algorithm, writing one block to disk during each iteration. During each iteration, it determines whether it will write the entire block or only part of it. If it writes only part of a block, it must first read the block from disk so as not to overwrite the parts that will remain the same, but if it writes the whole block, it need not read the block, since it will overwrite its previous contents anyway. The write proceeds block by block, but the kernel uses a *delayed write* (Section 3.4) to write the data to disk, caching it in case another process should *read* or *write* it soon and avoiding extra disk operations. Delayed write is probably most effective for pipes, because another process is reading the pipe and removing its data (Section 5.12). But even for regular files, delayed write is effective if the file is created temporarily and will be read soon. For example, many programs, such as editors and mail, create temporary files in the directory "/tmp" and quickly remove them. Use of delayed write can reduce the number of disk writes for temporary files.

5.4 FILE AND RECORD LOCKING

The original UNIX system developed by Thompson and Ritchie did not have an internal mechanism by which a process could insure exclusive access to a file. A locking mechanism was considered unnecessary because, as Ritchie notes, "we are not faced with large, single-file databases maintained by independent processes" (see [Ritchie 81]). To make the UNIX system more attractive to commercial users with database applications, System V now contains file and record locking mechanisms. File locking is the capability to prevent other processes from *read*ing or *writ*ing any part of an entire file, and record locking is the capability to prevent other processes from *read*ing or *writ*ing particular records (parts of a file between particular byte offsets). Exercise 5.9 explores the implementation of file and record locking.

5.5 ADJUSTING THE POSITION OF FILE I/O — LSEEK

The ordinary use of *read* and *write* system calls provides sequential access to a file, but processes can use the *lseek* system call to position the I/O and allow random access to a file. The syntax for the system call is

> position = lseek(fd, offset, reference);

where *fd* is the file descriptor identifying the file, *offset* is a byte offset, and *reference* indicates whether *offset* should be considered from the beginning of the file, from the current position of the read/write offset, or from the end of the file. The return value, *position*, is the byte offset where the next *read* or *write* will start. In the program in Figure 5.10, for example, a process *open*s a file, *read*s a byte, then invokes *lseek* to advance the file table offset value by 1023 (with *reference* 1), and loops. Thus, the program *read*s every 1024th byte of the file. If the value of *reference* is 0, the kernel seeks from the beginning of the file, and if its value is 2, the kernel seeks beyond the end of the file. The *lseek* system call has nothing to do with the seek operation that positions a disk arm over a particular disk sector. To implement *lseek*, the kernel simply adjusts the offset value in the file table; subsequent *read* or *write* system calls use the file table offset as their starting byte offset.

5.6 CLOSE

A process *close*s an *open* file when it no longer wants to access it. The syntax for the *close* system call is

```
#include  <fcntl.h>
main(argc, argv)
        int argc;
        char *argv[];
{
        int fd, skval;
        char c;

        if (argc != 2)
                exit();
        fd = open(argv[1], O_RDONLY);
        if (fd == -1)
                exit();
        while ((skval = read(fd, &c, 1)) == 1)
        {
                printf("char %c\n", c);
                skval = lseek(fd, 1023L, 1);
                printf("new seek val %d\n", skval);
        }
}
```

Figure 5.10. Program with Lseek System Call

```
close(fd);
```

where *fd* is the file descriptor for the *open* file. The kernel does the *close* operation
by manipulating the file descriptor and the corresponding file table and inode table
entries. If the reference count of the file table entry is greater than 1 because of
dup or *fork* calls, then other user file descriptors reference the file table entry, as
will be seen; the kernel decrements the count and the *close* completes. If the file
table reference count is 1, the kernel frees the entry and releases the in-core inode
originally allocated in the *open* system call (algorithm *iput*). If other processes still
reference the inode, the kernel decrements the inode reference count but leaves it
allocated; otherwise, the inode is free for reallocation because its reference count is
0. When the *close* system call completes, the user file descriptor table entry is
empty. Attempts by the process to use that file descriptor result in an error until
the file descriptor is reassigned as a result of another system call. When a process
exits, the kernel examines its active user file descriptors and internally *closes* each
one. Hence, no process can keep a file open after it terminates.

For example, Figure 5.11 shows the relevant table entries of Figure 5.4, after
the second process *closes* its files. The entries for file descriptors 3 and 4 in the
user file descriptor table are empty. The count fields of the file table entries are
now 0, and the entries are empty. The inode reference count for the files
"/etc/passwd" and "private" are also decremented. The inode entry for "private"
is on the free list because its reference count is 0, but its entry is not empty. If

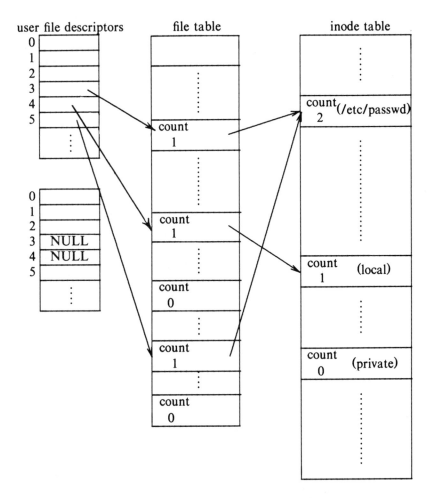

Figure 5.11. Tables after Closing a File

another process accesses the file "private" while the inode is still on the free list, the kernel will reclaim the inode, as explained in Section 4.1.2.

5.7 FILE CREATION

The *open* system call gives a process access to an existing file, but the *creat* system call creates a new file in the system. The syntax for the *creat* system call is

    fd = creat(pathname, modes);

where the variables *pathname*, *modes*, and *fd* mean the same as they do in the
open system call. If no such file previously existed, the kernel creates a new file
with the specified name and permission modes; if the file already existed, the kernel
truncates the file (releases all existing data blocks and sets the file size to 0) subject
to suitable file access permissions.[3] Figure 5.12 shows the algorithm for file
creation.

```
algorithm creat
input:   file name
         permission settings
output: file descriptor
{
        get inode for file name (algorithm namei);
        if (file already exists)
        {
                if (not permitted access)
                {
                        release inode (algorithm iput);
                        return(error);
                }
        }
        else       /* file does not exist yet */
        {
                assign free inode from file system (algorithm ialloc);
                create new directory entry in parent directory: include
                        new file name and newly assigned inode number;
        }
        allocate file table entry for inode, initialize count;
        if (file did exist at time of create)
                free all file blocks (algorithm free);
        unlock(inode);
        return(user file descriptor);
}
```

Figure 5.12. Algorithm for Creating a File

The kernel parses the path name using algorithm *namei*, following the
algorithm literally while parsing directory names. However, when it arrives at the
last component of the path name, namely, the file name that it will create, *namei*

---

3. The *open* system call specifies two flags, *O_CREAT* (create) and *O_TRUNC* (truncate): If a process
   specifies the *O_CREAT* flag on an *open* and the file does not exist, the kernel will create the file. If
   the file already exists, it will not be truncated unless the *O_TRUNC* flag is also set.

notes the byte offset of the first empty directory slot in the directory and saves the offset in the *u area*. If the kernel does not find the path name component in the directory, it will eventually write the name into the empty slot just found. If the directory has no empty slots, the kernel remembers the offset of the end of the directory and creates a new slot there. It also remembers the inode of the directory being searched in its *u area* and keeps the inode locked; the directory will become the parent directory of the new file. The kernel does not write the new file name into the directory yet, so that it has less to undo in event of later errors. It checks that the directory allows the process write permission: Because a process will write the directory as a result of the *creat* call, write permission for a directory means that processes are allowed to create files in the directory.

Assuming no file by the given name previously existed, the kernel assigns an inode for the new file, using algorithm *ialloc* (Section 4.6). It then writes the new file name component and the inode number of the newly allocated inode in the parent directory, at the byte offset saved in the *u area*. Afterwards, it releases the inode of the parent directory, having held it from the time it searched the directory for the file name. The parent directory now contains the name of the new file and its inode number. The kernel writes the newly allocated inode to disk (algorithm *bwrite*) before it writes the directory with the new name to disk. If the system crashes between the write operations for the inode and the directory, there will be an allocated inode that is not referenced by any path name in the system but the system will function normally. If, on the other hand, the directory were written before the newly allocated inode and the system crashed in the middle, the file system would contain a path name that referred to a bad inode. (See Section 5.16.1 for more detail.)

If the given file already existed before the *creat*, the kernel finds its inode while searching for the file name. The old file must allow write permission for a process to create a "new" file by the same name, because the kernel changes the file contents during the *creat* call: It truncates the file, freeing all its data blocks using algorithm *free*, so that the file looks like a newly created file. However, the owner and permission modes of the file are the same as they were for the original file: The kernel does not reassign ownership to the owner of the process, and it ignores the permission modes specified by the process. Finally, the kernel does not check that the parent directory of the existing file allows write permission, because it will not change the directory contents.

The *creat* system call proceeds according to the same algorithm as the *open* system call. The kernel allocates an entry in the file table for the created file so that the process can *write* the file, allocates an entry in the user file descriptor table, and eventually returns the index to the latter entry as the user file descriptor.

5.8 CREATION OF SPECIAL FILES

The system call *mknod* creates special files in the system, including named pipes, device files, and directories. It is similar to *creat* in that the kernel allocates an inode for the file. The syntax of the *mknod* system call is

   mknod(pathname, type and permissions, dev)

where *pathname* is the name of the node to be created, *type and permissions* give
the node type (directory, for example) and access permissions for the new file to be
created, and *dev* specifies the major and minor device numbers for block and
character special files (Chapter 10). Figure 5.13 depicts the algorithm *mknod* for
making a new node.

```
algorithm make new node
inputs: node (file name)
        file type
        permissions
        major, minor device number (for block, character special files)
output: none
{
        if (new node not named pipe and user not super user)
                return(error);
        get inode of parent of new node (algorithm namei);
        if (new node already exists)
        {
                release parent inode (algorithm iput);
                return(error);
        }
        assign free inode from file system for new node (algorithm ialloc);
        create new directory entry in parent directory: include new node
                name and newly assigned inode number;
        release parent directory inode (algorithm iput);
        if (new node is block or character special file)
                write major, minor numbers into inode structure;
        release new node inode (algorithm iput);
}
```

Figure 5.13. Algorithm for Making New Node

   The kernel searches the file system for the file name it is about to create. If the
file does not yet exist, the kernel assigns a new inode on the disk and writes the new
file name and inode number into the parent directory. It sets the file type field in
the inode to indicate that the file type is a pipe, directory or special file. Finally, if
the file is a *character special* or *block special* device file, it writes the major and
minor device numbers into the inode. If the *mknod* call is creating a directory
node, the node will exist after the system call completes but its contents will be in
the wrong format (there are no directory entries for "." and ".."). Exercise 5.33
considers the other steps needed to put a directory into the correct format.

```
algorithm change directory
input:   new directory name
output: none
{
        get inode for new directory name (algorithm namei);
        if (inode not that of directory or process not permitted access to file)
        {
                release inode (algorithm iput);
                return (error);
        }
        unlock inode;
        release "old" current directory inode (algorithm iput);
        place new inode into current directory slot in u area;
}
```

Figure 5.14. Algorithm for Changing Current Directory

5.9 CHANGE DIRECTORY AND CHANGE ROOT

When the system is first booted, process 0 makes the file system root its current directory during initialization. It executes the algorithm *iget* on the root inode, saves it in the *u area* as its current directory, and releases the inode lock. When a new process is created via the *fork* system call, the new process inherits the current directory of the old process in its *u area*, and the kernel increments the inode reference count accordingly.

The algorithm *chdir* (Figure 5.14) changes the current directory of a process. The syntax for the *chdir* system call is

chdir(pathname);

where *pathname* is the directory that becomes the new current directory of the process. The kernel parses the name of the target directory using algorithm *namei* and checks that the target file is a directory and that the process owner has access permission to the directory. It releases the lock to the new inode but keeps the inode allocated and its reference count incremented, releases the inode of the old current directory (algorithm *iput*) stored in the *u area*, and stores the new inode in the *u area*. After a process changes its current directory, algorithm *namei* uses the inode for the start directory to search for all path names that do not begin from root. After execution of the *chdir* system call, the inode reference count of the new directory is at least one, and the inode reference count of the previous current directory may be 0. In this respect, *chdir* is similar to the *open* system call, because both system calls access a file and leave its inode allocated. The inode allocated during the *chdir* system call is released only when the process executes another *chdir* call or when it *exits*.

A process usually uses the global file system root for all path names starting with "/". The kernel contains a global variable that points to the inode of the global root, allocated by *iget* when the system is booted. Processes can change their notion of the file system root via the *chroot* system call. This is useful if a user wants to simulate the usual file system hierarchy and run processes there. Its syntax is

chroot(pathname);

where *pathname* is the directory that the kernel subsequently treats as the process's root directory. When executing the *chroot* system call, the kernel follows the same algorithm as for changing the current directory. It stores the new root inode in the process *u area*, unlocking the inode on completion of the system call. However, since the default root for the kernel is stored in a global variable, it does not release the inode of the old root automatically, but only if it or an ancestor process had executed the *chroot* system call. The new inode is now the logical root of the file system for the process (and all its children), meaning that all path name searches in algorithm *namei* that start from root ("/") start from this inode, and that all attempts to use ".." over the root will leave the working directory of the process in the new root. A process bestows new child processes with its changed root, just as it bestows them with its current directory.

5.10 CHANGE OWNER AND CHANGE MODE

Changing the owner or mode (access permissions) of a file are operations on the inode, not on the file per se. The syntax of the calls is

chown(pathname, owner, group)
chmod(pathname, mode)

To change the owner of a file, the kernel converts the file name to an inode using algorithm *namei*. The process owner must be superuser or match that of the file owner (a process cannot give away something that does not belong to it). The kernel then assigns the new owner and group to the file, clears the set user and set group flags (see Section 7.5), and releases the inode via algorithm *iput*. After the change of ownership, the old owner loses "owner" access rights to the file. To change the mode of a file, the kernel follows a similar procedure, changing the mode flags in the inode instead of the owner numbers.

5.11 STAT AND FSTAT

The system calls *stat* and *fstat* allow processes to query the status of files, returning information such as the file type, file owner, access permissions, file size, number of links, inode number, and file access times. The syntax for the system calls is

```
stat(pathname, statbuffer);
fstat(fd, statbuffer);
```

where *pathname* is a file name, *fd* is a file descriptor returned by a previous *open* call, and *statbuffer* is the address of a data structure in the user process that will contain the status information of the file on completion of the call. The system calls simply write the fields of the inode into *statbuffer*. The program in Figure 5.33 will illustrate the use of *stat* and *fstat*.

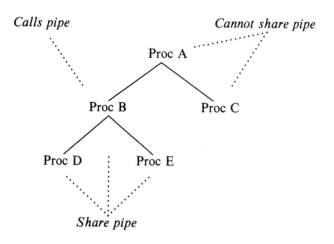

Figure 5.15.   Process Tree and Sharing Pipes

5.12 PIPES

Pipes allow transfer of data between processes in a first-in-first-out manner (*FIFO*), and they also allow synchronization of process execution. Their implementation allows processes to communicate even though they do not know what processes are on the other end of the pipe. The traditional implementation of pipes uses the file system for data storage. There are two kinds of pipes: *named pipes* and, for lack of a better term, *unnamed pipes*, which are identical except for the way that a process initially accesses them. Processes use the *open* system call for named pipes, but the *pipe* system call to create an unnamed pipe. Afterwards, processes use the regular system calls for files, such as *read*, *write*, and *close* when manipulating pipes. Only related processes, descendants of a process that issued the *pipe* call, can share access to unnamed pipes. In Figure 5.15 for example, if process B creates a pipe and then spawns processes D and E, the three processes share access to the pipe, but processes A and C do not. However, all processes can access a named pipe regardless of their relationship, subject to the usual file permissions.

Because unnamed pipes are more common, they will be presented first.

5.12.1 The Pipe System Call

The syntax for creation of a pipe is

   pipe(fdptr);

where *fdptr* is the pointer to an integer array that will contain the two file descriptors for *read*ing and *writ*ing the pipe. Because the kernel implements pipes in the file system and because a pipe does not exist before its use, the kernel must assign an inode for it on creation. It also allocates a pair of user file descriptors and corresponding file table entries for the pipe: one file descriptor for *read*ing from the pipe and the other for *writ*ing to the pipe. It uses the file table so that the interface for the *read*, *write* and other system calls is consistent with the interface for regular files. As a result, processes do not have to know whether they are *read*ing or *writ*ing a regular file or a pipe.

```
algorithm pipe
input:   none
output: read file descriptor
         write file descriptor
{
        assign new inode from pipe device (algorithm ialloc);
        allocate file table entry for reading, another for writing;
        initialize file table entries to point to new inode;
        allocate user file descriptor for reading, another for writing,
             initialize to point to respective file table entries;
        set inode reference count to 2;
        initialize count of inode readers, writers to 1;
}
```

Figure 5.16. Algorithm for Creation of (Unnamed) Pipes

Figure 5.16 shows the algorithm for creating unnamed pipes. The kernel assigns an inode for a pipe from a file system designated the *pipe device* using algorithm *ialloc*. A pipe device is just a file system from which the kernel can assign inodes and data blocks for pipes. System administrators specify a pipe device during system configuration, and it may be identical to another file system. While a pipe is active, the kernel cannot reassign the pipe inode and data blocks to another file.

The kernel then allocates two file table entries for the read and write descriptors, respectively, and updates the bookkeeping information in the in-core inode. Each file table entry records how many instances of the pipe are open for reading or writing, initially 1 for each file table entry, and the inode reference count indicates how many times the pipe was "opened," initially two — one for each file table entry. Finally, the inode records byte offsets in the pipe where the next read or write of the pipe will start. Maintaining the byte offsets in the inode allows convenient FIFO access to the pipe data and differs from regular files where the offset is maintained in the file table. Processes cannot adjust them via the *lseek* system call and so random access I/O to a pipe is not possible.

5.12.2 Opening a Named Pipe

A named pipe is a file whose semantics are the same as those of an unnamed pipe, except that it has a directory entry and is accessed by a path name. Processes *open* named pipes in the same way that they open regular files and, hence, processes that are not closely related can communicate. Named pipes permanently exist in the file system hierarchy (subject to their removal by the *unlink* system call), but unnamed pipes are transient: When all processes finish using the pipe, the kernel reclaims its inode.

The algorithm for opening a named pipe is identical to the algorithm for opening a regular file. However, before completing the system call, the kernel increments the read or write counts in the inode, indicating the number of processes that have the named pipe open for reading or writing. A process that *opens* the named pipe for reading will sleep until another process opens the named pipe for writing, and vice versa. It makes no sense for a pipe to be open for reading if there is no hope for it to receive data; the same is true for writing. Depending on whether the process *opens* the named pipe for reading or writing, the kernel awakens other processes that were asleep, waiting for a writer or reader process (respectively) on the named pipe.

If a process *opens* a named pipe for reading and a writing process exists, the *open* call completes. Or if a process *opens* a named pipe with the *no delay* option, the *open* returns immediately, even if there are no writing processes. But if neither condition is true, the process sleeps until a writer process *opens* the pipe. Similar rules hold for a process that *opens* a pipe for writing.

5.12.3 Reading and Writing Pipes

A pipe should be viewed as if processes *write* into one end of the pipe and *read* from the other end. As mentioned above, processes access data from a pipe in FIFO manner, meaning that the order that data is written into a pipe is the order that it is read from the pipe. The number of processes *read*ing from a pipe do not necessarily equal the number of processes *writ*ing the pipe; if the number of readers or writers is greater than 1, they must coordinate use of the pipe with other mechanisms. The kernel accesses the data for a pipe exactly as it accesses data for a regular file: It stores data on the pipe device and assigns blocks to the pipe as needed during *write* calls. The difference between storage allocation for a pipe and

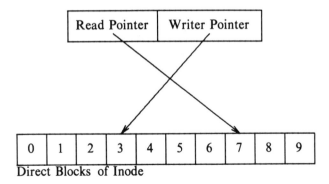

Figure 5.17. Logical View of Reading and Writing a Pipe

a regular file is that a pipe uses only the direct blocks of the inode for greater efficiency, although this places a limit on how much data a pipe can hold at a time. The kernel manipulates the direct blocks of the inode as a circular queue, maintaining read and write pointers internally to preserve the FIFO order (Figure 5.17).

Consider four cases for *read*ing and *writ*ing pipes: *writ*ing a pipe that has room for the data being written, *read*ing from a pipe that contains enough data to satisfy the *read*, *read*ing from a pipe that does not contain enough data to satisfy the *read*, and finally, *writ*ing a pipe that does not have room for the data being written.

Consider first the case that a process is writing a pipe and assume that the pipe has room for the data being written: The sum of the number of bytes being written and the number of bytes already in the pipe is less than or equal to the pipe's capacity. The kernel follows the algorithm for writing a regular file, except that it increments the pipe size automatically after every *write*, since by definition the amount of data in the pipe grows with every *write*. This differs from the growth of a regular file where the process increments the file size only when it *write*s data beyond the current end of file. If the next byte offset in the pipe were to require use of an indirect block, the kernel adjusts the file offset value in the *u area* to point to the beginning of the pipe (byte offset 0). The kernel never overwrites data in the pipe; it can reset the byte offset to 0 because it has already determined that the data will not overflow the pipe's capacity. When the writer process has written all its data into the pipe, the kernel updates the pipe's (inode) write pointer so that the next process to *write* the pipe will proceed from where the last *write* stopped. The kernel then awakens all other processes that fell asleep waiting to read data from the pipe.

When a process *read*s a pipe, it checks if the pipe is empty or not. If the pipe contains data, the kernel *read*s the data from the pipe as if the pipe were a regular file, following the regular algorithm for *read*. However, its initial offset is the pipe read pointer stored in the inode, indicating the extent of the previous *read*. After *read*ing each block, the kernel decrements the size of the pipe according to the number of bytes it read, and it adjusts the *u area* offset value to wrap around to the beginning of the pipe, if necessary. When the *read* system call completes, the kernel awakens all sleeping writer processes and saves the current read offset in the inode (not in the file table entry).

If a process attempts to *read* more data than is in the pipe, the *read* will complete successfully after returning all data currently in the pipe, even though it does not satisfy the user count. If the pipe is empty, the process will typically sleep until another process *write*s data into the pipe, at which time all sleeping processes that were waiting for data wake up and race to *read* the pipe. If, however, a process *open*s a named pipe with the *no delay* option, it will return immediately from a *read* if the pipe contains no data. The semantics of reading and writing pipes are similar to the semantics of reading and writing terminal devices (Chapter 10), allowing programs to ignore the type of file they are dealing with.

If a process *write*s a pipe and the pipe cannot hold all the data, the kernel marks the inode and goes to sleep waiting for data to drain from the pipe. When another process subsequently *read*s from the pipe, the kernel will notice that processes are asleep waiting for data to drain from the pipe, and it will awaken them, as explained above. The exception to this statement is when a process *write*s an amount of data greater than the pipe capacity (that is, the amount of data that can be stored in the inode direct blocks); here, the kernel *write*s as much data as possible to the pipe and puts the process to sleep until more room becomes available. Thus, it is possible that written data will not be contiguous in the pipe if other processes write their data to the pipe before this process resumes its write.

Analyzing the implementation of pipes, the process interface is consistent with that of regular files, but the implementation differs because the kernel stores the read and write offsets in the inode instead of in the file table. The kernel must store the offsets in the inode for named pipes so that processes can share their values: They cannot share values stored in file table entries because a process gets a new file table entry for each *open* call. However, the sharing of read and write offsets in the inode predates the implementation of named pipes. Processes with access to unnamed pipes share access to the pipe through common file table entries, so they could conceivably store the read and write offsets in the file table entry, as is done for regular files. This was not done, because the low-level routines in the kernel no longer have access to the file table entry: The code is simpler because the processes share offsets stored in the inode.

5.12.4 Closing Pipes

When closing a pipe, a process follows the same procedure it would follow for closing a regular file, except that the kernel does special processing before releasing the pipe's inode. The kernel decrements the number of pipe readers or writers, according to the type of the file descriptor. If the count of writer processes drops to

0 and there are processes asleep waiting to read data from the pipe, the kernel awakens them, and they return from their *read* calls without reading any data. If the count of reader processes drops to 0 and there are processes asleep waiting to write data to the pipe, the kernel awakens them and sends them a signal (Chapter 7) to indicate an error condition. In both cases, it makes no sense to allow the processes to continue sleeping when there is no hope that the state of the pipe will ever change. For example, if a process is waiting to read an unnamed pipe and there are no more writer processes, there will never be a writer process. Although it *is* possible to get new reader or writer processes for named pipes, the kernel treats them consistently with unnamed pipes. If no reader or writer processes access the pipe, the kernel frees all its data blocks and adjusts the inode to indicate that the pipe is empty. When it releases the inode of an ordinary pipe, it frees the disk copy for reassignment.

```
char string[] = "hello";
main()
{
        char buf[1024];
        char *cp1, *cp2;
        int fds[2];

        cp1 = string;
        cp2 = buf;
        while (*cp1)
                *cp2++ = *cp1++;
        pipe(fds);
        for (;;)
        {
                write(fds[1], buf, 6);
                read(fds[0], buf, 6);
        }
}
```

Figure 5.18. Reading and Writing a Pipe

5.12.5 Examples

The program in Figure 5.18 illustrates an artificial use of pipes. The process creates a pipe and goes into an infinite loop, *writ*ing the string "hello" to the pipe and *read*ing it from the pipe. The kernel does not know nor does it care that the process that writes the pipe is the same process that reads the pipe.

A process executing the program in Figure 5.19 creates a named pipe node called "fifo". If invoked with a second (dummy) argument, it continually *writes*

```
#include <fcntl.h>
char string[] = "hello";
main(argc, argv)
        int argc;
        char *argv[];
{
        int fd;
        char buf[256];

        /* create named pipe with read/write permission for all users */
        mknod("fifo", 010777, 0);
        if (argc == 2)
                fd = open("fifo", O_WRONLY);
        else
                fd = open("fifo", O_RDONLY);
        for (;;)
                if (argc == 2)
                        write(fd, string, 6);
                else
                        read(fd, buf, 6);
}
```

Figure 5.19. Reading and Writing a Named Pipe

the string "hello" into the pipe; if invoked without a second argument, it *read*s the named pipe. The two processes are invocations of the identical program and have secretly agreed to communicate through the named pipe "fifo", but they need not be related. Other users could execute the program and participate in (or interfere with) the conversation.

5.13 DUP

The *dup* system call copies a file descriptor into the first free slot of the user file descriptor table, returning the new file descriptor to the user. It works for all file types. The syntax of the system call is

    newfd = dup(fd);

where *fd* is the file descriptor being *dup*ed and *newfd* is the new file descriptor that references the file. Because *dup* duplicates the file descriptor, it increments the count of the corresponding file table entry, which now has one more file descriptor entry that points to it. For example, examination of the data structures depicted in Figure 5.20 indicates that the process did the following sequence of system calls: It *open*ed the file "/etc/passwd" (file descriptor 3), then *open*ed the file "local" (file descriptor 4), *open*ed the file "/etc/passwd" again (file descriptor 5), and finally,

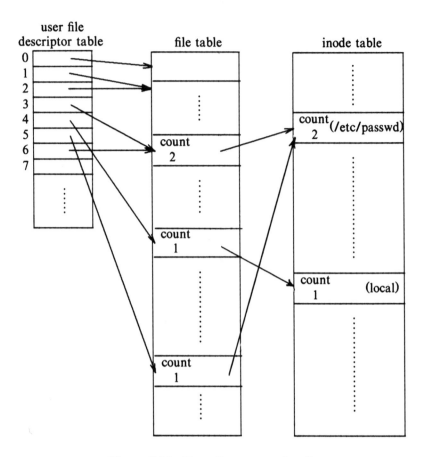

Figure 5.20. Data Structures after Dup

*dup*ed file descriptor 3, returning file descriptor 6.

Dup is perhaps an inelegant system call, because it assumes that the user knows that the system will return the lowest-numbered free entry in the user file descriptor table. However, it serves an important purpose in building sophisticated programs from simpler, building-block programs, as exemplified in the construction of shell pipelines (Chapter 7).

Consider the program in Figure 5.21. The variable i contains the file descriptor that the system returns as a result of opening the file "etc/passwd," and the variable j contains the file descriptor that the system returns as a result of *dup*ing the file descriptor i. In the *u area* of the process, the two user file descriptor entries represented by the user variables i and j point to one file table entry and therefore use the same file offset. The first two *read*s in the process thus read the data in sequence, and the two buffers, *buf1* and *buf2*, do not contain the same data.

```
#include  <fcntl.h>
main()
{
      int i, j;
      char buf1[512], buf2[512];

      i = open("/etc/passwd", O_RDONLY);
      j = dup(i);
      read(i, buf1, sizeof(buf1));
      read(j, buf2, sizeof(buf2));
      close(i);
      read(j, buf2, sizeof(buf2));
}
```

Figure 5.21. C Program Illustrating Dup

This differs from the case where a process *open*s the same file twice and *read*s the same data twice (Section 5.2). A process can *close* either file descriptor if it wants, but I/O continues normally on the other file descriptor, as illustrated in the example. In particular, a process can *close* its standard output file descriptor (file descriptor 1), *dup* another file descriptor so that it becomes file descriptor 1, then treat the file as its standard output. Chapter 7 presents a more realistic example of the use of *pipe* and *dup* when it describes the implementation of the shell.

5.14 MOUNTING AND UNMOUNTING FILE SYSTEMS

A physical disk unit consists of several logical sections, partitioned by the disk driver, and each section has a device file name. Processes can access data in a section by *open*ing the appropriate device file name and then *read*ing and *writ*ing the "file," treating it as a sequence of disk blocks. Chapter 10 gives details on this interface. A section of a disk may contain a logical file system, consisting of a boot block, super block, inode list, and data blocks, as described in Chapter 2. The *mount* system call connects the file system in a specified section of a disk to the existing file system hierarchy, and the *umount* system call disconnects a file system from the hierarchy. The *mount* system call thus allows users to access data in a disk section as a file system instead of a sequence of disk blocks.

The syntax for the *mount* system call is

mount(special pathname, directory pathname, options);

where *special pathname* is the name of the device special file of the disk section containing the file system to be mounted, *directory pathname* is the directory in the existing hierarchy where the file system will be mounted (called the *mount point*), and *options* indicate whether the file system should be mounted "read-only"

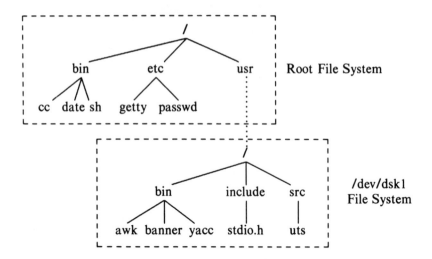

Figure 5.22. File System Tree Before and After Mount

(system calls such as *write* and *creat* that write the file system will fail). For example, if a process issues the system call

mount("/dev/dsk1", "/usr", 0);

the kernel attaches the file system contained in the portion of the disk called "/dev/dsk1" to directory "/usr" in the existing file system tree (see Figure 5.22). The file "/dev/dsk1" is a block special file, meaning that it is the name of a block device, typically a portion of a disk. The kernel assumes that the indicated portion of the disk contains a file system with a super block, inode list, and root inode. After completion of the *mount* system call, the root of the mounted file system is accessed by the name "/usr". Processes can access files on the mounted file system and ignore the fact that it is detachable. Only the *link* system call checks the file system of a file, because System V does not allow file links to span multiple file systems (see Section 5.15).

The kernel has a *mount table* with entries for every mounted file system. Each mount table entry contains

- a device number that identifies the mounted file system (this is the logical file system number mentioned previously);
- a pointer to a buffer containing the file system super block;
- a pointer to the root inode of the mounted file system ("/" of the "/dev/dsk1" file system in Figure 5.22);
- a pointer to the inode of the directory that is the mount point ("usr" of the root file system in Figure 5.22).

Association of the mount point inode and the root inode of the mounted file system, set up during the *mount* system call, allows the kernel to traverse the file system hierarchy gracefully, without special user knowledge.

```
algorithm mount
inputs: file name of block special file
        directory name of mount point
        options (read only)
output: none
{
        if (not super user)
                return(error);
        get inode for block special file (algorithm namei);
        make legality checks;
        get inode for "mounted on" directory name (algorithm namei);
        if (not directory, or reference count > 1)
        {
                release inodes (algorithm iput);
                return(error);
        }
        find empty slot in mount table;
        invoke block device driver open routine;
        get free buffer from buffer cache;
        read super block into free buffer;
        initialize super block fields;
        get root inode of mounted device (algorithm iget), save in mount table;
        mark inode of "mounted on" directory as mount point;
        release special file inode (algorithm iput);
        unlock inode of mount point directory;
}
```

Figure 5.23. Algorithm for Mounting a File System

Figure 5.23 depicts the algorithm for mounting a file system. The kernel only allows processes owned by a superuser to *mount* or *umount* file systems. Yielding permission for *mount* and *umount* to the entire user community would allow malicious (or not so malicious) users to wreak havoc on the file system. Super-users should wreak havoc only by accident.

The kernel finds the inode of the special file that represents the file system to be mounted, extracts the major and minor numbers that identify the appropriate disk section, and finds the inode of the directory on which the file system will be mounted. The reference count of the directory inode must not be greater than 1 (it must be at least 1 — why?), because of potentially dangerous side effects (see exercise 5.27). The kernel then allocates a free slot in the mount table, marks the slot in use, and assigns the device number field in the mount table. The above assignments are done immediately because the calling process could go to sleep in the ensuing device *open* procedure or in reading the file system super block, and another process could attempt to *mount* a file system. By having marked the mount table entry in use, the kernel prevents two *mounts* from using the same entry. By noting the device number of the attempted *mount*, the kernel can prevent other processes from *mount*ing the same file system again, because strange things could happen if a double mount were allowed (see exercise 5.26).

The kernel calls the *open* procedure for the block device containing the file system in the same way it invokes the procedure when opening the block device directly (Chapter 10). The device *open* procedure typically checks that the device is legal, sometimes initializing driver data structures and sending initialization commands to the hardware. The kernel then allocates a free buffer from the buffer pool (a variation of algorithm *getblk*) to hold the super block of the mounted file system and reads the super block using a variation of algorithm *read*. The kernel stores a pointer to the inode of the mounted-on directory of the original file tree to allow file path names containing ".." to traverse the mount point, as will be seen. It finds the root inode of the *mount*ed file system and stores a pointer to the inode in the mount table. To the user, the mounted-on directory and the root of the mounted file system are logically equivalent, and the kernel establishes their equivalence by their coexistence in the mount table entry. Processes can no longer access the inode of the mounted-on directory.

The kernel initializes fields in the file system super block, clearing the lock fields for the free block list and free inode list and setting the number of free inodes in the super block to 0. The purpose of the initializations is to minimize the danger of file system corruption when mounting the file system after a system crash: Making the kernel think that there are no free inodes in the super block forces algorithm *ialloc* to search the disk for free inodes. Unfortunately, if the linked list of free disk blocks is corrupt, the kernel does not fix the list internally (see Section 5.17 for file system maintenance). If the user *mounts* the file system *read-only* to disallow all write operations to the file system, the kernel sets a flag in the super block. Finally, the kernel marks the mounted-on inode as a mount point, so other processes can later identify it. Figure 5.24 depicts the various data structures at the conclusion of the *mount* call.

5.14.1 Crossing Mount Points in File Path Names

Let us reconsider algorithms *namei* and *iget* for the cases where a path name crosses a mount point. The two cases for crossing a mount point are: crossing from the mounted-on file system to the mounted file system (in the direction from the global system root towards a leaf node) and crossing from the mounted file system to the mounted-on file system. The following sequence of shell commands illustrates the two cases.

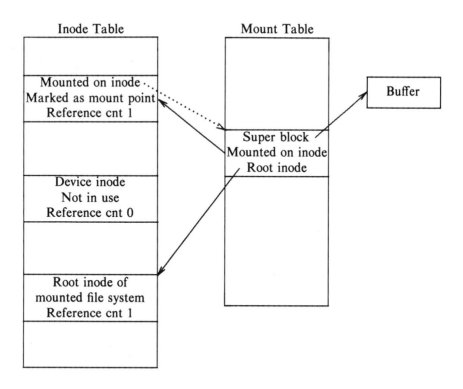

Figure 5.24. Data Structures after Mount

```
mount /dev/dsk1 /usr
cd /usr/src/uts
cd ../../..
```

The *mount* command invokes the *mount* system call after doing some consistency checks and mounts the file system in the disk section identified by "/dev/dsk1" onto the directory "/usr". The first *cd* (change directory) command causes the shell to execute the *chdir* system call, and the kernel parses the path name, crossing the mount point at "/usr". The second *cd* command results in the kernel parsing the path name and crossing the mount point at the third ".." in the path name.

For the case of crossing the mount point from the mounted-on file system to the mounted file system, consider the revised algorithm for *iget* in Figure 5.25, which is identical to that of Figure 4.3, except that it checks if the inode is a mount point: If the inode is marked "mounted-on," the kernel knows that it is a mount point. It finds the mount table entry whose mounted-on inode is the one just accessed and notes the device number of the mounted file system. Using the device number and the inode number for root, which is common to all file systems, it then accesses the

```
algorithm iget
input:   file system inode number
output: locked inode
{
      while (not done)
      {
            if (inode in inode cache)
            {
                  if (inode locked)
                  {
                        sleep (event inode becomes unlocked);
                        continue;        /* loop */
                  }
                  /* special processing for mount points———*/
                  if (inode a mount point)
                  {
                        find mount table entry for mount point;
                        get new file system number from mount table;
                        use root inode number in search;
                        continue;        /* loop again */
                  }
                  if (inode on inode free list)
                        remove from free list;
                  increment inode reference count;
                  return (inode);
            }

            /* inode not in inode cache */
            remove new inode from free list;
            reset inode number and file system;
            remove inode from old hash queue, place on new one;
            read inode from disk (algorithm bread);
            initialize inode (e.g. reference count to 1);
            return inode;
      }
}
```

Figure 5.25. Revised Algorithm for Accessing an Inode

root inode of the mounted device and returns that inode. In the first change directory example above, the kernel first accesses the inode for "/usr" in the mounted-on file system, finds that the inode is marked "mounted-on," finds the root inode of the mounted file system in the mount table, and accesses the root inode of the mounted file system.

```
algorithm namei            /* convert path name to inode */
input:  path name
output: locked inode
{
     if (path name starts from root)
          working inode = root inode (algorithm iget);
     else
          working inode = current directory inode (algorithm iget);
     while (there is more path name)
     {
          read next path name component from input;
          verify that inode is of directory, permissions;
          if (inode is of changed root and component is "..")
               continue;       /* loop */
component search:
          read inode (directory) (algorithms bmap, bread, brelse);
          if (component matches a directory entry)
          {
               get inode number for matched component;
               if (found inode of root and working inode is root and
                         and component name is "..")
               {
                    /* crossing mount point */
                    get mount table entry for working inode;
                    release working inode (algorithm iput);
                    working inode = mounted on inode;
                    lock mounted on inode;
                    increment reference count of working inode;
                    go to component search (for "..");
               }
               release working inode (algorithm iput);
               working inode = inode for new inode number (algorithm iget);
          }
          else     /* component not in directory */
               return (no inode);
     }
     return (working inode);
}
```

Figure 5.26. Revised Algorithm for Parsing a File Name

For the second case of crossing the mount point from the mounted file system to the mounted-on file system, consider the revised algorithm for *namei* in Figure 5.26. It is similar to that of Figure 4.11. However, after finding the inode number for a path name component in a directory, the kernel checks if the inode number is the root inode of a file system. If it is, and if the inode of the current working inode is also root, and the path name component is dot-dot (".."), the kernel identifies the inode as a mount point. It finds the mount table entry whose device number equals the device number of the last found inode, gets the inode of the mounted-on directory, and continues its search for dot-dot ("..") using the mounted-on inode as the working inode. At the root of the file system, however, ".." is the root.

In the example above (cd "../../.."), assume the starting current directory of the process is "/usr/src/uts". When parsing the path name in *namei*, the starting working inode is the current directory. The kernel changes the working inode to that of "/usr/src" as a result of parsing the first ".." in the path name. Then, it parses the second ".." in the path name, finds the root inode of the (previously) mounted file system, "usr", and makes it the working inode in *namei*. Finally, it parses the third ".." in the path name: It finds that the inode number for ".." is the root inode number, its working inode is the root inode, and ".." is the current path name component. The kernel finds the mount table entry for the "usr" mount point, releases the current working inode (the root of the "usr" file system), and allocates the mounted-on inode (the inode for directory "usr" in the root file system) as the new working inode. It then searches the directory structures in the mounted-on "/usr" for ".." and finds the inode number for the root of the file system ("/"). The *chdir* system call then completes as usual; the calling process is oblivious to the fact that it crossed a mount point.

5.14.2 Unmounting a File System

The syntax for the *umount* system call is

umount(special filename);

where *special filename* indicates the file system to be unmounted. When unmounting a file system (Figure 5.27), the kernel accesses the inode of the device to be unmounted, retrieves the device number for the special file, releases the inode (algorithm *iput*), and finds the mount table entry whose device number equals that of the special file. Before the kernel actually unmounts a file system, it makes sure that no files on that file system are still in use by searching the inode table for all files whose device number equals that of the file system being unmounted. Active files have a positive reference count and include files that are the current directory of some process, files with shared text that are currently being executed (Chapter 7), and open files that have not been closed. If any files from the file system are active, the *umount* call fails: if it were to succeed, the active files would be inaccessible.

The buffer pool may still contain "delayed write" blocks that were not written to disk, so the kernel flushes them from the buffer pool. The kernel removes shared text entries that are in the region table but not operational (see Chapter 7 for detail), writes out all recently modified super blocks to disk, and updates the disk copy of all inodes that need updating. It would suffice for the kernel to update the disk blocks, super block, and inodes for the unmounting file system only, but for

```
algorithm umount
input:   special file name of file system to be unmounted
output: none
{
        if (not super user)
                return(error);
        get inode of special file (algorithm namei);
        extract major, minor number of device being unmounted;
        get mount table entry, based on major, minor number,
                for unmounting file system;
        release inode of special file (algorithm iput);
        remove shared text entries from region table for files
                        belonging to file system; /* chap 7xxx */
        update super block, inodes, flush buffers;
        if (files from file system still in use)
                return(error);
        get root inode of mounted file system from mount table;
        lock inode;
        release inode (algorithm iput);   /* iget was in mount */
        invoke close routine for special device;
        invalidate buffers in pool from unmounted file system;
        get inode of mount point from mount table;
        lock inode;
        clear flag marking it as mount point;
        release inode (algorithm iput);         /* iget in mount */
        free buffer used for super block;
        free mount table slot;
}
```

Figure 5.27. Algorithm for Unmounting a File System

historical reasons it does so for all file systems. The kernel then releases the root inode of the mounted file system, held since its original access during the *mount* system call, and invokes the driver of the device that contains the file system to close the device. Afterwards, it goes through the buffers in the buffer cache and invalidates buffers for blocks on the now unmounted file system; there is no need to cache data in those blocks any longer. When invalidating the buffers, it moves the buffers to the beginning of the buffer free list, so that valid blocks remain in the buffer cache longer. It clears the "mounted-on" flag in the mounted-on inode set during the *mount* call and releases the inode. After marking the mount table entry free for general use, the *umount* call completes.

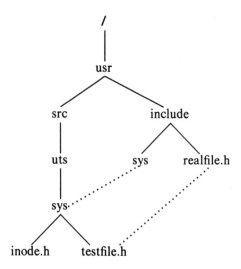

Figure 5.28. Linked Files in File System Tree

5.15 LINK

The *link* system call links a file to a new name in the file system directory structure, creating a new directory entry for an existing inode. The syntax for the *link* system call is

link(source file name, target file name);

where *source file name* is the name of an existing file and *target file name* is the new (additional) name the file will have after completion of the *link* call. The file system contains a path name for each link the file has, and processes can access the file by any of the path names. The kernel does not know which name was the original file name, so no file name is treated specially. For example, after executing the system calls

link("/usr/src/uts/sys", "/usr/include/sys");
link("/usr/include/realfile.h", "/usr/src/uts/sys/testfile.h");

the following three path names refer to the same file: "/usr/src/uts/sys/testfile.h", "/usr/include/sys/testfile.h", and "/usr/include/realfile" (see Figure 5.28).

The kernel allows only a superuser to *link* directories, simplifying the coding of programs that traverse the file system tree. If arbitrary users could *link* directories, programs designed to traverse the file hierarchy would have to worry about getting into an infinite loop if a user were to *link* a directory to a node name below it in the hierarchy. Superusers are presumably more careful about making such *links*. The capability to link directories had to be supported on early versions of the system, because the implementation of the *mkdir* command, which creates a new directory, relies on the capability to link directories. Inclusion of the *mkdir* system call eliminates the need to link directories.

```
algorithm link
input:   existing file name
         new file name
output: none
{
        get inode for existing file name (algorithm namei);
        if (too many links on file or linking directory without super user permission)
        {
                release inode (algorithm iput);
                return(error);
        }
        increment link count on inode;
        update disk copy of inode;
        unlock inode;
        get parent inode for directory to contain new file name (algorithm namei);
        if (new file name already exists or existing file, new file on
                                        different file systems)
        {
                undo update done above;
                return(error);
        }
        create new directory entry in parent directory of new file name:
                include new file name, inode number of existing file name;
        release parent directory inode (algorithm iput);
        release inode of existing file (algorithm iput);
}
```

Figure 5.29. Algorithm for Linking Files

Figure 5.29 shows the algorithm for *link*. The kernel first locates the inode for the source file using algorithm *namei*, increments its link count, updates the disk copy of the inode (for consistency, as will be seen), and unlocks the inode. It then searches for the target file; if the file is present, the *link* call fails, and the kernel decrements the link count incremented earlier. Otherwise, it notes the location of an empty slot in the parent directory of the target file, writes the target file name and the source file inode number into that slot, and releases the inode of the target file parent directory via algorithm *iput*. Since the target file did not originally exist, there is no other inode to release. The kernel concludes by releasing the source file inode: Its link count is 1 greater than it was at the beginning of the call, and another name in the file system allows access to it. The link count keeps count of the directory entries that refer to the file and is thus distinct from the inode reference count. If no other processes access the file at the conclusion of the *link* call, the inode reference count of the file is 0, and the link count of the file is at least 2.

For example, when executing

link("source", "dir/target");

the kernel locates the inode for file "source", increments its link count, remembers its inode number, say 74, and unlocks the inode. It locates the inode of "dir", the parent directory of "target", finds an empty directory slot in "dir", and writes the file name "target" and the inode number 74 into the empty directory slot. Finally, it releases the inode for "source" via algorithm *iput*. If the link count of "source" had been 1, it is now 2.

Two deadlock possibilities are worthy of note, both concerning the reason the process unlocks the source file inode after incrementing its link count. If the kernel did not unlock the inode, two processes could deadlock by executing the following system calls simultaneously.

process A: link("a/b/c/d", "e/f/g");
process B: link("e/f", "a/b/c/d/ee");

Suppose process A finds the inode for file "a/b/c/d" at the same time that process B finds the inode for "e/f". The phrase *at the same time* means that the system arrives at a state where each process has allocated its inode. Figure 5.30 illustrates an execution scenario. When process A now attempts to find the inode for directory "e/f", it would sleep awaiting the event that the inode for "f" becomes free. But when process B attempts to find the inode for directory "a/b/c/d", it would sleep awaiting the event that the inode for "d" becomes free. Process A would be holding a locked inode that process B wants, and process B would be holding a locked inode that process A wants. The kernel avoids this classic example of deadlock by releasing the source file's inode after incrementing its link count. Since the first resource (inode) is free when accessing the next resource, no deadlock can occur.

The last example showed how two processes could deadlock each other if the inode lock were not released. A single process could also deadlock itself. If it executed

link("a/b/c", "a/b/c/d");

it would allocate the inode for file "c" in the first part of the algorithm; if the kernel did not release the inode lock, it would deadlock when encountering the inode "c" in searching for the file "d". If two processes, or even one process, could not continue executing because of deadlock, what would be the effect on the system? Since inodes are finitely allocatable resources, receipt of a signal cannot awaken the process from its sleep (Chapter 7). Hence, the system could not break the deadlock without rebooting. If no other processes accessed the files over which the processes deadlock, no other processes in the system would be affected.

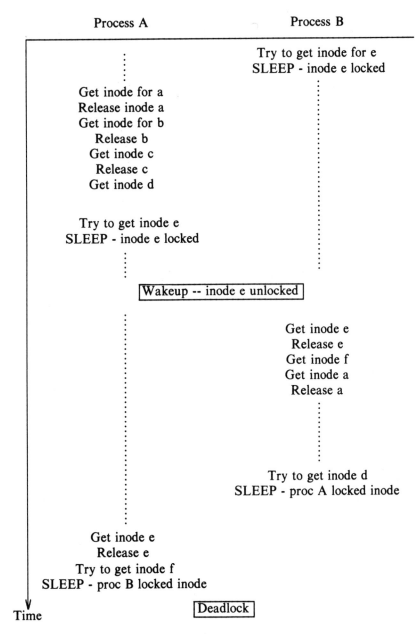

Figure 5.30. Deadlock Scenario for Link

However, any processes that accessed those files (or attempted to access other files via the locked directory) would deadlock. Thus, if the file were "/bin" or "/usr/bin" (typical depositories for commands) or "/bin/sh" (the shell) the effect on the system would be disastrous.

5.16 UNLINK

The *unlink* system call removes a directory entry for a file. The syntax for the *unlink* call is

    unlink(pathname);

where *pathname* identifies the name of the file to be *unlink*ed from the directory hierarchy. If a process *unlink*s a given file, no file is accessible by that name until another directory entry with that name is created. In the following code fragment, for example,

    unlink("myfile");
    fd = open("myfile", O_RDONLY);

the *open* call should fail, because the current directory no longer contains a file called *myfile*. If the file being *unlink*ed is the last link of the file, the kernel eventually frees its data blocks. However, if the file had several links, it is still accessible by its other names.

Figure 5.31 gives the algorithm for *unlink*ing a file. The kernel first uses a variation of algorithm *namei* to find the file that it must *unlink*, but instead of returning its inode, it returns the inode of the parent directory. It accesses the in-core inode of the file to be *unlink*ed, using algorithm *iget*. (The special case for unlinking the file "." is covered in an exercise.) After checking error conditions and, for executable files, removing inactive shared text entries from the region table (Chapter 7), the kernel clears the file name from the parent directory: Writing a 0 for the value of the inode number suffices to clear the slot in the directory. The kernel then does a synchronous write of the directory to disk to ensure that the file is inaccessible by its old name, decrements the link count, and releases the in-core inodes of the parent directory and the unlinked file via algorithm *iput*.

When releasing the in-core inode of the unlinked file in *iput*, if the reference count drops to 0, and if the link count is 0, the kernel reclaims the disk blocks occupied by the file. No file names refer to the inode any longer and the inode is not active. To reclaim the disk blocks, the kernel loops through the inode table of contents, freeing all direct blocks immediately (according to algorithm *free*). For the indirect blocks, it recursively frees all blocks that appear in the various levels of indirection, freeing the more direct blocks first. It zeroes out the block numbers in the inode table of contents and sets the file size in the inode to 0. It then clears the inode file type field to indicate that the inode is free and frees the inode with algorithm *ifree*. It updates the disk since the disk copy of the inode still indicated that the inode was in use; the inode is now free for assignment to other files.

```
algorithm unlink
input:   file name
output: none
{
        get parent inode of file to be unlinked (algorithm namei);
        /* if unlinking the current directory... */
        if (last component of file name is ".")
                increment inode reference count;
        else
                get inode of file to be unlinked (algorithm iget);
        if (file is directory but user is not super user)
        {
                release inodes (algorithm iput);
                return(error);
        }
        if (shared text file and link count currently 1)
                remove from region table;
        write parent directory: zero inode number of unlinked file;
        release inode parent directory (algorithm iput);
        decrement file link count;
        release file inode (algorithm iput);
                /* iput checks if link count is 0:  if so,
                 * releases file blocks (algorithm free) and
                 * frees inode (algorithm ifree);
                 */
}
```

Figure 5.31. Algorithm for Unlinking a File

5.16.1 File System Consistency

The kernel orders its writes to disk to minimize file system corruption in event of system failure. For instance, when it removes a file name from its parent directory, it writes the directory synchronously to the disk — before it destroys the contents of the file and frees the inode. If the system were to crash before the file contents were removed, damage to the file system would be minimal: There would be an inode that would have a link count 1 greater than the number of directory entries that access it, but all other paths to the file would still be legal. If the directory write were not synchronous, it would be possible for the directory entry on disk to point to a free (or reallocated!) inode after a system crash. Thus there would be more directory entries in the file system that refer to the inode than the inode would have link counts. In particular, if the file name was that of the last link to the file, it would refer to an unallocated inode. System damage is clearly less severe and easier to correct in the first case (see Section 5.18).

For example, suppose a file has two links with path names "a" and "b", and suppose a process *unlink*s "a". If the kernel orders the disk write operations, then it zeros the directory entry for "a" and writes it to disk. If the system crashes after the write to disk completes, file "b" has link count of 2, but file "a" does not exist because its old entry had been zeroed before the system crash. File "b" has an extra link count, but the system functions properly when rebooted.

Now suppose the kernel ordered the disk write operations in the reverse order and the system crashes: That is, it decrements the link count for the file "b" to 1, writes the inode to disk, and crashes before it could zero the directory entry for file "a". When the system is rebooted, entries for files "a" and "b" exist in their respective directories, but the link count for the file they reference is 1. If a process then *unlink*s file "a", the file link count drops to 0 even though file "b" still references the inode. If the kernel were later to reassign the inode as the result of a *creat* system call, the new file would have link count 1 but two path names that reference it. The system cannot rectify the situation except via maintenance programs (*fsck*, described in Section 5.18) that access the file system through the block or raw interface.

The kernel also frees inodes and disk blocks in a specific order to minimize corruption in event of system failure. When removing the contents of a file and clearing its inode, it is possible to free the blocks containing the file data first, or it is possible to free and write out the inode first. The result is usually identical for both cases, but it differs if the system crashes in the middle. Suppose the kernel first frees the disk blocks of a file and crashes. When the system is rebooted, the inode still contains references to the old disk blocks, which may no longer contain data relevant to the file. The kernel would see an apparently good file, but a user accessing the file would notice corruption. It is also possible that other files were assigned those disk blocks. The effort to clean the file system with the *fsck* program would be great. However, if the system first writes the inode to disk and the system crashes, a user would not notice anything wrong with the file system when the system is rebooted. The data blocks that previously belonged to the file would be inaccessible to the system, but users would notice no apparent corruption. The *fsck* program also finds the task of reclaiming unlinked disk blocks easier than the clean-up it would have to do for the first sequence of events.

5.16.2 Race Conditions

Race conditions abound in the *unlink* system call, particularly when unlinking directories. The *rmdir* command removes a directory after verifying that the directory contains no files (it *read*s the directory and checks that all directory entries have inode value 0). But since *rmdir* runs at user level, the actions of verifying that a directory is empty and removing the directory are not atomic; the system could do a context switch between execution of the *read* and *unlink* system calls. Hence, another process could *creat* a file in the directory after *rmdir* determined that the directory was empty. Users can prevent this situation only by use of file and record locking. Once a process begins execution of the *unlink* call, however, no other process can access the file being unlinked since the inodes of the parent directory and the file are locked.

Recall the algorithm for the *link* system call and how the kernel unlocks the inode before completion of the call. If another process should *unlink* the file while the inode lock is free, it would only decrement the link count; since the link count had been incremented before unlinking the inode, the count would still be greater than 0. Hence, the file cannot be removed, and the system is safe. The condition is equivalent to the case where the *unlink* happens immediately after the *link* call completes.

Another race condition exists in the case where one process is converting a file path name to an inode using algorithm *namei* and another process is removing a directory in that path. Suppose process A is parsing the path name "a/b/c/d" and goes to sleep while allocating the in-core inode for "c". It could go to sleep while trying to lock the inode or while trying to access the disk block in which the inode resides (see algorithms *iget* and *bread*). If process B wants to *unlink* the directory "c", it may go to sleep, possibly for the same reasons that process A is sleeping. Suppose the kernel later schedules process B to run before process A. Process B would run to completion, unlinking directory "c" and removing it and its contents (for the last link) before process A runs again. Later, process A would try to access an illegal in-core inode that had been removed. Algorithm *namei* therefore checks that the link count is not 0 before proceeding, reporting an error otherwise.

The check is not sufficient, however, because another process could conceivably create a new directory somewhere in the file system and allocate the inode that had previously been used for "c". Process A is tricked into thinking that it accessed the correct inode (see Figure 5.32). Nevertheless, the system maintains its integrity; the worst that could happen is that the wrong file is accessed — a possible security breach — but the race condition is rare in practice.

A process can *unlink* a file while another process has the file open. (The *unlink*ing process could even be the process that did the *open*). Since the kernel unlocks the inode at the end of the *open* call, the *unlink* call will succeed. The kernel will follow the *unlink* algorithm as if the file were not open, and it will remove the directory entry for the file. No other processes will be able to access the now *unlink*ed file. However, since the *open* system call had incremented the inode reference count, the kernel does not clear the file contents when executing the *iput* algorithm at the conclusion of the *unlink* call. So the opening process can do all the normal file operations with its file descriptor, including *read*ing and *writ*ing the file. But when it *close*s the file, the inode reference count drops to 0 in *iput*, and the kernel clears the contents of the file. In short, the process that had *open*ed the file proceeds as if the *unlink* did not occur, and the *unlink* happens as if the file were not open. Other system calls will continue to work for the opening process, too.

In Figure 5.33 for example, a process *open*s a file supplied as a parameter and then *unlink*s the file it just *open*ed. The *stat* call fails because the original path

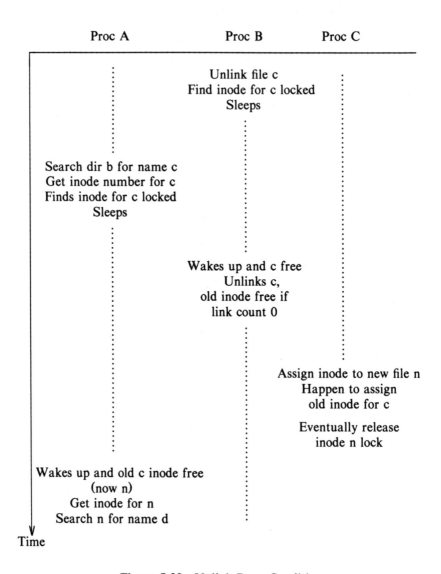

Figure 5.32. Unlink Race Condition

```
#include  <sys/types.h>
#include  <sys/stat.h>
#include  <fcntl.h>

main(argc, argv)
    int argc;
    char *argv[];
{
    int fd;
    char buf[1024];
    struct stat statbuf;

    if (argc != 2)              /* need a parameter */
        exit();
    fd = open(argv[1], O_RDONLY);
    if (fd == -1)               /* open fails */
        exit();
    if (unlink(argv[1]) == -1)      /* unlink file just opened */
        exit();
    if (stat(argv[1], &statbuf) == -1)     /* stat the file by name*/
        printf("stat %s fails as it should\n", argv[1]);
    else
        printf("stat %s succeeded!!!!\n", argv[1]);
    if (fstat(fd, &statbuf) == -1)           /* stat the file by fd */
        printf("fstat %s fails!!!\n", argv[1]);
    else
        printf("fstat %s succeeds as it should\n", argv[1]);
    while (read(fd, buf, sizeof(buf)) > 0)    /* read open/unlinked file */
        printf("%1024s", buf);         /* prints 1K byte field */
}
```

Figure 5.33. Unlinking an Opened File

name no longer refers to a file after the *unlink* (assuming no other process created a file by that name in the meantime), but the *fstat* call succeeds because it gets to the inode via the file descriptor. The process loops, *read*ing the file 1024 bytes at a time and printing the file to the standard output. When the *read* encounters the end of the file, the process *exit*s: After the close in *exit*, the file no longer exists. Processes commonly create temporary files and immediately unlink them; they can continue to read and write them, but the file name no longer appears in the directory hierarchy. If the process should fail for some reason, it leaves no trail of temporary files behind it.

5.17 FILE SYSTEM ABSTRACTIONS

Weinberger introduced *file system types* to support his network file system (see [Killian 84] for a brief description of this mechanism), and the latest release of System V supports a derivation of his scheme. File system types allow the kernel to support multiple file systems simultaneously, such as network file systems (Chapter 13) or even file systems of other operating systems. Processes use the usual UNIX system calls to access files, and the kernel maps a generic set of file operations into operations specific to each file system type.

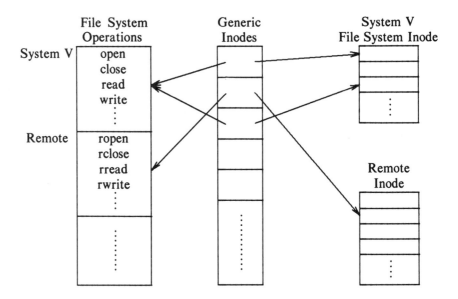

Figure 5.34. Inodes for File System Types

The inode is the interface between the abstract file system and the specific file system. A generic in-core inode contains data that is independent of particular file systems, and points to a file-system-specific inode that contains file-system-specific data. The file-system-specific inode contains information such as access permissions and block layout, but the generic inode contains the device number, inode number, file type, size, owner, and reference count. Other data that is file-system-specific includes the super block and directory structures. Figure 5.34 depicts the generic in-core inode table and two tables of file-system-specific inodes, one for System V file system structures and the other for a remote (network) inode. The latter inode presumably contains enough information to identify a file on a remote system. A file system may not have an inode-like structure; but the file-system-specific code manufactures an object that satisfies UNIX file system semantics and allocates its "inode" when the kernel allocates a generic inode.

Each file system type has a structure that contains the addresses of functions that perform abstract operations. When the kernel wants to access a file, it makes an indirect function call, based on the file system type and the operation (see Figure 5.34). Some abstract operations are to open a file, close it, read or write data, return an inode for a file name component (like *namei* and *iget*), release an inode (like *iput*), update an inode, check access permissions, set file attributes (permissions), and mount and unmount file systems. Chapter 13 will illustrate the use of file system abstractions in the description of a distributed file system.

5.18 FILE SYSTEM MAINTENANCE

The kernel maintains consistency of the file system during normal operation. However, extraordinary circumstances such as a power failure may cause a system crash that leaves a file system in an inconsistent state: most of the data in the file system is acceptable for use, but some inconsistencies exist. The command *fsck* checks for such inconsistencies and repairs the file system if necessary. It accesses the file system by its block or raw interface (Chapter 10) and bypasses the regular file access methods. This section describes several inconsistencies checked by *fsck*.

A disk block may belong to more than one inode or to the list of free blocks and an inode. When a file system is originally set up, all disk blocks are on the free list. When a disk block is assigned for use, the kernel removes it from the free list and assigns it to an inode. The kernel may not reassign the disk block to another inode until the disk block has been returned to the free list. Therefore, a disk block is either on the free list or assigned to a single inode. Consider the possibilities if the kernel freed a disk block in a file, returning the block number to the in-core copy of the super block, and allocated the disk block to a new file. If the kernel wrote the inode and blocks of the new file to disk but crashed before updating the inode of the old file to disk, the two inodes would address the same disk block number. Similarly, if the kernel wrote the super block and its free list to disk and crashed before writing the old inode out, the disk block would appear on the free list and in the old inode.

If a block number is not on the free list of blocks nor contained in a file, the file system is inconsistent because, as mentioned above, all blocks must appear somewhere. This situation could happen if a block was removed from a file and placed on the super block free list. If the old file was written to disk and the system crashed before the super block was written to disk, the block would not appear on any lists stored on disk.

An inode may have a non-0 link count, but its inode number may not exist in any directories in the file system. All files except (unnamed) pipes must exist in the file system tree. If the system crashes after creating a pipe or after creating a file but before creating its directory entry, the inode will have its link field set even though it does not appear to be in the file system. The problem could also arise if a directory were *unlink*ed before making sure that all files contained in the directory were *unlink*ed.

If the format of an inode is incorrect (for instance, if the file type field has an undefined value), something is wrong. This could happen if an administrator mounted an improperly formatted file system. The kernel accesses disk blocks that it thinks contain inodes but in reality contain data.

If an inode number appears in a directory entry but the inode is free, the file system is inconsistent because an inode number that appears in a directory entry should be that of an allocated inode. This could happen if the kernel was creating a new file and wrote the directory entry to disk but did not write the inode to disk before the crash. It could also occur if a process *unlink*ed a file and wrote the freed inode to disk, but did not write the directory element to disk before it crashed. These situations are avoided by ordering the write operations properly.

If the number of free blocks or free inodes recorded in the super block does not conform to the number that exist on disk, the file system is inconsistent. The summary information in the super block must always be consistent with the state of the file system.

5.19 SUMMARY

This chapter concludes the first part of the book, the explanation of the file system. It introduced three kernel tables: the user file descriptor table, the system file table, and the mount table. It described the algorithms for many system calls relating to the file system and their interaction. It introduced file system abstractions, which allow the UNIX system to support varied file system types. Finally, it described how *fsck* checks the consistency of the file system.

5.20 EXERCISES

1. Consider the program in Figure 5.35. What is the return value for all the *read*s and what is the contents of the buffer? Describe what is happening in the kernel during each *read*.

2. Reconsider the program in Figure 5.35 but suppose the statement

   lseek(fd, 9000L, 0);

   is placed before the first *read*. What does the process see and what happens inside the kernel?

3. A process can *open* a file in write-append mode, meaning that every write operations starts at the byte offset marking the current end of file. Therefore, two processes can *open* a file in write-append mode and write the file without overwriting data. What happens if a process *open*s a file in write-append mode and seeks to the beginning of the file?

4. The standard I/O library makes user reading and writing more efficient by buffering the data in the library and thus potentially saving the number of system calls a user has to make. How would you implement the library functions *fread* and *fwrite*? What should the library functions *fopen* and *fclose* do?

```
#include  <fcntl.h>
main()
{
        int fd;
        char buf[1024];
        fd = creat("junk", 0666);
        lseek(fd, 2000L, 2);                /* seek to byte 2000 */
        write(fd, "hello", 5);
        close(fd);

        fd = open("junk", O_RDONLY);
        read(fd, buf, 1024);              /* read zero's */
        read(fd, buf, 1024);              /* catch something */
        read(fd, buf, 1024);
}
```

Figure 5.35. Reading 0s and End of File

5. If a process is reading data consecutively from a file, the kernel notes the value of the read-ahead block in the in-core inode. What happens if several processes simultaneously read data consecutively from the same file?

```
#include  <fcntl.h>
main()
{
        int fd;
        char buf[256];

        fd = open("/etc/passwd", O_RDONLY);
        if (read(fd, buf, 1024) < 0)
                printf("read fails\n");
}
```

Figure 5.36. A Big Read in a Little Buffer

6. Consider the program in Figure 5.36. What happens when the program is executed? Why? What would happen if the declaration of *buf* were sandwiched between the declaration of two other arrays of size 1024? How does the kernel recognize that the *read* is too big for the buffer?

* 7. The BSD file system allows fragmentation of the last block of a file as needed, according to the following rules:

   • Structures similar to the super block keep track of free fragments;
   • The kernel does not keep a preallocated pool of free fragments but breaks a free block into fragments when necessary;

- The kernel can assign block fragments only for the last block of a file;
- If a block is partitioned into several fragments, the kernel can assign them to different files;
- The number of fragments in a block is fixed per file system;
- The kernel allocates fragments during the *write* system call.

Design an algorithm that allocates block fragments to a file. What changes must be made to the inode to allow for fragments? How advantageous is it from a performance standpoint to use fragments for files that use indirect blocks? Would it be more advantageous to allocate fragments during a *close* call instead of during a *write* call?

* 8. Recall the discussion in Chapter 4 for placing data in a file's inode. If the size of the inode is that of a disk block, design an algorithm such that the last data of a file is written in the inode block if it fits. Compare this method with that described in the previous problem.

* 9. System V uses the *fcntl* system call to implement file and record locking:

   fcntl(fd, cmd, arg);

   where *fd* is the file descriptor, *cmd* specifies the type of locking operation, and *arg* specifies various parameters, such as lock type (read or write) and byte offsets (see the appendix). The locking operations include
   - Test for locks belonging to other processes and return immediately, indicating whether other locks were found,
   - Set a lock and sleep until successful,
   - Set a lock but return immediately if unsuccessful.

   The kernel automatically releases locks set by a process when it *closes* the file. Describe an algorithm that implements file and record locking. If the locks are *mandatory*, other processes should be prevented from accessing the file. What changes must be made to *read* and *write*?

* 10. If a process goes to sleep while waiting for a file lock to become free, the possibility for deadlock exists: process A may lock file "one" and attempt to lock file "two," and process B may lock file "two" and attempt to lock file "one." Both processes are in a state where they cannot continue. Extend the algorithm of the previous problem so that the kernel detects the deadlock situation as it is about to occur and fails the system call. Is the kernel the right place to check for deadlocks?

11. Before the existence of a file locking system call, users could get cooperating processes to implement a locking mechanism by executing system calls that exhibited atomic features. What system calls described in this chapter could be used? What are the dangers inherent in using such methods?

12. Ritchie claims (see [Ritchie 81]) that file locking is not sufficient to prevent the confusion caused by programs such as editors that make a copy of a file while editing and then write the original file when done. Explain what he meant and comment.

13. Consider another method for locking files to prevent destructive update: Suppose the inode contains a new permission setting such that it allows only one process at a time to *open* the file for writing, but many processes can *open* the file for reading. Describe an implementation.

* 14. Consider the program in Figure 5.37 that creates a directory node in the wrong format (there are no directory entries for "." and ".."). Try a few commands on the new directory such as *ls −l*, *ls −ld*, or *cd*. What is happening?

```
main(argc, argv)
      int argc;
      char *argv[];
{
      if (argc != 2)
      {
            printf("try: command directory name\n");
            exit();
      }

      /* modes indicate: directory (04) rwx permission for all */
      /* only super user can do this */
      if (mknod(argv[1], 040777, 0) == -1)
            printf("mknod fails\n");
}
```

Figure 5.37. A Half-Baked Directory

15. Write a program that prints the owner, file type, access permissions, and access times of files supplied as parameters. If a file (parameter) is a directory, the program should *read* the directory and print the above information for all files in the directory.

16. Suppose a directory has read permission for a user but not execute permission. What happens when the directory is used as a parameter to *ls* with the "−i" option? What about the "−l" option? Explain the answers. Repeat the problem for the case that the directory has execute permission but not read permission.

17. Compare the permissions a process must have for the following operations and comment.
   - Creating a new file requires write permission in a directory.
   - Creating an existing file requires write permission on the file.
   - Unlinking a file requires write permission in the directory, not on the file.

* 18. Write a program that visits every directory, starting with the current directory. How should it handle loops in the directory hierarchy?

19. Execute the program in Figure 5.38 and describe what happens in the kernel. (Hint: Execute *pwd* when the program completes.)

20. Write a program that changes its root to a particular directory, and investigate the directory tree accessible to that program.

21. Why can't a process undo a previous *chroot* system call? Change the implementation so that it can change its root back to a previous root. What are the advantages and disadvantages of such a feature?

22. Consider the simple pipe example in Figure 5.19, where a process *writes* the string "hello" in the pipe then *reads* the string. What would happen if the count of data written to the pipe were 1024 instead of 6 (but the count of read data stays at 6)? What would happen if the order of the *read* and *write* system calls were reversed?

23. In the program illustrating the use of named pipes (Figure 5.19), what happens if *mknod* discovers that the named pipe already exists? How does the kernel implement this? What would happen if many reader and writer processes all attempted to

```
main(argc, argv)
    int argc;
    char *argv[];
{
    if (argc != 2)
    {
        printf("need 1 dir arg\n");
        exit();
    }

    if (chdir(argv[1]) == -1)
        printf("%s not a directory\n", argv[1]);
}
```

Figure 5.38. Sample Program with Chdir System Call

communicate through the named pipe instead of the one reader and one writer implicit in the text? How could the processes ensure that only one reader and one writer process were communicating?

24. When *open*ing a named pipe for reading, a process sleeps in the *open* until another process *open*s the pipe for writing. Why? Couldn't the process return successfully from the *open*, continue processing until it tried to *read* from the pipe, and sleep in the *read*?

25. How would you implement the *dup2* (from Version 7) system call with syntax

    dup2(oldfd, newfd);

    where *oldfd* is the file descriptor to be *dup*ed to file descriptor number *newfd*? What should happen if *newfd* already refers to an open file?

* 26. What strange things could happen if the kernel would allow two processes to mount the same file system simultaneously at two mount points?

27. Suppose a process changes its current directory to "/mnt/a/b/c" and a second process then *mount*s a file system onto "/mnt". Should the *mount* succeed? What happens if the first process executes *pwd*? The kernel does not allow the *mount* to succeed if the inode reference count of "/mnt" is greater than 1. Comment.

28. In the algorithm for crossing a mount point on recognition of ".." in the file path name, the kernel checks three conditions to see if it is at a mount point: that the found inode has the root inode number, that the working inode is root of the file system, and that the path name component is "..". Why must it check all three conditions? Show that checking any two conditions is insufficient to allow the process to cross the mount point.

29. If a user *mount*s a file system "read-only," the kernel sets a flag in the super block. How should it prevent write operations during the *write*, *creat*, *link*, *unlink*, *chown*, and *chmod* system calls? What write operations do all the above system calls do to the file system?

* 30. Suppose a process attempts to *umount* a file system and another process is simultaneously attempting to *creat* a new file on that file system. Only one system call can succeed. Explore the race condition.

* 31. When the *umount* system call checks that no more files are active on a file system, it has a problem with the file system root inode, allocated via *iget* during the *mount* system call and hence having reference count greater than 0. How can *umount* be sure there are no active files and take account for the file system root? Consider two cases:
   - *umount* releases the root inode with the *iput* algorithm before checking for active inodes. (How does it recover if there were active files after all?)
   - *umount* checks for active files before releasing the root inode but permits the root inode to remain active. (How active can the root inode get?)

32. When executing the command *ls* −*ld* on a directory, note that the number of links to the directory is never 1. Why?

33. How does the command *mkdir* (make a new directory) work? (Hint: When *mkdir* completes, what are the inode numbers for "." and ".."?)

* 34. Symbolic links refer to the capability to *link* files that exist on different file systems. A new type indicator specifies a symbolic link file; the data of the file is the path name of the file to which it is linked. Describe an implementation of symbolic links.

* 35. What happens when a process executes

   unlink(".");

   What is the current directory of the process? Assume superuser permissions.

36. Design a system call that truncates an existing file to arbitrary sizes, supplied as an argument, and describe an implementation. Implement a system call that allows a user to remove a file segment between specified byte offsets, compressing the file size. Without such system calls, encode a program that provides this functionality.

37. Describe all conditions where the reference count of an inode can be greater than 1.

38. In file system abstractions, should each file system type support a private lock operation to be called from the generic code, or does a generic lock operation suffice?

6

THE STRUCTURE
OF PROCESSES

Chapter 2 formulated the high-level characteristics of processes. This chapter presents the ideas more formally, defining the context of a process and showing how the kernel identifies and locates a process. Section 6.1 defines the process state model for the UNIX system and the set of state transitions. The kernel contains a process table with an entry that describes the state of every active process in the system. The *u area* contains additional information that controls the operation of a process. The process table entry and the *u area* are part of the context of a process. The aspect of the process context that most visibly distinguishes it from the context of another process is, of course, the contents of its address space. Section 6.2 describes the principles of memory management for processes and for the kernel and how the operating system and the hardware cooperate to do virtual memory address translation. Section 6.3 examines the components of the context of a process, and the rest of the chapter describes the low-level algorithms that manipulate the process context. Section 6.4 shows how the kernel saves the context of a process during an interrupt, system call, or context switch and how it later resumes execution of the suspended process. Section 6.5 gives various algorithms, used by the system calls described in the next chapter, that manipulate the process address space. Finally, Section 6.6 covers the algorithms for putting a process to sleep and for waking it up.

6.1 PROCESS STATES AND TRANSITIONS

As outlined in Chapter 2, the lifetime of a process can be conceptually divided into a set of states that describe the process. The following list contains the complete set of process states.

1. The process is executing in user mode.
2. The process is executing in kernel mode.
3. The process is not executing but is ready to run as soon as the kernel schedules it.
4. The process is sleeping and resides in main memory.
5. The process is ready to run, but the swapper (process 0) must swap the process into main memory before the kernel can schedule it to execute. Chapter 9 will reconsider this state in a paging system.
6. The process is sleeping, and the swapper has swapped the process to secondary storage to make room for other processes in main memory.
7. The process is returning from the kernel to user mode, but the kernel preempts it and does a context switch to schedule another process. The distinction between this state and state 3 ("ready to run") will be brought out shortly.
8. The process is newly created and is in a transition state; the process exists, but it is not ready to run, nor is it sleeping. This state is the start state for all processes except process 0.
9. The process executed the *exit* system call and is in the *zombie* state. The process no longer exists, but it leaves a record containing an exit code and some timing statistics for its parent process to collect. The zombie state is the final state of a process.

Figure 6.1 gives the complete process state transition diagram. Consider a typical process as it moves through the state transition model. The events depicted are artificial in that processes do not always experience them, but they illustrate various state transitions. The process enters the state model in the "created" state when the parent process executes the *fork* system call and eventually moves into a state where it is ready to run (3 or 5). For simplicity, assume the process enters the state "ready to run in memory." The process scheduler will eventually pick the process to execute, and the process enters the state "kernel running," where it completes its part of the *fork* system call.

When the process completes the system call, it may move to the state "user running," where it executes in user mode. After a period of time, the system clock may interrupt the processor, and the process enters state "kernel running" again. When the clock interrupt handler finishes servicing the clock interrupt, the kernel may decide to schedule another process to execute, so the first process enters state "preempted" and the other process executes. The state "preempted" is really the same as the state "ready to run in memory" (the dotted line in the figure that connects the two states emphasizes their equivalence), but they are depicted separately to stress that a process executing in kernel mode can be preempted only

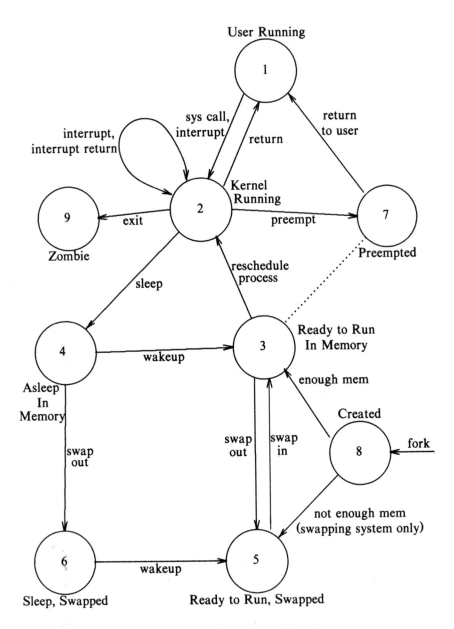

Figure 6.1. Process State Transition Diagram

when it is about to return to user mode. Consequently, the kernel could swap a process from the state "preempted" if necessary. Eventually, the scheduler will choose the process to execute, and it returns to the state "user running," executing in user mode again.

When a process executes a system call, it leaves the state "user running" and enters the state "kernel running." Suppose the system call requires I/O from the disk, and the process must wait for the I/O to complete. It enters the state "asleep in memory," putting itself to sleep until it is notified that the I/O has completed. When the I/O later completes, the hardware interrupts the CPU, and the interrupt handler awakens the process, causing it to enter the state "ready to run in memory."

Suppose the system is executing many processes that do not fit simultaneously into main memory, and the swapper (process 0) swaps out the process to make room for another process that is in the state "ready to run swapped." When evicted from main memory, the process enters the state "ready to run swapped." Eventually, the swapper chooses the process as the most suitable to swap into main memory, and the process reenters the state "ready to run in memory." The scheduler will eventually choose to run the process, and it enters the state "kernel running" and proceeds. When a process completes, it invokes the *exit* system call, thus entering the states "kernel running" and, finally, the "zombie" state.

The process has control over some state transitions at user-level. First, a process can create another process. However, the state transitions the process takes from the "created" state (that is, to the states "ready to run in memory" or "ready to run swapped") depend on the kernel: The process has no control over those state transitions. Second, a process can make system calls to move from state "user running" to state "kernel running" and enter the kernel of its own volition. However, the process has no control over when it will return from the kernel; events may dictate that it never returns but enters the zombie state (see Section 7.2 on signals). Finally, a process can *exit* of its own volition, but as indicated before, external events may dictate that it *exits* without explicitly invoking the *exit* system call. All other state transitions follow a rigid model encoded in the kernel, reacting to events in a predictable way according to rules formulated in this and later chapters. Some rules have already been cited: No process can preempt another process executing in the kernel, for example.

Two kernel data structures describe the state of a process: the process table entry and the *u area*. The process table contains fields that must always be accessible to the kernel, but the *u area* contains fields that need to be accessible only to the running process. Therefore, the kernel allocates space for the *u area* only when creating a process: It does not need *u area*s for process table entries that do not have processes.

The fields in the process table are the following.

- The *state* field identifies the process state.
- The process table entry contains fields that allow the kernel to locate the process and its *u area* in main memory or in secondary storage. The kernel uses the

information to do a *context switch* to the process when the process moves from
state "ready to run in memory" to the state "kernel running" or from the state
"preempted" to the state "user running." In addition, it uses this information
when swapping (or paging) processes to and from main memory (between the
two "in memory" states and the two "swapped" states). The process table
entry also contains a field that gives the process size, so that the kernel knows
how much space to allocate for the process.

- Several user identifiers (user IDs or UIDs) determine various process privileges.
  For example, the user ID fields delineate the sets of processes that can send
  signals to each other, as will be explained in the next chapter.
- Process identifiers (process IDs or PIDs) specify the relationship of processes to
  each other. These ID fields are set up when the process enters the state
  "created" in the *fork* system call.
- The process table entry contains an event descriptor when the process is in the
  "sleep" state. This chapter will examine its use in the algorithms for *sleep* and
  wakeup.
- Scheduling parameters allow the kernel to determine the order in which
  processes move to the states "kernel running" and "user running."
- A signal field enumerates the signals sent to a process but not yet handled
  (Section 7.2).
- Various timers give process execution time and kernel resource utilization, used
  for process accounting and for the calculation of process scheduling priority.
  One field is a user-set timer used to send an alarm signal to a process (Section
  8.3).

The *u area* contains the following fields that further characterize the process
states. Previous chapters have described the last seven fields, which are briefly
described again for completeness.

- A pointer to the process table identifies the entry that corresponds to the *u area*.
- The real and effective user IDs determine various privileges allowed the process,
  such as file access rights (see Section 7.6).
- Timer fields record the time the process (and its descendants) spent executing in
  user mode and in kernel mode.
- An array indicates how the process wishes to react to signals.
- The control terminal field identifies the "login terminal" associated with the
  process, if one exists.
- An error field records errors encountered during a system call.
- A return value field contains the result of system calls.
- I/O parameters describe the amount of data to transfer, the address of the
  source (or target) data array in user space, file offsets for I/O, and so on.
- The current directory and current root describe the file system environment of
  the process.
- The user file descriptor table records the files the process has *open*.

- Limit fields restrict the size of a process and the size of a file it can *write*.
- A permission modes field masks mode settings on files the process *creats*.

This section has described the process state transitions on a logical level. Each state has physical characteristics managed by the kernel, particularly the virtual address space of the process. The next section describes a model for memory management; later sections describe the states and state transitions at a physical level, focusing on the states "user running," "kernel running," "preempted," and "sleep (in memory)." The next chapter describes the states "created" and "zombie," and Chapter 8 describes the state "ready to run in memory." Chapter 9 discusses the two "swap" states and demand paging.

6.2 LAYOUT OF SYSTEM MEMORY

Assume that the physical memory of a machine is addressable, starting at byte offset 0 and going up to a byte offset equal to the amount of memory on the machine. As outlined in Chapter 2, a process on the UNIX system consists of three logical sections: text, data, and stack. (*Shared memory*, discussed in Chapter 11, should be considered part of the data section for purposes of this discussion.) The text section contains the set of instructions the machine executes for the process; addresses in the text section include text addresses (for branch instructions or subroutine calls), data addresses (for access to global data variables), or stack addresses (for access to data structures local to a subroutine). If the machine were to treat the generated addresses as address locations in physical memory, it would be impossible for two processes to execute concurrently if their set of generated addresses overlapped. The compiler could generate addresses that did not overlap between programs, but such a procedure is impractical for general-purpose computers because the amount of memory on a machine is finite and the set of all programs that could be compiled is infinite. Even if the compiler used heuristics to try to avoid unnecessary overlap of generated addresses, the implementation would be inflexible and therefore undesirable.

The compiler therefore generates addresses for a *virtual address space* with a given address range, and the machine's memory management unit translates the virtual addresses generated by the compiler into address locations in physical memory. The compiler does not have to know where in memory the kernel will later load the program for execution. In fact, several copies of a program can coexist in memory: All execute using the same virtual addresses but reference different physical addresses. The subsystems of the kernel and the hardware that cooperate to translate virtual to physical addresses comprise the *memory management* subsystem.

6.2.1 Regions

The System V kernel divides the virtual address space of a process into logical *regions*. A region is a contiguous area of the virtual address space of a process that can be treated as a distinct object to be shared or protected. Thus text, data, and stack usually form separate regions of a process. Several processes can share a region. For instance, several processes may execute the same program, and it is natural that they share one copy of the text region. Similarly, several processes may cooperate to share a common shared-memory region.

The kernel contains a region table and allocates an entry from the table for each active region in the system. Section 6.5 will describe the fields of the region table and region operations in greater detail, but for now, assume the region table contains the information to determine where its contents are located in physical memory. Each process contains a private *per process region table*, called a *pregion* for short. Pregion entries may exist in the process table, the *u area*, or in a separately allocated area of memory, dependent on the implementation, but for simplicity, assume that they are part of the process table entry. Each pregion entry points to a region table entry and contains the starting virtual address of the region in the process. Shared regions may have different virtual addresses in each process. The pregion entry also contains a permission field that indicates the type of access allowed the process: read-only, read-write, or read-execute. The pregion and the region structure are analogous to the file table and the inode structure in the file system: Several processes can share parts of their address space via a region, much as they can share access to a file via an inode; each process accesses the region via a private pregion entry, much as it accesses the inode via private entries in its user file descriptor table and the kernel file table.

Figure 6.2 depicts two processes, A and B, showing their regions, pregions, and the virtual addresses where the regions are connected. The processes share text region 'a' at virtual addresses 8K and 4K, respectively. If process A reads memory location 8K and process B reads memory location 4K, they read the identical memory location in region 'a'. The data regions and stack regions of the two processes are private.

The concept of the region is independent of the memory management policies implemented by the operating system. Memory management policy refers to the actions the kernel takes to insure that processes share main memory fairly. For example, the two memory management policies considered in Chapter 9 are process swapping and demand paging. The concept of the region is also independent of the memory management implementation: whether memory is divided into pages or segments, for example. To lay the foundation for the description of demand paging algorithms in Chapter 9, the discussion here assumes a memory architecture based on pages, but it does not assume that the memory management policy is based on demand paging algorithms.

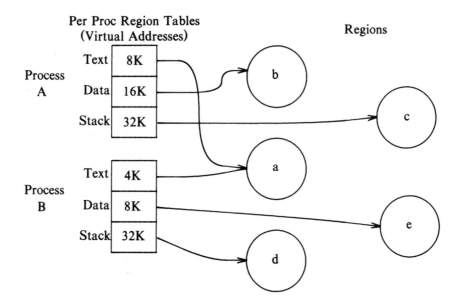

Figure 6.2. Processes and Regions

6.2.2 Pages and Page Tables

This section defines the memory model that will be used throughout this book, but it is not specific to the UNIX system. In a memory management architecture based on *pages*, the memory management hardware divides physical memory into a set of equal-sized blocks called pages. Typical page sizes range from 512 bytes to 4K bytes and are defined by the hardware. Every addressable location in memory is contained in a page and, consequently, every memory location can be addressed by a

(page number, byte offset in page)

pair. For example, if a machine has 2^{32} bytes of physical memory and a page size of 1K bytes, it has 2^{22} pages of physical memory; every 32-bit address can be treated as a pair consisting of a 22-bit page number and a 10-bit offset into the page (Figure 6.3).

When the kernel assigns physical pages of memory to a region, it need not assign the pages contiguously or in a particular order. The purpose of paged memory is to allow greater flexibility in assigning physical memory, analogous to the assignment of disk blocks to files in a file system. Just as the kernel assigns blocks to a file to increase flexibility and to reduce the amount of unused space caused by block fragmentation, so it assigns pages of memory to a region.

Hexadecimal Address	58432	
Binary	0101 1000 0100 0011 0010	
Page Number, Page Offset	01 0110 0001	00 0011 0010
In Hexadecimal	161	32

Figure 6.3. Addressing Physical Memory as Pages

Logical Page Number	Physical Page Number
0	177
1	54
2	209
3	17

Figure 6.4. Mapping of Logical to Physical Page Numbers

The kernel correlates the virtual addresses of a region to their physical machine addresses by mapping the logical page numbers in the region to physical page numbers on the machine, as shown in Figure 6.4. Since a region is a contiguous range of virtual addresses in a program, the logical page number is the index into an array of physical page numbers. The region table entry contains a pointer to a table of physical page numbers called a *page table*. Page table entries may also contain machine-dependent information such as permission bits to allow reading or writing of the page. The kernel stores page tables in memory and accesses them like all other kernel data structures.

Figure 6.5 shows a sample mapping of a process into physical memory. Assume that the size of a page is 1K bytes, and suppose the process wants to access virtual memory address 68,432. The pregion entries show that the virtual address is in the stack region starting at virtual address 64K (65,536 in decimal), assuming the direction of stack growth is towards higher addresses. Subtracting, address 68,432 is at byte offset 2896 in the region. Since each page consists of 1K bytes, the address is contained at byte offset 848 in page 2 (counting from 0) of the region, located at physical address 986K. Section 6.5.5 (loading a region) discusses the meaning of the page table entry marked "empty."

Modern machines use a variety of hardware registers and caches to speed up the address translation procedure just described, because the memory references and address calculations would otherwise be too slow. When resuming the execution of a process, the kernel therefore informs the memory management

Per Proc Region Table

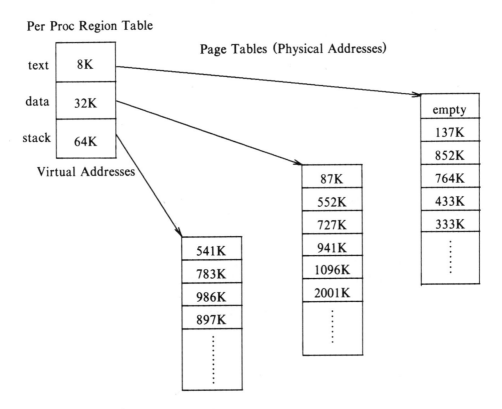

Figure 6.5. Mapping Virtual Addresses to Physical Addresses

hardware where the page tables and physical memory of the process reside by loading the appropriate registers. Since such operations are machine dependent and vary from one implementation to another, this text will not discuss them. The exercises at the end of the chapter cite specific machine architectures.

Let us use the following simple memory model in discussing memory management. Memory is organized in pages of 1K bytes, accessed via page tables as described earlier. The system contains a set of memory management register triples (assume a large supply), such that the first register in the triple contains the address of a page table in physical memory, the second register contains the first virtual address mapped via the triple, and the third register contains control information such as the number of pages in the page table and page access permissions (read-only, read-write). This model corresponds to the region model, just described. When the kernel prepares a process for execution, it loads the set of memory management register triples with the corresponding data stored in the pregion entries.

If a process addresses memory locations outside its virtual address space, the hardware causes an exception condition. For example, if the size of the text region in Figure 6.5 is 16K bytes and a process accesses virtual address 26K, the hardware will cause an exception that the operating system handles. Similarly, if a process tries to access memory without proper permissions, such as writing an address in its write-protected text region, the hardware will cause an exception. In both these examples, the process would normally *exit*; the next chapter provides more detail.

6.2.3 Layout of the Kernel

Although the kernel executes in the context of a process, the virtual memory mapping associated with the kernel is independent of all processes. The code and data for the kernel reside in the system permanently, and all processes share it. When the system is brought into service (booted), it loads the kernel code into memory and sets up the necessary tables and registers to map its virtual addresses into physical memory addresses. The kernel page tables are analogous to the page tables associated with a process, and the mechanisms used to map kernel virtual addresses are similar to those used for user addresses. In many machines, the virtual address space of a process is divided into several classes, including system and user, and each class has its own page tables. When executing in kernel mode, the system permits access to kernel addresses, but it prohibits such access when executing in user mode. Thus, when changing mode from user to kernel as a result of an interrupt or system call, the operating system collaborates with the hardware to permit kernel address references, and when changing mode back to user, the operating system and hardware prohibit such references. Other machines change the virtual address translation by loading special registers when executing in kernel mode.

Figure 6.6 gives an example of the virtual addresses of the kernel and a process, where kernel virtual addresses range from 0 to 4M−1 and user virtual addresses range from 4M up. There are two sets of memory management triples, one for kernel addresses and one for user addresses, and each triple points to a page table that contains the physical page numbers corresponding to the virtual page addresses. The system allows address references via the kernel register triples only when in kernel mode; hence, switching mode between kernel and user requires only that the system permit or deny address references via the kernel register triples.

Some system implementations load the kernel into memory such that most kernel virtual addresses are identical to their physical addresses and the virtual to physical memory map of those addresses is the identity function. However, the treatment of the *u area* requires virtual to physical address mapping in the kernel.

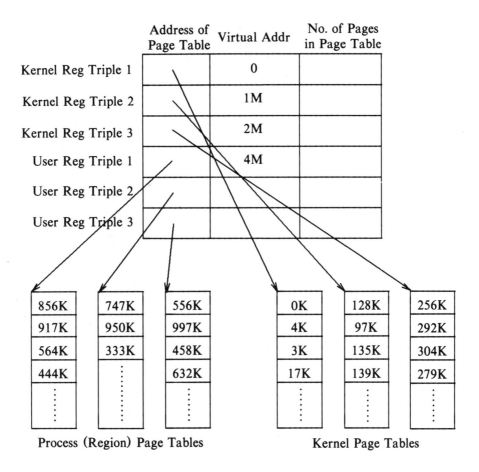

Figure 6.6. Changing Mode from User to Kernel

6.2.4 The U Area

Every process has a private *u area*, yet the kernel accesses it as if there were only one *u area* in the system, that of the running process. The kernel changes its virtual address translation map according to the executing process to access the correct *u area*. When compiling the operating system, the loader assigns the variable *u*, the name of the *u area*, a fixed virtual address. The value of the *u area* virtual address is known to other parts of the kernel, in particular, the module that does the context switch (Section 6.4.3). The kernel knows where in its memory management tables the virtual address translation for the *u area* is done, and it can dynamically change the address mapping of the *u area* to another physical address. The two physical addresses represent the *u area*s of two processes, but the kernel accesses them via the same virtual address.

A process can access its *u area* when it executes in kernel mode but not when it executes in user mode. Because the kernel can access only one *u area* at a time by its virtual address, the *u area* partially defines the context of the process that is running on the system. When the kernel schedules a process for execution, it finds the corresponding *u area* in physical memory and makes it accessible by its virtual address.

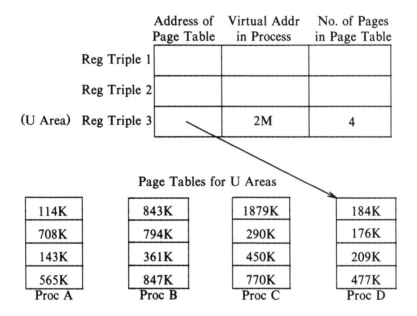

Figure 6.7. Memory Map of U Area in the Kernel

For example, suppose the *u area* is 4K bytes long and resides at kernel virtual address 2M. Figure 6.7 shows a sample memory layout, where the first two register triples refer to kernel text and data (the addresses and pointers are not shown), and the third triple refers to the *u area* for process D. If the kernel wants to access the *u area* of process A, it copies the appropriate page table information for the *u area* into the third register triple. At any instant, the third kernel register triple refers to the *u area* of the currently running process, but the kernel can refer to the *u area* of another process by overwriting the entries for the *u area* page table address with a new address. The entries for register triples 1 and 2 do not change for the kernel, because all processes share kernel text and data.

6.3 THE CONTEXT OF A PROCESS

The context of a process consists of the contents of its (user) address space and the contents of hardware registers and kernel data structures that relate to the process. Formally, the context of a process is the union of its *user-level context*, *register context*, and *system-level context*.[1] The user-level context consists of the process text, data, user stack, and shared memory that occupy the virtual address space of the process. Parts of the virtual address space of a process that periodically do not reside in main memory because of swapping or paging still constitute a part of the user-level context.

The register context consists of the following components.

- The program counter specifies the address of the next instruction the CPU will execute; the address is a virtual address in kernel or in user memory space.
- The processor status register (PS) specifies the hardware status of the machine as it relates to the process. For example, the PS usually contains subfields to indicate that the result of a recent computation resulted in a zero, positive or negative result, or that a register overflowed and a carry bit is set, and so on. The operations that caused the PS to be set were done for a particular process, hence the PS contains the hardware status of the machine as it relates to the process. Other important subfields typically found in the PS are those that indicate the current processor execution level (for interrupts) and the current and most recent modes of execution (such as kernel, user). The subfield that shows the current execution mode determines whether a process can execute privileged instructions and whether it can access kernel address space.
- The stack pointer contains the current address of the next entry in the kernel or user stack, determined by the mode of execution. Machine architectures dictate whether the stack pointer points to the next free entry on the stack or to the last used entry. Similarly, the machine dictates the direction of stack growth toward numerically higher or lower addresses, but such issues are immaterial for purposes of this discussion.
- The general-purpose registers contain data generated by the process during its execution. To simplify the following discussion, let us distinguish two general purpose registers, register 0 and register 1, for additional use in transmitting information between processes and the kernel.

The system-level context of a process has a "static part" (first three items of the following list) and a "dynamic part" (last two items). A process has one static part of the system-level context throughout its lifetime, but it can have a variable number of dynamic parts. The dynamic part of the system-level context should be

---

1. The terms *user-level context*, *register context*, *system-level context*, and *context layers* used in this section are the author's terminology.

viewed as a stack of *context layers* that the kernel pushes and pops on occurrence of various events. The system-level context consists of the following components.

- The process table entry of a process defines the state of a process, as described in Section 6.1, and contains control information that is always accessible to the kernel.
- The *u area* of a process contains process control information that need be accessed only in the context of the process. General control parameters such as the process priority are stored in the process table because they must be accessed outside the process context.
- Pregion entries, region tables and page tables, define the mapping from virtual to physical addresses and therefore define the text, data, stack, and other regions of a process. If several processes share common regions, the regions are considered part of the context of each process, because each process manipulates the regions independently. Part of the memory management task is to indicate which parts of the virtual address space of a process are not memory resident.
- The kernel stack contains the stack frames of kernel procedures as a process executes in kernel mode. Although all processes execute the identical kernel code, they have a private copy of the kernel stack that specifies their particular invocation of the kernel functions. For instance, one process may invoke the *creat* system call and go to sleep waiting for the kernel to assign a new inode, and another process may invoke the *read* system call and go to sleep awaiting the transfer of data from disk to memory. Both processes execute kernel functions, but they have separate stacks that contain their private function call sequence. The kernel must be able to recover the contents of the kernel stack and the position of the stack pointer to resume execution of a process in kernel mode. System implementations frequently place the kernel stack in the process *u area*, but it is logically independent and can exist in an independently allocated area of memory. The kernel stack is empty when the process executes in user mode.
- The dynamic part of the system-level context of a process consists of a set of layers, visualized as a last-in-first-out stack. Each *system-level context layer* contains the necessary information to recover the previous layer, including the register context of the previous level.

The kernel pushes a context layer when an interrupt occurs, when a process makes a system call, or when a process does a context switch. It pops a context layer when the kernel returns from handling an interrupt, when a process returns to user mode after the kernel completes execution of a system call, or when a process does a context switch. The context switch thus entails a push and a pop of a system-level context layer: The kernel pushes the context layer of the old process and pops the context layer of the new process. The process table entry stores the necessary information to recover the current context layer.

Figure 6.8 depicts the components that form the context of a process. The left side of the figure shows the static portion of the context. It consists of the user-

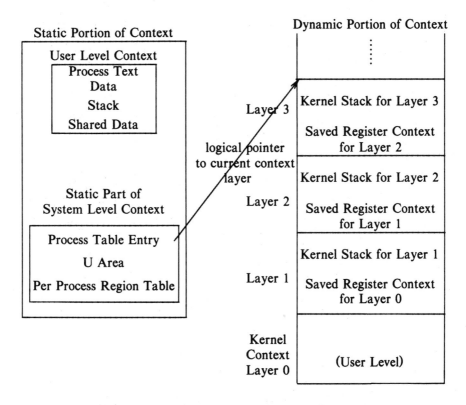

Figure 6.8. Components of the Context of a Process

level context, containing the process text (instructions), data, stack, and shared memory (if the process has any), and the static part of the system-level context, containing the process table entry, the *u area*, and the pregion entries (the virtual address mapping information for the user-level context). The right side of the figure shows the dynamic portion of the context. It consists of several stack frames, where each frame contains the saved register context of the previous layer, and the kernel stack as the kernel executes in that layer. System context layer 0 is a dummy layer that represents the user-level context; growth of the stack here is in the user address space, and the kernel stack is null. The arrow pointing from the static part of the system-level context to the top layer of the dynamic portion of the context represents the logical information stored in the process table entry to enable the kernel to recover the current context layer of the process.

    A process runs within its context or, more precisely, within its current context layer. The number of context layers is bounded by the number of interrupt levels the machine supports. For instance, if a machine supports different interrupt levels for software interrupts, terminals, disks, all other peripherals, and the clock, it supports 5 interrupt levels, and hence, a process can contain at most 7 context layers: 1 for each interrupt level, 1 for system calls, and 1 for user-level. The 7 layers are sufficient to hold all context layers even if interrupts occur in the "worst" possible sequence, because an interrupt of a given level is blocked (that is, the CPU defers it) while the kernel handles interrupts of that level or higher.

Although the kernel always executes in the context of some process, the logical function that it executes does not necessarily pertain to that process. For instance, if a disk drive interrupts the machine because it has returned data, it interrupts the running process and the kernel executes the interrupt handler in a new system-level context layer of the executing process, even though the data belongs to another process. Interrupt handlers do not generally access or modify the static parts of the process context, since those parts have nothing to do with the interrupt.

6.4 SAVING THE CONTEXT OF A PROCESS

As observed in previous sections, the kernel saves the context of a process whenever it pushes a new system context layer. In particular, this happens when the system receives an interrupt, when a process executes a system call, or when the kernel does a context switch. This section considers each case in detail.

6.4.1 Interrupts and Exceptions

The system is responsible for handling interrupts, whether they result from hardware (such as from the clock or from peripheral devices), from a programmed interrupt (execution of instructions designed to cause "software interrupts"), or from exceptions (such as page faults). If the CPU is executing at a lower processor execution level than the level of the interrupt, it accepts the interrupt before decoding the next instruction and raises the processor execution level, so that no other interrupts of that level (or lower) can happen while it handles the current interrupt, preserving the integrity of kernel data structures (see Section 2.2.2). The kernel handles the interrupt with the following sequence of operations:

1. It saves the current register context of the executing process and creates (pushes) a new context layer.
2. It determines the "source" or cause of the interrupt, identifying the type of interrupt (such as clock or disk) and the unit number of the interrupt, if applicable (such as which disk drive caused the interrupt). When the system receives an interrupt, it gets a number from the machine that it uses as an offset into a table, commonly called an *interrupt vector*. The contents of interrupt vectors vary from machine to machine, but they usually contain the address of the interrupt handler for the corresponding interrupt source and a way of finding a parameter for the interrupt handler. For example, consider the table of interrupt handlers in Figure 6.9. If a terminal interrupts the system, the kernel gets interrupt number 2 from the hardware and invokes the

Interrupt Number	Interrupt Handler
0	clockintr
1	diskintr
2	ttyintr
3	devintr
4	softintr
5	otherintr

Figure 6.9. Sample Interrupt Vector

terminal interrupt handler *ttyintr*.

3. The kernel invokes the interrupt handler. The kernel stack for the new context layer is logically distinct from the kernel stack of the previous context layer. Some implementations use the kernel stack of the executing process to store the interrupt handler stack frames, and other implementations use a global interrupt stack to store the frames for interrupt handlers that are guaranteed to return without switching context.

4. The interrupt handler completes it work and returns. The kernel executes a machine-specific sequence of instructions that restores the register context and kernel stack of the previous context layer as they existed at the time of the interrupt and then resumes execution of the restored context layer. The behavior of the process may be affected by the interrupt handler, since the interrupt handler may have altered global kernel data structures and awakened sleeping processes. Usually, however, the process continues execution as if the interrupt had never happened.

```
algorithm inthand          /* handle interrupts */
input:  none
output: none
{
        save (push) current context layer;
        determine interrupt source;
        find interrupt vector;
        call interrupt handler;
        restore (pop) previous context layer;
}
```

Figure 6.10. Algorithm for Handling Interrupts

Figure 6.10 summarizes how the kernel handles interrupts. Some machines do part of the sequence of operations in hardware or microcode to get better performance than if all operations were done by software, but there are tradeoffs, based on how much of the context layer must be saved and the speed of the hardware instructions doing the save. The specific operations required in a UNIX system implementation are therefore machine dependent.

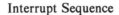

Interrupt Sequence

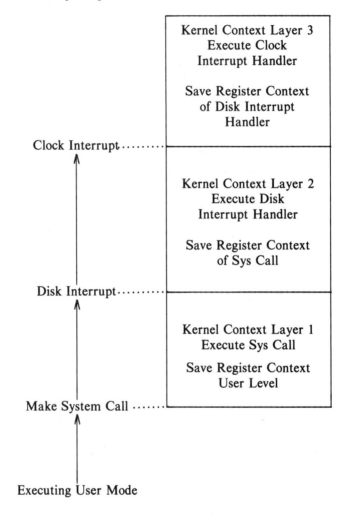

Figure 6.11. Example of Interrupts

Figure 6.11 shows an example where a process issues a system call (see the next section) and receives a disk interrupt while executing the system call. While executing the disk interrupt handler, the system receives a clock interrupt and executes the clock interrupt handler. Every time the system receives an interrupt (or makes a system call), it creates a new context layer and saves the register context of the previous layer.

6.4.2 System Call Interface

The system call interface to the kernel has been described in previous chapters as though it were a normal function call. Obviously, the usual calling sequence cannot change the mode of a process from user to kernel. The C compiler uses a predefined library of functions (the C library) that have the names of the system calls, thus resolving the system call references in the user program to what would otherwise be undefined names. The library functions typically invoke an instruction that changes the process execution mode to kernel mode and causes the kernel to start executing code for system calls. The ensuing discussion refers to the instruction as an *operating system trap*. The library routines execute in user mode, but the system call interface is, in short, a special case of an interrupt handler. The library functions pass the kernel a unique number per system call in a machine-dependent way — either as a parameter to the operating system trap, in a particular register, or on the stack — and the kernel thus determines the specific system call the user is invoking.

```
algorithm syscall              /* algorithm for invocation of system call */
input:   system call number
output: result of system call
{
        find entry in system call table corresponding to system call number;
        determine number of parameters to system call;
        copy parameters from user address space to u area;
        save current context for abortive return (described in section 6.4.4);
        invoke system call code in kernel;
        if (error during execution of system call)
        {
                set register 0 in user saved register context to error number;
                turn on carry bit in PS register in user saved register context;
        }
        else
                set registers 0, 1 in user saved register context
                                to return values from system call;
}
```

Figure 6.12. Algorithm for System Calls

In handling the operating system trap, the kernel looks up the system call number in a table to find the address of the appropriate kernel routine that is the entry point for the system call and to find the number of parameters the system call expects (Figure 6.12). The kernel calculates the (user) address of the first parameter to the system call by adding (or subtracting, depending on the direction of stack growth) an offset to the user stack pointer, corresponding to the number of parameters to the system call. Finally, it copies the user parameters to the *u area* and calls the appropriate system call routine. After executing the code for the system call, the kernel determines whether there was error. If so, it adjusts register locations in the saved user register context, typically setting the "carry" bit for the PS register and copying the error number into the register 0 location. If there were no errors in the execution of the system call, the kernel clears the "carry" bit in the PS register and copies the appropriate return values from the system call into the locations for registers 0 and 1 in the saved user register context. When the kernel returns from the operating system trap to user mode, it returns to the library instruction after the trap. The library interprets the return values from the kernel and returns a value to the user program.

For example, consider the program that creates a file with read and write permission for all users (mode 0666) in the first part of Figure 6.13. The second part of the figure shows an edited portion of the generated output for the program, as compiled and disassembled on a Motorola 68000 system. Figure 6.14 depicts the stack configurations during the system call. The compiler generates code to push the two parameters onto the user stack, where the first parameter pushed is the permission mode setting, 0666, and the second parameter pushed is the variable *name*.[2] The process then calls the library function for the *creat* system call (address 7a) from address 64. The return address from the function call is 6a, and the process pushes this number onto the stack. The library function for *creat* moves the constant 8 into register 0 and executes a *trap* instruction that causes the process to change from user mode to kernel mode and handle the system call. The kernel recognizes that the user is making a system call and recovers the number 8 from register 0 to determine that the system call is *creat*. Looking up an internal table, the kernel finds that the *creat* system call takes two parameters; recovering the stack register of the previous context layer, it copies the parameters from user space into the *u area*. Kernel routines that need the parameters can find them in predictable locations in the *u area*. When the kernel completes executing the code for *creat*, it returns to the system call handler, which checks if the *u area* error field is set (meaning there was some error in the system call); if so, the handler sets the carry bit in the PS register, places the error code into register 0, and returns. If there is no error, the kernel places the system return code into registers 0 and 1.

---

2. The order that the compiler evaluates and pushes function parameters is implementation dependent.

```
char name[] = "file";
main()
{
    int fd;
    fd = creat(name, 0666);
}
```

```
              Portions of Generated Motorola 68000 Assembler Code

  Addr    Instruction
                    .
                    .
                    .
  # code for main
                    .
  58:     mov     &0x1b6,(%sp)       # move 0666 onto stack
  5e:     mov     &0x204,-(%sp)      # move stack ptr
                                     # and move variable "name" onto stack
  64:     jsr     0x7a               # call C library for creat
                    .
                    .
  # library code for creat
  7a:     movq    &0x8,%d0           # move data value 8 into data register 0
  7c:     trap    &0x0               # operating system trap
  7e:     bcc     &0x6 <86>          # branch to addr 86 if carry bit clear
  80:     jmp     0x13c              # jump to addr 13c
  86:     rts                        # return from subroutine
                    .
                    .
  # library code for errors in system call
  13c:    mov     %d0,&0x20e         # move data reg 0 to location 20e (errno)
  142:    movq    &-0x1,%d0          # move constant -1 into data register 0
  144:    mova    %d0,%a0
  146:    rts                        # return from subroutine
```

Figure 6.13. Creat System Call and Generated Code for Motorola 68000

When returning from the system call handler to user mode, the C library checks
the carry bit in the PS register at address 7e: If it is set, the process jumps to
address 13c, takes the error code from register 0 and places it into the global
variable *errno* at address 20e, places a −1 in register 0, and returns to the next
instruction after the call at address 64. The return code for the function is −1,
signifying an error in the system call. If, when returning from kernel mode to user
mode, the carry bit in the PS register is clear, the process jumps from address 7e to
address 86 and returns to the caller (address 64): Register 0 contains the return
value from the system call.

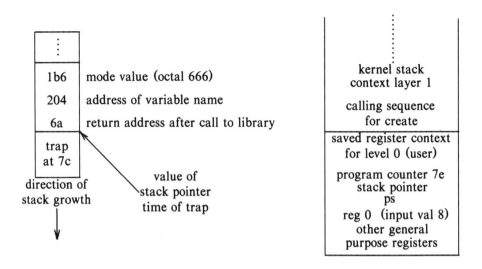

Figure 6.14. Stack Configuration for Creat System Call

Several library functions can map into one system call entry point. The system call entry point defines the true syntax and semantics for every system call, but the libraries frequently provide a more convenient interface. For example, there are several flavors of the *exec* system call, such as *execl* and *execle*, which provide slightly different interfaces for one system call. The libraries for these calls manipulate their parameters to implement the advertised features, but eventually, map into one kernel entry point.

6.4.3 Context Switch

Referring to the process state diagram in Figure 6.1, we see that the kernel permits a context switch under four circumstances: when a process puts itself to sleep, when it *exits*, when it returns from a system call to user mode but is not the most eligible process to run, or when it returns to user mode after the kernel completes handling an interrupt but is not the most eligible process to run. The kernel ensures integrity and consistency of internal data structures by prohibiting arbitrary context switches, as explained in Chapter 2. It makes sure that the state of its data structures is consistent before it does a context switch: that is, that all appropriate updates are done, that queues are properly linked, that appropriate locks are set to prevent intrusion by other processes, that no data structures are left unnecessarily locked, and so on. For example, if the kernel allocates a buffer, *read*s a block in a file, and goes to sleep waiting for I/O transmission from the disk to complete, it keeps the buffer locked so that no other process can tamper with the buffer. But if a process executes the *link* system call, the kernel releases the lock of the first inode before locking the second inode to avoid deadlocks.

The kernel must do a context switch at the conclusion of the *exit* system call, because there is nothing else for it to do. Similarly, the kernel allows a context switch when a process enters the sleep state, since a considerable amount of time may elapse until the process wakes up, and other processes can meanwhile execute. The kernel allows a context switch when a process is not the most eligible to run to permit fairer process scheduling: If a process completes a system call or returns from an interrupt and there is another process with higher priority waiting to run, it would be unfair to keep the high-priority process waiting.

The procedure for a context switch is similar to the procedures for handling interrupts and system calls, except that the kernel restores the context layer of a different process instead of the previous context layer of the same process. The reasons for the context switch are irrelevant. Similarly, the choice of which process to schedule next is a policy decision that does not affect the mechanics of the context switch.

1.	Decide whether to do a context switch, and whether a context switch is permissible now.
2.	Save the context of the "old" process.
3.	Find the "best" process to schedule for execution, using the process scheduling algorithm in Chapter 8.
4.	Restore its context.

Figure 6.15. Steps for a Context Switch

The code that implements the context switch on UNIX systems is usually the most difficult to understand in the operating system, because function calls give the appearance of not returning on some occasions and materializing from nowhere on others. This is because the kernel, in many implementations, saves the process context at one point in the code but proceeds to execute the context switch and scheduling algorithms in the context of the "old" process. When it later restores the context of the process, it resumes execution according to the previously saved context. To differentiate between the case where the kernel resumes the context of a new process and the case where it continues to execute in the old context after having saved it, the return values of critical functions may vary, or the program counter where the kernel executes may be set artificially.

Figure 6.16 shows a scenario for doing a context switch. The function *save_context* saves information about the context of the running process and returns the value 1. Among other pieces of information, the kernel saves the value of the current program counter (in the function *save_context*) and the value 0, to be used later as the return value in register 0 from *save_context*. The kernel continues to execute in the context of the old process (A), picking another process (B) to run

```
if (save_context())        /* save context of executing process */
{
        /* pick another process to run */
        .
        .
        .
        resume_context(new_process);
        /* never gets here ! */
}
/* resuming process executes from here */
```

Figure 6.16. Pseudo-Code for Context Switch

and calling *resume_context* to restore the new context (of B). After the new context is restored, the system is executing process B; the old process (A) is no longer executing but leaves its saved context behind (hence, the comment in the figure "never gets here"). Later, the kernel will again pick process A to run (except for the *exit* case, of course) when another process does a context switch, as just described. When process A's context is restored, the kernel will set the program counter to the value process A had previously saved in the function *save_context*, and it will also place the value 0, saved for the return value, into register 0. The kernel resumes execution of process A inside *save_context* even though it had executed the code up to the call to *resume_context* before the context switch. Finally, process A returns from the function *save_context* with the value 0 (in register 0) and resumes execution after the comment line "resuming process executes from here."

6.4.4 Saving Context for Abortive Returns

Situations arise when the kernel must abort its current execution sequence and immediately execute out of a previously saved context. Later sections dealing with *sleep* and *signals* describe the circumstances when a process must suddenly change its context; this section explains the mechanisms for executing a previous context. The algorithm to save a context is *setjmp* and the algorithm to restore the context is *longjmp*.[3] The method is identical to that described for the function *save_context* in the previous section, except that *save_context* pushes a new context layer, whereas *setjmp* stores the saved context in the *u area* and continues to execute in

---

3. These algorithms should not be confused with the library functions of the same name that users can call directly from their programs (see [SVID 85]). However, their functions are similar.

the old context layer. When the kernel wishes to resume the context it had saved in *setjmp*, it does a *longjmp*, restoring its context from the *u area* and returning a 1 from *setjmp*.

6.4.5 Copying Data between System and User Address Space

As presented so far, a process executes in kernel mode or in user mode with no overlap of modes. However, many system calls examined in the last chapter move data between kernel and user space, such as when copying system call parameters from user to kernel space or when copying data from I/O buffers in the *read* system call . Many machines allow the kernel to reference addresses in user space directly. The kernel must ascertain that the address being read or written is accessible as if it had been executing in user mode; otherwise, it could override the ordinary protection mechanisms and inadvertently read or write addresses outside the user address space (possibly kernel data structures). Therefore, copying data between kernel space and user space is an expensive proposition, requiring more than one instruction.

```
fubyte:                                # move byte from user space
          prober    $3,$1,*4(ap)       # byte accessible?
          beql      eret               # no
          movzbl    *4(ap),r0
          ret
eret:
          mnegl     $1,r0              # error return (−1)
          ret
```

Figure 6.17. Moving Data from User to System Space on a VAX

Figure 6.17 shows sample VAX code for moving one character from user address space to kernel address space. The *prober* instruction checks if one byte at address *argument pointer register+4* (*4(ap)) could be read in user mode (mode 3) and, if not, the kernel branches to address *eret*, stores −1 in register 0, and returns; the character move failed. Otherwise, the kernel moves one byte from the given user address to register 0 and returns that value to the caller. The procedure is expensive, requiring five instructions (with the function call to *fubyte*) to move 1 character.

6.5 MANIPULATION OF THE PROCESS ADDRESS SPACE

So far, this chapter has described how the kernel switches context between processes and how it pushes and pops context layers, viewing the user-level context as a static object that does not change during restoration of the process context.

However, various system calls manipulate the virtual address space of a process, as will be seen in the next chapter, doing so according to well defined operations on regions. This section describes the region data structure and the operations on regions; the next chapter deals with the system calls that use the region operations.

The region table entry contains the information necessary to describe a region. In particular, it contains the following entries:

- A pointer to the inode of the file whose contents were originally loaded into the region
- The region type (text, shared memory, private data or stack)
- The size of the region
- The location of the region in physical memory
- The status of a region, which may be a combination of
  - locked
  - in demand
  - in the process of being loaded into memory
  - valid, loaded into memory
- The reference count, giving the number of processes that reference the region.

The operations that manipulate regions are to lock a region, unlock a region, allocate a region, attach a region to the memory space of a process, change the size of a region, load a region from a file into the memory space of a process, free a region, detach a region from the memory space of a process, and duplicate the contents of a region. For example, the *exec* system call, which overlays the user address space with the contents of an executable file, detaches old regions, frees them if they were not shared, allocates new regions, attaches them, and loads them with the contents of the file. The remainder of this section describes the region operations in detail, assuming the memory management model described earlier (page tables and hardware register triples) and the existence of algorithms for allocation of page tables and pages of physical memory (Chapter 9).

6.5.1 Locking and Unlocking a Region

The kernel has operations to lock and unlock a region, independent of the operations to allocate and free a region, just as the file system has lock-unlock and allocate-release operations for inodes (algorithms *iget* and *iput*). Thus the kernel can lock and allocate a region and later unlock it without having to free the region. Similarly, if it wants to manipulate an allocated region, it can lock the region to prevent access by other processes and later unlock it.

6.5.2 Allocating a Region

The kernel allocates a new region (algorithm *allocreg*, Figure 6.18) during *fork*, *exec*, and *shmget* (shared memory) system calls. The kernel contains a region table whose entries appear either on a free linked list or on an active linked list. When it allocates a region table entry, the kernel removes the first available entry from the free list, places it on the active list, locks the region, and marks its type (shared or private). With few exceptions, every process is associated with an executable file as a result of a prior *exec* call, and *allocreg* sets the inode field in the region table entry to point to the inode of the executable file. The inode identifies the region to the kernel so that other processes can share the region if desired. The kernel increments the inode reference count to prevent other processes from removing its contents when *unlink*ing it, as will be explained in Section 7.5. *Allocreg* returns a locked, allocated region.

```
algorithm allocreg          /* allocate a region data structure */
input:   (1) inode pointer
         (2) region type
output: locked region
{
        remove region from linked list of free regions;
        assign region type;
        assign region inode pointer;
        if (inode pointer not null)
             increment inode reference count;
        place region on linked list of active regions;
        return(locked region);
}
```

Figure 6.18. Algorithm for Allocating a Region

6.5.3 Attaching a Region to a Process

The kernel attaches a region during the *fork*, *exec*, and *shmat* system calls to connect it to the address space of a process (algorithm *attachreg*, Figure 6.19). The region may be a newly allocated region or an existing region that the process will share with other processes. The kernel allocates a free pregion entry, sets its type field to text, data, shared memory, or stack, and records the virtual address where the region will exist in the process address space. The process must not exceed the system-imposed limit for the highest virtual address, and the virtual addresses of the new region must not overlap the addresses of existing regions. For example, if the system restricts the highest virtual address of a process to 8 megabytes, it would be illegal to attach a 1 megabyte-size region to virtual address 7.5M. If it is legal to attach the region, the kernel increments the size field in the process table entry according to the region size, and increments the region reference count.

```
algorithm attachreg          /* attach a region to a process */
input:   (1) pointer to (locked) region being attached
         (2) process to which region is being attached
         (3) virtual address in process where region will be attached
         (4) region type
output: per process region table entry
{
         allocate per process region table entry for process;
         initialize per process region table entry:
                 set pointer to region being attached;
                 set type field;
                 set virtual address field;
         check legality of virtual address, region size;
         increment region reference count;
         increment process size according to attached region;
         initialize new hardware register triple for process;
         return(per process region table entry);
}
```

Figure 6.19. Algorithm for Attachreg

Attachreg then initializes a new set of memory management register triples for the process: If the region is not already attached to another process, the kernel allocates page tables for it in a subsequent call to *growreg* (next section); otherwise, it uses the existing page tables. Finally, *attachreg* returns a pointer to the pregion entry for the newly attached region. For example, suppose the kernel wants to attach an existing (shared) text region of size 7K bytes to virtual address 0 of a process (Figure 6.20): it allocates a new memory management register triple and initializes the triple with the address of the region page table, the process virtual address (0), and the size of the page table (9 entries).

6.5.4 Changing the Size of a Region

A process may expand or contract its virtual address space with the *sbrk* system call. Similarly, the stack of a process automatically expands (that is, the process does not make an explicit system call) according to the depth of nested procedure calls. Internally, the kernel invokes the algorithm *growreg* to change the size of a region (Figure 6.21). When a region expands, the kernel makes sure that the virtual addresses of the expanded region do not overlap those of another region and that the growth of the region does not cause the process size to become greater than the maximum allowed virtual memory space. The kernel never invokes *growreg* to increase the size of a shared region that is already attached to several processes; therefore, it does not have to worry about increasing the size of a region

Per Process Region Table

	Page Table Addr	Proc Virt Addr	Size and Protect
Entry for Text		0	9

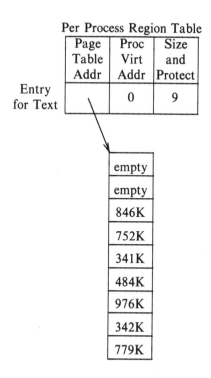

empty
empty
846K
752K
341K
484K
976K
342K
779K

Figure 6.20. Example of Attaching to an Existing Text Region

for one process and causing another process to grow beyond the system limit for process size. The two cases where the kernel uses *growreg* on an existing region are *sbrk* on the data region of a process and automatic growth of the user stack. Both regions are private. Text regions and shared memory regions cannot grow after they are initialized. These cases will become clear in the next chapter.

The kernel now allocates page tables (or extends existing page tables) to accommodate the larger region and allocates physical memory on systems that do not support demand paging. When allocating physical memory, it makes sure such memory is available before invoking *growreg*; if the memory is unavailable, it resorts to other measures to increase the region size, as will be covered in Chapter 9. If the process contracts the region, the kernel simply releases memory assigned to the region. In both cases, it adjusts the process size and region size and reinitializes the pregion entry and memory management register triples to conform to the new mapping.

For example, suppose the stack region of a process starts at virtual address 128K and currently contains 6K bytes, and the kernel wants to extend the size of the region by 1K bytes (1 page). If the process size is acceptable and virtual

```
algorithm growreg        /* change the size of a region */
input:   (1) pointer to per process region table entry
         (2) change in size of region (may be positive or negative)
output: none
{
    if (region size increasing)
    {
        check legality of new region size;
        allocate auxiliary tables (page tables);
        if (not system supporting demand paging)
        {
            allocate physical memory;
            initialize auxiliary tables, as necessary;
        }
    }
    else       /* region size decreasing */
    {
        free physical memory, as appropriate;
        free auxiliary tables, as appropriate;
    }

    do (other) initialization of auxiliary tables, as necessary;
    set size field in process table;
}
```

Figure 6.21. Algorithm Growreg for Changing the Size of a Region

addresses 134K to 135K − 1 do not belong to another region attached to the process, the kernel extends the size of the region. It extends the page table, allocates a page of memory, and initializes the new page table entry. Figure 6.22 illustrates this case.

6.5.5 Loading a Region

In a system that supports demand paging, the kernel can "map" a file into the process address space during the *exec* system call, arranging to read individual physical pages later on demand, as will be explained in Chapter 9. If the kernel does not support demand paging, it must copy the executable file into memory, loading the process regions at virtual addresses specified in the executable file. It may attach a region at a different virtual address from where it loads the contents of the file, creating a gap in the page table (recall Figure 6.20). For example, this feature is used to cause memory faults when user programs access address 0 illegally. Programs with pointer variables sometimes use them erroneously without checking that their value is 0 and, hence, that they are illegal for use as a pointer

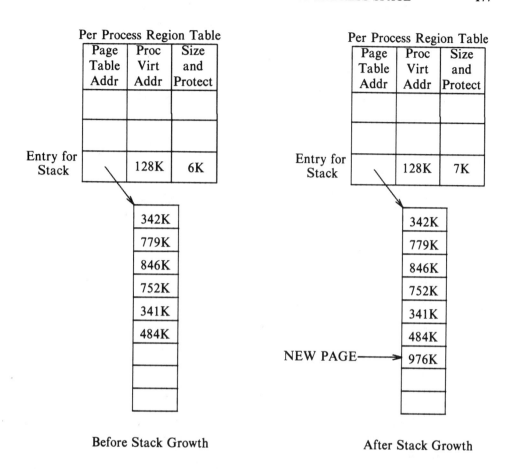

Figure 6.22. Growing the Stack Region by 1K Bytes

reference. By protecting the page containing address 0 appropriately, processes that errantly access address 0 incur a fault and abort, allowing programmers to discover such bugs more quickly.

To load a file into a region, *loadreg* (Figure 6.23) accounts for the gap between the virtual address where the region is attached to the process and the starting virtual address of the region data and expands the region according to the amount of memory the region requires. Then it places the region in the state "being loaded into memory" and reads the region data into memory from the file, using an internal variation of the *read* system call algorithm.

If the kernel is loading a text region that can be shared by several processes, it is possible that another process could find the region and attempt to use it before its contents were fully loaded, because the first process could sleep while reading the

```
algorithm loadreg        /* load a portion of a file into a region */
input:   (1) pointer to per process region table entry
         (2) virtual address to load region
         (3) inode pointer of file for loading region
         (4) byte offset in file for start of region
         (5) byte count for amount of data to load
output: none
{
        increase region size according to eventual size of region
                (algorithm growreg);
        mark region state: being loaded into memory;
        unlock region;
        set up u area parameters for reading file:
                target virtual address where data is read to,
                start offset value for reading file,
                count of bytes to read from file;
        read file into region (internal variant of read algorithm);
        lock region;
        mark region state: completely loaded into memory;
        awaken all processes waiting for region to be loaded;
}
```

Figure 6.23. Algorithm for Loadreg

file. The details of how this could happen and why locks cannot be used are left for the discussion of *exec* in the next chapter and in Chapter 9. To avoid a problem, the kernel checks a region state flag to see if the region is completely loaded and, if the region is not loaded, the process sleeps. At the end of *loadreg*, the kernel awakens processes that were waiting for the region to be loaded and changes the region state to valid and in memory.

For example, suppose the kernel wants to load text of size 7K into a region that is attached at virtual address 0 of a process but wants to leave a gap of 1K bytes at the beginning of the region (Figure 6.24). By this time, the kernel will have allocated a region table entry and will have attached the region at address 0 using algorithms *allocreg* and *attachreg*. Now it invokes *loadreg*, which invokes *growreg* twice — first, to account for the 1K byte gap at the beginning of the region, and second, to allocate storage for the contents of the region — and *growreg* allocates a page table for the region. The kernel then sets up fields in the *u area* to read the file: It reads 7K bytes from a specified byte offset in the file (supplied as a parameter by the kernel) into virtual address 1K of the process.

Per Process Region Table

Page Table Addr	Proc Virt Addr	Size and Protect
Text —		0

(a) Original Region Entry

Per Process Region Table

Page Table Addr	Proc Virt Addr	Size and Protect
	0	1

empty

(b) After First Growreg
Page Table with One Entry
for Gap

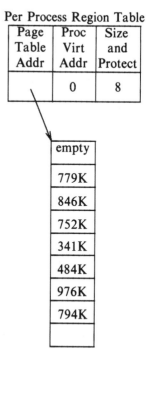

Per Process Region Table

Page Table Addr	Proc Virt Addr	Size and Protect
	0	8

empty
779K
846K
752K
341K
484K
976K
794K

(c) After 2nd Growreg

Figure 6.24. Loading a Text Region

6.5.6 Freeing a Region

When a region is no longer attached to any processes, the kernel can free the region and return it to the list of free regions (Figure 6.25). If the region is associated with an inode, the kernel releases the inode using algorithm *iput*, corresponding to the increment of the inode reference count in *allocreg*. The kernel releases physical resources associated with the region, such as page tables and memory pages. For example, suppose the kernel wants to free the stack region in Figure 6.22. Assuming the region reference count is 0, it releases the 7 pages of physical memory and the page table.

```
algorithm freereg        /* free an allocated region */
input:   pointer to a (locked) region
output: none
{
        if (region reference count non zero)
        {
                /* some process still using region */
                release region lock;
                if (region has an associated inode)
                        release inode lock;
                return;
        }
        if (region has associated inode)
                release inode (algorithm iput);
        free physical memory still associated with region;
        free auxiliary tables associated with region;
        clear region fields;
        place region on region free list;
        unlock region;
}
```

Figure 6.25. Algorithm for Freeing a Region

```
algorithm detachreg        /* detach a region from a process */
input:   pointer to per process region table entry
output: none
{
        get auxiliary memory management tables for process,
                    release as appropriate;
        decrement process size;
        decrement region reference count;
        if (region reference count is 0 and region not sticky bit)
                free region (algorithm freereg);
        else        /* either reference count non-0 or region sticky bit on */
        {
                free inode lock, if applicable (inode associated with region);
                free region lock;
        }
}
```

Figure 6.26. Algorithm Detachreg

6.5.7 Detaching a Region from a Process

The kernel detaches regions in the *exec*, *exit*, and *shmdt* (detach shared memory) system calls. It updates the pregion entry and severs the connection to physical memory by invalidating the associated memory management register triple (algorithm *detachreg*, Figure 6.26). The address translation mechanisms thus invalidated apply specifically to the *process*, not to the region (as in algorithm *freereg*). The kernel decrements the region reference count and the size field in the process table entry according to the size of the region. If the region reference count drops to 0 and if there is no reason to leave the region intact (the region is not a shared memory region or a text region with the *sticky bit* on, as will be described in Section 7.5), the kernel frees the region using algorithm *freereg*. Otherwise, it releases the region and inode locks, which had been locked to prevent race conditions as will be described in Section 7.5 but leaves the region and its resources allocated.

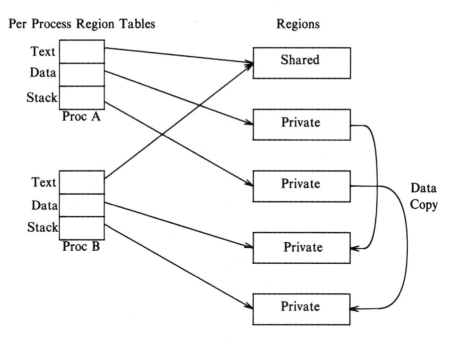

Figure 6.27. Duplicating a Region

```
algorithm dupreg          /* duplicate an existing region */
input:   pointer to region table entry
output: pointer to a region that looks identical to input region
{
        if (region type shared)
                /* caller will increment region reference count
                 * with subsequent attachreg call
                 */
                return(input region pointer);
        allocate new region (algorithm allocreg);
        set up auxiliary memory management structures, as currently
                exists in input region;
        allocate physical memory for region contents;
        "copy" region contents from input region to newly allocated
                region;
        return(pointer to allocated region);
}
```

Figure 6.28. Algorithm for Dupreg

6.5.8 Duplicating a Region

The *fork* system call requires that the kernel duplicate the regions of a process. If a region is shared (shared text or shared memory), however, the kernel need not physically copy the region; instead, it increments the region reference count, allowing the parent and child processes to share the region. If the region is not shared and the kernel must physically copy the region, it allocates a new region table entry, page table, and physical memory for the region. In Figure 6.27 for example, process A *fork*ed process B and duplicated its regions. The text region of process A is shared, so process B can share it with process A. But the data and stack regions of process A are private, so process B duplicates them by copying their contents to newly allocated regions. Even for private regions, a physical copy of the region is not always necessary, as will be seen (Chapter 9). Figure 6.28 shows the algorithm for *dupreg*.

6.6 SLEEP

So far, this chapter has covered all the low-level functions that are executed for the transitions to and from the state "kernel running" except for the functions that move a process into the sleep state. It will conclude with a presentation of the algorithms for *sleep*, which changes the process state from "kernel running" to "asleep in memory," and *wakeup*, which changes the process state from "asleep" to "ready to run" in memory or swapped.

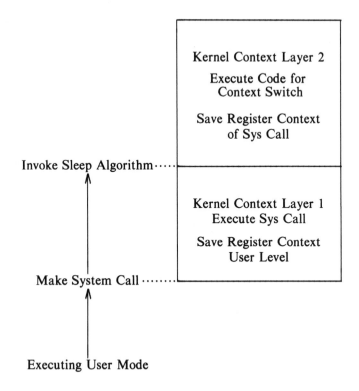

Figure 6.29. Typical Context Layers of a Sleeping Process

When a process goes to sleep, it typically does so during execution of a system call: The process enters the kernel (context layer 1) when it executes an operating system trap and goes to sleep awaiting a resource. When the process goes to sleep, it does a context switch, pushing its current context layer and executing in kernel context layer 2 (Figure 6.29). Processes also go to sleep when they incur page faults as a result of accessing virtual addresses that are not physically loaded; they sleep while the kernel reads in the contents of the pages.

6.6.1 Sleep Events and Addresses

Recall from Chapter 2 that processes are said to sleep on an event, meaning that they are in the sleep state until the event occurs, at which time they wake up and enter a "ready-to-run" state (in memory or swapped out). Although the system uses the abstraction of sleeping on an event, the implementation maps the set of events into a set of (kernel) virtual addresses. The addresses that represent the events are coded into the kernel, and their only significance is that the kernel

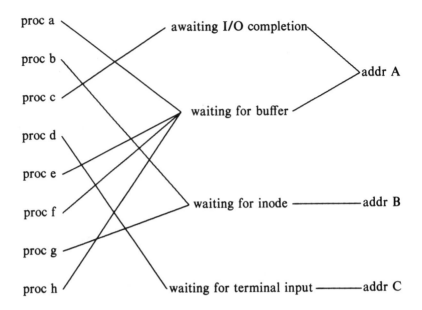

Figure 6.30. Processes Sleeping on Events and Events Mapping into Addresses

expects an event to map into a particular address. The abstraction of the event does not distinguish how many processes are awaiting the event, nor does the implementation. As a result, two anomalies arise. First, when an event occurs and a wakeup call is issued for processes that are sleeping on the event, they *all* wake up and move from a sleep state to a ready-to-run state. The kernel does not wake up one process at a time, even though they may contend for a single locked structure, and many may go back to sleep after a brief visit to the kernel running state (recall the discussion in Chapters 2 and 3). Figure 6.30 shows several processes sleeping on events.

The second anomaly in the implementation is that several events may map into one address. In Figure 6.30, for example, the events "waiting for the buffer" to become free and "awaiting I/O completion" map into the address of the buffer ("addr A"). When I/O for the buffer completes, the kernel wakes up all processes sleeping on both events. Since a process waiting for I/O keeps the buffer locked, other processes waiting for the buffer to become free will go back to sleep if the buffer is still locked when they execute. It would be more efficient if there would be a one-to-one mapping of events to addresses. In practice, however, performance is not hurt, because the mapping of multiple events into one address is rare and because the running process usually frees the locked resource before the other processes are scheduled to run. Stylistically, however, it would make the kernel a little easier to understand if the mapping were one-to-one.

```
algorithm sleep
input:   (1) sleep address
         (2) priority
output: 1 if process awakened as a result of a signal that process catches,
         longjump algorithm if process awakened as a result of a signal
                              that it does not catch,
         0 otherwise;
{
        raise processor execution level to block all interrupts;
        set process state to sleep;
        put process on sleep hash queue, based on sleep address;
        save sleep address in process table slot;
        set process priority level to input priority;
        if (process sleep is NOT interruptible)
        {
                do context switch;
                /* process resumes execution here when it wakes up */
                reset processor priority level to allow interrupts as when
                        process went to sleep;
                return(0);
        }

        /* here, process sleep is interruptible by signals */
        if (no signal pending against process)
        {
                do context switch;
                /* process resumes execution here when it wakes up */
                if (no signal pending against process)
                {
                        reset processor priority level to what it was when
                                process went to sleep;
                        return(0);
                }
        }
        remove process from sleep hash queue, if still there;

        reset processor priority level to what it was when process went to sleep;
        if (process sleep priority set to catch signals)
                return(1)
        do longjmp algorithm;
}
```

Figure 6.31. Sleep Algorithm

6.6.2 Algorithms for Sleep and Wakeup

Figure 6.31 shows the algorithm for *sleep*. The kernel first raises the processor execution level to block out all interrupts so that there can be no race conditions when it manipulates the sleep queues, and it saves the old processor execution level so that it can be restored when the process later wakes up. It marks the process state "asleep," saves the sleep address and priority in the process table, and puts it onto a hashed queue of sleeping processes. In the simple case (sleep cannot be interrupted), the process does a context switch and is safely asleep. When a sleeping process wakes up, the kernel later schedules it to run: The process returns from its context switch in the *sleep* algorithm, restores the processor execution level to the value it had when the process entered the algorithm, and returns.

```
algorithm wakeup                    /* wake up a sleeping process */
input:   sleep address
output: none
{
        raise processor execution level to block all interrupts;
        find sleep hash queue for sleep address;
        for (every process asleep on sleep address)
        {
                remove process from hash queue;
                mark process state "ready to run";
                put process on scheduler list of processes ready to run;
                clear field in process table entry for sleep address;
                if (process not loaded in memory)
                        wake up swapper process (0);
                else if (awakened process is more elligible to run than
                                        currently running process)
                        set scheduler flag;
        }
        restore processor execution level to original level;
}
```

Figure 6.32. Algorithm for Wakeup

To wake up sleeping processes, the kernel executes the *wakeup* algorithm (Figure 6.32), either during the usual system call algorithms or when handling an interrupt. For instance, the algorithm *iput* releases a locked inode and awakens all processes waiting for the lock to become free. Similarly, the disk interrupt handler awakens a process waiting for I/O completion. The kernel raises the processor execution level in *wakeup* to block out interrupts. Then for every process sleeping on the input sleep address, it marks the process state field "ready to run," removes the process from the linked list of sleeping processes, places it on a linked list of processes eligible for scheduling, and clears the field in the process table that marked its sleep address. If a process that woke up was not loaded in memory, the kernel awakens the swapper process to swap the process into memory (assuming the system is one that does not support demand paging); otherwise, if the awakened process is more eligible to run than the currently executing process, the kernel sets a scheduler flag so that it will go through the process scheduling algorithm when the process returns to user mode (Chapter 8). Finally, the kernel restores the processor execution level. It cannot be stressed enough: *wakeup* does *not* cause a process to be scheduled immediately; it only makes the process eligible for scheduling.

The discussion above is the simple case of the *sleep* and *wakeup* algorithms, because it assumes that the process sleeps until the proper event occurs. Processes frequently sleep on events that are "sure" to happen, such as when awaiting a locked resource (inodes or buffers) or when awaiting completion of disk I/O. The process is sure to wake up because the use of such resources is designed to be temporary. However, a process may sometimes sleep on an event that is not sure to happen, and if so, it must have a way to regain control and continue execution. For such cases, the kernel "interrupts" the sleeping process immediately by sending it a *signal*. The next chapter explains *signal*s in great detail; for now, assume that the kernel can (selectively) wake up a sleeping process as a result of the signal, and that the process can recognize that it has been sent a signal.

For instance, if a process issues a *read* system call to a terminal, the kernel does not satisfy the call until a user types data on the terminal keyboard (Chapter 10). However, the user that started the process may leave the terminal for an all-day meeting, leaving the process asleep and waiting for input, and another user may want to use the terminal. If the second user resorts to drastic measures (such as turning the terminal off), the kernel needs a way to recover the disconnected process: As a first step, it must awaken the process from its sleep as the result of a signal. Parenthetically, there is nothing wrong with processes sleeping for a long time. Sleeping process occupy a slot in the process table and could thus lengthen the search times for certain algorithms, but they do not use CPU time, so their overhead is small.

To distinguish the types of sleep states, the kernel sets the scheduling priority of the sleeping process when it enters the sleep state, based on the sleep priority parameter. That is, it invokes the *sleep* algorithm with a priority value, based on its knowledge that the sleep event is sure to occur or not. If the priority is above a threshold value, the process will not wake up prematurely on receipt of a signal but will sleep until the event it is waiting for happens. But if the priority value is below the threshold value, the process will awaken immediately on receipt of the signal.[4]

---

4. The terms "above" and "below" refer to the normal usage of the terms high priority and low priority. However, the kernel implementation uses integers to measure the priority value, with lower values implying higher priority.

If a signal is already set against a process when it enters the *sleep* algorithm, the conditions just stated determine whether the process ever gets to sleep. For instance, if the sleep priority is above the threshold value, the process goes to sleep and waits for an explicit wakeup call. If the sleep priority is below the threshold value, however, the process does not go to sleep but responds to the signal as if the signal had arrived while it was asleep. If the kernel did not check for signals before going to sleep, the signal may not arrive again and the process would never wake up.

When a process is awakened as a result of a signal (or if it never gets to sleep because of existence of a signal), the kernel may do a *longjmp*, depending on the reason the process originally went to sleep. The kernel does a *longjmp* to restore a previously saved context if it has no way to complete the system call it is executing. For instance, if a terminal *read* call is interrupted because a user turns the terminal off, the *read* should not complete but should return with an error indication. This holds for all system calls that can be interrupted while they are asleep. The process should not continue normally after waking up from its sleep, because the sleep event was not satisfied. The kernel saves the process context at the beginning of most system calls using *setjmp* in anticipation of the need for a later *longjmp*.

There are occasions when the kernel wants the process to wake up on receipt of a signal but not do a *longjmp*. The kernel invokes the *sleep* algorithm with a special priority parameter that suppresses execution of the *longjmp* and causes the *sleep* algorithm to return the value 1. This is more efficient than doing a *setjmp* immediately before the *sleep* call and then a *longjmp* to restore the context of the process as it was before entering the sleep state. The purpose is to allow the kernel to clean up local data structures. For example, a device driver may allocate private data structures and then go to sleep at an interruptible priority; if it wakes up because of a signal, it should free the allocated data structures, then *longjmp* if necessary. The user has no control over whether a process does a *longjmp*; that depends on the reason the process was sleeping and whether kernel data structures need modification before the process returns from the system call.

6.7 SUMMARY

This chapter has defined the context of a process. Processes in the UNIX system move between various logical states according to well-defined transition rules, and state information is saved in the process table and the *u area*. The context of a process consists of its user-level context and its system-level context. The user-level context consists of the process text, data, (user) stack, and shared memory regions, and the system-level context consists of a static part (process table entry, *u area*, and memory mapping information) and a dynamic part (kernel stack and saved registers of previous system context layer) that is pushed and popped as the process executes system calls, handles interrupts, and does context switches. The user-level context of a process is divided into separate regions, comprising contiguous ranges of virtual addresses that are treated as distinct objects for protection and sharing.

The memory management model used to describe the virtual address layout of a process assumes the use of a page table for each process region. The kernel contains various algorithms that manipulate regions. Finally, the chapter described the algorithms for *sleep* and *wakeup*. The following chapters use the low-level structures and algorithms described here, in the explanation of the system calls for process management, process scheduling, and the implementation of memory management policies.

6.8 EXERCISES

1. Design an algorithm that translates virtual addresses to physical addresses, given the virtual address and the address of the pregion entry.
2. The AT&T 3B2 computer and the NSC Series 32000 use a two-tiered (segmented) translation scheme to translate virtual addresses to physical addresses. That is, the system contains a pointer to a table of page table pointers, and each entry in the table can address a fixed portion of the process address space, according to its offset in the table. Compare the algorithm for virtual address translation on these machines to the algorithm discussed for the memory model in the text. Consider issues of performance and the space needed for auxiliary tables.
3. The VAX-11 architecture contains two sets of base and limit registers that the machine uses for user address translation. The scheme is the same as that described in the previous problem, except that the number of page table pointers is two. Given that processes have three regions, text, data, and stack, what is a good way of mapping the regions into page tables and using the two sets of registers? The stack in the VAX-11 architecture grows towards lower virtual addresses. What should the stack region look like? Chapter 11 will describe another region for shared memory: How should it fit into the VAX-11 architecture?
4. Design an algorithm for allocating and freeing memory pages and page tables. What data structures would allow best performance or simplest implementation?
5. The MC68451 memory management unit for the Motorola 68000 Family of Microprocessors allows allocation of memory segments with sizes ranging from 256 bytes to 16 megabytes in powers of 2. Each (physical) memory management unit contains 32 segment descriptors. Describe an efficient method for memory allocation. What should the implementation of regions look like?
6. Consider the virtual address map in Figure 6.5. Suppose the kernel swaps the process out (in a swapping system) or swaps out many pages in the stack region (in a paging system). If the process later reads (virtual) address 68,432, must it read the identical location in physical memory that it would have read before the swap or paging operation? If the lower levels of memory management were implemented with page tables, must the page tables be located in the same locations of physical memory?
* 7. It is possible to implement the system such that the kernel stack grows on top of the user stack. Discuss the advantages and disadvantages of such an implementation.
8. When attaching a region to a process, how can the kernel check that the region does not overlap virtual addresses in regions already attached to the process?
9. Consider the algorithm for doing a context switch. Suppose the system contains only one process that is ready to run. In other words, the kernel picks the process that just saved its context to run. Describe what happens.

10. Suppose a process goes to sleep and the system contains no processes ready to run. What happens when the (about to be) sleeping process does its context switch?

11. Suppose that a process executing in user mode uses up its time slice and, as a result of a clock interrupt, the kernel schedules a new process to run. Show that the context switch takes place at kernel context layer 2.

12. In a paging system, a process executing in user mode may incur a page fault because it is attempting to access a page that is not loaded in memory. In the course of servicing the interrupt, the kernel reads the page from a swap device and goes to sleep. Show that the context switch (during the sleep) takes place at kernel context layer 2.

13. A process executes the system call

    read(fd, buf, 1024);

    on a paging system. Suppose the kernel executes algorithm *read* to the point where it has read the data into a system buffer, but it incurs a page fault when trying to copy the data into the user address space because the page containing *buf* was paged out. The kernel handles the interrupt by reading the offending page into memory. What happens in each kernel context layer? What happens if the page fault handler goes to sleep while waiting for the page to be written into main memory?

14. When copying data from user address space to the kernel in Figure 6.17, what would happen if the user supplied address was illegal?

* 15. In algorithms *sleep* and *wakeup*, the kernel raises the processor execution level to prevent interrupts. What bad things could happen if it did not raise the processor execution level? (Hint: The kernel frequently awakens sleeping processes from interrupt handlers.)

* 16. Suppose a process attempts to go to sleep on event A but has not yet executed the code in the *sleep* algorithm to block interrupts; suppose an interrupt occurs before the process raises the processor execution level in *sleep*, and the interrupt handler attempts to awaken all processes asleep on event A. What will happen to the process attempting to go to sleep? Is this a dangerous situation? If so, how can the kernel avoid it?

17. What happens if the kernel issues a *wakeup* call for all processes asleep on address A, but no processes are asleep on that address at the time?

18. Many processes can sleep on an address, but the kernel may want to wake up selected processes that receive a signal. Assume the signal mechanism can identify the particular processes. Describe how the *wakeup* algorithm should be changed to wake up one process on a sleep address instead of all the processes.

19. The Multics system contains algorithms for *sleep* and *wakeup* with the following syntax:

    sleep(event);
    wakeup(event, priority);

    That is, the *wakeup* algorithm assigns a priority to the process it is awakening. Compare these calls to the *sleep* and *wakeup* calls in the UNIX system.

7

PROCESS
CONTROL

The last chapter defined the context of a process and explained the algorithms that manipulate it; this chapter will describe the use and implementation of the system calls that control the process context. The *fork* system call creates a new process, the *exit* call terminates process execution, and the *wait* call allows a *parent* process to synchronize its execution with the *exit* of a *child* process. Signals inform processes of asynchronous events. Because the kernel synchronizes execution of *exit* and *wait* via signals, the chapter presents signals before *exit* and *wait*. The *exec* system call allows a process to invoke a "new" program, overlaying its address space with the executable image of a file. The *brk* system call allows a process to allocate more memory dynamically; similarly, the system allows the user stack to grow dynamically by allocating more space when necessary, using the same mechanisms as for *brk*. Finally, the chapter sketches the construction of the major loops of the shell and of *init*.

Figure 7.1 shows the relationship between the system calls described in this chapter and the memory management algorithms described in the last chapter. Almost all calls use *sleep* and *wakeup*, not shown in the figure. Furthermore, *exec* interacts with the file system algorithms described in Chapters 4 and 5.

System Calls Dealing with Memory Management				System Calls Dealing with Synchronization			Miscellaneous	
fork	exec	brk	exit	wait	signal	kill	setpgrp	setuid
dupreg attachreg	detachreg allocreg attachreg growreg loadreg mapreg	growreg	detachreg					

Figure 7.1. Process System Calls and Relation to Other Algorithms

7.1 PROCESS CREATION

The only way for a user to create a new process in the UNIX operating system is to invoke the *fork* system call. The process that invokes *fork* is called the *parent* process, and the newly created process is called the *child* process. The syntax for the *fork* system call is

   pid = fork();

On return from the *fork* system call, the two processes have identical copies of their user-level context except for the return value *pid*. In the parent process, *pid* is the child process ID; in the child process, *pid* is 0. Process 0, created internally by the kernel when the system is booted, is the only process not created via *fork*.

   The kernel does the following sequence of operations for *fork*.

1. It allocates a slot in the process table for the new process.
2. It assigns a unique ID number to the child process.
3. It makes a logical copy of the context of the parent process. Since certain portions of a process, such as the text region, may be shared between processes, the kernel can sometimes increment a region reference count instead of copying the region to a new physical location in memory.
4. It increments file and inode table counters for files associated with the process.
5. It returns the ID number of the child to the parent process, and a 0 value to the child process.

The implementation of the *fork* system call is not trivial, because the child process appears to start its execution sequence out of thin air. The algorithm for *fork* varies slightly for demand paging and swapping systems; the ensuing discussion is based on traditional swapping systems but will point out the places that change for demand paging systems. It also assumes that the system has enough main memory available to store the child process. Chapter 9 considers the case where not enough memory is available for the child process, and it also describes the implementation of *fork* on a paging system.

```
algorithm fork
input:   none
output: to parent process, child PID number
         to child process, 0
{
        check for available kernel resources;
        get free proc table slot, unique PID number;
        check that user not running too many processes;
        mark child state "being created;"
        copy data from parent proc table slot to new child slot;
        increment counts on current directory inode and changed root (if applicable);
        increment open file counts in file table;
        make copy of parent context (u area, text, data, stack) in memory;
        push dummy system level context layer onto child system level context;
                dummy context contains data allowing child process
                to recognize itself, and start running from here
                when scheduled;
        if (executing process is parent process)
        {
                change child state to "ready to run;"
                return(child ID);        /* from system to user */
        }
        else      /* executing process is the child process */
        {
                initialize u area timing fields;
                return(0);        /* to user */
        }
}
```

Figure 7.2. Algorithm for Fork

Figure 7.2 shows the algorithm for *fork*. The kernel first ascertains that it has available resources to complete the *fork* successfully. On a swapping system, it needs space either in memory or on disk to hold the child process; on a paging system, it has to allocate memory for auxiliary tables such as page tables. If the resources are unavailable, the *fork* call fails. The kernel finds a slot in the process table to start constructing the context of the child process and makes sure that the user doing the *fork* does not have too many processes already running. It also picks a unique ID number for the new process, one greater than the most recently assigned ID number. If another process already has the proposed ID number, the kernel attempts to assign the next higher ID number. When the ID numbers reach a maximum value, assignment starts from 0 again. Since most processes execute for a short time, most ID numbers are not in use when ID assignment wraps around.

The system imposes a (configurable) limit on the number of processes a user can simultaneously execute so that no user can steal many process table slots, thereby preventing other users from creating new processes. Similarly, ordinary users cannot create a process that would occupy the last remaining slot in the process table, or else the system could effectively deadlock. That is, the kernel cannot guarantee that existing processes will *exit* naturally and, therefore, no new processes could be created, because all the process table slots are in use. On the other hand, a superuser can execute as many processes as it likes, bounded by the size of the process table, and a superuser process *can* occupy the last available slot in the process table. Presumably, a superuser could take drastic action and spawn a process that forces other processes to *exit* if necessary (see Section 7.2.3 for the *kill* system call).

The kernel next initializes the child's process table slot, copying various fields from the parent slot. For instance, the child "inherits" the parent process real and effective user ID numbers, the parent process group, and the parent *nice* value, used for calculation of scheduling priority. Later sections discuss the meaning of these fields. The kernel assigns the parent process ID field in the child slot, putting the child in the process tree structure, and initializes various scheduling parameters, such as the initial priority value, initial CPU usage, and other timing fields. The initial state of the process is "being created" (recall Figure 6.1).

The kernel now adjusts reference counts for files with which the child process is automatically associated. First, the child process resides in the current directory of the parent process. The number of processes that currently access the directory increases by 1 and, accordingly, the kernel increments its inode reference count. Second, if the parent process or one of its ancestors had ever executed the *chroot* system call to change its root, the child process inherits the changed root and increments its inode reference count. Finally, the kernel searches the parent's user file descriptor table for open files known to the process and increments the global file table reference count associated with each open file. Not only does the child process inherit access rights to open files, but it also shares access to the files with the parent process because both processes manipulate the same file table entries. The effect of *fork* is similar to that of *dup* vis-a-vis open files: A new entry in the user file descriptor table points to the entry in the global file table for the open file. For *dup*, however, the entries in the user file descriptor table are in one process; for *fork*, they are in different processes.

The kernel is now ready to create the user-level context of the child process. It allocates memory for the child process *u area*, regions, and auxiliary page tables, duplicates every region in the parent process using algorithm *dupreg*, and attaches every region to the child process using algorithm *attachreg*. In a swapping system, it copies the contents of regions that are not shared into a new area of main memory. Recall from Section 6.2.4 that the *u area* contains a pointer to its process table slot. Except for that field, the contents of the child *u area* are initially the same as the contents of the parent process *u area*, but they can diverge after completion of the *fork*. For instance, the parent process may *open* a new file after the *fork*, but the child process does not have automatic access to it.

So far, the kernel has created the static portion of the child context; now it creates the dynamic portion. The kernel copies the parent context layer 1, containing the user saved register context and the kernel stack frame of the *fork* system call. If the implementation is one where the kernel stack is part of the *u area*, the kernel automatically creates the child kernel stack when it creates the child *u area*. Otherwise, the parent process must copy its kernel stack to a private area of memory associated with the child process. In either case, the kernel stacks for the parent and child processes are identical. The kernel then creates a dummy context layer (2) for the child process, containing the saved register context for context layer (1). It sets the program counter and other registers in the saved register context so that it can "restore" the child context, even though it had never executed before, and so that the child process can recognize itself as the child when it runs. For instance, if the kernel code tests the value of register 0 to decide if the process is the parent or the child, it writes the appropriate value in the child saved register context in layer 1. The mechanism is similar to that discussed for a context switch in the previous chapter.

When the child context is ready, the parent completes its part of *fork* by changing the child state to "ready to run (in memory)" and by returning the child process ID to the user. The kernel later schedules the child process for execution via the normal scheduling algorithm, and the child process "completes" *its* part of the *fork*. The context of the child process was set up by the parent process; to the kernel, the child process appears to have awakened after awaiting a resource. The child process executes part of the code for the *fork* system call, according to the program counter that the kernel restored from the saved register context in context layer 2, and returns a 0 from the system call.

Figure 7.3 gives a logical view of the parent and child processes and their relationship to other kernel data structures immediately after completion of the *fork* system call. To summarize, both processes share files that the parent had open at the time of the *fork*, and the file table reference count for those files is one greater than it had been. Similarly, the child process has the same current directory and changed root (if applicable) as the parent, and the inode reference count of those directories is one greater than it had been. The processes have identical copies of the text, data, and (user) stack regions; the region type and the system implementation determine whether the processes can share a physical copy of the text region.

Consider the program in Figure 7.4, an example of sharing file access across a *fork* system call. A user should invoke the program with two parameters, the name of an existing file and the name of a new file to be created. The process *open*s the

Parent Process

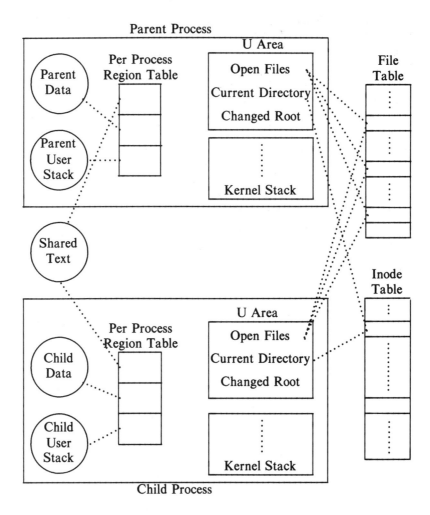

Figure 7.3. Fork Creating a New Process Context

existing file, *creat*s the new file, and — assuming it encounters no errors — *fork*s and creates a child process. Internally, the kernel makes a copy of the parent context for the child process, and the parent process executes in one address space and the child process executes in another. Each process can access private copies of the global variables *fdrd*, *fdwt*, and *c* and private copies of the stack variables *argc* and *argv*, but neither process can access the variables of the other process. However, the kernel copied the *u area* of the original process to the child process during the *fork*, and the child thus inherits access to the parent files (that is, the files the parent originally *open*ed and *creat*ed) using the same file descriptors.

```
#include <fcntl.h>
int fdrd, fdwt;
char c;

main(argc, argv)
     int argc;
     char *argv[];
{
     if (argc != 3)
          exit(1);
     if ((fdrd = open(argv[1], O_RDONLY)) == -1)
          exit(1);
     if ((fdwt = creat(argv[2], 0666)) == -1)
          exit(1);

     fork();
     /* both procs execute same code */
     rdwrt();
     exit(0);
}

rdwrt()
{
     for (;;)
     {
          if (read(fdrd, &c, 1) != 1)
               return;
          write(fdwt, &c, 1);
     }
}
```

Figure 7.4. Program where Parent and Child Share File Access

The parent and child processes call the function *rdwrt*, independently, of course, and execute a loop, *read*ing one byte from the source file and *writ*ing it to the target file. The function *rdwrt* returns when the *read* system call encounters the end of file. The kernel had incremented the file table counts of the source and target files, and the file descriptors in both processes refer to the *same* file table entries. That is, the file descriptors *fdrd* for both processes refer to the file table entry for the source file, and the file descriptors *fdwt* for both processes refer to the file table entry for the target file. Therefore, the two processes never *read* or *write* the same file offset values, because the kernel increments them after each *read* and *write* call. Although the processes appear to copy the source file twice as fast because they share the work load, the contents of the target file depend on the order that the kernel scheduled the processes. If it schedules the processes such that they alternate execution of their system calls, or even if they alternate the execution of pairs of *read-write* system calls, the contents of the target file would be identical to the contents of the source file. But consider the following scenario where the processes are about to *read* the two character sequence "ab" in the source file. Suppose the parent process *read*s the character 'a', and the kernel does a context switch to execute the child process before the parent does the *write*. If the child process *read*s the character 'b' and *write*s it to the target file before the parent is rescheduled, the target file will not contain the string "ab" in the proper place, but "ba". The kernel does not guarantee the relative rates of process execution.

Now consider the program in Figure 7.5, which inherits file descriptors 0 and 1 (standard input and standard output) from its parent. The execution of each *pipe* system call allocates two more file descriptors in the arrays *to_par* and *to_chil*, respectively. The process *fork*s and makes a copy of its context: each process can access its own data, as in the previous example. The parent process *close*s its standard output file (file descriptor 1), and *dup*s the write descriptor returned for the pipe *to_chil*. Because the first free slot in the parent file descriptor table is the slot just cleared by the *close*, the kernel copies the pipe write descriptor to slot 1 in the file descriptor table, and the standard output file descriptor becomes the pipe write descriptor for *to_chil*. The parent process does a similar operation to make its standard input descriptor the pipe read descriptor for *to_par*. Similarly, the child process closes its standard input file (descriptor 0) and *dup*s the pipe read descriptor for *to_chil*. Since the first free slot in the file descriptor table is the previous standard input slot, the child standard input becomes the pipe read descriptor for *to_chil*. The child does a similar set of operations to make its standard output the pipe write descriptor for *to_par*. Both processes *close* the file descriptors returned from *pipe* — good programming practice, as will be explained. As a result, when the parent *write*s its standard output, it is *writ*ing the pipe *to_chil* and sending data to the child process, which *read*s the pipe on its standard input. When the child *write*s its standard output, it is *writ*ing the pipe *to_par* and sending data to the parent process, which *read*s the pipe on its standard input. The processes thus exchange messages over the two pipes.

The results of this example are invariant, regardless of the order that the processes execute their respective system calls. That is, it makes no difference whether the parent returns from the *fork* call before the child or afterwards. Similarly, it makes no difference in what relative order the processes execute the system calls until they enter their loops: The kernel structures are identical. If the child process executes its *read* system call before the parent does its *write*, the child process will sleep until the parent *write*s the pipe and awakens it. If the parent process *write*s the pipe before the child *read*s the pipe, the parent will not complete its *read* of standard input until the child *read*s *its* standard input and *write*s its standard output. From then on, the order of execution is fixed: Each process completes a *read* and *write* system call and cannot complete its next *read* system call until the other process completes a *read* and *write* system call. The parent

```
#include  <string.h>
char string[] = "hello world";
main()
{
    int count, i;
    int to_par[2], to_chil[2];        /* for pipes to parent, child */
    char buf[256];
    pipe(to_par);
    pipe(to_chil);
    if (fork() == 0)
    {
        /* child process executes here */
        close(0);            /* close old standard input */
        dup(to_chil[0]);    /* dup pipe read to standard input */
        close(1);            /* close old standard output */
        dup(to_par[1]);      /* dup pipe write to standard out */
        close(to_par[1]);   /* close unnecessary pipe descriptors */
        close(to_chil[0]);
        close(to_par[0]);
        close(to_chil[1]);
        for (;;)
        {
            if ((count = read(0, buf, sizeof(buf))) == 0)
                exit();
            write(1, buf, count);
        }
    }
    /* parent process executes here */
    close(1);         /* rearrange standard in, out */
    dup(to_chil[1]);
    close(0);
    dup(to_par[0]);
    close(to_chil[1]);
    close(to_par[0]);
    close(to_chil[0]);
    close(to_par[1]);
    for (i = 0;  i < 15;  i++)
    {
        write(1, string, strlen(string));
        read(0, buf, sizeof(buf));
    }
}
```

Figure 7.5. Use of Pipe, Dup, and Fork

*exit*s after 15 iterations through the loop; the child then *read*s "end-of-file" because the pipe has no writer processes and *exit*s. If the child were to *write* the pipe after the parent had *exit*ed, it would receive a signal for writing a pipe with no reader processes.

We mentioned above that it is good programming practice to *close* superfluous file descriptors. This is true for three reasons. First, it conserves file descriptors in view of the system-imposed limit. Second, if a child process *exec*s, the file descriptors remain assigned in the new context, as will be seen. Closing extraneous files before an *exec* allows programs to execute in a clean, surprise-free environment, with only standard input, standard output, and standard error file descriptors open. Finally, a *read* of a pipe returns end-of-file only if no processes have the pipe open for writing. If a reader process keeps the pipe write descriptor open, it will never know when the writer processes *close* their end of the pipe. The example above would not work properly unless the child *close*s its write pipe descriptors before entering its loop.

7.2 SIGNALS

Signals inform processes of the occurrence of asynchronous events. Processes may send each other *signals* with the *kill* system call, or the kernel may send signals internally. There are 19 signals in the System V (Release 2) UNIX system that can be classified as follows (see the description of the signal system call in [SVID 85]):

- Signals having to do with the termination of a process, sent when a process *exit*s or when a process invokes the *signal* system call with the *death of child* parameter;
- Signals having to do with process induced exceptions such as when a process accesses an address outside its virtual address space, when it attempts to write memory that is read-only (such as program text), or when it executes a privileged instruction or for various hardware errors;
- Signals having to do with the unrecoverable conditions during a system call, such as running out of system resources during *exec* after the original address space has been released (see Section 7.5);
- Signals caused by an unexpected error condition during a system call, such as making a nonexistent system call (the process passed a system call number that does not correspond to a legal system call), writing a pipe that has no reader processes, or using an illegal "reference" value for the *lseek* system call. It would be more consistent to return an error on such system calls instead of generating a signal, but the use of signals to abort misbehaving processes is more pragmatic;[1]

- Signals originating from a process in user mode, such as when a process wishes to receive an *alarm* signal after a period of time, or when processes send arbitrary signals to each other with the *kill* system call;
- Signals related to terminal interaction such as when a user hangs up a terminal (or the "carrier" signal drops on such a line for any reason), or when a user presses the "break" or "delete" keys on a terminal keyboard;
- Signals for tracing execution of a process.

The discussion in this and in following chapters explains the circumstances under which signals of the various classes are used.

The treatment of signals has several facets, namely how the kernel sends a signal to a process, how the process handles a signal, and how a process controls its reaction to signals. To send a signal to a process, the kernel sets a bit in the signal field of the process table entry, corresponding to the type of signal received. If the process is asleep at an interruptible priority, the kernel awakens it. The job of the sender (process or kernel) is complete. A process can remember different types of signals, but it has no memory of how many signals it receives of a particular type. For example, if a process receives a hangup signal and a kill signal, it sets the appropriate bits in the process table signal field, but it cannot tell how many instances of the signals it receives.

The kernel checks for receipt of a signal when a process is about to return from kernel mode to user mode and when it enters or leaves the sleep state at a suitably low scheduling priority (see Figure 7.6). The kernel handles signals only when a process returns from kernel mode to user mode. Thus, a signal does not have an instant effect on a process running in kernel mode. If a process is running in user mode, and the kernel handles an interrupt that causes a signal to be sent to the process, the kernel will recognize and handle the signal when it returns from the interrupt. Thus, a process never executes in user mode before handling outstanding signals.

Figure 7.7 shows the algorithm the kernel executes to determine if a process received a signal. The case for "death of child" signals will be treated later in the chapter. As will be seen, a process can choose to ignore signals with the *signal* system call. In the algorithm *issig*, the kernel simply turns off the signal indication for signals the process wants to ignore but notes the existence of signals it does not ignore.

---

1. The use of signals in some circumstances uncovers errors in programs that do not check for failure of system calls (private communication from D. Ritchie).

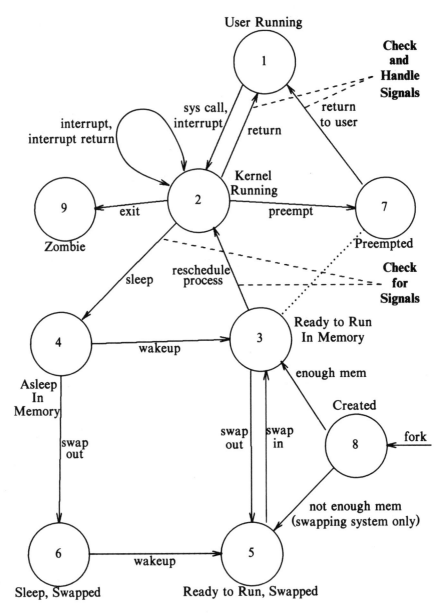

Figure 7.6. Checking and Handling Signals in the Process State Diagram

```
algorithm issig                    /* test for receipt of signals */
input:  none
output: true, if process received signals that it does not ignore
        false otherwise
{
        while (received signal field in process table entry not 0)
        {
                find a signal number sent to the process;
                if (signal is death of child)
                {
                        if (ignoring death of child signals)
                                free process table entries of zombie children;
                        else if (catching death of child signals)
                                return(true);
                }
                else if (not ignoring signal)
                        return(true);
                turn off signal bit in received signal field in process table;
        }
        return(false);
}
```

Figure 7.7. Algorithm for Recognizing Signals

7.2.1 Handling Signals

The kernel handles signals in the context of the process that receives them so a process must run to handle signals. There are three cases for handling signals: the process *exits* on receipt of the signal, it ignores the signal, or it executes a particular (user) function on receipt of the signal. The default action is to call *exit* in kernel mode, but a process can specify special action to take on receipt of certain signals with the *signal* system call.

The syntax for the *signal* system call is

oldfunction = signal(signum, function);

where *signum* is the signal number the process is specifying the action for, *function* is the address of the (user) function the process wants to invoke on receipt of the signal, and the return value *oldfunction* was the value of *function* in the most recently specified call to *signal* for *signum*. The process can pass the values 1 or 0 instead of a function address: The process will ignore future occurrences of the signal if the parameter value is 1 (Section 7.4 deals with the special case for ignoring the "death of child" signal) and *exit* in the kernel on receipt of the signal if its value is 0 (the default value). The *u area* contains an array of signal-handler fields, one for each signal defined in the system. The kernel stores the address of the user function in the field that corresponds to the signal number. Specification

```
algorithm psig     /* handle signals after recognizing their existence */
input:  none
output: none
{
      get signal number set in process table entry;
      clear signal number in process table entry;
      if (user had called signal sys call to ignore this signal)
            return;              /* done */
      if (user specified function to handle the signal)
      {
            get user virtual address of signal catcher stored in u area;
            /* the next statement has undesirable side-effects */
            clear u area entry that stored address of signal catcher;
            modify user level context:
                    artificially create user stack frame to mimic
                    call to signal catcher function;
            modify system level context:
                    write address of signal catcher into program
                    counter field of user saved register context;
            return;
      }
      if (signal is type that system should dump core image of process)
      {
            create file named "core" in current directory;
            write contents of user level context to file "core";
      }
      invoke exit algorithm immediately;
}
```

Figure 7.8. Algorithm for Handling Signals

to handle signals of one type has no effect on handling signals of other types.

When handling a signal (Figure 7.8) the kernel determines the signal type and turns off the appropriate signal bit in the process table entry, set when the process received the signal. If the signal handling function is set to its default value, the kernel will dump a "core" image of the process (see exercise 7.7) for certain types of signals before *exit*ing. The dump is a convenience to programmers, allowing them to ascertain its causes and, thereby, to debug their programs. The kernel dumps core for signals that imply something is wrong with a process, such as when a process executes an illegal instruction or when it accesses an address outside its virtual address space. But the kernel does not dump core for signals that do not imply a program error. For instance, receipt of an interrupt signal, sent when a user hits the "delete" or "break" key on a terminal, implies that the user wants to terminate a process prematurely, and receipt of a hangup signal implies that the login terminal is no longer "connected." These signals do not imply that anything is wrong with the process. The *quit* signal, however, induces a core dump even though it is initiated outside the running process. Usually sent by typing the control-vertical-bar character at the terminal, it allows the programmer to obtain a core dump of a running process, useful for one that is in an infinite loop.

When a process receives a signal that it had previously decided to ignore, it continues as if the signal had never occurred. Because the kernel does not reset the field in the *u area* that shows the signal is ignored, the process will ignore the signal if it happens again, too. If a process receives a signal that it had previously decided to catch, it executes the user specified signal handling function immediately when it returns to user mode, after the kernel does the following steps.

1. The kernel accesses the user saved register context, finding the program counter and stack pointer that it had saved for return to the user process.
2. It clears the signal handler field in the *u area*, setting it to the default state.
3. The kernel creates a new stack frame on the user stack, writing in the values of the program counter and stack pointer it had retrieved from the user saved register context and allocating new space, if necessary. The user stack looks as if the process had called a user-level function (the signal catcher) at the point where it had made the system call or where the kernel had interrupted it (before recognition of the signal).
4. The kernel changes the user saved register context: It resets the value for the program counter to the address of the signal catcher function and sets the value for the stack pointer to account for the growth of the user stack.

After returning from the kernel to user mode, the process will thus execute the signal handling function; when it returns from the signal handling function, it returns to the place in the user code where the system call or interrupt originally occurred, mimicking a return from the system call or interrupt.

For example, Figure 7.9 contains a program that catches interrupt signals (*SIGINT*) and sends itself an interrupt signal (the result of the *kill* call here), and Figure 7.10 contains relevant parts of a disassembly of the load module on a VAX 11/780. When the system executes the process, the call to the *kill* library routine comes from address (hexadecimal) ee, and the library routine executes the *chmk* (change mode to kernel) instruction at address 10a to call the *kill* system call. The return address from the system call is 10c. In executing the system call, the kernel sends an interrupt signal to the process. The kernel notices the interrupt signal when it is about to return to user mode, removes the address 10c from the user saved register context, and places it on the user stack. The kernel takes the address of the function *catcher*, 104, and puts it into the user saved register context. Figure 7.11 illustrates the states of the user stack and saved register context.

Several anomalies exist in the algorithm described here for the treatment of signals. First and most important, when a process handles a signal but before it returns to user mode, the kernel clears the field in the *u area* that contains the address of the user signal handling function. If the process wants to handle the signal again, it must call the *signal* system call again. This has unfortunate

```
#include <signal.h>
main()
{
    extern catcher();
    signal(SIGINT, catcher);
    kill(0, SIGINT);
}

catcher()
{
}
```

Figure 7.9. Source Code for a Program that Catches Signals

```
****   VAX    DISASSEMBLER   ****

_main()
            e4:
            e6:    pushab    0x18(pc)
            ec:    pushl     $0x2
    # next line calls signal
            ee:    calls     $0x2,0x23(pc)
            f5:    pushl     $0x2
            f7:    clrl      —(sp)
    # next line calls kill library routine
            f9:    calls     $0x2,0x8(pc)
            100:   ret
            101:   halt
            102:   halt
            103:   halt
_catcher()
            104:
            106:   ret
            107:   halt
_kill()
            108:
    # next line traps into kernel
            10a:   chmk      $0x25
            10c:   bgequ     0x6 <0x114>
            10e:   jmp       0x14(pc)
            114:   clrl      r0
            116:   ret
```

Figure 7.10. Disassembly of Program that Catches Signals

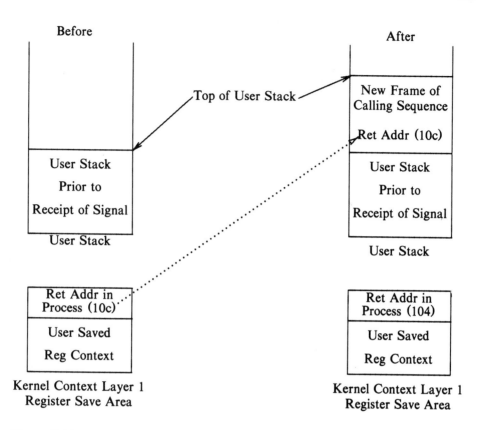

Figure 7.11. User Stack and Kernel Save Area Before and After Receipt of Signal

ramifications: A race condition results because a second instance of the signal may arrive before the process has a chance to invoke the system call. Since the process is executing in user mode, the kernel could do a context switch, increasing the chance that the process will receive the signal before resetting the signal catcher.

The program in Figure 7.12 illustrates the race condition. The process calls the *signal* system call to arrange to catch interrupt signals and execute the function *sigcatcher*. It then creates a child process, invokes the *nice* system call to lower its scheduling priority relative to the child process (see Chapter 8), and goes into an infinite loop. The child process suspends execution for 5 seconds to give the parent process time to execute the *nice* system call and lower its priority. The child process then goes into a loop, sending an interrupt signal (via *kill*) to the parent process during each iteration. If the *kill* returns because of an error, probably because the parent process no longer exists, the child process *exits*. The idea is that the parent process should invoke the signal catcher every time it receives an interrupt signal. The signal catcher prints a message and calls *signal* again to

```
#include <signal.h>
sigcatcher()
{
      printf("PID %d caught one\n", getpid());      /* print proc id */
      signal(SIGINT, sigcatcher);
}

main()
{
      int ppid;

      signal(SIGINT, sigcatcher);

      if (fork() == 0)
      {
            /* give enough time for both procs to set up */
            sleep(5);          /* lib function to delay 5 secs */
            ppid = getppid();       /* get parent id */
            for (;;)
                    if (kill(ppid, SIGINT) == -1)
                            exit();
      }

      /* lower priority, greater chance of exhibiting race */
      nice(10);
      for (;;)
            ;
}
```

Figure 7.12. Program Demonstrating Race Condition in Catching Signals

catch the next occurrence of an interrupt signal, and the parent continues to execute in the infinite loop.

It is possible for the following sequence of events to occur, however.

1. The child process sends an interrupt signal to the parent process.
2. The parent process catches the signal and calls the signal catcher, but the kernel preempts the process and switches context before it executes the *signal* system call again.
3. The child process executes again and sends another interrupt signal to the parent process.
4. The parent process receives the second interrupt signal, but it has not made arrangements to catch the signal. When it resumes execution, it *exits*.

The program was written to encourage such behavior, since invocation of the *nice* system call by the parent process induces the kernel to schedule the child process more frequently. However, it is indeterminate when this result will occur.

According to Ritchie (private communication), signals were designed as events that are fatal or ignored, not necessarily handled, and hence the race condition was not fixed in early releases. However, it poses a serious problem to programs that want to catch signals. The problem would be solved if the signal field were not cleared on receipt of the signal. But such a solution could result in a new problem: If signals keep arriving and are caught, the user stack could grow out of bounds because of the nested calls to the signal catcher. Alternatively, the kernel could reset the value of the signal-handling function to ignore signals of that type until the user again specifies what to do for such signals. Such a solution implies a loss of information, because the process has no way of knowing how many signals it receives. However, the loss of information is no more severe than it is for the case where the process receives many signals of one type before it has a chance to handle them. Finally, the BSD system allows a process to block and unblock receipt of signals with a new system call; when a process unblocks signals, the kernel sends pending signals that had been blocked to the process. When a process receives a signal, the kernel automatically blocks further receipt of the signal until the signal handler completes. This is analogous to how the kernel reacts to hardware interrupts: it blocks report of new interrupts while it handles previous interrupts.

A second anomaly in the treatment of signals concerns catching signals that occur while the process is in a system call, sleeping at an interruptible priority. The signal causes the process to take a *longjmp* out of its sleep, return to user mode, and call the signal handler. When the signal handler returns, the process appears to return from the system call with an error indicating that the system call was interrupted. The user can check for the error return and restart the system call, but it would sometimes be more convenient if the kernel automatically restarted the system call, as is done in the BSD system.

A third anomaly exists for the case where the process ignores a signal. If the signal arrives while the process is asleep at an interruptible sleep priority level, the process will wake up but will not do a *longjmp*. That is, the kernel realizes that the process ignores the signal only after waking it up and running it. A more consistent policy would be to leave the process asleep. However, the kernel stores the signal function address in the *u area*, and the *u area* may not be accessible when the signal is sent to the process. A solution to this problem would be to store the signal function address in the process table entry, where the kernel could check whether it should awaken the process on receipt of the signal. Alternatively, the process could immediately go back to sleep in the *sleep* algorithm, if it discovers that it should not have awakened. Nevertheless, user processes never realize that the process woke up, because the kernel encloses entry to the *sleep* algorithm in a "while" loop (recall from Chapter 2), putting the process back to sleep if the sleep event did not really occur.

Finally, the kernel does not treat "death of child" signals the same as other signals. In particular, when the process recognizes that it has received a "death of child" signal, it turns off the notification of the signal in the process table entry signal field and in the default case, it acts as if no signal had been sent. The effect of a "death of child" signal is to wake up a process sleeping at interruptible priority. If the process catches "death of child" signals, it invokes the user handler as it does for other signals. The operations that the kernel does if the process ignores "death of child" signals will be discussed in Section 7.4. Finally, if a process invokes the *signal* system call with "death of child" parameter, the kernel sends the calling process a "death of child" signal if it has child processes in the zombie state. Section 7.4 discusses the rationale for calling *signal* with the "death of child" parameter.

7.2.2 Process Groups

Although processes on a UNIX system are identified by a unique ID number, the system must sometimes identify processes by "group." For instance, processes with a common ancestor process that is a login shell are generally related, and therefore all such processes receive signals when a user hits the "delete" or "break" key or when the terminal line hangs up. The kernel uses the *process group ID* to identify groups of related processes that should receive a common signal for certain events. It saves the group ID in the process table; processes in the same process group have identical group ID's.

The *setpgrp* system call initializes the process group number of a process and sets it equal to the value of its process ID. The syntax for the system call is

grp = setpgrp();

where *grp* is the new process group number. A child retains the process group number of its parent during *fork*. *Setpgrp* also has important ramifications for setting up the control terminal of a process (see Section 10.3.5).

7.2.3 Sending Signals from Processes

Processes use the *kill* system call to send signals. The syntax for the system call is

kill(pid, signum)

where *pid* identifies the set of processes to receive the signal, and *signum* is the signal number being sent. The following list shows the correspondence between values of *pid* and sets of processes.

- If *pid* is a positive integer, the kernel sends the signal to the process with process ID *pid*.
- If *pid* is 0, the kernel sends the signal to all processes in the sender's process group.
- If *pid* is −1, the kernel sends the signal to all processes whose real user ID equals the effective user ID of the sender (Section 7.6 will define real and

effective user ID's). If the sending process has effective user ID of superuser, the kernel sends the signal to all processes except processes 0 and 1.

- If *pid* is a negative integer but not −1, the kernel sends the signal to all processes in the process group equal to the absolute value of *pid*.

In all cases, if the sending process does not have effective user ID of superuser, or its real or effective user ID do not match the real or effective user ID of the receiving process, *kill* fails.

```
#include  <signal.h>
main()
{
      register int i;

      setpgrp();
      for (i = 0;  i < 10;  i++)
      {
            if (fork() == 0)
            {
                  /* child proc */
                  if (i & 1)
                        setpgrp();
                  printf("pid = %d pgrp = %d\n", getpid(), getpgrp());
                  pause();        /* sys call to suspend execution */
            }
      }
      kill(0, SIGINT);
}
```

Figure 7.13. Sample Use of Setpgrp

In the program in Figure 7.13, the process resets its process group number and creates 10 child processes. When created, each child process has the same process group number as the parent process, but processes created during odd iterations of the loop reset their process group number. The system calls *getpid* and *getpgrp* return the process ID and the group ID of the executing process, and the *pause* system call suspends execution of the process until it receives a signal. Finally, the parent executes the *kill* system call and sends an interrupt signal to all processes in its process group. The kernel sends the signal to the 5 "even" processes that did not reset their process group, but the 5 "odd" processes continue to loop.

7.3 PROCESS TERMINATION

Processes on a UNIX system terminate by executing the *exit* system call. An *exit*ing process enters the zombie state (recall Figure 6.1), relinquishes its resources, and dismantles its context except for its slot in the process table. The syntax for the call is

    exit(status);

where the value of *status* is returned to the parent process for its examination. Processes may call *exit* explicitly or implicitly at the end of a program: the startup routine linked with all C programs calls *exit* when the program returns from the *main* function, the entry point of all programs. Alternatively, the kernel may invoke *exit* internally for a process on receipt of uncaught signals as discussed above. If so, the value of *status* is the signal number.

The system imposes no time limit on the execution of a process, and processes frequently exist for a long time. For instance, processes 0 (the swapper) and 1 (*init*) exist throughout the lifetime of a system. Other examples are *getty* processes, which monitor a terminal line, waiting for a user to log in, and special-purpose administrative processes.

```
algorithm exit
input:   return code for parent process
output: none
{
      ignore all signals;
      if (process group leader with associated control terminal)
      {
            send hangup signal to all members of process group;
            reset process group for all members to 0;
      }
      close all open files (internal version of algorithm close);
      release current directory (algorithm iput);
      release current (changed) root, if exists (algorithm iput);
      free regions, memory associated with process (algorithm freereg);
      write accounting record;
      make process state zombie
      assign parent process ID of all child processes to be init process (1);
            if any children were zombie, send death of child signal to init;
      send death of child signal to parent process;
      context switch;
}
```

Figure 7.14. Algorithm for Exit

Figure 7.14 shows the algorithm for *exit*. The kernel first disables signal handling for the process, because it no longer makes any sense to handle signals. If the *exit*ing process is a *process group leader* associated with a control terminal (see Section 10.3.5), the kernel assumes the user is not doing any useful work and sends a "hangup" signal to all processes in the process group. Thus, if a user types "end of file" (control-d character) in the login shell while some processes associated with the terminal are still alive, the *exit*ing process will send them a hangup signal. The kernel also resets the process group number to 0 for processes in the process group, because it is possible that another process will later get the process ID of the process that just *exit*ed and that it too will be a process group leader. Processes that belonged to the old process group will not belong to the later process group. The kernel then goes through the open file descriptors, *clos*ing each one internally with algorithm *close*, and releases the inodes it had accessed for the current directory and changed root (if it exists) via algorithm *iput*.

The kernel now releases all user memory by freeing the appropriate regions with algorithm *detachreg* and changes the process state to zombie. It saves the *exit* status code and the accumulated user and kernel execution time of the process and its descendants in the process table. The description of *wait* in Section 7.4 shows how a process gets the timing data for descendant processes. The kernel also *write*s an accounting record to a global accounting file, containing various run-time statistics such as user ID, CPU and memory usage, and amount of I/O for the process. User-level programs can later read the accounting file to gather various statistics, useful for performance monitoring and customer billing. Finally, the kernel disconnects the process from the process tree by making process 1 (*init*) adopt all its child processes. That is, process 1 becomes the legal parent of all live children that the *exit*ing process had created. If any of the children are zombie, the exiting process sends *init* a "death of child" signal so that *init* can remove them from the process table (see Section 7.9); the *exit*ing process sends its parent a "death of child" signal, too. In the typical scenario, the parent process executes a *wait* system call to synchronize with the *exit*ing child. The now-zombie process does a context switch so that the kernel can schedule another process to execute; the kernel never schedules a zombie process to execute.

In the program in Figure 7.15, a process creates a child process, which prints its PID and executes the *pause* system call, suspending itself until it receives a signal. The parent prints the child's PID and *exit*s, returning the child's PID as its status code. If the *exit* call were not present, the startup routine calls *exit* when the process returns from *main*. The child process spawned by the parent lives on until it receives a signal, even though the parent process is gone.

7.4 AWAITING PROCESS TERMINATION

A process can synchronize its execution with the termination of a child process by executing the *wait* system call. The syntax for the system call is

```
main()
{
      int child;

      if ((child = fork()) == 0)
      {
            printf("child PID %d\n", getpid());
            pause();        /* suspend execution until signal */
      }
      /* parent */
      printf("child PID %d\n", child);
      exit(child);
}
```

Figure 7.15. Example of Exit

$$pid = wait(stat\_addr);$$

where *pid* is the process ID of the zombie child, and *stat_addr* is the address in user space of an integer that will contain the *exit* status code of the child.

Figure 7.16 shows the algorithm for *wait*. The kernel searches for a zombie child of the process and, if there are no children, returns an error. If it finds a zombie child, it extracts the PID number and the parameter supplied to the child's *exit* call and returns those values from the system call. An *exit*ing process can thus specify various return codes to give the reason it *exit*ed, but many programs do not consistently set it in practice. The kernel adds the accumulated time the child process executed in user and in kernel mode to the appropriate fields in the parent process *u area* and, finally, releases the process table slot formerly occupied by the zombie process. The slot is now available for a new process.

If the process executing *wait* has child processes but none are zombie, it sleeps at an interruptible priority until the arrival of a signal. The kernel does not contain an explicit wake up call for a process sleeping in *wait*: such processes only wake up on receipt of signals. For any signal except "death of child," the process will react as described above. However, if the signal is "death of child," the process may respond differently.

- In the default case, it will wake up from its sleep in *wait*, and *sleep* invokes algorithm *issig* to check for signals. *Issig* (Figure 7.7) recognizes the special case of "death of child" signals and returns "false." Consequently, the kernel does not "long jump" from *sleep*, but returns to *wait*. The kernel will restart the *wait* loop, find a zombie child — at least one is guaranteed to exist, release the child's process table slot, and return from the *wait* system call.
- If the process catches "death of child" signals, the kernel arranges to call the user signal-handler routine, as it does for other signals.

```
algorithm wait
input:   address of variable to store status of exiting process
output: child ID, child exit code
{
        if (waiting process has no child processes)
              return(error);

        for (;;)       /* loop until return from inside loop */
        {
              if (waiting process has zombie child)
              {
                    pick arbitrary zombie child;
                    add child CPU usage to parent;
                    free child process table entry;
                    return(child ID, child exit code);
              }
              if (process has no children)
                    return error;
              sleep at interruptible priority (event child process exits);
        }
}
```

Figure 7.16. Algorithm for Wait

- If the process ignores "death of child" signals, the kernel restarts the *wait* loop, frees the process table slots of zombie children, and searches for more children.

For example, a user gets different results when invoking the program in Figure 7.17 with or without a parameter. Consider first the case where a user invokes the program without a parameter (*argc* is 1, the program name). The (parent) process creates 15 child processes that eventually *exit* with return code *i*, the value of the loop variable when the child was created. The kernel, executing *wait* for the parent, finds a zombie child process and returns its process ID and *exit* code. It is indeterminate which child process it finds. The C library code for the *exit* system call stores the *exit* code in bits 8 to 15 of *ret_code* and returns the child process ID for the *wait* call. Thus *ret_code* equals 256*i*, depending on the value of *i* for the child process, and *ret_val* equals the value of the child process ID.

If a user invokes the above program with a parameter (*argc* > 1), the (parent) process calls *signal* to ignore "death of child" signals. Assume the parent process sleeps in *wait* before any child processes *exit*: When a child process *exits*, it sends a "death of child" signal to the parent process; the parent process wakes up because its sleep in *wait* is at an interruptible priority. When the parent process eventually runs, it finds that the outstanding signal was for "death of child"; but because it ignores "death of child" signals, the kernel removes the entry of the zombie child from the process table and continues executing *wait* as if no signal had happened.

```
#include  <signal.h>
main(argc, argv)
      int argc;
      char *argv[];
{
      int i, ret_val, ret_code;

      if (argc >= 1)
            signal(SIGCLD, SIG_IGN);          /* ignore death of children */
      for (i = 0;  i < 15;  i++)
            if (fork() == 0)
            {
                  /* child proc here */
                  printf("child proc %x\n", getpid());
                  exit(i);
            }
      ret_val = wait(&ret_code);
      printf("wait ret_val %x ret_code %x\n", ret_val, ret_code);
}
```

Figure 7.17. Example of Wait and Ignoring Death of Child Signal

The kernel does the above procedure each time the parent receives a "death of child" signal, until it finally goes through the *wait* loop and finds that the parent has no children. The *wait* system call then returns a −1. The difference between the two invocations of the program is that the parent process *wait*s for the termination of *any* child process in the first case but *wait*s for the termination of *all* child processes in the second case.

Older versions of the UNIX system implemented the *exit* and *wait* system calls without the "death of child" signal. Instead of sending a "death of child" signal, *exit* would wake up the parent process. If the parent process was sleeping in the *wait* system call, it would wake up, find a zombie child, and return. If it was not sleeping in the *wait* system call, the wake up would have no effect; it would find a zombie child on its next *wait* call. Similarly, the *init* process would sleep in *wait*, and *exit*ing processes would wake it up if it were to adopt new zombie processes.

The problem with that implementation is that it is impossible to clean up zombie processes unless the parent executes *wait*. If a process creates many children but never executes *wait*, the process table will become cluttered with zombie children when the children *exit*. For example, consider the dispatcher program in Figure 7.18. The process *read*s its standard input file until it encounters the end of file, creating a child process for each *read*. However, the parent process does not *wait* for the termination of the child process, because it wants to dispatch processes as fast as possible and the child process may take too long until it *exit*s. If the parent makes the *signal* call to ignore "death of child"

```
#include  <signal.h>
main(argc, argv)
{
       char buf[256];

       if (argc != 1)
              signal(SIGCLD, SIG_IGN);       /* ignore death of children */
       while (read(0, buf, 256))
              if (fork() == 0)
              {
                     /* child proc here typically does something with buf */
                     exit(0);
              }
}
```

Figure 7.18. Example Depicting the Reason for Death of Child Signal

signals, the kernel will release the entries for the zombie processes automatically. Otherwise, zombie processes would eventually fill the maximum allowed slots of the process table.

7.5 INVOKING OTHER PROGRAMS

The *exec* system call invokes another program, overlaying the memory space of a process with a copy of an executable file. The contents of the user-level context that existed before the *exec* call are no longer accessible afterward except for *exec*'s parameters, which the kernel copies from the old address space to the new address space. The syntax for the system call is

    execve(filename, argv, envp)

where *filename* is the name of the executable file being invoked, *argv* is a pointer to an array of character pointers that are parameters to the executable program, and *envp* is a pointer to an array of character pointers that are the *environment* of the executed program. There are several library functions that call the *exec* system call such as *execl*, *execv*, *execle*, and so on. All call *execve* eventually, hence it is used here to specify the *exec* system call. When a program uses command line parameters, as in

    main(argc, argv)

the array *argv* is a copy of the *argv* parameter to *exec*. The character strings in the environment are of the form "name=value" and may contain useful information for programs, such as the user's home directory and a path of directories to search for executable programs. Processes can access their environment via the global

```
algorithm exec
input:  (1) file name
        (2) parameter list
        (3) environment variables list
output: none
{
        get file inode (algorithm namei);
        verify file executable, user has permission to execute;
        read file headers, check that it is a load module;
        copy exec parameters from old address space to system space;
        for (every region attached to process)
                detach all old regions (algorithm detach);
        for (every region specified in load module)
        {
                allocate new regions (algorithm allocreg);
                attach the regions (algorithm attachreg);
                load region into memory if appropriate (algorithm loadreg);
        }
        copy exec parameters into new user stack region;
        special processing for setuid programs, tracing;
        initialize user register save area for return to user mode;
        release inode of file (algorithm iput);
}
```

Figure 7.19. Algorithm for Exec

variable *environ*, initialized by the C startup routine.

Figure 7.19 shows the algorithm for the *exec* system call. *Exec* first accesses the file via algorithm *namei* to determine if it is an executable, regular (nondirectory) file and to determine if the user has permission to execute the program. The kernel then reads the file header to determine the layout of the executable file.

Figure 7.20 shows the logical format of an executable file as it exists in the file system, typically generated by the assembler or loader. It consists of four parts:

1. The primary header describes how many sections are in the file, the start address for process execution, and the *magic number*, which gives the type of the executable file.
2. Section headers describe each section in the file, giving the section size, the virtual addresses the section should occupy when running in the system, and other information.
3. The sections contain the "data," such as text, that are initially loaded in the process address space.
4. Miscellaneous sections may contain symbol tables and other data, useful for debugging.

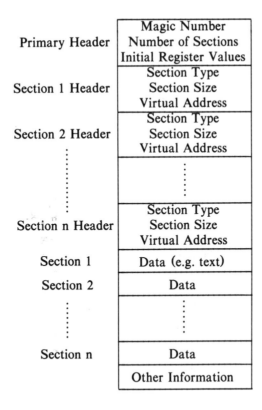

Primary Header	Magic Number
	Number of Sections
	Initial Register Values
Section 1 Header	Section Type
	Section Size
	Virtual Address
Section 2 Header	Section Type
	Section Size
	Virtual Address
⋮	⋮
Section n Header	Section Type
	Section Size
	Virtual Address
Section 1	Data (e.g. text)
Section 2	Data
⋮	⋮
Section n	Data
	Other Information

Figure 7.20. Image of an Executable File

Specific formats have evolved through the years, but all executable files have contained a primary header with a magic number.

The magic number is a short integer, which identifies the file as a load module and enables the kernel to distinguish run-time characteristics about it. For example, use of particular magic numbers on a PDP 11/70 informed the kernel that processes could use up to 128K bytes of memory instead of 64K bytes,[2] but the magic number still plays an important role in paging systems, as will be seen in Chapter 9.

---

2. The values of the magic numbers were the values of PDP 11 jump instructions; original versions of the system *executed* the instructions, and the program counter jumped to various locations depending on the size of the header and on the type of executable file being executed! This feature was no longer in use by the time the system was written in C.

At this point, the kernel has accessed the inode for the executable file and has verified that it can execute it. It is about to free the memory resources that currently form the user-level context of the process. But since the parameters to the new program are contained in the memory space about to be freed, the kernel first copies the arguments from the old memory space to a temporary buffer until it attaches the regions for the new memory space.

Because the parameters to *exec* are user addresses of arrays of character strings, the kernel copies the address of the character string and then the character string to kernel space for each character string. It may choose several places to store the character strings, dependent on the implementation. The more popular places are the kernel stack (a local array in a kernel routine), unallocated areas (such as pages) of memory that can be borrowed temporarily, or secondary memory such as a swapping device.

The simplest implementation for copying parameters to the new user-level context is to use the kernel stack. But because system configurations usually impose a limit on the size of the kernel stack and because the *exec* parameters can have arbitrary length, the scheme must be combined with another. Of the other choices, implementations use the fastest method. If it is easy to allocate pages of memory, such a method is preferable since access to primary memory is faster than access to secondary memory (such as a swapping device).

After copying the *exec* parameters to a holding place in the kernel, the kernel detaches the old regions of the process using algorithm *detachreg*. Special treatment for text regions will be discussed later in this section. At this point the process has no user-level context, so any errors that it incurs from now on result in its termination, caused by a signal. Such errors include running out of space in the kernel region table, attempting to load a program whose size exceeds the system limit, attempting to load a program whose region addresses overlap, and others. The kernel allocates and attaches regions for text and data, loading the contents of the executable file into main memory (algorithms *allocreg*, *attachreg*, and *loadreg*). The data region of a process is (initially) divided into two parts: data initialized at compile time and data not initialized at compile time ("bss"). The initial allocation and attachment of the data region is for the initialized data. The kernel then increases the size of the data region using algorithm *growreg* for the "bss" data, and initializes the value of the memory to 0. Finally, it allocates a region for the process stack, attaches it to the process, and allocates memory to store the *exec* parameters. If the kernel has saved the *exec* parameters in memory pages, it can use those pages for the stack. Otherwise, it copies the *exec* parameters to the user stack.

The kernel clears the addresses of user signal catchers from the *u area*, because those addresses are meaningless in the new user-level context. Signals that are ignored remain ignored in the new context. Then the kernel sets the saved register context for user mode, specifically setting the initial user stack pointer and program counter: The loader had written the initial program counter in the file header. The kernel takes special action for *setuid* programs and for process tracing, covered in the next section and in Chapter 11, respectively. Finally, it invokes algorithm *iput*, releasing the inode that was originally allocated in the *namei* algorithm at the beginning of *exec*. The use of *namei* and *iput* in *exec* corresponds to their use in *open*ing and *clos*ing a file; the state of a file during the *exec* call resembles that of an open file except for the absence of a file table entry. When the process "returns" from the *exec* system call, it executes the code of the new program. However, it is the same process it was before the *exec*; its process ID number does not change, nor does its position in the process hierarchy. Only the user-level context changes.

```
main()
{
        int status;
        if (fork() == 0)
                execl("/bin/date", "date", 0);
        wait(&status);
}
```

Figure 7.21. Use of Exec

For example, the program in Figure 7.21 creates a child process that invokes the *exec* system call. Immediately after the parent and child processes return from *fork*, they execute independent copies of the program. When the child process is about to invoke the *exec* call, its text region consists of the instructions for the program, its data region consists of the strings "/bin/date" and "date", and its stack contains the stack frames the process pushed to get to the *exec* call. The kernel finds the file "/bin/date" in the file system, finds that all users can execute it, and determines that it is an executable load module. By convention, the first parameter of the argument list *argv* to *exec* is the (last component of the) path name of the executable file. The process thus has access to the program name at user-level, sometimes a useful feature.[3] The kernel then copies the strings "/bin/date" and "date" to an internal holding area and frees the text, data, and stack regions occupied by the process. It allocates new text, data, and stack regions for the process, copies the instruction section of the file "/bin/date" into the text region, and copies the data section of the file into the data region. The kernel reconstructs the original parameter list (here, the character string "date") and puts it in the stack region. After the *exec* call, the child process no longer executes the

---

3. On System V for instance, the standard programs for renaming a file (*mv*), copying a file (*cp*), and linking a file (*ln*) are one executable file because they execute similar code. The process looks at the name the user used to invoke it to determine what it should do.

old program but executes the program "date": When the "date" program completes, the parent process receives its exit status from the *wait* call.

Until now, we have assumed that process text and data occupy separate sections of an executable program and, hence, separate regions of a running process. There are two advantages for keeping text and data separate: protection and sharing. If text and data were in the same region, the system could not prevent a process from overwriting its instructions, because it would not know which addresses contain instructions and which contain data. But if text and data are in separate regions, the kernel can set up hardware protection mechanisms to prevent processes from overwriting their text space. If a process mistakenly attempts to overwrite its text space, it incurs a protection fault that typically results in termination of the process.

```
#include  <signal.h>
main()
{
       int i, *ip;
       extern f(), sigcatch();

       ip = (int *)f;        /* assign ip to address of function f */
       for (i = 0;  i < 20;  i++)
              signal(i, sigcatch);
       *ip = 1;                 /* attempt to overwrite address of f */
       printf("after assign to ip\n");
       f();
}

f()
{
}

sigcatch(n)
       int n;
{
       printf("caught sig %d\n", n);
       exit(1);
}
```

Figure 7.22. Example of Program Overwriting its Text

For example, the program in Figure 7.22 assigns the pointer *ip* to the address of the function *f* and then arranges to catch all signals. If the program is compiled so that text and data are in separate regions, the process executing the program incurs a protection fault when it attempts to write the contents of *ip*, because it is writing its write-protected text region. The kernel sends a *SIGBUS* signal to the process on an AT&T 3B20 computer, although other implementations may send other signals. The process catches the signal and *exits* without executing the print statement in *main*. However, if the program were compiled so that the program text and data were part of one region (the data region), the kernel would not realize that a process was overwriting the address of the function *f*. The address of *f* contains the value 1! The process executes the print statement in *main* but executes an illegal instruction when it calls *f*. The kernel sends it a *SIGILL* signal, and the process *exits*.

Having instructions and data in separate regions makes it easier to protect against addressing errors. Early versions of the UNIX system allowed text and data to be in the same region, however, because of process size limitations imposed by PDP machines: Programs were smaller and required fewer "segmentation" registers if text and data occupied the same region. Current versions of the system do not have such stringent size limitations on processes, and future compilers will not support the option to load text and data in one region.

The second advantage of having separate regions for text and data is to allow sharing of regions. If a process cannot write its text region, its text does not change from the time the kernel loads it from the executable file. If several processes execute a file they can, therefore, share one text region, saving memory. Thus, when the kernel allocates a text region for a process in *exec*, it checks if the executable file allows its text to be shared, indicated by its magic number. If so, it follows algorithm *xalloc* to find an existing region for the file text or to assign a new one (see Figure 7.23).

In *xalloc*, the kernel searches the active region list for the file's text region, identifying it as the one whose inode pointer matches the inode of the executable file. If no such region exists, the kernel allocates a new region (algorithm *allocreg*), attaches it to the process (algorithm *attachreg*), loads it into memory (algorithm *loadreg*), and changes its protection to read-only. The latter step causes a memory protection fault if a process attempts to write the text region. If, in searching the active region list, the kernel locates a region that contains the file text, it makes sure that the region is loaded into memory (it sleeps otherwise) and attaches it to the process. The kernel unlocks the region at the conclusion of *xalloc* and decrements the region count later, when it executes *detachreg* during *exit* or *exec*. Traditional implementations of the system contain a *text table* that the kernel manipulates in the way just described for text regions. The set of text regions can thus be viewed as a modern version of the old text table.

Recall that when allocating a region for the first time in *allocreg* (Section 6.5.2), the kernel increments the reference count of the inode associated with the region, after it had incremented the reference count in *namei* (invoking *iget*) at the beginning of *exec*. Because the kernel decrements the reference count once in *iput* at the end of *exec*, the inode reference count of a (shared text) file being executed is at least 1: Therefore, if a process *unlinks* the file, its contents remain intact. The kernel no longer needs the file after loading it into memory, but it needs the pointer to the in-core inode in the region table to identify the file that corresponds

```
algorithm xalloc                /* allocate and initialize text region */
input:   inode of executable file
output: none
{
        if (executable file does not have separate text region)
                return;
        if (text region associated with text of inode)
        {
                /* text region already exists...attach to it */
                lock region;
                while (contents of region not ready yet)
                {
                        /* manipulation of reference count prevents total
                         * removal of the region.
                         */
                        increment region reference count;
                        unlock region;
                        sleep (event contents of region ready);
                        lock region;
                        decrement region reference count;
                }
                attach region to process (algorithm attachreg);
                unlock region;
                return;
        }
        /* no such text region exists---create one */
        allocate text region (algorithm allocreg); /* region is locked */
        if (inode mode has sticky bit set)
                turn on region sticky flag;
        attach region to virtual address indicated by inode file header
                                (algorithm attachreg);
        if (file specially formatted for paging system)
                /* Chapter 9 discusses this case */
        else      /* not formatted for paging system */
                read file text into region (algorithm loadreg);
        change region protection in per process region table to read only;
        unlock region;
}
```

Figure 7.23. Algorithm for Allocation of Text Regions

to the region. If the reference count were to drop to 0, the kernel could reallocate the in-core inode to another file, compromising the meaning of the inode pointer in the region table: If a user were to *exec* the new file, the kernel would find the text region of the old file by mistake. The kernel avoids this problem by incrementing the inode reference count in *allocreg*, preventing reassignment of the in-core inode.

When the process detaches the text region during *exit* or *exec*, the kernel decrements the inode reference count an extra time in *freereg*, unless the inode has the sticky-bit mode set, as will be seen.

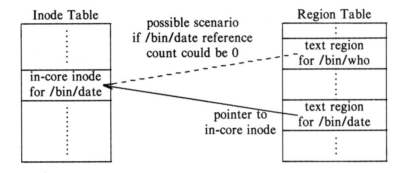

Figure 7.24. Relationship of Inode Table and Region Table for Shared Text

For example, reconsider the *exec* of "/bin/date" in Figure 7.21, and assume that the file has separate text and data sections. The first time a process executes "/bin/date", the kernel allocates a region table entry for the text (Figure 7.24) and leaves the inode reference count at 1 (after the *exec* completes). When "/bin/date" *exits*, the kernel invokes *detachreg* and *freereg*, decrementing the inode reference count to 0. However, if the kernel had not incremented the inode reference count for "/bin/date" the first time it was *exec*ed, its reference count would be 0 and the inode would be on the free list while the process was running. Suppose another process *execs* the file "/bin/who", and the kernel allocates the in-core inode previously used for "/bin/date" to "/bin/who". The kernel would search the region table for the inode for "/bin/who" but find the inode for "/bin/date" instead. Thinking that the region contains the text for "/bin/who", it would execute the wrong program. Consequently, the inode reference count for running, shared text files is at least 1, so that the kernel cannot reallocate the inode.

The capability to share text regions allows the kernel to decrease the startup time of an *exec*ed program by using the *sticky-bit*. System administrators can set the sticky-bit file mode with the *chmod* system call (and command) for frequently used executable files. When a process executes a file that has its sticky-bit set, the kernel does not release the memory allocated for text when it later detaches the region during *exit* or *exec*, even if the region reference count drops to 0. The kernel leaves the text region intact with *inode* reference count 1, even though it is no longer attached to any processes. When another process *execs* the file, it finds the region table entry for the file text. The process startup time is small, because it does not have to read the text from the file system: If the text is still in memory, the kernel does not do any I/O for the text; if the kernel has swapped the text to a swap device, it is faster to load the text from a swap device than from the file system, as will be seen in Chapter 9.

The kernel removes the entries for sticky-bit text regions in the following cases:

1. If a process *opens* the file for writing, the *write* operations will change the contents of the file, invalidating the contents of the region.
2. If a process changes the permission modes of the file (*chmod*) such that the sticky-bit is no longer set, the file should not remain in the region table.
3. If a process *unlinks* the file, no process will be able to *exec* it any more because the file has no entry in the file system; hence no new processes will access the file's region table entry. Because there is no need for the text region, the kernel can remove it to free some resources.
4. If a process unmounts the file system, the file is no longer accessible and no processes can *exec* it, so the logic of the previous case applies.
5. If the kernel runs out of space on the swap device, it attempts to free available space by freeing sticky-bit regions that are currently unused. Although other processes may need the text region soon, the kernel has more immediate needs.

The sticky text region must be removed in the first two cases because it no longer reflects the current state of the file. The kernel removes the sticky entries in the last three cases because it is pragmatic to do so. Of course, the kernel frees the region *only* if no processes currently use it (its reference count is 0); otherwise, the system calls *open*, *unlink*, and *umount* (cases 1, 3 and 4) fail.

The scenario for *exec* is slightly more complicated if a process *execs* itself. If a user types

    sh script

the shell *forks* and the child process *execs* the shell and executes the commands in the file "script". If a process *execs* itself and allows sharing of its text region, the kernel must avoid deadlocks over the inode and region locks. That is, the kernel cannot lock the "old" text region, hold the lock, and then attempt to lock the "new" text region, because the old and new regions are one region. Instead, the kernel simply leaves the old text region attached to the process, since it will be reused anyway.

Processes usually invoke *exec* after *fork*; the child process thus copies the parent address space during the *fork*, discards it during the *exec*, and executes a different program image than the parent process. Would it not be more natural to combine the two system calls into one to invoke a program and run it as a new process? Ritchie surmises that *fork* and *exec* exist as separate system calls because, when designing the UNIX system, he and Thompson were able to add the *fork* system call without having to change much code in the existing kernel (see page 1584 of [Ritchie 84a]). But separation of the *fork* and *exec* system calls is functionally important too, because the processes can manipulate their standard input and standard output file descriptors independently to set up pipes more elegantly than if the two system calls were combined. The example of the shell in Section 7.8 highlights this feature.

7.6 THE USER ID OF A PROCESS

The kernel associates two user IDs with a process, independent of the process ID: the *real user ID* and the *effective user ID* or *setuid* (set user ID). The real user ID identifies the user who is responsible for the running process. The effective user ID is used to assign ownership of newly created files, to check file access permissions, and to check permission to send signals to processes via the *kill* system call. The kernel allows a process to change its effective user ID when it *execs* a *setuid* program or when it invokes the *setuid* system call explicitly.

A *setuid* program is an executable file that has the *setuid* bit set in its permission mode field. When a process *execs* a *setuid* program, the kernel sets the effective user ID fields in the process table and *u area* to the owner ID of the file. To distinguish the two fields, let us call the field in the process table the *saved* user ID. An example illustrates the difference between the two fields.

The syntax for the *setuid* system call is

setuid(uid)

where *uid* is the new user ID, and its result depends on the current value of the effective user ID. If the effective user ID of the calling process is superuser, the kernel resets the real and effective user ID fields in the process table and *u area* to *uid*. If the effective user ID of the calling process is not superuser, the kernel resets the effective user ID in the *u area* to *uid* if *uid* has the value of the real user ID or if it has the value of the saved user ID. Otherwise, the system call returns an error. Generally, a process inherits its real and effective user IDs from its parent during the *fork* system call and maintains their values across *exec* system calls.

The program in Figure 7.25 demonstrates the *setuid* system call. Suppose the executable file produced by compiling the program has owner "maury" (user ID 8319), its *setuid* bit is on, and all users have permission to execute it. Further, assume that users "mjb" (user ID 5088) and "maury" own the files of their respective names, and that both files have read-only permission for their owners. User "mjb" sees the following output when executing the program:

```
uid 5088 euid 8319
fdmjb −1 fdmaury 3
after setuid(5088): uid 5088 euid 5088
fdmjb 4 fdmaury −1
after setuid(8319): uid 5088 euid 8319
```

The system calls *getuid* and *geteuid* return the real and effective user IDs of the process, 5088 and 8319 respectively for user "mjb". Therefore, the process cannot *open* file "mjb", because its effective user ID (8319) does not have read permission

```
#include  <fcntl.h>
main()
{
        int uid, euid, fdmjb, fdmaury;

        uid = getuid();              /* get real UID */
        euid = geteuid();        /* get effective UID */
        printf("uid %d euid %d\n", uid, euid);

        fdmjb = open("mjb", O_RDONLY);
        fdmaury = open("maury", O_RDONLY);
        printf("fdmjb %d fdmaury %d\n", fdmjb, fdmaury);

        setuid(uid);
        printf("after setuid(%d): uid %d euid %d\n", uid, getuid(), geteuid());

        fdmjb = open("mjb", O_RDONLY);
        fdmaury = open("maury", O_RDONLY);
        printf("fdmjb %d fdmaury %d\n", fdmjb, fdmaury);

        setuid(euid);
        printf("after setuid(%d): uid %d euid %d\n", euid, getuid(), geteuid());
}
```

Figure 7.25. Example of Execution of Setuid Program

for the file, but the process can *open* file "maury". After calling *setuid* to reset the effective user ID of the process to the real user ID ("mjb"), the second print statement prints values 5088 and 5088, the user ID of "mjb". Now the process can *open* the file "mjb", because its effective user ID has read permission on the file, but the process cannot open file "maury". Finally, after calling *setuid* to reset the effective user ID to the saved *setuid* value of the program (8319), the third print statement prints values 5088 and 8319 again. The last case shows that a process can *exec* a *setuid* program and toggle its effective user ID between its real user ID and its *exec*ed *setuid*.

User "maury" sees the following output when executing the program:

```
uid 8319 euid 8319
fdmjb −1 fdmaury 3
after setuid(8319): uid 8319 euid 8319
fdmjb −1 fdmaury 4
after setuid(8319): uid 8319 euid 8319
```

The real and effective user IDs are always 8319: the process can never *open* file "mjb", but it can *open* file "maury". The effective user ID stored in the *u area* is the result of the most recent *setuid* system call or the *exec* of a *setuid* program; it is solely responsible for determining file access permissions. The *saved* user ID in the process table allows a process to reset its effective user ID to it by executing the *setuid* system call, thus recalling its original, effective user ID.

The *login* program executed by users when logging into the system is a typical program that calls the *setuid* system call. *Login* is *setuid* to root (superuser) and therefore runs with *effective user ID* root. It queries the user for various information such as name and password and, when satisfied, invokes the *setuid* system call to set its real and effective user ID to that of the user trying to log in (found in fields in the file "/etc/passwd"). *Login* finally *execs* the shell, which runs with its real and effective user IDs set for the appropriate user.

The *mkdir* command is a typical *setuid* program. Recall from Section 5.8 that only a process with effective user ID superuser can create a directory. To allow ordinary users the capability to create directories, the *mkdir* command is a *setuid* program owned by root (superuser permission). When executing *mkdir*, the process runs with superuser access rights, creates the directory for the user via *mknod*, and then changes the owner and access permissions of the directory to that of the real user.

7.7 CHANGING THE SIZE OF A PROCESS

A process may increase or decrease the size of its data region by using the *brk* system call. The syntax for the *brk* system call is

    brk(endds);

where *endds* becomes the value of the highest virtual address of the data region of the process (called its *break* value). Alternatively, a user can call

    oldendds = sbrk(increment);

where *increment* changes the current break value by the specified number of bytes, and *oldendds* is the break value before the call. *Sbrk* is a C library routine that calls *brk*. If the data space of the process increases as a result of the call, the newly allocated data space is virtually contiguous to the old data space; that is, the virtual address space of the process extends continuously into the newly allocated data space. The kernel checks that the new process size is less than the system maximum and that the new data region does not overlap previously assigned virtual address space (Figure 7.26). If all checks pass, the kernel invokes *growreg* to allocate auxiliary memory (e.g., page tables) for the data region and increments the process size field. On a swapping system, it also attempts to allocate memory for the new space and clear its contents to zero; if there is no room in memory, it swaps the process out to get the new space (explained in detail in Chapter 9). If the process is calling *brk* to free previously allocated space, the kernel releases the memory; if the process accesses virtual addresses in pages that it had released, it incurs a memory fault.

```
algorithm brk
input:   new break value
output: old break value
{
        lock process data region;
        if (region size increasing)
                if (new region size is illegal)
                {
                        unlock data region;
                        return(error);
                }
        change region size (algorithm growreg);
        zero out addresses in new data space;
        unlock process data region;
}
```

Figure 7.26. Algorithm for Brk

Figure 7.27 shows a program that uses *brk* and sample output when run on an AT&T 3B20 computer. After arranging to catch *segmentation violation* signals by calling *signal*, the process calls *sbrk* and prints out its initial *break* value. Then it loops, incrementing a character pointer and writing its contents, until it attempts to write an address beyond its data region, causing a *segmentation violation* signal. Catching the signal, *catcher* calls *sbrk* to allocate another 256 bytes in the data region; the process continues from where it was interrupted in the loop, writing into the newly acquired data space. When it loops beyond the data region again, the entire procedure repeats. An interesting phenomenon occurs on machines whose memory is allocated by pages, as on the 3B20. A page is the smallest unit of memory that is protected by the hardware and so the hardware cannot detect when a process writes addresses that are beyond its *break* value but still on a "semilegal" page. This is shown by the output in Figure 7.27: the first *sbrk* call returns 140924, meaning that there are 388 bytes left on the page, which contain 2K bytes on a 3B20. But the process will fault only when it addresses the next page, at address 141312. *Catcher* adds 256 to the *break* value, making it 141180, still below the address of the next page. Hence, the process immediately faults again, printing the same address, 141312. After the next *sbrk*, the kernel allocates a new page of memory, so the process can address another 2K bytes, to 143360, even though the *break* value is not that high. When it faults, it will call *sbrk* 8 times until it can continue. Thus, a process can sometimes cheat beyond its official *break* value, although it is poor programming style.

The kernel automatically extends the size of the user stack when it overflows, following an algorithm similar to that for *brk*. A process originally contains enough (user) stack space to hold the *exec* parameters, but it overflows its initial stack area as it pushes data onto the stack during execution. When it overflows its

```
#include  <signal.h>
char *cp;
int callno;

main()
{
      char *sbrk();
      extern catcher();

      signal(SIGSEGV, catcher);
      cp = sbrk(0);
      printf("original brk value %u\n", cp);
      for (;;)
              *cp++ = 1;
}

catcher(signo)
      int signo;
{

      callno++;
      printf("caught sig %d %dth call at addr %u\n", signo, callno, cp);
      sbrk(256);
      signal(SIGSEGV, catcher);
}
```

```
original brk value 140924
caught sig 11 1th call at addr 141312
caught sig 11 2th call at addr 141312
caught sig 11 3th call at addr 143360
        . . . (same address printed out to 10th call)
caught sig 11 10th call at addr 143360
caught sig 11 11th call at addr 145408
        . . . (same address printed out to 18th call)
caught sig 11 18th call at addr 145408
caught sig 11 19th call at addr 145408
                    .
                    .
```

Figure 7.27. Use of Brk and Sample Output

stack, the machine incurs a memory fault, because the process is attempting to access a location outside its address space. The kernel determines that the reason for the memory fault was because of stack overflow by comparing the value of the (faulted) stack pointer to the size of the stack region. The kernel allocates new space for the stack region exactly as it allocates space for *brk*, above. When it

```
/* read command line until "end of file" */
while (read(stdin, buffer, numchars))
{
      /* parse command line */
      if (/* command line contains & */)
            amper = 1;
      else
            amper = 0;
      /* for commands not part of the shell command language */
      if (fork() == 0)
      {
            /* redirection of IO? */
            if (/* redirect output */)
            {
                  fd = creat(newfile, fmask);
                  close(stdout);
                  dup(fd);
                  close(fd);
                  /* stdout is now redirected */
            }
            if (/* piping */ )
            {
                  pipe(fildes);
```

Figure 7.28. Main Loop of the Shell

returns from the interrupt, the process has the necessary stack space to continue.

7.8 THE SHELL

This chapter has covered enough material to explain how the *shell* works. The shell is more complex than described here, but the process relationships are illustrative of the real program. Figure 7.28 shows the main loop of the shell and demonstrates asynchronous execution, redirection of output, and pipes.

The shell *read*s a command line from its standard input and interprets it according to a fixed set of rules. The standard input and standard output file descriptors for the login shell are usually the terminal on which the user logged in, as will be seen in Chapter 10. If the shell recognizes the input string as a built-in command (for example, commands *cd*, *for*, *while* and others), it executes the command internally without creating new processes; otherwise, it assumes the command is the name of an executable file.

```
                    if (fork() == 0)
                    {
                        /* first component of command line */
                        close(stdout);
                        dup(fildes[1]);
                        close(fildes[1]);
                        close(fildes[0]);
                        /* stdout now goes to pipe */
                        /* child process does command */
                        execlp(command1, command1, 0);
                    }
                    /* 2nd command component of command line */
                    close(stdin);
                    dup(fildes[0]);
                    close(fildes[0]);
                    close(fildes[1]);
                    /* standard input now comes from pipe */
                }
                execve(command2, command2, 0);
            }
            /* parent continues over here...
             * waits for child to exit if required
             */
            if (amper == 0)
                retid = wait(&status);
    }
```

Figure 7.28. Main Loop of the Shell (continued)

The simplest command lines contain a program name and some parameters, such as

who
grep −n include *.c
ls −l

The shell *fork*s and creates a child process, which *exec*s the program that the user specified on the command line. The parent process, the shell that the user is using, *wait*s until the child process *exit*s from the command and then loops back to *read* the next command.

To run a process asynchronously (in the background), as in

nroff −mm bigdocument &

the shell sets an internal variable *amper* when it parses the ampersand character. If it finds the variable set at the end of the loop, it does not execute *wait* but immediately restarts the loop and *read*s the next command line.

The figure shows that the child process has access to a copy of the shell command line after the *fork*. To redirect standard output to a file, as in

nroff —mm bigdocument > output

the child *creat*s the output file specified on the command line; if the *creat* fails (for creating a file in a directory with wrong permissions, for example), the child would *exit* immediately. But if the *creat* succeeds, the child *closes* its previous standard output file and *dups* the file descriptor of the new output file. The standard output file descriptor now refers to the redirected output file. The child process *closes* the file descriptor obtained from *creat* to conserve file descriptors for the *exec*ed program. The shell redirects standard input and standard error files in a similar way.

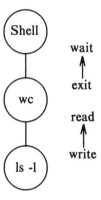

Figure 7.29. Relationship of Processes for ls —l | wc

The code shows how the shell could handle a command line with a single *pipe*, as in

ls —l | wc

After the parent process *fork*s and creates a child process, the child creates a *pipe*. The child process then *fork*s; it and its child each handle one component of the command line. The grandchild process created by the second *fork* executes the first command component (*ls*): It writes to the *pipe*, so it closes its standard output file descriptor, *dups* the pipe write descriptor, and *closes* the original pipe write descriptor since it is unnecessary. The parent (*wc*) of the last child process (*ls*) is the child of the original shell process (see Figure 7.29). This process (*wc*) *closes* its standard input file and *dups* the pipe read descriptor, causing it to become the standard input file descriptor. It then *closes* the original pipe read descriptor since it no longer needs it, and *exec*s the second command component of the original command line. The two processes that execute the command line execute asynchronously, and the output of one process goes to the input of the other process. The parent shell meanwhile *wait*s for its child process (*wc*) to *exit*, then proceeds as usual: The entire command line completes when *wc exit*s. The shell loops and *read*s the next command.

7.9 SYSTEM BOOT AND THE INIT PROCESS

To initialize a system from an inactive state, an administrator goes through a "bootstrap" sequence: The administrator "boots" the system. Boot procedures vary according to machine type, but the goal is common to all machines: to get a copy of the operating system into machine memory and to start executing it. This is usually done in a series of stages; hence the name bootstrap. The administrator may set switches on the computer console to specify the address of a special hard-coded bootstrap program or just push a single button that instructs the machine to load a bootstrap program from its microcode. This program may consist of only a few instructions that instruct the machine to execute another program. On UNIX systems, the bootstrap procedure eventually reads the boot block (block 0) of a disk, and loads it into memory. The program contained in the boot block loads the kernel from the file system (from the file "/unix", for example, or another name specified by an administrator). After the kernel is loaded in memory, the boot program transfers control to the start address of the kernel, and the kernel starts running (algorithm *start*, Figure 7.30).

The kernel initializes its internal data structures. For instance, it constructs the linked lists of free buffers and inodes, constructs hash queues for buffers and inodes, initializes region structures, page table entries, and so on. After completing the initialization phase, it *mount*s the root file system onto root ("/") and fashions the environment for process 0, creating a *u area*, initializing slot 0 in the process table and making root the current directory of process 0, among other things.

When the environment of process 0 is set up, the system is running as process 0. Process 0 *fork*s, invoking the *fork* algorithm directly from the kernel, because it is executing in kernel mode. The new process, process 1, running in kernel mode, creates its user-level context by allocating a data region and attaching it to its address space. It grows the region to its proper size and copies code (described shortly) from the kernel address space to the new region: This code now forms the user-level context of process 1. Process 1 then sets up the saved user register context, "returns" from kernel to user mode, and executes the code it had just copied from the kernel. Process 1 is a user-level process as opposed to process 0, which is a kernel-level process that executes in kernel mode. The text for process 1, copied from the kernel, consists of a call to the *exec* system call to execute the program "/etc/init". Process 1 calls *exec* and executes the program in the normal fashion. Process 1 is commonly called *init* because it is responsible for initialization of new processes.

Why does the kernel copy the code for the *exec* system call to the user address space of process 1? It could invoke an internal version of *exec* directly from the

```
algorithm start                /* system startup procedure */
input:  none
output: none
{
        initialize all kernel data structures;
        pseudo-mount of root;
        hand-craft environment of process 0;
        fork process 1:
        {
                /* process 1 in here */
                allocate region;
                attach region to init address space;
                grow region to accommodate code about to copy in;
                copy code from kernel space to init user space to exec init;
                change mode: return from kernel to user mode;
                /* init never gets here---as result of above change mode,
                 * init exec's /etc/init and becomes a "normal" user process
                 * with respect to invocation of system calls
                 */
        }
        /* proc 0 continues here */
        fork kernel processes;
        /* process 0 invokes the swapper to manage the allocation of
         * process address space to main memory and the swap devices.
         * This is an infinite loop;  process 0 usually sleeps in the
         * loop unless there is work for it to do.
         */
        execute code for swapper algorithm;
}
```

Figure 7.30. Algorithm for Booting the System

kernel, but that would be more complicated than the implementation just described. To follow the latter procedure, *exec* would have to parse file names in kernel space, not just in user space, as in the current implementation. Such generality, needed only for *init*, would complicate the *exec* code and slow its performance in more common cases.

The *init* process (Figure 7.31) is a process dispatcher, spawning processes that allow users to log in to the system, among others. *Init* reads the file "/etc/inittab" for instructions about which processes to spawn. The file "/etc/inittab" contains lines that contain an "id," a state identifier (single user, multi-user, etc.), an "action" (see exercise 7.43), and a program specification (see Figure 7.32). *Init* reads the file and, if the *state* in which it was invoked matches the state identifier of a line, creates a process that executes the given program specification. For example, when invoking *init* for the multi-user state (state 2), *init* typically spawns

```
algorithm init          /* init process, process 1 of the system */
input:  none
output: none
{
     fd = open("/etc/inittab", O_RDONLY);
     while (line_read(fd, buffer))
     {
          /* read every line of file */
          if (invoked state != buffer state)
               continue;        /* loop back to while */
          /* state matched */
          if (fork() == 0)
          {
               execl("process specified in buffer");
               exit();
          }
          /* init process does not wait */
          /* loop back to while */
     }

     while ((id = wait((int *) 0)) != -1)
     {
          /* check here if a spawned child died;
           * consider respawning it */
          /* otherwise, just continue */
     }
}
```

Figure 7.31. Algorithm for Init

```
Format: identifier, state, action, process specification
Fields separated by colons.
Comment at end of line preceded by '#'


co::respawn:/etc/getty console console          # Console in machine room
46:2:respawn:/etc/getty -t 60 tty46 4800H       # comments here
```

Figure 7.32. Sample Inittab File

getty processes to monitor the terminal lines configured on a system. When a user successfully logs in, *getty* goes through a *login* procedure and *execs* a login shell, described in Chapter 10. Meanwhile, *init* executes the *wait* system call, monitoring the death of its child processes and the death of processes "orphaned" by *exit*ing parents.

Processes in the UNIX system are either user processes, daemon processes, or kernel processes. Most processes on typical systems are user processes, associated with users at a terminal. *Daemon* processes are not associated with any users but do system-wide functions, such as administration and control of networks, execution of time-dependent activities, line printer spooling, and so on. *Init* may spawn daemon processes that exist throughout the lifetime of the system or, on occasion, users may spawn them. They are like user processes in that they run at user mode and make system calls to access system services.

Kernel processes execute only in kernel mode. Process 0 spawns kernel processes, such as the page-reclaiming process *vhand*, and then becomes the *swapper* process. Kernel processes are similar to daemon processes in that they provide system-wide services, but they have greater control over their execution priorities since their code is part of the kernel. They can access kernel algorithms and data structures directly without the use of system calls, so they are extremely powerful. However, they are not as flexible as daemon processes, because the kernel must be recompiled to change them.

7.10 SUMMARY

This chapter has discussed the system calls that manipulate the process context and control its execution. The *fork* system call creates a new process by duplicating all the regions attached to the parent process. The tricky part of the *fork* implementation is to initialize the saved register context of the child process, so that it starts executing inside the *fork* system call and recognizes that it is the child process. All processes terminate in a call to the *exit* system call, which detaches the regions of a process and sends a "death of child" signal to its parent. A parent process can synchronize execution with the termination of a child process with the *wait* system call. The *exec* system call allows a process to invoke other programs, overlaying its address space with the contents of an executable file. The kernel detaches the old process regions and allocates new regions, corresponding to the executable file. Shared-text files and use of the sticky-bit mode improve memory utilization and the startup time of *exec*ed programs. The system allows ordinary users to execute with the privileges of other users, possibly superuser, with *setuid* programs and use of the *setuid* system call. The *brk* system call allows a process to change the size of its data region. Processes control their reaction to signals with the *signal* system call. When they catch a signal, the kernel changes the user stack and the user saved register context to set up the call to the signal handler. Processes can send signals with the *kill* system call, and they can control receipt of signals designated for particular process groups through the *setpgrp* system call.

The shell and *init* use standard system calls to provide sophisticated functions normally found in the kernel of other systems. The shell uses the system calls to interpret user commands, redirecting standard input, standard output and standard error, spawning processes, setting up pipes between spawned processes, synchronizing execution with child processes, and recording the exit status of commands. Similarly, *init* spawns various processes, particularly to control terminal execution. When such a process *exits*, *init* can respawn a new process for the same function, if so specified in the file "/etc/inittab".

7.11 EXERCISES

1. Run the program in Figure 7.33 at the terminal. Redirect its standard output to a file and compare the results.

```
main()
{
        printf("hello\n");
        if (fork() == 0)
                printf("world\n");
}
```

Figure 7.33. Fork and the Standard I/O Package

2. Describe what happens in the program in Figure 7.34 and compare to the results of Figure 7.4.
3. Reconsider the program in Figure 7.5, where two processes exchange messages through a pair of pipes. What happens if they try to exchange messages through one pipe?
4. In general, could there be any loss of information if a process receives several instances of a signal before it has a chance to react? (Consider a process that counts the number of interrupt signals it receives.) Should this problem be fixed?
5. Describe an implementation of the *kill* system call.
6. The program in Figure 7.35 catches "death of child" signals, and like many signal-catcher functions, resets the signal catcher. What happens in the program?
7. When a process receives certain signals and does not handle them, the kernel dumps an image of the process as it existed when it received the signal. The kernel creates a file called "core" in the current directory of the process and copies the *u area*, text, data, and stack regions into the file. A user can subsequently investigate the dumped image of the process with standard debugging tools. Describe an algorithm the kernel could follow to create a core file. What should the algorithm do if a file "core" already exists in the current directory? What should the kernel do if multiple processes dump "core" files in one directory?
8. Reconsider the program in Figure 7.12 where a process bombards another process with signals that the second process catches. Discuss what would happen if the signal-handling algorithm were changed in either of the following two ways:

```
#include   <fcntl.h>
int fdrd, fdwt;
char c;

main(argc, argv)
        int argc;
        char *argv[];
{
        if (argc != 3)
                exit(1);
        fork();



        if ((fdrd = open(argv[1], O_RDONLY)) == -1)
                exit(1);
        if ((((fdwt = creat(argv[2], 0666)) == -1) &&
                        ((fdwt = open(argv[2], 0_WRONLY)) == -1))
                exit(1);
        rdwrt();
}
rdwrt()
{
        for (;;)
        {
                if (read(fdrd, &c, 1) != 1)
                        return;
                write(fdwt, &c, 1);
        }
}
```

Figure 7.34. Program where Parent and Child Do Not Share File Access

- The kernel does not change the signal-handling function until the user explicitly requests to do so;
- The kernel causes the process to ignore the signal until the user calls *signal* again.

9. Redesign the algorithm for handling signals such that the kernel automatically arranges for a process to ignore further instances of a signal it is handling until the signal handler returns. How can the kernel find out when the signal handler, running in user mode, returns? This specification is closer to the treatment of signals on BSD systems.

* 10. If a process receives a signal while sleeping at an interruptible priority in a system call, it *longjmp*s out of the system call. The kernel arranges for the process to execute its signal handler, if specified; when the process returns from the signal handler, it appears to have returned from the system call with an error indication (interrupted) on System V. The BSD system automatically restarts the system call for the process. How can this feature be implemented?

```
#include  <signal.h>
main()
{
        extern catcher();

        signal(SIGCLD, catcher);
        if (fork() == 0)
                exit();
        /* pause suspends execution until receipt of a signal */
        pause();
}

catcher()
{
        printf("parent caught sig\n");
        signal(SIGCLD, catcher);
}
```

Figure 7.35. Catching Death of Child Signals

11. The conventional implementation of the *mkdir* command invokes the *mknod* system call to create the directory node, then calls the *link* system call twice to link the directory entries "." and ".." to the directory node and its parent directory. Without the three operations, the directory will not be in the correct format. What happens if *mkdir* receives a signal while executing? What if the signal is *SIGKILL*, which cannot be caught? Reconsider this problem if the system were to implement a *mkdir* system call.

12. A process checks for signals when it enters or leaves the sleep state (if it sleeps at an interruptible priority) and when it returns to user mode from the kernel after completion of a system call or after handling an interrupt. Why does the process not have to check for signals when entering the system for execution of a system call?

* 13. Suppose a process is about to return to user mode after executing a system call, and it finds that it has no outstanding signals. Immediately after checking, the kernel handles an interrupt and sends the process a signal. (For instance, a user hits the "break" key.) What does the process do when the kernel returns from the interrupt?

* 14. If several signals are sent to a process simultaneously, the kernel handles them in the order that they are listed in the manual. Given the three possibilities for responding to receipt of a signal — catching the signals, *exit*ing after dumping a core image of the process, and *exit*ing without dumping a core image of the process — is there a better order for handling simultaneous signals? For example, if a process receives a quit signal (causes a core dump) and an interrupt signal (no core dump), does it make more sense to handle the quit signal or the interrupt signal first?

15. Implement a new system call

        newpgrp(pid, ngrp);

that resets the process group of another process, identified by process ID *pid* to *ngrp*. Discuss possible uses and dangers of such a system call.

16. Comment on the following statement: A process can sleep on any event in the *wait* algorithm, and the system would work correctly.

17. Consider implementation of a new system call,

    nowait(pid);

    where the process ID *pid* identifies a child of the process issuing the call. When issuing the call, the process informs the kernel that it will never *wait* for the child process to *exit*, so that the kernel can immediately clean up the child process slot when the child dies. How could the kernel implement such a solution? Discuss the merits of such a system call and compare it to the use of "death of child" signals.

18. The C loader automatically includes a startup routine that calls the function *main* in the user program. If the user program does not call *exit* internally, the startup routine calls *exit* for the user after the return from *main*. What would happen if the call to *exit* were missing from the startup routine (because of a bug in the loader) when the process returns from *main*?

19. What information does *wait* find when the child process invokes *exit* without a parameter? That is, the child process calls *exit()* instead of *exit(n)*. If a programmer consistently invokes *exit* without a parameter, how predictable is the value that *wait* examines? Demonstrate and prove your claim.

20. Describe what happens when a process executing the program in Figure 7.36 *execs* itself. How does the kernel avoid deadlocks over locked inodes?

```
main(argc, argv)
     int argc;
     char *argv[];
{
     execl(argv[0], argv[0], 0);
}
```

Figure 7.36. An Interesting Program

21. By convention, the first argument to *exec* is the (last component of the) file name that the process executes. What happens when a user executes the program in Figure 7.37. What happens if "a.out" is the load module produced by compiling the program in Figure 7.36?

22. Suppose the C language supported a new data type "read-only," such that a process incurs a protection fault whenever it attempts to write "read-only" data. Describe an implementation. (Hint: Compare to shared text.) What algorithms in the kernel change? What other objects could one consider for implementation as regions?

23. Describe how the algorithms for *open*, *chmod*, *unlink*, and *unmount* change for sticky-bit files. For example, what should the kernel do with a sticky-bit file when the file is *unlink*ed?

24. The superuser is the only user who has permission to *write* the password file "/etc/passwd", preventing malicious or errant users from corrupting its contents. The *passwd* program allows users to change their password entry, but it must make sure that they do not change other people's entries. How should it work?

```
main()
{
        if (fork() == 0)
        {
                execl("a.out", 0);
                printf("exec failed\n");
        }
}
```

Figure 7.37. An Unconventional Program

* 25. Explain the security problem that exists if a *setuid* program is not write-protected.
26. Execute the following sequence of shell commands, where the file "a.out" is an executable file.

    chmod 4777 a.out
    chown root a.out

The *chmod* command turns on the *setuid* bit (the 4 in 4777), and the owner "root" is conventionally the superuser. Can execution of such a sequence allow a simple breach of security?
27. What happens if you run the program in Figure 7.38? Why?

```
main()
{
        char *endpt;
        char *sbrk();
        int brk();

        endpt = sbrk(0);
        printf("endpt = %ud after sbrk\n", (int) endpt);

        while (endpt--)
        {
                if (brk(endpt) == -1)
                {
                        printf("brk of %ud failed\n", endpt);
                        exit();
                }
        }
}
```

Figure 7.38. A Tight Squeeze

28. The library routine *malloc* allocates more data space to a process by invoking the *brk* system call, and the library routine *free* releases memory previously allocated by malloc. The syntax for the calls is

```
ptr = malloc(size);
free(ptr);
```

where *size* is an unsigned integer representing the number of bytes to allocate, and *ptr* is a character pointer that points to the newly acquired space. When used as a parameter for free, *ptr* must have been previously returned by malloc. Implement the library routines.

29. What happens when running the program in Figure 7.39? Compare to the results predicted by the system manual.

```
main()
{
        int i;
        char *cp;
        extern char *sbrk();

        cp = sbrk(10);
        for (i = 0;  i < 10;  i++)
              *cp++ = 'a' + i;
        sbrk(-10);
        cp = sbrk(10);
        for (i = 0;  i < 10;  i++)
              printf("char %d = '%c'\n", i, *cp++);
}
```

Figure 7.39. A Simple Sbrk Example

30. When the shell creates a new process to execute a command, how does it know that the file is executable? If it is executable, how does it distinguish between a shell script and a file produced by a compilation? What is the correct sequence for checking the above cases?

31. The shell symbol ">>" appends output to the specified file: for example,

    run >> outfile

*creat*s the file "outfile" if it does not already exist and *write*s the file, or it *open*s the file and *write*s after the existing data. Write code to implement this.

```
main()
{
      exit(0);
}
```

Figure 7.40. Truth Program

32. The shell tests the *exit* return from a process, treating a 0 value as true and a non-0 value as false (note the inconsistency with C). Suppose the name of the executable file corresponding to the program in Figure 7.40 is *truth*. Describe what happens

when the shell executes the following loop. Enhance the sample shell code to handle this case.

```
while truth
do
truth &
done
```

33. Why must the shell create the processes to handle the two command components of a pipeline in the indicated order (Figure 7.29)?

34. Make the sample code for the shell loop more general in how it handles pipes. That is, allow it to handle an arbitrary number of pipes on the command line.

35. The environment variable PATH describes the ordered set of directories that the shell should search for executable files. The library functions *execlp* and *execvp* prepend directories listed in PATH to file name arguments that do not begin with a slash character. Implement these functions.

* 36. A superuser should set up the PATH environment variable so that the shell does *not* search for executable files in the current directory. What security problem exists if it attempts to execute files in the current directory?

37. How does the shell handle the *cd* (change directory) command? For the command line

```
cd pathname &
```

what does the shell do?

38. When the user types a "delete" or "break" key at the terminal, the terminal driver sends an interrupt signal to all processes in the process group of the login shell. The user intends to stop processes spawned by the shell but probably does not want to log off. How should the shell loop in Figure 7.28 be enhanced?

39. The user can type the command

```
nohup command_line
```

to disallow receipt of hangup signals and quit signals in the processes generated for "command_line." How should the shell loop in Figure 7.28 handle this?

40. Consider the sequence of shell commands

```
nroff −mm bigfile1 > big1out &
nroff −mm bigfile2 > big2out
```

and reexamine the shell loop shown in Figure 7.28. What would happen if the first *nroff* finished executing before the second one? How should the code for the shell loop be modified to handle this case correctly?

41. When executing untested programs from the shell, a common error message printed by the shell is "Bus error — core dumped." The program apparently did something illegal; how does the shell know that it should print an error message?

42. Only one *init* process can execute as process 1 on a system. However, a system administrator can change the state of the system by invoking *init*. For example, the system comes up in single user state when it is booted, meaning that the system console is active but user terminals are not. A system administrator types the command

    init 2

at the console to change the state of *init* to state 2 (multi-user). The console shell *forks* and *execs* *init*. What should happen in the system, given that only one *init* process should be active?

43. The format of entries in the file "/etc/inittab" allows specification of an action associated with each generated process. For example, the action typically associated with *getty* is *respawn*, meaning that *init* should recreate the process if it dies. Practically, this means that *init* will spawn another *getty* process when a user logs off, allowing another user to access the now inoperative terminal line. How can *init* implement the respawn action?

44. Several kernel algorithms require a search of the process table. The search time can be improved by use of parent, child, and sibling pointers: The parent pointer points to the parent of the process, the child pointer points to any child process, and the sibling pointer points to another process with the same parent. A process finds all its children by following its child pointer and then following the sibling pointers (loops are illegal). What algorithms benefit from this implementation? What algorithms must remain the same?

8

PROCESS SCHEDULING AND TIME

On a time sharing system, the kernel allocates the CPU to a process for a period of time called a time slice or time quantum, preempts the process and schedules another one when the time slice expires, and reschedules the process to continue execution at a later time. The scheduler function on the UNIX system uses relative time of execution as a parameter to determine which process to schedule next. Every active process has a scheduling priority; the kernel switches context to that of the process with the highest priority when it does a context switch. The kernel recalculates the priority of the running process when it returns from kernel mode to user mode, and it periodically readjusts the priority of every "ready-to-run" process in user mode.

Some user processes also have a need to know about time: For example, the *time* command prints the time it took for another command to execute, and the *date* command prints the date and time of day. Various time-related system calls allow processes to set or retrieve kernel time values or to ascertain the amount of process CPU usage. The system keeps time with a hardware clock that interrupts the CPU at a fixed, hardware-dependent rate, typically between 50 and 100 times a second. Each occurrence of a clock interrupt is called a *clock tick*. This chapter explores time related activities on the UNIX system, considering process scheduling, system calls for time, and the functions of the clock interrupt handler.

8.1 PROCESS SCHEDULING

The scheduler on the UNIX system belongs to the general class of operating system schedulers known as *round robin with multilevel feedback*, meaning that the kernel allocates the CPU to a process for a time quantum, preempts a process that exceeds its time quantum, and feeds it back into one of several priority queues. A process may need many iterations through the "feedback loop" before it finishes. When the kernel does a context switch and restores the context of a process, the process resumes execution from the point where it had been suspended.

```
algorithm schedule_process
input:  none
output: none
{
        while (no process picked to execute)
        {
                for (every process on run queue)
                        pick highest priority process that is loaded in memory;
                if (no process eligible to execute)
                        idle the machine;
                        /* interrupt takes machine out of idle state */
        }
        remove chosen process from run queue;
        switch context to that of chosen process, resume its execution;
}
```

Figure 8.1. Algorithm for Process Scheduling

8.1.1 Algorithm

At the conclusion of a context switch, the kernel executes the algorithm to schedule a process (Figure 8.1), selecting the highest priority process from those in the states "ready to run and loaded in memory" and "preempted." It makes no sense to select a process if it is not loaded in memory, since it cannot execute until it is swapped in. If several processes tie for highest priority, the kernel picks the one that has been "ready to run" for the longest time, following a round robin scheduling policy. If there are no processes eligible for execution, the processor idles until the next interrupt, which will happen in at most one clock tick; after handling that interrupt, the kernel again attempts to schedule a process to run.

8.1.2 Scheduling Parameters

Each process table entry contains a priority field for process scheduling. The priority of a process in user mode is a function of its recent CPU usage, with processes getting a lower priority if they have recently used the CPU. The range of process priorities can be partitioned into two classes (see Figure 8.2): user priorities and kernel priorities. Each class contains several priority values, and each priority has a queue of processes logically associated with it. Processes with user-level priorities were preempted on their return from the kernel to user mode, and processes with kernel-level priorities achieved them in the *sleep* algorithm. User-level priorities are below a threshold value, and kernel-level priorities are above the threshold value. Kernel-level priorities are further subdivided: Processes with low kernel priority wake up on receipt of a signal, but processes with high kernel priority continue to sleep (see Section 7.2.1).

Figure 8.2 shows the threshold priority between user priorities and kernel priorities as the double line between priorities "waiting for child exit" and "user level 0." The priorities called "swapper," "waiting for disk I/O," "waiting for buffer," and "waiting for inode" are high, noninterruptible system priorities, with 1, 3, 2, and 1 processes queued on the respective priority level, and the priorities called "waiting for tty input," "waiting for tty output," and "waiting for child exit" are low, interruptible system priorities with 4, 0, and 2 processes queued, respectively. The figure distinguishes user priorities, calling them "user level 0," "user level 1," to "user level n,"[1] containing 0, 4, and 1 processes, respectively.

The kernel calculates the priority of a process in specific process states.

* It assigns priority to a process about to go to sleep, correlating a fixed, priority value with the reason for sleeping. The priority does not depend on the run-time characteristics of the process (I/O bound or CPU bound), but instead is a constant value that is hard-coded for each call to sleep, dependent on the reason the process is sleeping. Processes that sleep in lower-level algorithms tend to cause more system bottlenecks the longer they are inactive; hence they receive a higher priority than processes that would cause fewer system bottlenecks. For instance, a process sleeping and waiting for the completion of disk I/O has a higher priority than a process waiting for a free buffer for several reasons: First, the process waiting for completion of disk I/O already has a buffer; when it wakes up, there is a chance that it will do enough processing to release the buffer and, possibly, other resources. The more resources it frees, the better the chances are that other processes will not block waiting for resources. The system will have fewer context switches and, consequently, process response

---

1. The highest priority value on the system is 0. Thus, user level 0 has higher priority than user level 1, and so on.

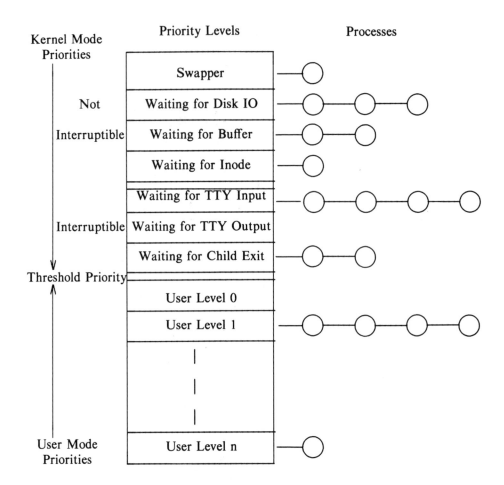

Figure 8.2. Range of Process Priorities

time and system throughput are better. Second, a process waiting for a free buffer may be waiting for a buffer held by the process waiting for completion of I/O. When the I/O completes, both processes wake up because they sleep on the same address. If the process waiting for the buffer were to run first, it would sleep again anyway until the other process frees the buffer; hence its priority is lower.
• The kernel adjusts the priority of a process that returns from kernel mode to user mode. The process may have previously entered the sleep state, changing its priority to a kernel-level priority that must be lowered to a user-level priority when returning to user mode. Also, the kernel penalizes the executing process in fairness to other processes, since it had just used valuable kernel resources.

- The clock handler adjusts the priorities of all processes in user mode at 1 second intervals (on System V) and causes the kernel to go through the scheduling algorithm to prevent a process from monopolizing use of the CPU.

The clock may interrupt a process several times during its time quantum; at every clock interrupt, the clock handler increments a field in the process table that records the recent CPU usage of the process. Once a second, the clock handler also adjusts the recent CPU usage of each process according to a decay function,

$$decay(CPU) = CPU/2;$$

on System V. When it recomputes recent CPU usage, the clock handler also recalculates the priority of every process in the "preempted but ready-to-run" state according to the formula

$$priority = (\text{"recent CPU usage"}/2) + (\text{base level user priority})$$

where "base level user priority" is the threshold priority between kernel and user mode described above. A numerically low value implies a high scheduling priority. Examining the functions for recomputation of recent CPU usage and process priority, the slower the decay rate for recent CPU usage, the longer it will take for the priority of a process to reach its base level; consequently, processes in the "ready-to-run" state will tend to occupy more priority levels.

The effect of priority recalculation once a second is that processes with user-level priorities move between priority queues, as illustrated in Figure 8.3. Comparing this figure to Figure 8.2, one process has moved from the queue for user-level priority 1 to the queue for user-level priority 0. In a real system, all processes with user-level priorities in the figure would change priority queues, but only one has been depicted. The kernel does not change the priority of processes in kernel mode, nor does it allow processes with user-level priority to cross the threshold and attain kernel-level priority, unless they make a system call and go to sleep.

The kernel attempts to recompute the priority of all active processes once a second, but the interval can vary slightly. If the clock interrupt had come while the kernel was executing a critical region of code (that is, while the processor execution level was raised but, obviously, not raised high enough to block out the clock interrupt), the kernel does not recompute priorities, since that would keep the kernel in the critical region for too long a time. Instead, the kernel remembers that it should have recomputed process priorities and does so at a succeeding clock interrupt when the "previous" processor execution level is sufficiently low. Periodic recalculation of process priority assures a round-robin scheduling policy for processes executing in user mode. The kernel responds naturally to interactive requests such as for text editors or form entry programs: such processes have a high idle-time-to-CPU usage ratio, and consequently their priority value naturally rises when they are ready for execution (see page 1937 of [Thompson 78]). Other implementations of the scheduling mechanism vary the time quantum between 0 and 1 second dynamically, depending on system load. Such implementations can

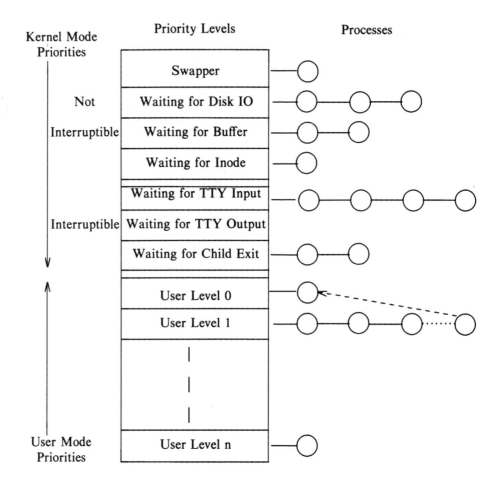

Figure 8.3. Movement of a Process on Priority Queues

thus give quicker response to processes, because they do not have to wait up to a second to run; on the other hand, the kernel has more overhead because of extra context switches.

8.1.3 Examples of Process Scheduling

Figure 8.4 shows the scheduling priorities on System V for 3 processes A, B, and C, under the following assumptions: They are created simultaneously with initial priority 60, the highest user-level priority is 60, the clock interrupts the system 60 times a second, the processes make no system calls, and no other processes are

Time	Proc A		Proc B		Proc C	
	Priority	Cpu Count	Priority	Cpu Count	Priority	Cpu Count
0	60	0	60	0	60	0
		1				
		2				
		⋮				
		60				
1	75	30	60	0	60	0
				1		
				2		
				⋮		
				60		
2	67	15	75	30	60	0
						1
						2
						⋮
						60
3	63	7	67	15	75	30
		8				
		9				
		⋮				
		67				
4	76	33	63	7	67	15
				8		
				9		
				⋮		
				67		
5	68	16	76	33	63	7

Figure 8.4. Example of Process Scheduling

ready to run. The kernel calculates the decay of the CPU usage by

$$CPU = decay(CPU) = CPU/2;$$

and the process priority as

$$priority = (CPU/2) + 60;$$

Assuming process A is the first to run and that it starts running at the beginning of a time quantum, it runs for 1 second: During that time the clock interrupts the system 60 times and the interrupt handler increments the CPU usage field of process A 60 times (to 60). The kernel forces a context switch at the 1-second mark and, after recalculating the priorities of all processes, schedules process B for execution. The clock handler increments the CPU usage field of process B 60 times during the next second and then recalculates the CPU usage and priority of all processes and forces a context switch. The pattern repeats, with the processes taking turns to execute.

Now consider the processes with priorities shown in Figure 8.5, and assume other processes are in the system. The kernel may preempt process A, leaving it in the state "ready to run," after it had received several time quanta in succession on the CPU, and its user-level priority may therefore be low (Figure 8.5a). As time progresses, process B may enter the "ready-to-run" state, and its user-level priority may be higher than that of process A at that instant (Figure 8.5b). If the kernel does not schedule either process for a while (it schedules other processes), both processes could eventually be at the same user priority level, although process B would probably enter that level first since its starting level was originally closer (Figures 8.5c and 8.5d). Nevertheless, the kernel would choose to schedule process A ahead of process B because it was in the state "ready to run" for a longer time (Figure 8.5e): This is the tie-breaker rule for processes with equal priority.

Recall from Section 6.4.3 that the kernel schedules a process at the conclusion of a context switch: A process must do a context switch when it goes to sleep or *exits*, and it has the *opportunity* to do a context switch when returning to user mode from kernel mode. The kernel preempts a process about to return to user mode if a process with higher priority is ready to run. Such a process exists if the kernel awakened a process with higher priority than the currently running process, or if the clock handler changed the priority of all "ready-to-run" processes. In the first case, the current process should not run in user mode given that a higher-priority kernel mode process is available. In the second case, the clock handler decides that the process used up its time quantum, and since many processes had their priorities changed, the kernel does a context switch to reschedule.

8.1.4 Controlling Process Priorities

Processes can exercise crude control of their scheduling priority by using the *nice* system call:

  nice(value);

where *value* is added in the calculation of process priority:

  priority=("recent CPU usage"/constant) + (base priority) + (nice value)

The *nice* system call increments or decrements the *nice* field in the process table by the value of the parameter, although only the superuser can supply *nice* values that increase the process priority. Similarly, only the superuser can supply a *nice* value below a particular threshold. Users who invoke the *nice* system call to lower their process priority when executing computation-intensive jobs are "nice" to other users

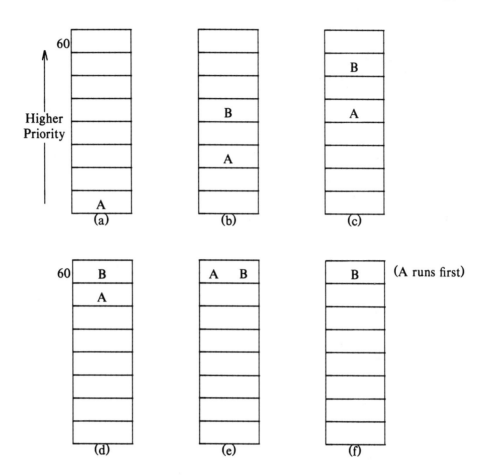

Figure 8.5. Round Robin Scheduling and Process Priorities

on the system, hence the name. Processes inherit the *nice* value of their parent during the *fork* system call. The *nice* system call works for the running process only; a process cannot reset the *nice* value of another process. Practically, this means that if a system administrator wishes to lower the priority values of various processes because they consume too much time, there is no way to do so short of *kill*ing them outright.

8.1.5 Fair Share Scheduler

The scheduler algorithm described above does not differentiate between classes of users. That is, it is impossible to allocate half of the CPU time to a particular set of processes, if desired. However, such considerations are important in a computer center environment, where a set of users may want to buy half of the CPU time of a machine on a guaranteed basis, to ensure a certain level of response. This section describes a scheme called the Fair Share Scheduler, implemented in the AT&T Bell Laboratories Indian Hill Computer Center [Henry 84].

The principle of the fair share scheduler is to divide the user community into a set of fair share groups, such that the members of each group are subject to the constraints of the regular process scheduler relative to other processes in the group. However, the system allocates its CPU time proportionally to each group, regardless of how many processes are in the groups. For example, suppose there are four fair share groups on a system, each with an allocated CPU share of 25%, and that the groups contain 1, 2, 3, and 4 CPU bound processes that never willingly give up the processor (they are in an infinite loop, for instance). Assuming there are no other processes on the system, each process in the four groups would get 10% of the CPU time (there are 10 processes) using the regular scheduling algorithm, because there is no way to distinguish them from each other. But using the fair share scheduler, the process in group 1 will receive twice as much CPU time as each process in group 2, 3 times as much CPU time as each process in group 3, and 4 times as much CPU time as each process in group 4. In this example, the CPU time of all processes in a group should be equal over time, because they are all in an infinite loop.

Implementation of this scheme is simple, a feature that makes it attractive: Another term is added to the formula for computation of process priority, namely, a "fair share group priority." Each process has a new field in its *u area* that points to a fair share CPU usage field, shared by all processes in the fair share group. The clock interrupt handler increments the fair share group CPU usage field for the running process, just as it increments the CPU usage field of the running process and decays the values of all fair share group CPU usage fields once a second. When calculating process priorities, a new component of the calculation is the group CPU usage, normalized according to the amount of CPU time allocated to the fair share group. The more CPU time processes in a group received recently, the higher the numerical value of the group CPU usage field is and, therefore, the lower the priority for all the processes in the fair share group.

For example, consider the three processes depicted in Figure 8.6 and suppose that process A is in one group and processes B and C are in another. Assuming the kernel schedules process A first, it will increment the CPU and group usage fields for process A over the next second. On recomputation of process priorities at the 1-second mark, processes B and C have the highest priority; assume the kernel schedules process B. During the next second, the CPU usage field of process B goes up to 60, as does the group usage field for processes B and C. Hence, on recomputation of process priorities at the 2-second mark, process C will have priority 75 (compare to Figure 8.4), and the kernel will schedule process A, with priority 74. The figure shows how the pattern repeats: the kernel schedules the processes in the order A, B, A, C, A, B, and so on.

Time	Proc A Priority	CPU	Group	Proc B Priority	CPU	Group	Proc C Priority	CPU	Group
0	60	0	0	60	0	0	60	0	0
		1	1						
		2	2						
		:	:						
		60	60						
1	90	30	30	60	0	0	60	0	0
					1	.1			1
					2	2			2
					:	:			:
					60	60			60
2	74	15	15	90	30	30	75	0	30
		16	16						
		17	17						
		:	:						
		75	75						
3	96	37	37	74	15	15	67	0	15
						16		1	16
						17		2	17
						:		:	:
						75		60	75
4	78	18	18	81	7	37	93	30	37
		19	19						
		20	20						
		:	:						
		78	78						
5	98	39	39	70	3	18	76	15	18

Figure 8.6. Example of Fair Share Scheduler — Three Processes, Two Groups

8.1.6 Real-Time Processing

Real-time processing implies the capability to provide immediate response to specific external events and, hence, to schedule particular processes to run within a specified time limit after occurrence of an event. For example, a computer may monitor the life-support systems of hospital patients to take instant action on a change in status of a patient. Processes such as text editors are not considered real-time processes: It is desirable that response to the user be quick, but it is not that critical that a user cannot wait a few extra seconds (although the user may have other ideas). The scheduler algorithms described above were designed for use in a time-sharing environment and are inappropriate in a real-time environment, because they cannot guarantee that the kernel can schedule a particular process within a fixed time limit. Another impediment to the support of real-time processing is that the kernel is nonpreemptive; the kernel cannot schedule a real-time process in user mode if it is currently executing another process in kernel mode, unless major changes are made. Currently, system programmers must insert real-time processes into the kernel to achieve real-time response. A true solution to the problem must allow real-time processes to exist dynamically (that is, not be hard-coded in the kernel), providing them with a mechanism to inform the kernel of their real-time constraints. No standard UNIX system has this capability today.

8.2 SYSTEM CALLS FOR TIME

There are several time-related system calls, *stime*, *time*, *times*, and *alarm*. The first two deal with global system time, and the latter two deal with time for individual processes.

Stime allows the superuser to set a global kernel variable to a value that gives the current time:

    stime(pvalue);

where *pvalue* points to a long integer that gives the time as measured in seconds from midnight before (00:00:00) January 1, 1970, GMT. The clock interrupt handler increments the kernel variable once a second. *Time* retrieves the time as set by *stime*:

    time(tloc);

where *tloc* points to a location in the user process for the return value. *Time* returns this value from the system call, too. Commands such as *date* use *time* to determine the current time.

Times retrieves the cumulative times that the calling process spent executing in user mode and kernel mode and the cumulative times that all zombie children had executed in user mode and kernel mode. The syntax for the call is

    times(tbuffer)
    struct tms *tbuffer;

where the structure *tms* contains the retrieved times and is defined by

•

```
#include  <sys/types.h>
#include  <sys/times.h>
extern long times();

main()
{
      int i;
      /* tms is data structure containing the 4 time elements */
      struct tms pb1, pb2;
      long pt1, pt2;

      pt1 = times(&pb1);
      for (i = 0;  i < 10;  i++)
            if (fork() == 0)
                  child(i);

      for (i = 0;  i < 10;  i++)
            wait((int *) 0);
      pt2 = times(&pb2);
      printf("parent real %u user %u sys %u cuser %u csys %u\n",
            pt2 - pt1, pb2.tms_utime - pb1.tms_utime, pb2.tms_stime - pb1.tms_stime,
            pb2.tms_cutime - pb1.tms_cutime, pb2.tms_cstime - pb1.tms_cstime);
}

child(n)
      int n;
{
      int i;
      struct tms cb1, cb2;
      long t1, t2;

      t1 = times(&cb1);
      for (i = 0;  i < 10000;  i++)
            ;
      t2 = times(&cb2);
      printf("child %d: real %u user %u sys %u\n", n, t2 - t1,
            cb2.tms_utime - cb1.tms_utime, cb2.tms_stime - cb1.tms_stime);
      exit();
}
```

•

Figure 8.7. Program Using Times

```
struct tms {
      /* time_t is the data structure for time */
      time_t  tms_utime;          /* user time of process */
      time_t  tms_stime;          /* kernel time of process */
```

```
        time_t  tms_cutime;         /* user time of children */
        time_t  tms_cstime          /* kernel time of children */
};
```

Times returns the elapsed time "from an arbitrary point in the past," usually the time of system boot.

In the program in Figure 8.7, a process creates 10 child processes, and each child loops 10,000 times. The parent process calls *times* before creating the children and after they all *exit*, and the child processes call *times* before and after their loops. One would naively expect the parent *child user* and *child system* times to equal the respective sums of the child processes' *user* and *system* times, and the parent *real time* to equal the sum of the child processes' *real time*. However, the child times do not include time spent in the *fork* and *exit* system calls, and all times can be distorted by time spent handling interrupts or doing context switches.

User processes can schedule alarm signals using the *alarm* system call. For example, the program in Figure 8.8 checks the access time of a file every minute and prints a message if the file had been accessed. To do so, it enters an infinite loop: During each iteration, it calls *stat* to report the last time the file was accessed and, if accessed during the last minute, prints a message. The process then calls *signal* to catch alarm signals, calls *alarm* to schedule an alarm signal in 60 seconds, and calls *pause* to suspend its activity until receipt of a signal. After 60 seconds, the alarm signal goes off, the kernel sets up the process user stack to call the signal catcher function *wakeup*, the function returns to the position in the code after the *pause* call, and the process executes the loop again.

The common factor in all the time related system calls is their reliance on the system clock: the kernel manipulates various time counters when handling clock interrupts and initiates appropriate action.

8.3 CLOCK

The functions of the clock interrupt handler are to

- restart the clock,
- schedule invocation of internal kernel functions based on internal timers,
- provide execution profiling capability for the kernel and for user processes,
- gather system and process accounting statistics,
- keep track of time,
- send alarm signals to processes on request,
- periodically wake up the swapper process (see the next chapter),
- control process scheduling.

Some operations are done every clock interrupt, whereas others are done after several clock ticks. The clock handler runs with the processor execution level set high, preventing other events (such as interrupts from peripheral devices) from happening while the handler is active. The clock handler is therefore fast, so that

```
#include  <sys/types.h>
#include  <sys/stat.h>
#include  <sys/signal.h>

main(argc, argv)
      int argc;
      char *argv[];
{
      extern unsigned alarm();
      extern wakeup();
      struct stat statbuf;
      time_t axtime;

      if (argc != 2)
      {
            printf("only 1 arg\n");
            exit();
      }

      axtime = (time_t) 0;
      for (;;)
      {
            /* find out file access time */
            if (stat(argv[1], &statbuf) == -1)
            {
                  printf("file %s not there\n", argv[1]);
                  exit();
            }
            if (axtime != statbuf.st_atime)
            {
                  printf("file %s accessed\n", argv[1]);
                  axtime = statbuf.st_atime;
            }
            signal(SIGALRM, wakeup);        /* reset for alarm */
            alarm(60);
            pause();                /* sleep until signal */
      }
}

wakeup()
{
}
```

Figure 8.8. Program Using Alarm Call

```
algorithm clock
input:   none
output: none
{
        restart clock;                    /* so that it will interrupt again */
        if (callout table not empty)
        {
                adjust callout times;
                schedule callout function if time elapsed;
        }
        if (kernel profiling on)
                note program counter at time of interrupt;
        if (user profiling on)
                note program counter at time of interrupt;
        gather system statistics;
        gather statistics per process;
        adjust measure of process CPU utilitization;
        if (1 second or more since last here and interrupt not in critical
                                                region of code)
        {
                for (all processes in the system)
                {
                        adjust alarm time if active;
                        adjust measure of CPU utilization;
                        if (process to execute in user mode)
                                adjust process priority;
                }
                wakeup swapper process is necessary;
        }
}
```

Figure 8.9. Algorithm for the Clock Handler

the critical time periods when other interrupts are blocked is as small as possible. Figure 8.9 shows the algorithm for handling clock interrupts.

8.3.1 Restarting the Clock

When the clock interrupts the system, most machines require that the clock be reprimed by software instructions so that it will interrupt the processor again after a suitable interval. Such instructions are hardware dependent and will not be discussed.

8.3.2 Internal System Timeouts

Some kernel operations, particularly device drivers and network protocols, require invocation of kernel functions on a real-time basis. For instance, a process may put a terminal into raw mode so that the kernel satisfies user *read* requests at fixed intervals instead of waiting for the user to type a carriage return (see Section 10.3.3). The kernel stores the necessary information in the *callout* table (Figure 8.9), which consists of the function to be invoked when time expires, a parameter for the function, and the time in clock ticks until the function should be called.

The user has no direct control over the entries in the callout table; various kernel algorithms make entries as needed. The kernel sorts entries in the callout table according to their respective "time to fire," independent of the order they are placed in the table. Because of the time ordering, the time field for each entry in the callout table is stored as the amount of time to fire after the previous element fires. The total time to fire for a given element in the table is the sum of the times to fire of all entries up to and including the element.

Function	Time to Fire
a()	-2
b()	3
c()	10

Function	Time to Fire
a()	-2
b()	3
f()	2
c()	8

Before   After

Figure 8.10. Callout Table and New Entry for f

Figure 8.10 shows an instance of the *callout* table before and after addition of a new entry for the function *f*. (The negative time field for function *a* will be explained shortly.) When making a new entry, the kernel finds the correct (timed) position for the new entry and appropriately adjusts the time field of the entry immediately after the new entry. In the figure, the kernel arranges to invoke function *f* after 5 clock ticks: it creates an entry for *f* after the entry for *b* with the value of its time field 2 (the sum of the time fields for *b* and *f* is 5), and changes the time field for *c* to 8 (*c* will still fire in 13 clock ticks). Kernel implementations can use a linked list for each entry of the callout table, or they can readjust position of the entries when changing the table. The latter option is not that expensive if the kernel does not use the callout table too much.

At every clock interrupt, the clock handler checks if there are any entries in the callout table and, if there are any, decrements the time field of the first entry. Because of the way the kernel keeps time in the callout table, decrementing the time field for the first entry effectively decrements the time field for all entries in the table. If the time field of the first entry in the list is less than or equal to 0, then the specified function should be invoked. The clock handler does not invoke the function directly so that it does not inadvertently block later clock interrupts: The processor priority level is currently set to block out clock interrupts, but the kernel has no idea how long the function will take to complete. If the function were to last longer than a clock tick, the next clock interrupt (and all other interrupts that occur) would be blocked. Instead, the clock handler typically schedules the function by causing a "software interrupt," sometimes called a "programmed interrupt" because it is caused by execution of a particular machine instruction. Because software interrupts are at a lower priority level than other interrupts, they are blocked until the kernel finishes handling all other interrupts. Many interrupts, including clock interrupts, could occur between the time the kernel is ready to call a function in the callout table and the time the software interrupt occurs and, therefore, the time field of the first callout entry can have a negative value. When the software interrupt finally happens, the interrupt handler removes entries from the callout table whose time fields have expired and calls the appropriate function.

Since it is possible that the time field of the first entries in the callout table are 0 or negative, the clock handler must find the first entry whose time field is positive and decrement it. In Figure 8.10 for example, the time field of the entry for function a is -2, meaning that the system took 2 clock interrupts after a was eligible to be called. Assuming the entry for b was in the table 2 ticks ago, the kernel skipped the entry for a and decremented the time field for b.

8.3.3 Profiling

Kernel profiling gives a measure of how much time the system is executing in user mode versus kernel mode, and how much time it spends executing individual routines in the kernel. The kernel profile driver monitors the relative performance of kernel modules by sampling system activity at the time of a clock interrupt. The profile driver has a list of kernel addresses to sample, usually addresses of kernel functions; a process had previously down-loaded these addresses by *writing* the profile driver. If kernel profiling is enabled, the clock interrupt handler invokes the interrupt handler of the profile driver, which determines whether the processor mode at the time of the interrupt was user or kernel. If the mode was user, the profiler increments a count for user execution, but if the mode was kernel, it increments an internal counter corresponding to the program counter. User processes can read the profile driver to obtain the kernel counts and do statistical measurements.

Algorithm	Address	Count
bread	100	5
breada	150	0
bwrite	200	0
brelse	300	2
getblk	400	1
user	–	2

Figure 8.11. Sample Addresses of Kernel Algorithms

For example, Figure 8.11 shows hypothetical addresses of several kernel routines. If the sequence of program counter values sampled over 10 clock interrupts is 110, 330, 145, address in user space, 125, 440, 130, 320, address in user space, and 104, the figure shows the counts the kernel would save. Examining these figures, one would conclude that the system spends 20% of its time in user mode and 50% of its time executing the kernel algorithm *bread*.

If kernel profiling is done for a long time period, the sampled pattern of program counter values converges toward a true proportion of system usage. However, the mechanism does not account for time spent executing the clock handler and code that blocks out clock-level interrupts, because the clock cannot interrupt such critical regions of code and therefore cannot invoke the profile interrupt handler there. This is unfortunate since such critical regions of kernel code are frequently those that are the most important to profile. Hence, results of kernel profiling must be taken with a grain of salt. Weinberger [Weinberger 84] describes a scheme for generating counters into basic blocks of code, such as the body of "if-then" and "else" statements, to provide exact counts of how many times they are executed. However, the method increases CPU time anywhere from 50% to 200%, so its use as a permanent kernel profiling mechanism is not practical.

Users can profile execution of processes at user-level with the *profil* system call:

profil(buff, bufsize, offset, scale);

where *buff* is the address of an array in user space, *bufsize* is the size of the array, *offset* is the virtual address of a user subroutine (usually, the first), and *scale* is a factor that maps user virtual addresses into the array. The kernel treats *scale* as a fixed-point binary fraction with the binary point at the extreme "left": The hexadecimal value 0xffff gives a one to one mapping of program counters to words in *buff*, 0x7fff maps pairs of program addresses into a single *buff* word, 0x3fff maps groups of 4 program addresses into a single *buff* word, and so on. The kernel stores the system call parameters in the process *u area*. When the clock interrupts the process while in user mode, the clock handler examines the user program counter at the time of the interrupt, compares it to *offset*, and increments a location in *buff* whose address is a function of *bufsize* and *scale*.

```
#include  <signal.h>
int buffer[4096];
main()
{
      int offset, endof, scale, eff, gee, text;
      extern theend(), f(), g();
      signal(SIGINT, theend);
      endof = (int) theend;
      offset = (int) main;
      /* calculates number of words of program text */
      text = (endof − offset + sizeof(int) − 1)/sizeof(int);
      scale = 0xffff;
      printf("offset %d endof %d text %d\n", offset, endof, text);
      eff = (int) f;
      gee = (int) g;
      printf("f %d  g %d  fdiff %d gdiff %d\n", eff, gee, eff−offset, gee−offset);
      profil(buffer, sizeof(int)*text, offset, scale);
      for (;;)
      {
            f();
            g();
      }
}
f()
{
}
g()
{
}
theend()
{
      int i;
      for (i = 0;  i < 4096;  i++)
            if (buffer[i])
                  printf("buf[%d] = %d\n", i, buffer[i]);
      exit();
}
```

Figure 8.12. Program Invoking Profil System Call

For example, consider the program in Figure 8.12, profiling execution of a program that calls the two functions *f* and *g* successively in an infinite loop. The process first invokes *signal* to arrange to call the function *theend* on occurrence of an interrupt signal and then calculates the range of text addresses it wishes to profile, extending from the address of the function *main* to the address of the function *theend*, and, finally, invokes *profil* to inform the kernel that it wishes to

```
offset 212 endof 440 text 57
f 416  g 428  fdiff 204 gdiff 216
buf[46] = 50
buf[48] = 8585216
buf[49] = 151
buf[51] = 12189799
buf[53] = 65
buf[54] = 10682455
buf[56] = 67
```

Figure 8.13. Sample Output for Profil Program

profile its execution. Running the program for about 10 seconds on a lightly loaded AT&T 3B20 computer gave the output shown in Figure 8.13. The address of f is 204 greater than the 0th profiling address; because the size of the text of f is 12 bytes and the size of an integer is 4 on an AT&T 3B20 computer, the addresses of f map into *buf* entries 51, 52, and 53. Similarly, the addresses of g map into *buf* entries 54, 55, and 56. The *buf* entries 46, 48, and 49 are for addresses in the loop in function *main*. In typical usage, the range of addresses to be profiled is determined by examination of the text addresses in the symbol table of the program being profiled. Users are discouraged from using the *profil* call directly because it is complicated; instead, an option on the C compiler directs the compiler to generate code to profile processes.

8.3.4 Accounting and Statistics

When the clock interrupts the system, the system may be executing in kernel mode, executing in user mode, or idle (not executing any processes). It is idle if all processes are sleeping, awaiting the occurrence of an event. The kernel keeps internal counters for each processor state and adjusts them during each clock interrupt, noting the current mode of the machine. User processes can later analyze the statistics gathered in the kernel.

Every process has two fields in its *u area* to keep a record of elapsed kernel and user time. When handling clock interrupts, the kernel updates the appropriate field for the executing process, depending on whether the process was executing in kernel mode or in user mode. Parent processes gather statistics for their child processes in the *wait* system call when accumulating execution statistics for *exit*ing child processes.

Every process has one field in its *u area* for the kernel to log its memory usage. When the clock interrupts a running process, the kernel calculates the total memory used by a process as a function of its private memory regions and its proportional usage of shared memory regions. For example, if a process shares a text region of size 50K bytes with four other processes and uses data and stack regions of size

25K and 40K bytes, respectively, the kernel charges the process for 75K bytes (50K/5 + 25K + 40K). For a paging system, it calculates the memory usage by counting the number of valid pages in each region. Thus, if the interrupted process uses two private regions and shares another region with another process, the kernel charges it for the number of valid pages in the private regions plus half the number of valid pages in the shared region. The kernel writes the information in an accounting record when the process *exits*, and the information can be used for customer billing.

8.3.5 Keeping Time

The kernel increments a timer variable at every clock interrupt, keeping time in clock ticks from the time the system was booted. The kernel uses the timer variable to return a time value for the *time* system call, and to calculate the total (real time) execution time of a process. The kernel saves the process start time in its *u area* when a process is created in the *fork* system call, and it subtracts that value from the current time when the process *exits*, giving the real execution time of the process. Another timer variable, set by the *stime* system call and updated once a second, keeps track of calendar time.

8.4 SUMMARY

This chapter has described the basic algorithm for process scheduling on the UNIX system. The kernel associates a scheduling priority with every process in the system, assigning the value when a process goes to sleep or, periodically, in the clock interrupt handler. The priority assigned when a process goes to sleep is a fixed value, dependent on the kernel algorithm the process was executing. The priority assigned in the clock handler (or when a process returns from kernel mode to user mode) depends on how much time the process has recently used the CPU: It receives a lower priority if it has used the CPU recently and a higher priority, otherwise. The *nice* system call allows a process to adjust one parameter used in computation of process priority.

This chapter also described system calls dealing with time: setting and retrieving kernel time, retrieving process execution times, and setting process alarm signals. Finally, it described the functions of the clock interrupt handler, which keeps track of system time, manages the callout table, gathers statistics, and arranges for invocation of the process scheduler, process swapper, and page stealer. The swapper and page stealer are the topics of the next chapter.

8.5 EXERCISES

1. In assigning priorities when a process goes to sleep, the kernel assigns a higher priority to a process waiting for a locked inode than to a process waiting for a locked buffer.

Similarly, it assigns higher priority to processes waiting to read terminal input than to processes waiting to write terminal output. Justify both cases.

* 2. The algorithm for the clock interrupt handler recalculates process priorities and reschedules processes in 1-second intervals. Discuss an algorithm that dynamically changes the interval depending on system load. Is the gain worth the added complexity?

3. The Sixth Edition of the UNIX system uses the following formula to adjust the recent CPU usage of a process:

$$\text{decay}(CPU) = \max(\text{threshold priority}, CPU - 10);$$

and the Seventh Edition uses the formula:

$$\text{decay}(CPU) = .8 * CPU;$$

Both systems calculate process priority by the formula

$$\text{priority} = CPU/16 + (\text{base level priority});$$

Try the example in Figure 8.4 using these decay functions.

4. Repeat the example in Figure 8.4 with seven processes instead of three. Repeat the example assuming there are 100 clock interrupts per second instead of 60. Comment.

5. Design a scheme such that the system puts a time limit on how long a process executes, forcing it to exit if it exceeds the time limit. How should the user distinguish such processes from processes that should run for ever? If the only requirement was to run such a scheme from the shell, what would have to be done?

6. When a process executes the *wait* system call and finds a zombie process, the kernel adds the child's CPU usage field to the parent's. What is the rationale for penalizing the parent?

7. The command *nice* causes the subsequent command to be invoked with the given nice value, as in

    nice 6 nroff —mm big_memo > output

Write C code for the *nice* command.

8. Trace the scheduling of the processes in Figure 8.4 given that the *nice* value of process A is 5 or −5.

9. Implement a system call, *renice x y*, where *x* is a process ID (of an active process) and *y* is the value that its *nice* value should take.

10. Reconsider the example in Figure 8.6 for the fair share scheduler. Suppose the group containing process A pays for 33% of the CPU and the group containing processes B and C pays for 66% of the CPU time. What should the sequence of scheduled processes look like? Generalize the computation of process priorities so that it normalizes the value of the group CPU usage field.

11. Implement the command *date*: with no arguments, the command prints the system's opinion of the current date; using a parameter, as in

    date mmddhhmmyy

a (super) user can set the system's opinion of the current date to the corresponding month, day, year, hour, and minute. For example,

    date 0911205084

sets the system date to September 11, 1984, 8:50 p.m.

12. Programs can use a user-level *sleep* function

    sleep(seconds);

    to suspend execution for the indicated number of seconds. Implement the function using the *alarm* and *pause* system calls. What should happen if the process had called *alarm* before calling *sleep*? Consider two possibilities: that the previous *alarm* call would expire while the process was sleeping, and that it would expire after the *sleep* completed.

* 13. Refering to the last problem, the kernel could do a context switch between the *alarm* and *pause* calls in the *sleep* function, and the process could receive the *alarm* signal before it calls *pause*. What would happen? How can this race condition be fixed?

9

MEMORY MANAGEMENT POLICIES

The CPU scheduling algorithm described in the last chapter is strongly influenced by memory management policies. At least part of a process must be contained in primary memory to run; the CPU cannot execute a process that exists entirely in secondary memory. However, primary memory is a precious resource that frequently cannot contain all active processes in the system. For instance, if a system contains 8 megabytes of primary memory, nine 1-megabyte processes will not fit there simultaneously. The memory management subsystem decides which processes should reside (at least partially) in main memory, and manages the parts of the virtual address space of a process that are not core resident. It monitors the amount of available primary memory and may periodically write processes to a secondary memory device called the *swap device* to provide more space in primary memory. At a later time, the kernel reads the data from the swap device back to main memory.

Historically, UNIX systems transferred entire processes between primary memory and the swap device, but did not transfer parts of a process independently, except for shared text. Such a memory management policy is called *swapping*. It made sense to implement such a policy on the PDP 11, where the maximum process size was 64K bytes. For this policy, the size of a process is bounded by the amount of physical memory available on a system. The BSD system (release 4.0) was the first major implementation of a *demand paging* policy, transferring memory pages instead of processes to and from a secondary device; recent releases of UNIX System V also support demand paging. The entire process does not have to reside in main memory to execute, and the kernel loads pages for a process on demand when the process references the pages. The advantage of a demand paging policy is that it permits greater flexibility in mapping the virtual address space of a process into the physical memory of a machine, usually allowing the size of a process to be greater than the amount of available physical memory and allowing more processes to fit simultaneously in main memory. The advantage of a swapping policy is that it is easier to implement and results in less system overhead. This chapter discusses the two memory management policies, swapping and paging.

9.1 SWAPPING

There are three parts to the description of the swapping algorithm: managing space on the swap device, swapping processes out of main memory, and swapping processes into main memory.

9.1.1 Allocation of Swap Space

The swap device is a block device in a configurable section of a disk. Whereas the kernel allocates space for files one block at a time, it allocates space on the swap device in groups of contiguous blocks. Space allocated for files is used statically; since it will exist for a long time, the allocation scheme is flexible to reduce the amount of fragmentation and, hence, unallocatable space in the file system. But the allocation of space on the swap device is transitory, depending on the pattern of process scheduling. A process that resides on the swap device will eventually migrate back to main memory, freeing the space it had occupied on the swap device. Since speed is critical and the system can do I/O faster in one multiblock operation than in several single block operations, the kernel allocates contiguous space on the swap device without regard for fragmentation.

Because the allocation scheme for the swap device differs from the allocation scheme for file systems, the data structures that catalog free space differ too. The kernel maintains free space for file systems in a linked list of free blocks, accessible from the file system super block, but it maintains the free space for the swap device in an in-core table, called a *map*. Maps, used for other resources besides the swap device (some device drivers, for example), allow a first-fit allocation of contiguous "blocks" of a resource.

A map is an array where each entry consists of an address of an allocatable resource and the number of resource units available there; the kernel interprets the address and units according to the type of map. Initially, a map contains one entry that indicates the address and the total number of resources. For instance, the kernel treats each unit of the swap map as a group of disk blocks, and it treats the address as a block offset from the beginning of the swap area. Figure 9.1 illustrates an initial swap map that consists of 10,000 blocks starting at address 1.

Address   Units

1	10000

Figure 9.1. Initial Swap Map

```
algorithm malloc        /* algorithm to allocate map space */
input:   (1) map address        /* indicates which map to use */
         (2) requested number of units
output: address, if successful
         0, otherwise
{
      for (every map entry)
      {
            if (current map entry can fit requested units)
            {
                  if (requested units == number of units in entry)
                        delete entry from map;
                  else
                        adjust start address of entry;
                  return (original address of entry);
            }
      }
      return(0);
}
```

Figure 9.2. Algorithm for Allocating Space from Maps

As the kernel allocates and frees resources, it updates the map so that it continues to contain accurate information about free resources.

Figure 9.2 gives the algorithm *malloc* for allocating space from maps. The kernel searches the map for the first entry that contains enough space to accommodate the request. If the request consumes all the resources of the map entry, the kernel removes the entry from the array and compresses the map (that is, the map has one fewer entries). Otherwise, it adjusts the address and unit fields of the entry according to the amount of resources allocated. Figure 9.3 shows the sequence of swap map configurations after allocating 100 units, 50 units, then 100 units again. The kernel adjusts the swap map to show that the first 250 units have been allocated, and that it now contains 9750 free units starting at address 251.

When freeing resources, the kernel finds their proper position in the map by address. Three cases are possible:

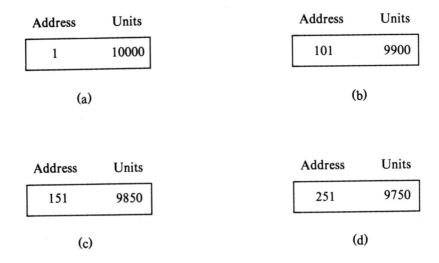

Figure 9.3. Allocating Swap Space

1. The freed resources completely fill a hole in the map: they are contiguous to the entries whose addresses would immediately precede them and follow them in the map. In this case, the kernel combines the newly freed resources and the existing (two) entries into one entry in the map.
2. The freed resources partially fill a hole in the map. If the address of the freed resources are contiguous with the map entry that would immediately precede them or with the entry that would immediately follow them (but not both), the kernel adjusts the address and units fields of the appropriate entry to account for the resources just freed. The number of entries in the map remains the same.
3. The freed resources partially fill a hole but are not contiguous to any resources in the map. The kernel creates a new entry for the map and inserts it in the proper position.

Returning to the previous example, if the kernel frees 50 units of the swap resource starting at address 101, the swap map contains a new entry for the freed resources, since the returned resources are not contiguous to existing entries in the map. If the kernel then frees 100 units of the swap resource starting at address 1, it adjusts the first entry of the swap map since the freed resources are contiguous to those in the first entry. Figure 9.4 shows the sequence of swap map configurations corresponding to these events.

Suppose the kernel now requests 200 units of swap space. Because the first entry in the swap map only contains 150 units, the kernel satisfies the request from the second entry (see Figure 9.5). Finally, suppose the kernel frees 350 units of

Address Units

251	9750

(a)

Address Units

101	50
251	9750

(b)

Address Units

1	150
251	9750

(c)

Figure 9.4. Freeing Swap Space

Address Units

1	150
251	9750

(a)

Address Units

1	150
451	9550

(b)

Figure 9.5. Allocating Swap Space from the Second Entry in the Map

swap space starting at address 151. Although the 350 units were allocated separately, there is no reason the kernel could not free them at once. (It does not do so for swap space, since requests for swap space are independent of each other.) The kernel realizes that the freed resources fit neatly into the hole between the first and second entries in the swap map and creates one entry for the former two (and the freed resources).

Traditional implementations of the UNIX system use one swap device, but the latest implementations of System V allow multiple swap devices. The kernel chooses the swap device in a round robin scheme, provided it contains enough contiguous memory. Administrators can create and remove swap devices dynamically. If a swap device is being removed, the kernel does not swap data to it; as data is swapped from it, it empties out until it is free and can be removed.

9.1.2 Swapping Processes Out

The kernel swaps a process out if it needs space in memory, which may result from any of the following:

1. The *fork* system call must allocate space for a child process,
2. The *brk* system call increases the size of a process,
3. A process becomes larger by the natural growth of its stack,
4. The kernel wants to free space in memory for processes it had previously swapped out and should now swap in.

The case of *fork* stands out, because it is the only case where the in-core memory previously occupied by the process is *not* relinquished.

When the kernel decides that a process is eligible for swapping from main memory, it decrements the reference count of each region in the process and swaps the region out if its reference count drops to 0. The kernel allocates space on a swap device and locks the process in memory (for cases 1–3), preventing the swapper from swapping it out (see exercise 9.12) while the current swap operation is in progress. The kernel saves the swap address of the region in the region table entry.

The kernel swaps as much data as possible per I/O operation directly between the swap device and user address space, bypassing the buffer cache. If the hardware cannot transfer multiple pages in one operation, the kernel software must iteratively transfer one page of memory at a time. The exact rate of data transfer and its mechanics therefore depend on the capabilities of the disk controller and the implementation of memory management, among other factors. For instance, if memory is organized in pages, the data to be swapped out is likely to be discontiguous in physical memory. The kernel must gather the page addresses of data to be swapped out, and the disk driver may use the collection of page addresses to set up the I/O. The swapper waits for each I/O operation to complete before swapping out other data.

It is not necessary that the kernel write the entire virtual address space of a process to a swap device. Instead, it copies the physical memory assigned to a process to the allocated space on the swap device, ignoring unassigned virtual addresses. When the kernel swaps the process back into memory, it knows the virtual address map of the process, so it can reassign the process to the correct virtual addresses. The kernel eliminates an extra copy from a data buffer to physical memory by reading the data into the physical memory locations that were previously set up to conform to the virtual address locations.

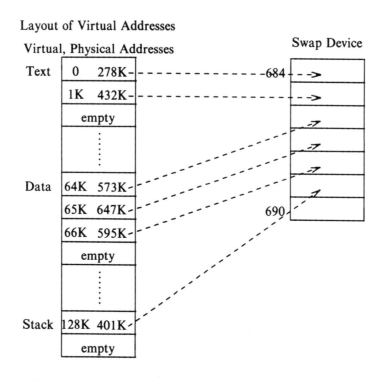

Figure 9.6. Mapping Process Space onto the Swap Device

Figure 9.6 gives an example of mapping the in-core image of a process onto a swap device.[1] The process contains three regions for text, data, and stack: the text region ends at virtual address 2K, and the data region starts at virtual address 64K, leaving a gap of 62K bytes in the virtual address space. When the kernel swaps the process out, it swaps the pages for virtual addresses 0, 1K, 64K, 65K, 66K, and 128K; it does not allocate swap space for the empty 62K bytes between the text and data regions or the empty 61K bytes between the data and stack regions but fills the swap space contiguously. When the kernel swaps the process back in, it knows that the process has a 62K-byte hole by consulting the process memory map, and it assigns physical memory accordingly. Figure 9.7 demonstrates this case. Comparison of Figures 9.6 and 9.7 shows that the physical addresses occupied by

---

1. For simplicity, the virtual address space of a process is depicted as a linear array of page table entries in this and in later figures, disregarding the fact that each region usually has a separate page table.

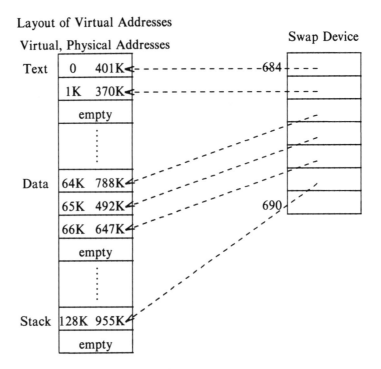

Figure 9.7. Swapping a Process into Memory

the process before and after the swap are not the same; however, the process does not notice a change at user-level, because the contents of its virtual space are the same.

Theoretically, all memory space occupied by a process, including its *u area* and kernel stack, is eligible to be swapped out, although the kernel may temporarily lock a region into memory while a sensitive operation is underway. Practically, however, kernel implementations do not swap the *u area* if the *u area* contains the address translation tables for the process. The implementation also dictates whether a process can swap itself out or whether it must request another process to swap it out (see exercise 9.4).

9.1.2.1 Fork Swap

The description of the *fork* system call (Section 7.1) assumed that the parent process found enough memory to create the child context. Otherwise, the kernel swaps the process out without freeing the memory occupied by the in-core (parent) copy. When the swap is complete, the child process exists on the swap device; the parent places the child in the "ready-to-run" state (see Figure 6.1) and returns to user mode. Since the child is in the "ready-to-run" state, the swapper will eventually swap it into memory, where the kernel will schedule it; the child will complete its part of the *fork* system call and return to user mode.

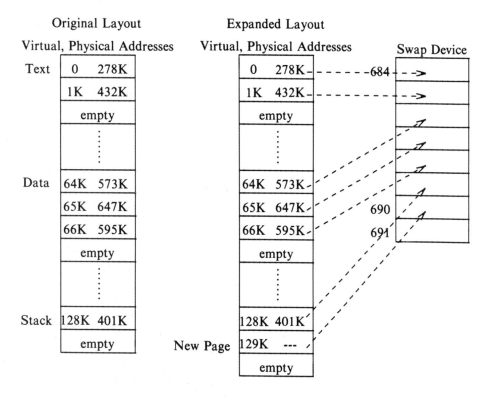

Figure 9.8. Adjusting Memory Map for Expansion Swap

9.1.2.2 Expansion Swap

If a process requires more physical memory than is currently allocated to it, either as a result of user stack growth or invocation of the *brk* system call and if it needs more memory than is currently available, the kernel does an *expansion swap* of the process. It reserves enough space on the swap device to contain the memory space of the process, including the newly requested space. Then, it adjusts the address translation mapping of the process to account for the new virtual memory but does not assign physical memory (since none was available). Finally, it swaps the process out in a normal swapping operation, zeroing out the newly allocated space on the swap device (see Figure 9.8). When the kernel later swaps the process into memory, it will allocate physical memory according to the new (augmented size) address translation map. When the process resumes execution, it will have enough memory.

9.1.3 Swapping Processes In

Process 0, the swapper, is the only process that swaps processes into memory from swap devices. At the conclusion of system initialization, the swapper goes into an infinite loop, where its only task is to do process swapping, as mentioned in Section 7.9. It attempts to swap processes in from the swap device, and it swaps processes out if it needs space in main memory. The swapper sleeps if there is no work for it to do (for example, if there are no processes to swap in) or if it is unable to do any work (there are no processes eligible to swap out); the kernel periodically wakes it up, as will be seen. The kernel schedules the swapper to execute just as it schedules other processes, albeit at higher priority, but the swapper executes only in kernel mode. The swapper makes no system calls but uses internal kernel functions to do swapping; it is the archetype of all kernel processes.

As mentioned briefly in Chapter 8, the clock handler measures the time that each process has been in core or swapped out. When the swapper wakes up to swap processes in, it examines all processes that are in the state "ready to run but swapped out" and selects one that has been swapped out the longest (see Figure 9.9). If there is enough free memory available, the swapper swaps the process in, reversing the operation done for swapping out: It allocates physical memory, reads the process from the swap device, and frees the swap space.

If the swapper successfully swaps in a process, it searches the set of "ready-to-run but swapped out" processes for others to swap in and repeats the above procedure. One of the following situations eventually arises:

- No "ready-to-run" processes exist on the swap device: The swapper goes to sleep until a process on the swap device wakes up or until the kernel swaps out a process that is "ready to run." (Recall the state diagram in Figure 6.1.)
- The swapper finds an eligible process to swap in but the system does not contain enough memory: The swapper attempts to swap another process out and, if successful, restarts the swapping algorithm, searching for a process to swap in.

If the swapper must swap a process out, it examines every process in memory: Zombie processes do not get swapped out, because they do not take up any physical memory; processes locked in memory, doing region operations, for example, are also not swapped out. The kernel swaps out sleeping processes rather than those "ready to run," because "ready-to-run" processes have a greater chance of being scheduled soon. The choice of which sleeping process to swap out is a function of the process priority and the time the process has been in memory. If there are no sleeping processes in memory, the choice of which "ready-to-run" process to swap out is a function of the process *nice* value and the time the process has been in memory.

```
algorithm swapper        /* swap in swapped out processes,
                         * swap out other processes to make room */
input:  none
output: none
{
   loop:
      for (all swapped out processes that are ready to run)
            pick process swapped out longest;
      if (no such process)
      {
            sleep (event must swap in);
            goto loop;
      }
      if (enough room in main memory for process)
      {
            swap process in;
            goto loop;
      }
   /* loop2: here in revised algorithm (see page 285) */
      for (all processes loaded in main memory, not zombie and not locked in memory)
      {
            if (there is a sleeping process)
                  choose process such that priority + residence time
                        is numerically highest;
            else  /* no sleeping processes */
                  choose process such that residence time + nice
                        is numerically highest;
      }
      if (chosen process not sleeping or residency requirements not
                        satisfied)
            sleep (event must swap process in);
      else
            swap out process;
      goto loop;         /* goto loop2 in revised algorithm */
}
```

Figure 9.9. Algorithm for the Swapper

A "ready-to-run" process must be core resident for at least 2 seconds before being swapped out, and a process to be swapped in must have been swapped out for at least 2 seconds. If the swapper cannot find any processes to swap out or if neither the process to be swapped in nor the process to be swapped out have accumulated more than 2 seconds[2] residence time in their environment, then the swapper sleeps on the event that it wants to swap a process into memory but cannot find room for it. The clock will awaken the swapper once a second in that state. The kernel also awakens the swapper if another process goes to sleep, since it may be more eligible for swapping out than the processes previously considered by the swapper. If the swapper swaps out a process or if it sleeps because it could not swap out a process, it will resume execution at the beginning of the swapping algorithm, attempting to swap in eligible processes.

Figure 9.10 depicts five processes and the time they spend in memory or on the swap device as they go through a sequence of swapping operations. For simplicity, assume that all processes are CPU intensive and that they do not make any system calls; hence, a context switch happens only as a result of clock interrupts at 1-second intervals. The swapper runs at highest scheduling priority, so it always runs briefly at 1-second intervals if it has work to do. Further, assume that the processes are the same size and the system can contain at most two processes simultaneously in main memory. Initially, processes A and B are in main memory and the other processes are swapped out. The swapper cannot swap any processes during the first 2 seconds, because none have been in memory or on the swap device for 2 seconds (the residency requirement), but at the 2-second mark, it swaps out processes A and B and swaps in processes C and D. It attempts to swap in process E, too, but fails because there is no more room in main memory. At the 3 second mark, process E is eligible for swapping because it has been on the swap device for 3 seconds, but the swapper cannot swap processes out of main memory because their residency time is under 2 seconds. At the 4-second mark, the swapper swaps out processes C and D and swaps in processes E and A.

The swapper chooses processes to swap in based on the amount of time the processes had been swapped out. Another criterion could have been to swap in the highest-priority process that is ready to run, since such processes deserve a better chance to execute. It has been demonstrated that such a policy results in "slightly" better throughput under heavy system load (see [Peachey 84]).

The algorithm for choosing a process to swap out to make room in memory has more serious flaws, however. First, the swapper swaps out a process based on its priority, memory-residence time, and *nice* value. Although it swaps out a process only to make room for a process being swapped in, it may swap out a process that does not provide enough memory for the incoming process. For instance, if the swapper attempts to swap in a process that occupies 1 megabyte of memory and the system contains no free memory, it is futile to swap out a process that occupies only 2K bytes of memory. An alternative strategy would be to swap out groups of

---

2. The Version 6 implementation of the UNIX system did not swap a process out to make room for an incoming process until the incoming process had been disk resident for 3 seconds. The outgoing process had to reside in memory at least 2 seconds. The choice of the time interval cuts down on thrashing and increases system throughput.

Time	Proc A	B	C	D	E
0	0 / runs	0	swap out / 0	swap out / 0	swap out / 0
1	1	1 / runs	1	1	1
2	2 / swap out / 0	2 / swap out / 0	2 / swap in / 0 / runs	2 / swap in / 0	2
3	1	1	1	1 / runs	3
4	2 / swap in / 0	2	2 / swap out / 0	2 / swap out / 0	4 / swap in / 0 / runs
5	1 / runs	3	1	1	1
6	2 / swap out / 0	4 / swap in / 0 / runs	2 / swap in / 0	2	2 / swap out / 0

Figure 9.10. Sequence of Swapping Operations

Time	Proc A	B	C	D	E
0	0 runs	0	swap out 0	nice 25 swap out 0	swap out 0
1	1	1 runs	1	1	1
2	2 swap out 0	2 swap out 0	2 swap in 0 runs	2 swap in 0	2
3	1	1	1	1 swap out 0	3 swap in 0 runs
4	2 swap in 0 runs	2	2 swap out 0	1	1
5	1	3 swap in 0 runs	1	2	2 swap out 0
6	2 swap out 0	1	2	3 swap in 0 runs	1

Figure 9.11. Thrashing due to Swapping

processes only if they provide enough memory for the incoming process. Experiments using a PDP 11/23 computer have shown that such a strategy can increase system throughput by about 10 percent under heavy loads (see [Peachey 84]).

Second, if the swapper sleeps because it could not find enough memory to swap in a process, it searches again for a process to swap in although it had previously chosen one. The reason is that other swapped processes may have awakened in the meantime and they may be more eligible for swapping in than the previously chosen process. But that is small solace to the original process still trying to be swapped in. In some implementations, the swapper tries to swap out many smaller processes to make room for the big process to be swapped in before searching for another process to swap in; this is the revision in the swapper algorithm shown by the comments in Figure 9.9.

Third, if the swapper chooses a "ready-to-run" process to swap out, it is possible that the process had not executed since it was previously swapped in. Figure 9.11 depicts such a case, where the kernel swaps in process D at the 2-second mark, schedules process C, and then swaps out process D at the 3-second mark in favor of process E (because of the interaction of the *nice* value) even though process D had never run. Such thrashing is clearly undesirable.

One final danger is worthy of mention. If the swapper attempts to swap out a process but cannot find space on the swap device, a system deadlock could arise if the following four conditions are met: All processes in main memory are asleep, all "ready-to-run" processes are swapped out, there is no room on the swap device for new processes, and there is no room in main memory for incoming processes. Exercise 9.5 explores this situation. Interest in fixing problems with the swapper has declined in recent years as demand paging algorithms have been implemented for UNIX systems.

9.2 DEMAND PAGING

Machines whose memory architecture is based on pages and whose CPU has restartable instructions[3] can support a kernel that implements a demand paging algorithm, swapping pages of memory between main memory and a swap device. Demand paging systems free processes from size limitations otherwise imposed by the amount of physical memory available on a machine. For instance, machines that contain 1 or 2 megabytes of physical memory can execute processes whose sizes are 4 or 5 megabytes. The kernel still imposes a limit on the virtual size of a process, dependent on the amount of virtual memory the machine can address. Since a process may not fit into physical memory, the kernel must load its relevant portions into memory dynamically and execute it even though other parts are not loaded. Demand paging is transparent to user programs except for the virtual size

---

3. If a machine executes "part" of an instruction and incurs a page fault, the CPU must restart the instruction after handling the fault, because intermediate computations done before the page fault may have been lost.

permissible to a process.

Processes tend to execute instructions in small portions of their text space, such as program loops and frequently called subroutines, and their data references tend to cluster in small subsets of the total data space of the process. This is known as the principle of "locality." Denning [Denning 68] formalized the notion of the *working set* of a process, which is the set of pages that the process has referenced in its last n memory references; the number n is called the *window* of the working set. Because the working set is a fraction of the entire process, more processes may fit simultaneously into main memory than in a swapping system, potentially increasing system throughput because of reduced swapping traffic. When a process addresses a page that is not in its working set, it incurs a page fault; in handling the fault, the kernel updates the working set, reading in pages from a secondary device if necessary.

Figure 9.12 shows a sequence of page references a process could make, depicting the working sets for various window sizes and following a least recently used replacement policy. As a process executes, its working set changes, depending on the pattern of memory references the process makes; a larger window size yields a larger working set, implying that a process will not fault as often. It is impractical to implement a pure working set model, because it is expensive to remember the order of page references. Instead, systems approximate a working set model by setting a *reference* bit whenever a process accesses a page and by sampling memory references periodically: If a page was recently referenced, it is part of a working set; otherwise, it "ages" in memory until it is eligible for swapping.

When a process accesses a page that is not part of its working set, it incurs a *validity page fault*. The kernel suspends execution of the process until it reads the page into memory and makes it accessible to the process. When the page is loaded in memory, the process restarts the instruction it was executing when it incurred the fault. Thus, the implementation of a paging subsystem has two parts: swapping rarely used pages to a swapping device and handling page faults. This general description of paging schemes extends to non-UNIX systems, too. The rest of this chapter examines the paging scheme for UNIX System V in detail.

9.2.1 Data Structures for Demand Paging

The kernel contains 4 major data structures to support low-level memory management functions and demand paging: page table entries, *disk block descriptors*, the *page frame data table* (called *pfdata* for short), and the swap-use table. The kernel allocates space for the pfdata table once for the lifetime of the system but allocates memory pages for the other structures dynamically.

Recall from Chapter 6 that a region contains page tables to access physical memory. Each entry of a page table (Figure 9.13) contains the physical address of the page, protection bits indicating whether processes can read, write or execute from the page, and the following bit fields to support demand paging:

Sequence of Page References	Working Sets		Window Sizes	
	2	3	4	5
24	24	24	24	24
15	15 24	15 24	15 24	15 24
18	18 15	18 15 24	18 15 24	18 15 24
23	23 18	23 18 15	23 18 15 24	23 18 15 24
24	24 23	24 23 18	⋮	⋮
17	17 24	17 24 23	17 24 23 18	17 24 23 18 15
18	18 17	18 17 24	⋮	⋮
24	24 18	⋮	⋮	⋮
18	18 24	⋮	⋮	⋮
17	17 18	⋮	⋮	⋮
17	17	⋮	⋮	⋮
15	15 17	15 17 18	15 17 18 24	⋮
24	24 15	24 15 17	⋮	⋮
17	17 24	⋮	⋮	⋮
24	24 17	⋮	⋮	⋮
18	18 24	18 24 17	⋮	⋮

Figure 9.12. Working Set of a Process

- Valid
- Reference
- Modify
- Copy on write
- Age

The kernel turns on the *valid* bit to indicate that the contents of a page are legal, but the page reference is not necessarily illegal if the *valid* bit is off, as will be seen. The *reference* bit indicates whether a process recently referenced a page, and the *modify* bit indicates whether a process recently modified the contents of a page. The *copy on write* bit, used in the *fork* system call, indicates that the kernel must create a new copy of the page when a process modifies its contents. Finally, the kernel manipulates the *age* bits to indicate how long a page has been a member of the working set of a process. Assume the kernel manipulates the valid, copy on write, and age bits, and the hardware sets the reference and modify bits of the page table entry; Section 9.2.4 will consider hardware that does not have these capabilities.

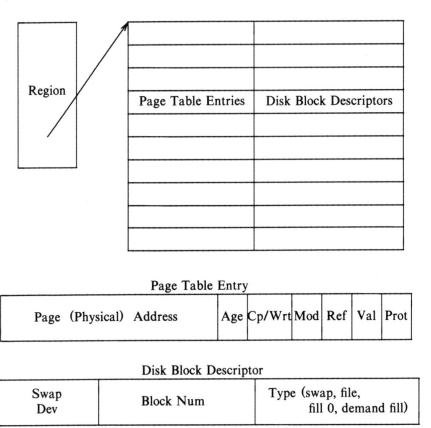

Page Table Entry

Page (Physical) Address	Age	Cp/Wrt	Mod	Ref	Val	Prot

Disk Block Descriptor

Swap Dev	Block Num	Type (swap, file, fill 0, demand fill)

Figure 9.13. Page Table Entries and Disk Block Descriptors

Each page table entry is associated with a disk block descriptor, which describes the disk copy of the virtual page (Figure 9.13). Processes that share a region therefore access common page table entries and disk block descriptors. The contents of a virtual page are either in a particular block on a swap device, in an executable file, or not on a swap device. If the page is on a swap device, the disk block descriptor contains the logical device number and block number containing the page contents. If the page is contained in an executable file, the disk block descriptor contains the logical block number in the file that contains the page; the kernel can quickly map this number into its disk address. The disk block descriptor also indicates two special conditions set during *exec*: that a page is "demand fill" or "demand zero." Section 9.2.1.2 will explain these conditions.

The pfdata table describes each page of *physical* memory and is indexed by page number. The fields of an entry are

- The page state, indicating that the page is on a swap device or executable file, that DMA is currently underway for the page (reading data from a swap device), or that the page can be reassigned.
- The number of processes that reference the page. The reference count equals the number of valid page table entries that reference the page. It may differ from the number of processes that share regions containing the page, as will be described below when reconsidering the algorithm for *fork*.
- The logical device (swap or file system) and block number that contains a copy of the page.
- Pointers to other pfdata table entries on a list of free pages and on a hash queue of pages.

The kernel links entries of the pfdata table onto a free list and a hashed list, analogous to the linked lists of the buffer cache. The free list is a cache of pages that are available for reassignment, but a process may fault on an address and still find the corresponding page intact on the free list. The free list thus allows the kernel to avoid unnecessary read operations from the swap device. The kernel allocates new pages from the list in least recently used order. The kernel also hashes the pfdata table entry according to its (swap) device number and block number. Thus, given a device and block number, the kernel can quickly locate a page if it is in memory. To assign a physical page to a region, the kernel removes a free page frame entry from the head of the free list, updates its swap device and block numbers, and puts it onto the correct hash queue.

The swap-use table contains an entry for every page on a swap device. The entry consists of a reference count of how many page table entries point to a page on a swap device.

Figure 9.14 shows the relationship between page table entries, disk block descriptors, pfdata table entries, and the swap-use count table. Virtual address 1493K of a process maps into a page table entry that points to physical page 794; the disk block descriptor for the page table entry shows that a copy of the page exists at disk block 2743 on swap device 1. The pfdata table entry for physical page 794 also shows that a copy of the page exists at disk block 2743 on swap device 1, and its in-core reference count is 1. Section 9.2.4.1 will explain why the disk block number is duplicated in the pfdata table and the disk block descriptor. The swap use count for the virtual page is 1, meaning that one page table entry points to the swap copy.

9.2.1.1 Fork in a Paging System

As explained in Section 7.1, the kernel duplicates every region of the parent process during the *fork* system call and attaches it to the child process. Traditionally, the

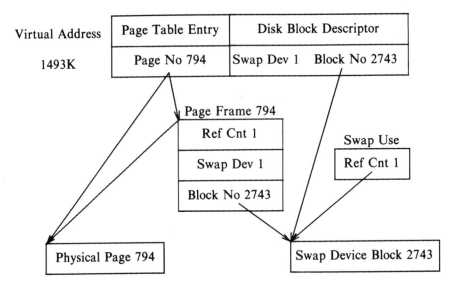

Figure 9.14. Relationship of Data Structures for Demand Paging

kernel of a swapping system makes a physical copy of the parent's address space, usually a wasteful operation, because processes often call *exec* soon after the *fork* call and immediately free the memory just copied. On the System V paging system, the kernel avoids copying the page by manipulating the region tables, page table entries, and pfdata table entries: It simply increments the region reference count of shared regions. For private regions such as data and stack, however, it allocates a new region table entry and page table and then examines each parent page table entry: If a page is valid, it increments the reference count in the pfdata table entry, indicating the number of processes that share the page via *different* regions (as opposed to the number that share the page by sharing the region). If the page exists on a swap device, it increments the swap-use table reference count for the page.

The page can now be referenced through both regions, which share the page until a process writes to it. The kernel then copies the page so that each region has a private version. To do this, the kernel turns on the "copy on write" bit for every page table entry in private regions of the parent and child processes during *fork*. If either process writes the page, it incurs a protection fault, and in handling the fault, the kernel makes a new copy of the page for the faulting process. The physical copying of the page is thus deferred until a process really needs it.

Figure 9.15 shows the data structures when a process *fork*s. The processes share access to the page table of the shared text region T, so the region reference count is 2 and the pfdata reference count for pages in the text region is 1. The

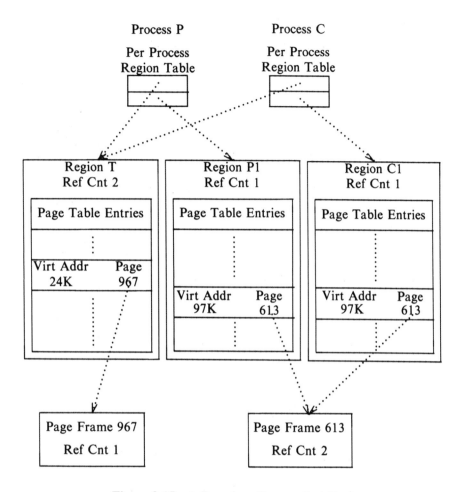

Figure 9.15. A Page in a Process that Forks

kernel allocates a new child data region, *C1*, a copy of region *P1* in the parent process. The page table entries of the two regions are identical, as illustrated by the entry for virtual address 97K. The page table entries point to pfdata table entry 613, whose reference count is 2, indicating that two regions reference the page.

The implementation of the *fork* system call in the BSD system makes a physical copy of the pages of the parent process. Recognizing the performance improvement gained by not having to do the copy, however, the BSD system also contains the *vfork* system call, which assumes that a child process will immediately invoke *exec* on return from the *vfork* call. *Vfork* does not copy page tables so it is faster than the System V *fork* implementation. But the child process executes in the same physical address space as the parent process (until an *exec* or *exit*) and can thus overwrite the parent's data and stack. A dangerous situation could arise if a programmer uses *vfork* incorrectly, so the onus for calling *vfork* lies with the programmer. The difference between the System V approach and the BSD approach is philosophical: Should the kernel hide idiosyncrasies of its implementation from users, or should it allow sophisticated users the opportunity to take advantage of the implementation to do a logical function more efficiently?

```
int global;
main()
{
        int local;

        local = 1;
        if (vfork() == 0)
        {
                /* child */
                global = 2;       /* write parent data space */
                local = 3;        /* write parent stack */
                _exit();
        }
        printf("global %d local %d\n", global, local);
}
```

Figure 9.16. Vfork and Corruption of Process Memory

For example, consider the program in Figure 9.16. After the *vfork* call, the child process does not *exec*, but resets the variables *global* and *local* and exits.[4] The system guarantees that the parent process is suspended until the child process *execs* or *exits*. When the parent process finally resumes execution, it finds that the values of the two variables are not the same as they were before the *vfork*! More spectacular effects can occur if the child process returns from the function that had called *vfork* (see exercise 9.8).

---

4. The call to *_exit* is used, because *exit* "cleans up" the standard I/O (user-level) data structures for the parent *and* child processes, preventing the parent's *printf* statement from working correctly — another unfortunate side effect of *vfork*.

9.2.1.2 Exec in a Paging System

When a process invokes the *exec* system call, the kernel reads the executable file into memory from the file system, as described in Chapter 7. On a demand paged system, however, the executable file may be too large to fit in the available main memory. The kernel, therefore, does not preassign memory to the executable file but "faults" it in, assigning memory as needed. It first assigns the page tables and disk block descriptors for the executable file, marking the page table entries "demand fill" (for non-bss data) or "demand zero" (for bss data). Following a variant of the *read* algorithm for reading the file into memory, the process incurs a validity fault as it reads each page. The fault handler notes whether the page is "demand fill," meaning its contents will immediately be overwritten with the contents of the executable file so it need not be cleared, or that it is "demand zero," meaning that its contents should be cleared. The description of the validity fault handler in Section 9.2.3 will show how this is done. If the process cannot fit into memory, the page-stealer process periodically swaps pages from memory, making room for the incoming file.

There are obvious inefficiencies in this scheme. First, a process incurs a page fault when reading each page of the executable file, even though it may never access the page. Second, the page stealer may swap pages from memory before the *exec* is done, resulting in two extra swap operations per page if the process needs the page early. To make *exec* more efficient, the kernel can demand page directly from the executable file if the data is properly aligned, as indicated by a special magic number. However, use of standard algorithms (such as *bmap*, in Chapter 4) to access a file would make it expensive to demand page from indirect blocks because of the multiple buffer cache accesses necessary to read a block. Furthermore, consistency problems could arise because *bmap* is not reentrant. The kernel sets various I/O parameters in the *u area* during the *read* system call. If a process incurs a page fault during a *read* system call when attempting to copy data to user space, it would overwrite these fields in the *u area* to read the page from the file system. Therefore, the kernel cannot use the regular algorithms to fault in pages from the file system. The algorithms are, of course, reentrant in regular cases, because each process has a separate *u area* and a process cannot simultaneously execute multiple system calls.

To page directly from an executable file, the kernel finds all the disk block numbers of the executable file when it does the *exec* and attaches the list to the file inode. When setting up the page tables for such an executable file, the kernel marks the disk block descriptor with the logical block number (starting from block 0 in the file) containing the page; the validity fault handler later uses this information to load the page from the file. Figure 9.17 shows a typical arrangement, where the disk block descriptor indicates that the page is at logical block offset 84 in the file. The kernel follows the pointer from the region to the inode and looks up the appropriate disk block number (279).

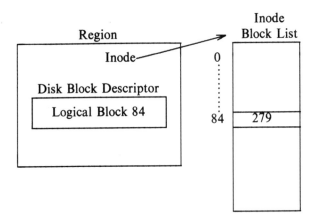

Figure 9.17. Mapping a File into a Region

9.2.2 The Page-Stealer Process

The page stealer is a kernel process that swaps out memory pages that are no longer part of the working set of a process. The kernel creates the page stealer during system initialization and invokes it throughout the lifetime of the system when low on free pages. It examines every active, unlocked region, skipping locked regions in the expectation of examining them during its next pass through the region list, and increments the age field of all valid pages. The kernel locks a region when a process faults on a page in the region, so that the page stealer cannot steal the page being faulted in.

There are two paging states for a page in memory: The page is aging and is not yet eligible for swapping, or the page is eligible for swapping and is available for reassignment to other virtual pages. The first state indicates that a process recently accessed the page, and the page is therefore in its working set. Some machines set a *reference* bit when they reference a page, but software methods can be substituted if the hardware does not have this feature (Section 9.2.4). The page stealer turns off the *reference* bit for such pages but remembers how many examinations have passed since the page was last referenced. The first state thus consists of several substates, corresponding to the number of passes the page stealer makes before the page is eligible for swapping (see Figure 9.18). When the number exceeds a threshold value, the kernel puts the page into the second state, ready to be swapped. The maximum period that a page can age before it is eligible to be swapped is implementation dependent, constrained by the number of bits available in the page table entry.

Figure 9.19 depicts the interaction between processes accessing a page and examinations by the page stealer. The page starts out in main memory, and the figure shows the number of examinations by the page stealer between memory

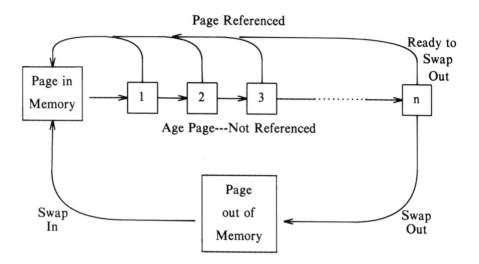

Figure 9.18. State Diagram for Page Aging

references. A process referenced the page after the second examination, dropping its age to 0. Similarly, a process referenced the page again after one more examination. Finally, the page stealer examined the page three times without an intervening reference and swapped the page out.

If two or more processes share a region, they update the *reference* bits of the same set of page table entries. Pages can thus be part of the working set of more than one process, but that does not matter to the page stealer. If a page is part of the working set of any process, it remains in memory; if it is not part of the working set of any process, it is eligible for swapping. It does not matter if one region has more pages in memory than others: the page stealer does not attempt to swap out equal numbers of pages from all active regions.

The kernel wakes up the page stealer when the available free memory in the system is below a low-water mark, and the page stealer swaps out pages until the available free memory in the system exceeds a high-water mark. The use of high- and low-water marks reduces thrashing: If the kernel were only to use one threshold, it would swap out enough pages to get above the threshold (of free pages), but as a result of faulting pages back into memory, the number would soon drop below the threshold. The page stealer would effectively thrash about the threshold. By swapping out pages until the number of free pages exceeds a high-water mark, it takes longer until the number of free pages drops below the low-water mark, so the page stealer does not run as often. Administrators can configure the values of the high- and low-water marks for best performance.

When the page stealer decides to swap out a page, it considers whether a copy of the page is on a swap device. There are three possibilities.

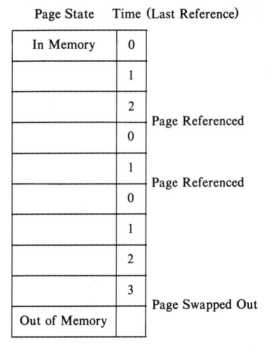

Figure 9.19. Example of Aging a Page

1. If no copy of the page is on a swap device, the kernel "schedules" the page for swapping: The page stealer places the page on a list of pages to be swapped out and continues; the swap is logically complete. When the list of pages to be swapped reaches a limit (dependent on the capabilities of the disk controller), the kernel writes the pages to the swap device.
2. If a copy of the page is already on a swap device and no process had modified its in-core contents (the page table entry *modify* bit is clear), the kernel clears the page table entry *valid* bit, decrements the reference count in the pfdata table entry, and puts the entry on the free list for future allocation.
3. If a copy of the page is on a swap device but a process had modified its contents in memory, the kernel schedules the page for swapping, as above, and frees the space it currently occupies on the swap device.

The page stealer copies the page to a swap device if case 1 or case 3 is true.

    To illustrate the differences between the last two cases, suppose a page is on a swap device and is swapped into main memory after a process incurs a validity fault. Assume the kernel does not automatically remove the disk copy. Eventually, the page stealer decides to swap the page out again. If no process has written the page since it was swapped in, the memory copy is identical to the disk copy and there is no need to write the page to the swap device. If a process has written the page, however, the memory copy differs from the disk copy, so the kernel must write the page to the swap device, after freeing the space on the swap device previously occupied by the page. It does not reuse the space on the swap device immediately, so that it can keep swap space contiguous for better performance.

The page stealer fills a list of pages to be swapped, possibly from different regions, and swaps them to a swap device when the list is full. Every page of a process need not be swapped: Some pages may not have aged sufficiently, for example. This differs from the policy of the swapping process, which swaps every page of a process from memory, but the method for writing data to the swap device is identical to that described in Section 9.1.2 for a swapping system. If no swap device contains enough contiguous space, the kernel swaps out one page at a time, which is clearly more costly. There is more fragmentation of a swap device in the paging scheme than in a swapping scheme, because the kernel swaps out blocks of pages but swaps in only one page at a time.

When the kernel writes a page to a swap device, it turns off the *valid* bit in its page table entry and decrements the use count of its pfdata table entry. If the count drops to 0, it places the pfdata table entry at the end of the free list, caching it until reassignment. If the count is not 0, several processes are sharing the page as a result of a previous *fork* call, but the kernel still swaps the page out. Finally, the kernel allocates swap space, saves the swap address in the disk block descriptor, and increments the swap-use table count for the page. If a process incurs a page fault while the page is on the free list, however, the kernel can rescue the page from memory instead of having to retrieve it from the swap device. However, the page is still swapped if it is on the swap list.

For example, suppose the page stealer swaps out 30, 40, 50 and 20 pages from processes A, B, C, and D, respectively, and that it writes 64 pages to the swap device in one disk write operation. Figure 9.20 shows the sequence of page-swapping operations that would occur if the page stealer examines pages of the processes in the order A, B, C, and D. The page stealer allocates space for 64 pages on the swap device and swaps out the 30 pages of process A and 34 pages of process B. It then allocates more space on the swap device for another 64 pages and swaps out the remaining 6 pages of process B, the 50 pages of process C, and 8 pages of process D. The two areas of the swap device for the two write operations need not be contiguous. The page stealer keeps the remaining 12 pages of process D on the list of pages to be swapped but does not swap them until the list is full. As processes fault in pages from the swap device or when the pages are no longer in use (processes *exit*), free space develops on the swap device.

To summarize, there are two phases to swapping a page from memory. First, the page stealer finds the page eligible for swapping and places the page number on a list of pages to be swapped. Second, the kernel copies the page to a swap device when convenient, turns off the *valid* bit in the page table entry, decrements the pfdata table entry reference count, and places the pfdata table entry at the end of

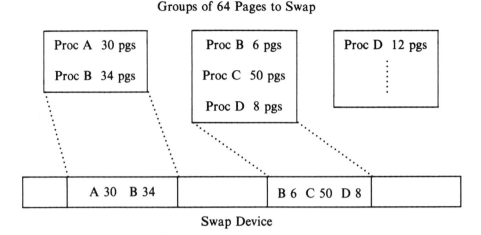

Figure 9.20. Allocation of Swap Space in Paging Scheme

the free list if its reference count is 0. The contents of the physical page in memory are valid until the page is reassigned.

9.2.3 Page Faults

The system can incur two types of page faults: validity faults and protection faults. Because the fault handlers may have to read a page from disk to memory and sleep during the I/O operation, fault handlers are an exception to the general rule that interrupt handlers cannot sleep. However, because the fault handler sleeps in the context of the process that caused the memory fault, the fault relates to the running process; hence, no arbitrary processes are put to sleep.

9.2.3.1 Validity Fault Handler

If a process attempts to access a page whose *valid* bit is not set, it incurs a validity fault and the kernel invokes the validity fault handler (Figure 9.21). The *valid* bit is not set for pages outside the virtual address space of a process, nor is it set for pages that are part of the virtual address space but do not currently have a physical page assigned to them. The hardware supplies the kernel with the virtual address that was accessed to cause the memory fault, and the kernel finds the page table entry and disk block descriptor for the page. The kernel locks the region containing the page table entry to prevent race conditions that would occur if the page stealer attempted to swap the page out. If the disk block descriptor has no record of the

```
algorithm vfault         /* handler for validity faults */
input:   address where process faulted
output: none
{
      find region, page table entry, disk block descriptor
                  corresponding to faulted address, lock region;
      if (address outside virtual address space)
      {
            send signal (SIGSEGV: segmentation violation) to process;
            goto out;
      }
      if (address now valid)         /* process may have slept above */
            goto out;
      if (page in cache)
      {
            remove page from cache;
            adjust page table entry;
            while (page contents not valid) /* another proc faulted first */
                  sleep (event contents become valid);
      }
      else      /* page not in cache */
      {
            assign new page to region;

            put new page in cache, update pfdata entry;
            if (page not previously loaded and page "demand zero")
                  clear assigned page to 0;
            else
            {
                  read virtual page from swap dev or exec file;
                  sleep (event I/O done);
            }
            awaken processes (event page contents valid);
      }
      set page valid bit;
      clear page modify bit, page age;
      recalculate process priority;
  out: unlock region;
}
```

Figure 9.21. Algorithm for Validity Fault Handler

faulted page, the attempted memory reference is invalid and the kernel sends a "segmentation violation" signal to the offending process (recall Figure 7.25). This is the same procedure a swapping system follows when a process accesses an invalid address, except that it recognizes the error immediately because all legal pages are memory resident. If the memory reference was legal, the kernel allocates a page of memory to read in the page contents from the swap device or from the executable file.

The page that caused the fault is in one of five states:

1. On a swap device and not in memory,
2. On the free page list in memory,
3. In an executable file,
4. Marked "demand zero,"
5. Marked "demand fill."

Let us consider each case in detail.

If a page is on a swap device and not in memory (case 1), it once resided in main memory but the page stealer had swapped it out. From the disk block descriptor, the kernel finds the swap device and block number where the page is stored and verifies that the page is not in the page cache. The kernel updates the page table entry so that it points to the page about to be read in, places the pfdata table entry on a hash list to speed later operation of the fault handler, and reads the page from the swap device. The faulting process sleeps until the I/O completes, when the kernel awakens other processes who were waiting for the contents of the page to be read in.

For example, consider the page table entry for virtual address 66K in Figure 9.22. If a process incurs a validity fault when accessing the page, the fault handler examines the disk block descriptor and sees that the page is contained in block 847 of the swap device (assume there is only one swap device): Hence, the virtual address is legal. The fault handler then searches the page cache but fails to find an entry for disk block 847. Therefore, there is no copy of the virtual page in memory, and the fault handler must read it from the swap device. The kernel assigns page 1776 (Figure 9.23), reads the contents of the virtual page from the swap device into the new page, and updates the page table entry to refer to page 1776. Finally, it updates the disk block descriptor to indicate that the page is still swapped and the pfdata table entry for page 1776 to indicate that block 847 of the swap device contains a duplicate copy of the virtual page.

The kernel does not always have to do an I/O operation when it incurs a validity fault, even though the disk block descriptor indicates that the page is swapped (case 2). It is possible that the kernel had never reassigned the physical page after swapping it out, or that another process had faulted the virtual page into another physical page. In either case, the fault handler finds the page in the page cache, keying off the block number in the disk block descriptor. It reassigns the page table entry to point to the page just found, increments its page reference count, and removes the page from the free list, if necessary. For example, suppose

Virt Addr	Page Table Entries			Disk Block Descriptors		Page Frames		
	Phys Page	State		State	Block	Page	Disk Block	Count
0								
1K	1648	Inv		File	3			
2K								
3K	None	Inv		DF	5			
4K						1036	387	0
⋮						⋮		
						1648	1618	1
64K	1917	Inv		Disk	1206	⋮		
65K	None	Inv		DZ				
66K	1036	Inv		Disk	847	1861	1206	0
67K								

Figure 9.22. Occurrence of a Validity Fault

a process faults when accessing virtual address 64K in Figure 9.22. Searching the page cache, the kernel finds that page frame 1861 is associated with disk block 1206, as is the disk block descriptor. It resets the page table entry for virtual address 64K to point to page 1861, sets the *valid* bit, and returns. The disk block number thus associates a page table entry with a pfdata table entry, explaining why both tables save it.

Similarly, the fault handler does not have to read the page into memory if another process had faulted on the same page but had not completely read it in yet. The fault handler finds the region containing the page table entry locked by another instance of the fault handler. It sleeps until the other instance of the fault handler completes, finds the page now valid, and returns. Figure 9.24 depicts such a scenario.

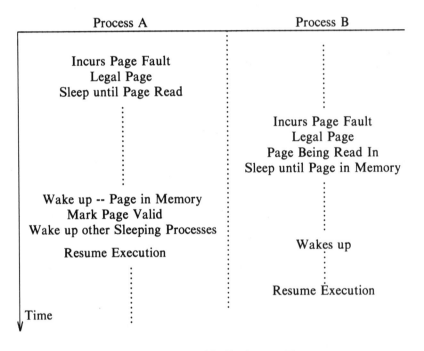

Virt Addr	Page Table Entries			Disk Block Descriptors		Page Frames		
	Phys Page	State		State	Block	Page	Disk Block	Count
66K	1776	Val		Disk	847	1776	847	1

Figure 9.23. After Swapping Page into Memory

Process A	Process B
Incurs Page Fault	
Legal Page	
Sleep until Page Read	
	Incurs Page Fault
	Legal Page
	Page Being Read In
	Sleep until Page in Memory
Wake up -- Page in Memory	
Mark Page Valid	
Wake up other Sleeping Processes	
Resume Execution	Wakes up
	Resume Execution
Time	

Figure 9.24. Double Fault on a Page

If a copy of the page does not exist on a swap device but is in the original executable file (case 3), the kernel reads the page from the original file. The fault handler examines the disk block descriptor, finds the logical block number in the file that contains the page, and finds the inode associated with the region table entry. It uses the logical block number as an offset into the array of disk block numbers attached to the inode during *exec*. Knowing the disk block number, it reads the page into memory. For example, the disk block descriptor for virtual address 1K in Figure 9.22 shows that the page contents are in logical block 3 in the executable file.

If a process incurs a page fault for a page marked "demand fill" or "demand zero" (cases 4 and 5), the kernel allocates a free page in memory and updates the appropriate page table entry. For "demand zero," it also clears the page to zero. Finally, it clears the "demand fill" or "demand zero" flags: The page is now valid in memory and its contents are not duplicated on a swap device or in a file system. This would happen when accessing virtual addresses 3K and 65K in Figure 9.22: No process had accessed those pages since the file was *exec*ed.

The validity fault handler concludes by setting the *valid* bit of the page and clearing the *modify* bit. It recalculates the process priority, because the process may have slept in the fault handler at a kernel-level priority, giving it an unfair scheduling advantage when returning to user mode. Finally, if returning to user mode, it checks for receipt of any signals that occurred while handling the page fault.

9.2.3.2 Protection Fault Handler

The second kind of memory fault that a process can incur is a *protection* fault, meaning that the process accessed a valid page but the permission bits associated with the page did not permit access. (Recall the example of a process attempting to write its text space, in Figure 7.22.) A process also incurs a protection fault when it attempts to write a page whose *copy on write* bit was set during the *fork* system call. The kernel must determine whether permission was denied because the page requires a *copy on write* or whether something truly illegal happened.

The hardware supplies the protection fault handler with the virtual address where the fault occurred, and the fault handler finds the appropriate region and page table entry (Figure 9.25). It locks the region so that the page stealer cannot steal the page while the protection fault handler operates on it. If the fault handler determines that the fault was caused because the *copy on write* bit was set, and if the page is shared with other processes, the kernel allocates a new page and copies the contents of the old page to it; the other processes retain their references to the old page. After copying the page and updating the page table entry with the new page number, the kernel decrements the reference count of the old pfdata table entry. Figure 9.26 illustrates the scenario: Three processes share physical page 828. Process B writes the page but incurs a protection fault, because the *copy on write* bit is set. The protection fault handler allocates page 786, copies the contents of page 828 to the new page, decrements the reference count of page 828, and updates the page table entry accessed by process B to point to page 786.

If the *copy on write* bit is set but no other processes share the page, the kernel allows the process to reuse the physical page. It turns off the *copy on write* bit and disassociates the page from its disk copy, if one exists, because other processes may share the disk copy. It then removes the pfdata table entry from the page queue, because the new copy of the virtual page is not on the swap device. Then, it

```
algorithm pfault                /* protection fault handler */
input:      address where process faulted
output:       none
{
        find region, page table entry, disk block descriptor,
                    page frame for address, lock region;
        if (page not valid in memory)
                goto out;
        if (copy on write bit not set)
                goto out;              /* real program error — signal */
        if (page frame reference count > 1)
        {
                allocate a new physical page;
                copy contents of old page to new page;
                decrement old page frame reference count;
                update page table entry to point to new physical page;
        }
        else      /* "steal" page, since nobody else is using it */
        {
                if (copy of page exists on swap device)
                        free space on swap device, break page association;
                if (page is on page hash queue)
                        remove from hash queue;
        }
        set modify bit, clear copy on write bit in page table entry;
        recalculate process priority;
        check for signals;
   out: unlock region;
}
```

Figure 9.25. Algorithm for Protection Fault Handler

decrements the swap-use count for the page and, if the count drops to 0, frees the swap space (see exercise 9.11).

If a page table entry is invalid and its *copy on write* bit is set to cause a protection fault, let us assume that the system handles the validity fault first when a process accesses the page (exercise 9.17 covers the reverse case). Nevertheless, the protection fault handler must check that a page is still valid, because it could sleep when locking a region, and the page stealer could meanwhile swap the page from memory. If the page is invalid (the *valid* bit is clear), the fault handler returns immediately, and the process will incur a validity fault. The kernel handles the validity fault, but the process will incur the protection fault again. More than likely, it will handle the final protection fault without any more interference, because it will take a long time until the page will age sufficiently to be swapped out. Figure 9.27 illustrates this sequence of events.

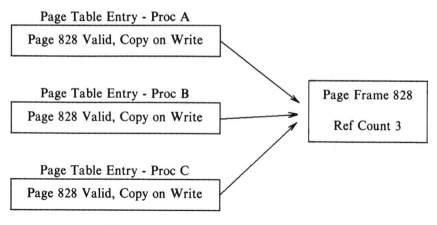

(a) Before Proc B Incurs Protection Fault

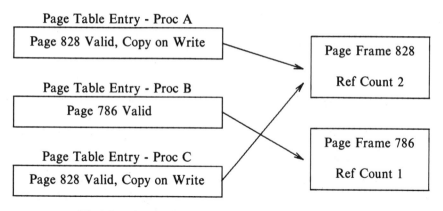

(b) After Protection Fault Handler Runs for Proc B

Figure 9.26. Protection Fault with Copy on Write Set

When the protection fault handler finishes executing, it sets the *modify* and *protection* bits, but clears the *copy on write* bit. It recalculates the process priority and checks for signals, as is done at the end of the validity fault handler.

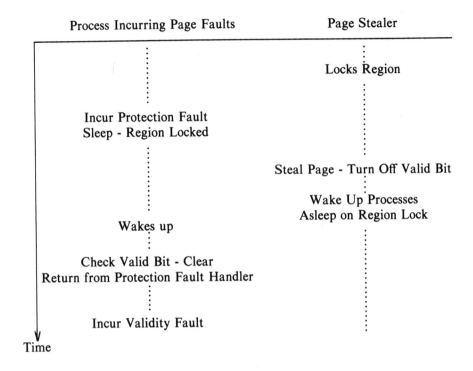

Figure 9.27. Interaction of Protection Fault and Validity Fault

9.2.4 Demand Paging on Less-Sophisticated Hardware

The algorithms for demand paging are most efficient if the hardware sets the *reference* and *modify* bits and causes a protection fault when a process writes a page whose *copy on write* bit is set. However, it is possible to implement the paging algorithms described here if the hardware recognizes only the *valid* and protection bits. If the *valid* bit is duplicated by a *software-valid* bit that indicates whether the page is really valid or not, then the kernel could turn off the hardware *valid* bit and simulate the setting of the other bits in software. For example, the VAX-11 hardware does not have a reference bit (see [Levy 82]). The kernel can turn off the hardware *valid* bit for the page and follow this scenario: If a process references the page, it incurs a page fault because the hardware *valid* bit is off, and the page fault interrupt handler examines the page. Because the *software-valid* bit is set, the kernel knows that the page is really valid and in memory; it sets the software *reference* bit and turns the hardware *valid* bit on, but it will have acquired the knowledge that the page had been referenced. Subsequent references to the page will not incur a fault because the hardware *valid* bit is on. When the page stealer examines the page, it turns off the hardware *valid* bit again, causing

Hardware Valid	Software Valid	Software Reference
Off	On	Off

(a) Before Modifying Page

Hardware Valid	Software Valid	Software Reference
On	On	On

(b) After Modifying Page

Figure 9.28. Mimicking Hardware Modify Bit in Software

processes to fault when referencing the page, repeating the cycle. Figure 9.28 depicts this case.

9.3 A HYBRID SYSTEM WITH SWAPPING AND DEMAND PAGING

Although demand paging systems treat memory more flexibly than swapping systems, situations can arise where the page stealer and validity fault handler thrash because of a shortage of memory. If the sum of the working sets of all processes is greater than the physical memory on a machine, the fault handler will usually sleep, because it cannot allocate pages for a process. The page stealer will not be able to steal pages fast enough, because all pages are in a working set. System throughput suffers because the kernel spends too much time in overhead, rearranging memory at a frantic pace.

The System V kernel runs swapping and demand paging algorithms to avoid thrashing problems. When the kernel cannot allocate pages for a process, it wakes up the swapper and puts the calling process into a state that is the equivalent of "ready to run but swapped." Several processes may be in this state simultaneously. The swapper swaps out entire processes until available memory exceeds the high-water mark. For each process swapped out, it makes one "ready-to-run but swapped" process ready to run. It does not swap those processes in via the normal swapping algorithm but lets them fault in pages as needed. Later iterations of the swapper will allow other processes to be faulted in if there is sufficient memory in the system. This method slows down the system fault rate and reduces thrashing; it is similar in philosophy to methods used in the VAX/VMS operating system ([Levy 82]).

9.4 SUMMARY

This chapter has explored the UNIX System V algorithms for process swapping and demand paging. The swapping algorithm swaps entire processes between main memory and a swap device. The kernel swaps processes from memory if their size grows such that there is no more room in main memory (as a result of a *fork*, *exec*, or *sbrk* system call or as a result of normal stack growth), or if it has to make room for a process being swapped in. The kernel swaps processes in via the special swapper process, process 0, invoking it whenever there exists a "ready-to-run" process on the swap device. The swapper swaps in all such processes until there are no more processes on the swap device or until there is no more room in memory. In the latter case, it attempts to swap processes from main memory, but it reduces the amount of thrashing by prohibiting swapping of processes that do not satisfy residency requirements; hence, the swapper is not always successful in swapping all processes into memory during each pass. The clock handler wakes up the swapper every second if it has work to do.

The implementation of demand paging allows processes to execute even though their entire virtual address space is not loaded in memory; therefore the virtual size of a process can exceed the amount of physical memory available in a system. When the kernel runs low on free pages, the page stealer goes through the active pages of every region, marks pages eligible for stealing if they have aged sufficiently, and eventually copies them to a swap device. When a process addresses a virtual page that is currently swapped out, it incurs a validity fault. The kernel invokes the validity fault handler to assign a new physical page to the region and copies the contents of the virtual page to main memory.

With the implementation of the demand paging algorithm, several features improve system performance. First, the kernel uses the *copy on write* bit for *fork*ing processes, removing the need to make physical copies of pages in most cases. Second, the kernel can demand page contents of an executable file from the file system, eliminating the need for *exec* to read the file into memory immediately. This helps performance because such pages may never be needed during the lifetime of a process, and it eliminates extra thrashing caused if the page stealer were to swap such pages from memory before they are used.

9.5 EXERCISES

1. Sketch the design of an algorithm *mfree*, which frees space and returns it to a *map*.
2. Section 9.1.2 states that the system locks a process being swapped so that no other process can swap it while the first operation is underway. What would happen if the system did not lock the process?
3. Suppose the *u area* contains the segment tables and page tables for a process. How can the kernel swap the *u area* out?
4. If the kernel stack is inside the *u area*, why can't a process swap itself out? How would you encode a kernel process to swap out other processes and how should it be invoked?
* 5. Suppose the kernel attempts to swap out a process to make room for processes on a swap device. If there is not enough space on any swap devices, the swapper sleeps until more space becomes available. Is it possible for all processes in memory to be asleep and for all ready-to-run processes to be on the swap device? Describe such a scenario. What should the kernel do to rectify the situation?

6. Reconsider the swapping example in Figure 9.10 if there is room for only 1 process in memory.

7. Reconsider the swapping example in Figure 9.11. Construct an example where a process is permanently starved from use of the CPU. Is there any way to prevent this?

```
main()
{
        f();
        g();
}

f()
{
        vfork();
}

g()
{
        int blast[100], i;
        for (i = 0;  i < 100;  i++)
                blast[i] = i;
}
```

Figure 9.29. Vfork and More Corruption

8. What happens when executing the program in Figure 9.29 on a 4.2 BSD system? What happens to the parent's stack?

9. Why is it advantageous to schedule the child process before the parent after a *fork* call if *copy on write* bits are set on shared pages? How can the kernel force the child to run first?

* 10. The validity fault algorithm presented in the text swaps in one page at a time. Its efficiency can be improved by prepaging other pages around the page that caused the fault. Enhance the page fault algorithm to allow prepaging.

11. The algorithms for the page stealer and for the validity fault handler assume that the size of a page equals the size of a disk block. How should the algorithms be enhanced to handle the cases where the respective sizes are not equal?

* 12. When a process *fork*s, the page use count in the pfdata table is incremented for all shared pages. Suppose the page stealer swaps a (shared) page to a swap device, and one process (say, the parent) later faults it in. The virtual page now resides in a physical page. Explain why the child process will always be able to find a legal copy of the page, even after the parent writes the page. If the parent writes the page, why must it disassociate itself from the disk copy immediately?

13. What should a fault handler do if the system runs out of pages?

* 14. Design an algorithm that pages out infrequently used parts of the kernel. What parts of the kernel cannot be paged and how should they be identified?

15. Devise an algorithm that tracks the allocation of space on a swap device by means of a bit map instead of the maps described in the chapter. Compare the efficiency of the two methods.

16. Suppose a machine has no hardware *valid* bit but has protection bits to allow read, write, and execute from a page. Simulate manipulation of a software *valid* bit.

17. The VAX-11 hardware checks for protection faults before validity faults. What ramifications does this have for the algorithms for the fault handlers?

18. The *plock* system call allows superusers to lock and unlock the text and data regions of the calling process into memory. The swapper and page stealer processes cannot remove locked pages from memory. Processes that use this call never have to wait to be swapped in, assuring them faster response than other processes. How should the system call be implemented? Should there be an option to lock the stack region into memory too? What should happen if the total memory space of *plock*ed regions is greater than the available memory on the machine?

19. What is the program in Figure 9.30 doing? Consider an alternative paging policy, where each process has a maximum allowed number of pages in its working set.

```
struct fourmeg
{
      int page[512];          /* assume int is 4 bytes */
} fourmeg[2048];

main()
{
      for (;;)
      {
            switch(fork())
            {
            case -1:     /* parent can't fork---too many children */
            case 0:      /* child */
                  func();
            default:
                  continue;
            }
      }
}

func()
{
      int i;

      for (;;)
      {
            printf("proc %d loops again\n", getpid());
            for (i = 0;  i < 2048;  i++)
                  fourmeg[i].page[0] = i;
      }
}
```

Figure 9.30. A Misbehaving Program

10

THE I/O
SUBSYSTEM

The I/O subsystem allows a process to communicate with peripheral devices such as disks, tape drives, terminals, printers, and networks, and the kernel modules that control devices are known as *device drivers*. There is usually a one-to-one correspondence between device drivers and device types: Systems may contain one disk driver to control all disk drives, one terminal driver to control all terminals, and one tape driver to control all tape drives. Installations that have devices from more than one manufacturer — for example, two brands of tape drives — may treat the devices as two different device types and have two separate drivers, because such devices may require different command sequences to operate properly. A device driver controls many physical devices of a given type. For example, one terminal driver may control all terminals connected to the system. The driver distinguishes among the many devices it controls: Output intended for one terminal must not be sent to another.

The system supports "software devices," which have no associated physical device. For example, it treats physical memory as a device to allow a process access to physical memory outside its address space, even though memory is not a peripheral device. The *ps* command, for instance, *read*s kernel data structures from physical memory to report process statistics. Similarly, drivers may write trace records useful for debugging, and a trace driver may allow users to read the records. Finally, the kernel profiler described in Chapter 8 is implemented as a driver: A process *write*s addresses of kernel routines found in the kernel symbol table and *read*s profiling results.

This chapter examines the interfaces between processes and the I/O subsystem and between the machine and the device drivers. It investigates the general structure and function of device drivers, then treats disk drivers and terminal drivers as detailed examples of the general interface. It concludes with a description of a new method for implementing device drivers called *streams*.

10.1 DRIVER INTERFACES

The UNIX system contains two types of devices, *block* devices and *raw* or *character* devices. As defined in Chapter 2, block devices, such as disks and tapes, look like random access storage devices to the rest of the system; character devices include all other devices such as terminals and network media. Block devices may have a character device interface, too.

The user interface to devices goes through the file system (recall Figure 2.1): Every device has a name that looks like a file name and is accessed like a file. The device special file has an inode and occupies a node in the directory hierarchy of the file system. The device file is distinguished from other files by the file type stored in its inode, either "block" or "character special," corresponding to the device it represents. If a device has both a block and character interface, it is represented by two device files: its block device special file and its character device special file. System calls for regular files, such as *open*, *close*, *read*, and *write*, have an appropriate meaning for devices, as will be explained later. The *ioctl* system call provides an interface that allows processes to control character devices, but it is not applicable to regular files.[1] However, each device driver need not support every system call interface. For example, the trace driver mentioned earlier allows users to *read* records written by other drivers, but it does not allow users to *write* it.

10.1.1 System Configuration

System configuration is the procedure by which administrators specify parameters that are installation dependent. Some parameters specify the sizes of kernel tables, such as the process table, inode table, and file table, and the number of buffers to be allocated for the buffer pool. Other parameters specify device configuration, telling the kernel which devices are included in the installation and their "address." For instance, a configuration may specify that a terminal board is plugged into a

---

1. Conversely, the *fcntl* system call provides control of operations at the file descriptor level, not the device level. Other implementations interpret *ioctl* for all file types.

particular slot on the hardware backplane.

There are three stages at which device configuration can be specified. First, administrators can hard-code configuration data into files that are compiled and linked when building the kernel code. The configuration data is typically specified in a simple format, and a configuration program converts it into a file suitable for compilation. Second, administrators can supply configuration information after the system is already running; the kernel updates internal configuration tables dynamically. Finally, self-identifying devices permit the kernel to recognize which devices are installed. The kernel reads hardware switches to configure itself. The details of system configuration are beyond the scope of this book, but in all cases, the configuration procedure generates or fills in tables that form part of the code of the kernel.

The kernel to driver interface is described by the *block device switch* table and the *character device switch* table (Figure 10.1). Each device type has entries in the table that direct the kernel to the appropriate driver interfaces for the system calls. The *open* and *close* system calls of a device file funnel through the two device switch tables, according to the file type. The *mount* and *umount* system calls also invoke the device open and close procedures for block devices. *Read*, *write*, and *ioctl* system calls of character special files pass through the respective procedures in the character device switch table. *Read* and *write* system calls of block devices and of files on mounted file systems invoke the algorithms of the buffer cache, which invoke the device strategy procedure. Some drivers invoke the strategy procedure internally from their read and write procedures, as will be seen. The next section explores each driver interface in greater detail.

The hardware to driver interface consists of machine-dependent control registers or I/O instructions for manipulating devices and interrupt vectors: When a device interrupt occurs, the system identifies the interrupting device and calls the appropriate interrupt handler. Obviously, software devices such as the kernel profiler driver (Chapter 8) do not have a hardware interface, but other interrupt handlers may call a "software interrupt handler" directly. For example, the clock interrupt handler calls the kernel profiler interrupt handler.

Administrators set up device special files with the *mknod* command, supplying file type (block or character) and major and minor numbers. The *mknod* command invokes the *mknod* system call to create the device file. For example, in the command line

    mknod /dev/tty13 c 2 13

"/dev/tty13" is the file name of the device, *c* specifies that it is a character special file (*b* specifies a block special file), 2 is the major number, and 13 is the minor number. The major number indicates a device type that corresponds to the appropriate entry in the block or character device switch tables, and the minor number indicates a unit of the device. If a process *open*s the block special file "/dev/dsk1" and its major number is 0, the kernel calls the routine *gdopen* in entry 0 of the block device switch table (Figure 10.2); if a process *read*s the character

File Subsystem

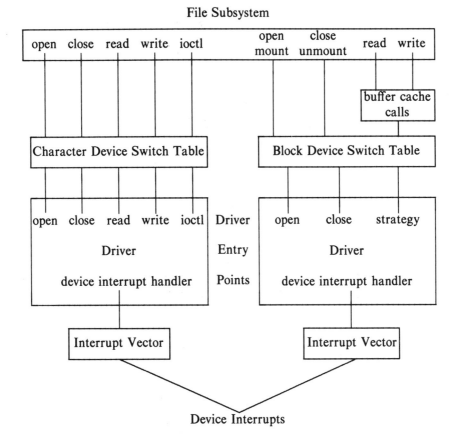

Figure 10.1. Driver Entry Points

special file "/dev/mem" and its major number is 3, the kernel calls the routine *mmread* in entry 3 of the character device switch table. The routine *nulldev* is an "empty" routine, used when there is no need for a particular driver function. Many peripheral devices can be associated with a major device number; the minor device number distinguishes them from each other. Device special files do not have to be created every time the system is booted; they need be changed only if the configuration changes, such as when adding devices to an installation.

10.1.2 System Calls and the Driver Interface

This section describes the interface between the kernel and device drivers. For system calls that use file descriptors, the kernel follows pointers from the user file

block device switch table			
entry	open	close	strategy
0	gdopen	gdclose	gdstrategy
1	gtopen	gtclose	gtstrategy

character device switch table					
entry	open	close	read	write	ioctl
0	conopen	conclose	conread	conwrite	conioctl
1	dzbopen	dzbclose	dzbread	dzbwrite	dzbioctl
2	syopen	nulldev	syread	sywrite	syioctl
3	nulldev	nulldev	mmread	mmwrite	nodev
4	gdopen	gdclose	gdread	gdwrite	nodev
5	gtopen	gtclose	gtread	gtwrite	nodev

Figure 10.2. Sample Block and Character Device Switch Tables

descriptor to the kernel file table and inode, where it examines the file type and accesses the block or character device switch table, as appropriate. It extracts the major and minor numbers from the inode, uses the major number as an index into the appropriate table, and calls the driver function according to the system call being made, passing the minor number as a parameter. An important difference between system calls for devices and regular files is that the inode of a special file is *not* locked while the kernel executes the driver. Drivers frequently sleep, waiting for hardware connections or for the arrival of data, so the kernel cannot determine how long a process will sleep. If the inode was locked, other processes that access the inode (via the *stat* system call, for example) would sleep indefinitely because another process is asleep in the driver.

The device driver interprets the parameters of the system call as appropriate for the device. A driver maintains data structures that describe the state of each unit that it controls; driver functions and interrupt handlers execute according to the state of the driver and the action being done (for example, data being input or output). Each interface will now be described in greater detail.

10.1.2.1 Open

The kernel follows the same procedure for *open*ing a device as it does for *open*ing regular files (see Section 5.1), allocating an in-core inode, incrementing its reference count, and assigning a file table entry and user file descriptor. The kernel eventually returns the user file descriptor to the calling process, so that *open*ing a device looks like *open*ing a regular file. However, it invokes the device-specific *open* procedure before returning to user mode, (Figure 10.3). For a block device, it

```
algorithm open                 /* for device drivers */
input:   pathname
         openmode
output: file descriptor
{
        convert pathname to inode, increment inode reference count,
        allocate entry in file table, user file descriptor,
                as in open of regular file;

        get major, minor number from inode;

        save context (algorithm setjmp) in case of long jump from driver;

        if (block device)
        {
                use major number as index to block device switch table;
                call driver open procedure for index:
                        pass minor number, open modes;
        }
        else
        {
                use major number as index to character device switch table;
                call driver open procedure for index:
                        pass minor number, open modes;
        }

        if (open fails in driver)
                decrement file table, inode counts;
}
```

Figure 10.3. Algorithm for Opening a Device

invokes the *open* procedure encoded in the block device switch table, and for a character device, it invokes the *open* procedure in the character device switch table. If a device is both a block and a character device, the kernel will invoke the appropriate *open* procedure depending on the particular device file the user *open*ed: The two open procedures may even be identical, depending on the driver.

The device-specific *open* procedure establishes a connection between the calling process and the *open*ed device and initializes private driver data structures. For a terminal, for example, the *open* procedure may put the process to sleep until the machine detects a (hardware) carrier signal indicating that a user is trying to log in. It then initializes driver data structures according to appropriate terminal settings (such as the terminal baud rate). For software devices such as system memory, the *open* procedure may have no initialization to do.

If a process must sleep for some external reason when *open*ing a device, it is possible that the event that should awaken the process from its sleep may never occur. For example, if no user ever logs in to a particular terminal, the *getty* process that *open*ed the terminal (Section 7.9) sleeps until a user attempts to log in, potentially a long time. The kernel must be able to awaken the process from its sleep and cancel the *open* call on receipt of a signal: It must reset the inode, file table entry, and user file descriptor that it had allocated before entry into the driver, because the *open* fails. Hence, the kernel saves the process context using algorithm *setjmp* (Section 6.4.4) before entering the device-specific *open* routine; if the process awakens from its sleep because of a signal, the kernel restores the process context to its state before entering the driver using algorithm *longjmp* (Section 6.4.4) and releases all data structures it had allocated for the *open*. Similarly, the driver can catch the signal and clean up private data structures, if necessary. The kernel also readjusts the file system data structures when the driver encounters error conditions, such as when a user attempts to access a device that was not configured. The *open* call fails in such cases.

Processes may specify various options to qualify the device *open*. The most common option is "no delay," meaning that the process will not sleep during the *open* procedure if the device is not ready. The *open* system call returns immediately, and the user process has no knowledge of whether a hardware connection was made or not. *Open*ing a device with the "no delay" option also affects the semantics of the *read* system call, as will be seen (Section 10.3.4).

If a device is *open*ed many times, the kernel manipulates the user file descriptors and the inode and file table entries as described in Chapter 5, invoking the device specific *open* procedure for each *open* system call. The device driver can thus count how many times a device was *open*ed and fail the *open* call if the count is inappropriate. For example, it makes sense to allow multiple processes to *open* a terminal for writing so that users can exchange messages. But it does not make sense to allow multiple processes to *open* a printer for writing simultaneously, since they could overwrite each other's data. The differences are practical rather than implementational: allowing simultaneous writing to terminals fosters communication between users; preventing simultaneous writing to printers increases the chance of getting readable printouts.[2]

10.1.2.2 Close

A process severs its connection to an *open* device by *clos*ing it. However, the kernel invokes the device-specific *close* procedure only for the last *close* of the

---

2. In practice, printers are usually controlled by special spooler processes, and permissions are set up so that only the spooler can access the printer. But the analogy is still applicable.

device, that is, only if no other processes have the device *open*, because the device *close* procedure terminates hardware connections; clearly this must wait until no processes are accessing the device. Because the kernel invokes the device *open* procedure during every *open* system call but invokes the device *close* procedure only once, the device driver is never sure how many processes are still using the device. Drivers can easily put themselves out of state if not coded carefully: If they sleep in the *close* procedure and another process *open*s the device before the close completes, the device can be rendered useless if the combination of open and close results in an unrecognized state.

```
algorithm close                /* for devices */
input:   file descriptor
output: none
{
        do regular close algorithm (chapter 5xxx);
        if (file table reference count not 0)
                goto finish;
        if (there is another open file and its major, minor numbers
                        are same as device being closed)
                goto finish;              /* not last close after all */
        if (character device)
        {
                use major number to index into character device switch table;
                call driver close routine:  parameter minor number;
        }
        if (block device)
        {
                if (device mounted)
                        goto finish;
                write device blocks in buffer cache to device;
                use major number to index into block device switch table;
                call driver close routine:  parameter minor number;
                invalidate device blocks still in buffer cache;
        }
    finish:
        release inode;
}
```

Figure 10.4. Algorithm for Closing a Device

The algorithm for *clos*ing a device is similar to the algorithm for closing a regular file (Figure 10.4). However, before the kernel releases the inode it does operations specific to device files.

1. It searches the file table to make sure that no other processes still have the device *open*. It is not sufficient to rely on the file table count to indicate the

last close of a device, because several processes may access the device via a different file table entry. It is also not sufficient to rely on the inode table count, because several device files may specify the same device. For example, the results of the following *ls −l* command show two character device files (the first "c" on the line) that refer to one device, because their major and minor numbers (9 and 1) are equal. The link count of 1 for each file implies that there are two inodes.

```
crw−−w−−w−      1 root    vis    9, 1  Aug 6 1984    /dev/tty01
crw−−w−−w−      1 root    unix   9, 1  May 3 15:02   /dev/fty01
```

If processes *open* the two files independently, they access different inodes but the same device.

2. For a character device, the kernel invokes the device *close* procedure and returns to user mode. For a block device, the kernel searches the mount table to make sure that the device does not contain a mounted file system. If there is a mounted file system from the block device, the kernel cannot invoke the device close procedure, because it is not the last *close* of the device. Even if the device does not contain a mounted file system, the buffer cache could still contain blocks of data that were left over from a previously mounted file system and never written to the device, because they were marked "delayed write." The kernel therefore searches the buffer cache for such blocks and writes them to the device before invoking the device *close* procedure. After *clos*ing the device, the kernel again goes through the buffer cache and invalidates all buffers that contain blocks for the now *close*d device, allowing buffers with useful data to stay in the cache longer.

3. The kernel releases the inode of the device file.

To summarize, the device *close* procedure severs the device connection and reinitializes driver data structures and device hardware, so that the kernel can reopen the device later on.

10.1.2.3 Read and Write

The kernel algorithms for *read* and *write* of a device are similar to those for a regular file. If the process is *read*ing or *writ*ing a character device, the kernel invokes the device driver *read* or *write* procedure. Although there are important cases where the kernel transmits data directly between the user address space and the device, device drivers may buffer data internally. For example, terminal drivers use *clist*s to buffer data (Section 10.3.1). In such cases, the device driver allocates a "buffer," copies data from user space during a *write*, and outputs the data from the "buffer" to the device. The driver write procedure throttles the amount of data being output (called flow control): If processes generate data faster than the device can output it, the write procedure puts processes to sleep until the device can accept more data. For a *read*, the device driver receives the data from the device in a

Memory

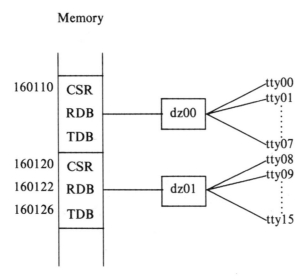

Figure 10.5. Memory Mapped I/O with the VAX DZ11 Controller

buffer and copies the data from the buffer to the user address specified in the system call.

The precise method in which a driver communicates with a device depends on the hardware. Some machines provide *memory mapped I/O*, meaning that certain addresses in the kernel address space are not locations in physical memory but are special registers that control particular devices. By writing control parameters to specified registers according to hardware specifications, the driver controls the device. For example, I/O controllers for the VAX-11 computer contain special registers for recording device status (*control and status registers*) and for data transmission (*data buffer registers*), which are configured at specific addresses in physical memory. In particular, the VAX DZ11 terminal controller controls 8 asynchronous lines for terminal communication (see [Levy 80] for more detail on the VAX architecture). Assume that the *control and status register* of a particular DZ11 is at address 160120, the *transmit data buffer register* is at address 160126, and the *receive data buffer register* is at address 160122 (Figure 10.5). To write a character to terminal "/dev/tty09", the terminal driver writes the number 1 (1 = 9 modulo 8) to a specified bit position in the *control and status register* and then writes the character to the *transmit data buffer register*. The operation of writing the *transmit data buffer register* transmits the data. The DZ11 controller sets a *done* bit in the *control and status register* when it is ready to accept more data. The driver can optionally set a *transmit interrupt enable* bit in the *control and status register*, which causes the DZ11 controller to interrupt the system when it is ready to accept more data. Reading data from the DZ11 is similar.

Other machines have *programmed I/O*, meaning that the machine contains instructions to control devices. Drivers control devices by executing the appropriate instructions. For example, the IBM 370 computer has a *Start I/O* instruction to initiate an I/O operation to a device. The method a driver uses to communicate with peripherals is transparent to the user.

Because the interface between device drivers and the underlying hardware is machine dependent, no standard interfaces exist at this level. For both memory-mapped I/O and programmed I/O, a driver can issue control sequences to a device to set up *direct memory access (DMA)* between the device and memory. The system allows bulk DMA transfer of data between the device and memory in parallel to CPU operations, and the device interrupts the system when such a transfer has completed. The driver sets up the virtual memory mapping so that the correct locations in memory are used for DMA.

High-speed devices can sometimes transfer data directly between the device and the user's address space, without intervention of a kernel buffer. This results in higher transfer speed because there is one less copy operation in the kernel, and the amount of data transmitted per transfer operation is not bounded by the size of kernel buffers. Drivers that make use of this "raw" I/O transfer usually invoke the block strategy interface from the character read and write procedures if they have a block counterpart.

10.1.2.4 Strategy Interface

The kernel uses the *strategy* interface to transmit data between the buffer cache and a device, although as mentioned above, the read and write procedures of character devices sometimes use their (block counterpart) *strategy* procedure to transfer data directly between the device and the user address space. The strategy procedure may queue I/O jobs for a device on a work list or do more sophisticated processing to schedule I/O jobs. Drivers can set up data transmission for one physical address or many, as appropriate. The kernel passes a buffer header address to the driver strategy procedure; the header contains a list of (page) addresses and sizes for transmission of data to or from the device. This is also how the swapping operations discussed in Chapter 9 work. For the buffer cache, the kernel transmits data from one data address; when swapping, the kernel transmits data from many data addresses (pages). If data is being copied to or from the user's address space, the driver must lock the process (or at least, the relevant pages) in memory until the I/O transfer is complete.

For example, after *mount*ing a file system, the kernel identifies every file in the file system by its device number and inode number. The device number is an encoding of the device major and minor numbers. When the kernel accesses a block from a file, it copies the device number and block number into the buffer header, as described in Chapter 3. When the buffer cache algorithms (*bread* or *bwrite*, for example) access the disk, they invoke the strategy procedure indicated by the device major number. The strategy procedure uses the minor number and block number fields in the buffer header to identify where to find the data on the device, and it uses the buffer address to identify where the data should be transferred. Similarly, if a process accesses a block device directly (that is, the process *open*s the block device and *read*s or *write*s it), it uses the buffer cache algorithms, and the interface works as just described.

10.1.2.5 Ioctl

The *ioctl* system call is a generalization of the terminal-specific *stty* (set terminal settings) and *gtty* (get terminal settings) system calls available in earlier versions of the UNIX system. It provides a general, catch-all entry point for device specific commands, allowing a process to set hardware options associated with a device and software options associated with the driver. The specific actions specified by the *ioctl* call vary per device and are defined by the device driver. Programs that use *ioctl* must know what type of file they are dealing with, because they are device-specific. This is an exception to the general rule that the system does not differentiate between different file types. Section 10.3.3 provides more detail on the use of *ioctl* for terminals.

The syntax of the system call is

ioctl(fd, command, arg);

where *fd* is the file descriptor returned by a prior *open* system call, *command* is a request of the driver to do a particular action, and *arg* is a parameter (possibly a pointer to a structure) for the *command*. Commands are driver specific; hence, each driver interprets commands according to internal specifications, and the format of the data structure *arg* depends on the command. Drivers can read the data structure *arg* from user space according to predefined formats, or they can write device settings into user address space at *arg*. For instance, the *ioctl* interface allows users to set terminal baud rates; it allows users to rewind tapes on a tape drive; finally, it allows network operations such as specifying virtual circuit numbers and network addresses.

10.1.2.6 Other File System Related Calls

File system calls such as *stat* and *chmod* work for devices as they do for regular files; they manipulate the inode without accessing the driver. Even the *lseek* system call works for devices. For example, if a process *lseek*s to a particular byte offset on a tape, the kernel updates the file table offset but does no driver-specific operations. When the process later *read*s or *write*s, the kernel moves the file table offset to the *u area*, as is done for regular files, and the device *physically* seeks to the correct offset indicated in the *u area*. An example in Section 10.3 illustrates this case.

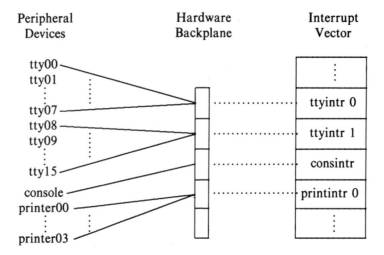

Figure 10.6. Device Interrupts

10.1.3 Interrupt Handlers

As previously explained (Section 6.4.1), occurrence of an interrupt causes the kernel to execute an interrupt handler, based on the correlation of the interrupting device and an offset in the interrupt vector table. The kernel invokes the device specific interrupt handler, passing it the device number or other parameters to identify the specific unit that caused the interrupt. For example, Figure 10.6 shows two entries in an interrupt vector table for handling terminal interrupts ("ttyintr"), each handling interrupts for 8 terminals. If device *tty09* interrupts the system, the system calls the interrupt handler associated with the hardware position of the interrupting device. Because many physical devices can be associated with one interrupt vector entry, the driver must be able to resolve which device caused the interrupt. In the figure, the two interrupt vector entries for "ttyintr" are labeled 0 and 1, implying that the system distinguishes between the two vector entries in some way when calling the interrupt handler, such as using that number as a parameter to the call. The interrupt handler would use that number and other information passed by the interrupt mechanism to ascertain that device *tty09* interrupted the system and not *tty12*, for example. This example is a simplification of what happens on real systems, where several levels of controllers and their interrupt handlers enter the picture, but it illustrates the general principles.

In summary, the device number used by the interrupt handler identifies a hardware unit, and the minor number in the device file identifies a device for the kernel. The device driver correlates the minor device number to the hardware unit number.

10.2 DISK DRIVERS

Historically, disk units on UNIX systems have been configured into sections that contain individual file systems, allowing "the [disk] pack to be broken up into more manageable pieces" (see [System V 84b]). For instance, if a disk contains four file systems, an administrator may leave one unmounted, *mount* another "read-only," and *mount* the last two "read-write." Even though all the file systems coexist on one physical unit, users cannot access files in the unmounted file system using the access methods described in Chapters 4 and 5, nor can any users write files in the "read-only" file system. Furthermore, since each section (and hence file system) spans contiguous tracks and cylinders of the disk, it is easier to copy entire file systems than if they were dispersed throughout an entire disk volume.

The disk driver translates a file system address, consisting of a logical device number and block number, to a particular sector on the disk. The driver gets the address in one of two ways: Either the strategy procedure uses a buffer from the buffer pool and the buffer header contains the device and block number, or the *read* and *write* procedures are passed the logical (minor) device number as a parameter; they convert the byte offset saved in the *u area* to the appropriate block address. The disk driver uses the device number to identify the physical drive and particular section to be used, maintaining internal tables to find the sector that marks the beginning of a disk section. Finally, it adds the block number of the file system to the start sector number to identify the sector used for the I/O transmission.

Section	Start Block	Length in Blocks
Size of block = 512 bytes		
0	0	64000
1	64000	944000
2	168000	840000
3	336000	672000
4	504000	504000
5	672000	336000
6	840000	168000
7	0	1008000

Figure 10.7. Disk Sections for RP07 Disk

Historically, the sizes and lengths of disk sections have been fixed according to the disk type. For instance, the DEC RP07 disk is partitioned into the sections shown in Figure 10.7. Suppose the files "/dev/dsk0", "/dev/dsk1", "/dev/dsk2" and "/dev/dsk3" correspond to sections 0 through 3 of an RP07 disk and have minor numbers 0 through 3. Assume the size of a logical file system block is the same as that of a disk block. If the kernel attempts to access block 940 in the file system contained in "/dev/dsk3", the disk driver converts the request to access block 336940 (section 3 starts at block 336000; 336000 + 940 = 336940) on the disk.

The sizes of disk sections vary, and administrators configure file systems in sections of the appropriate size: Large file systems go into large sections, and so on. Sections may overlap on disk. For example, Sections 0 and 1 in the RP07 disk are disjoint, but together they cover blocks 0 to 1008000, the entire disk. Section 7 also covers the entire disk. The overlap of sections does not matter, provided that the file systems contained in the sections are configured such that *they* do not overlap. It is advantageous to have one section include the entire disk, since the entire volume can thus be quickly copied.

The use of fixed sections restricts the flexibility of disk configuration. The hard-coded knowledge of disk sections should not be put into the disk driver but should be placed in a configurable volume table of contents on the disk. However, it is difficult to find a generic position on all disks for the volume table of contents and retain compatibility with previous versions of the system. Current implementations of System V expect the boot block of the first file system on a disk to occupy the first sector of the volume, although that is the most logical place for a volume table of contents. Nevertheless, the disk driver could contain hard-coded information on where the volume table of contents is stored for that particular disk, allowing variable sized disk sections.

Because of the high level of disk traffic typical of UNIX systems, the disk driver must maximize data throughput to get the best system performance. Most modern disk controllers take care of disk job scheduling, positioning the disk arm, and transferring data between the disk and the CPU; otherwise, the disk driver must do these tasks.

Utility programs can use either the raw or block interface to access disk data directly, bypassing the regular file system access method investigated in Chapters 4 and 5. Two important programs that deal directly with the disk are *mkfs* and *fsck*. *Mkfs* formats a disk section for a UNIX file system, creating a super block, inode list, linked list of free disk blocks, and a root directory on the new file system. *Fsck* checks the consistency of an existing file system and corrects errors, as presented in Chapter 5.

Consider the program in Figure 10.8 and the files "/dev/dsk15" and "/dev/rdsk15", and suppose the *ls* command prints the following information.

ls −l /dev/dsk15 /dev/rdsk15

```
br--------    2 root    root    0, 21 Feb 12 15:40    /dev/dsk15
crw-rw----    2 root    root    7, 21 Mar  7 09:29    /dev/rdsk15
```

It shows that "/dev/dsk15" is a block device owned by "root," and only "root" can *read* it directly. Its major number is 0, and its minor number is 21. The file "/dev/rdsk15" is a character device owned by "root" but allows read and write permission for the owner and group (both root here). Its major number is 7, and its minor number is 21. A process *open*ing the files gains access to the device via

```
#include "fcntl.h"
main()
{
        char buf1[4096], buf2[4096];
        int fd1, fd2, i;

        if (((fd1 = open("/dev/dsk5", O_RDONLY)) == -1) ||
                   ((fd2 = open("/dev/rdsk5", O_RDONLY)) == -1))
        {
                printf("failure on open\n");
                exit();
        }

        lseek(fd1, 8192L, 0);
        lseek(fd2, 8192L, 0);

        if ((read(fd1, buf1, sizeof(buf1)) == -1) || (read(fd2, buf2, sizeof(buf2)) == -1))
        {
                printf("failure on read\n");
                exit();
        }

        for (i = 0;  i < sizeof(buf1);  i++)
                if (buf1[i] != buf2[i])
                {
                        printf("different at offset %d\n", i);
                        exit();
                }
        printf("reads match\n");
}
```

Figure 10.8. Reading Disk Data Using Block and Raw Interface

the block device switch table and the character device switch table, respectively, and the minor number 21 informs the driver which disk section is being accessed — for example, physical drive 2, section 1. Because the minor numbers are identical for each file, both refer to the same disk section, assuming this is one device.[3] Thus, a process executing the program *open*s the same driver twice (through different interfaces), *lseek*s to byte offset 8192 in the devices, and *read*s data from that

---

3. There is no way to verify that a character driver and a block driver refer to the same device, except by examination of the system configuration tables and the driver code.

position. The results of the *read* calls should be identical, assuming no other file system activity.

Programs that *read* and *write* the disk directly are dangerous because they can read or write sensitive data, jeopardizing system security. Administrators must protect the block and raw interfaces by putting the appropriate permissions on the disk device files. For example, the disk files "/dev/dsk15" and "/dev/rdsk15" should be owned by "root," and their permissions should allow "root" to read the file but should not allow any other users to read or write.

Programs that *read* and *write* the disk directly can also destroy the consistency of file system data. The file system algorithms explained in Chapters 3, 4, and 5 coordinate disk I/O operations to maintain a consistent view of disk data structures, including linked lists of free disk blocks and pointers from inodes to direct and indirect data blocks. Processes that access the disk directly bypass these algorithms. Even if they are carefully encoded, there is still a consistency problem if they run while other file system activity is going on. For this reason, *fsck* should not be run on an active file system.

The difference between the two disk interfaces is whether they deal with the buffer cache. When accessing the block device interface, the kernel follows the same algorithm as for regular files, except that after converting the logical byte offset into a logical block offset (recall algorithm *bmap* in Chapter 4), it treats the logical block offset as a physical block number in the file system. It then accesses the data via the buffer cache and, ultimately, the driver strategy interface. However, when accessing the disk via the raw interface, the kernel does not convert the byte offset into the file but passes the offset immediately to the driver via the *u area*. The driver *read* or *write* routine converts the byte offset to a block offset and copies the data directly to the user address space, bypassing kernel buffers.

Thus, if one process *write*s a block device and a second process then *read*s a raw device at the same address, the second process may not read the data that the first process had written, because the data may still be in the buffer cache and not on disk. However, if the second process had *read* the block device, it would automatically pick up the new data, as it exists in the buffer cache.

Use of the raw interface may also introduce strange behavior. If a process *read*s or *write*s a raw device in units smaller than the block size, for example, results are driver-dependent. For instance, when issuing 1-byte *write*s to a tape drive, each byte may appear in different tape blocks.

The advantage of using the raw interface is speed, assuming there is no advantage to caching data for later access. Processes accessing block devices transfer blocks of data whose size is constrained by the file system logical block size. For example, if a file system has a logical block size of 1K bytes, at most 1K bytes are transferred per I/O operation. However, processes accessing the disk as a raw device can transfer many disk blocks during a disk operation, subject to the capabilities of the disk controller. Functionally, the process sees the same result, but the raw interface may be much faster. In Figure 10.8 for example, when a process *read*s 4096 bytes using the block interface for a file system with 1K bytes per block, the kernel loops internally four times and accesses the disk during each iteration before returning from the system call, but when it *reads* the raw interface, the driver may satisfy the *read* with one disk operation. Furthermore, use of the block interface entails an extra copy of data between user address space and kernel buffers, which is avoided in the raw interface.

10.3 TERMINAL DRIVERS

Terminal drivers have the same function as other drivers: to control the transmission of data to and from terminals. However, terminals are special, because they are the user's interface to the system. To accommodate interactive use of the UNIX system, terminal drivers contain an internal interface to *line discipline* modules, which interpret input and output. In *canonical* mode, the line discipline converts raw data sequences typed at the keyboard to a canonical form (what the user really meant) before sending the data to a receiving process; the line discipline also converts raw output sequences written by a process to a format that the user expects. In *raw* mode, the line discipline passes data between processes and the terminal without such conversions.

For example, programmers are notoriously fast but error-prone typists. Terminals provide an "erase" key (or such a key can be so designated) such that the user can logically erase part of the typed sequence and enter corrections. The terminal sends the entire sequence to the machine, including the erase characters.[4] In canonical mode, the line discipline buffers the data into lines (the sequence of characters until a carriage-return[5] character) and processes erase characters internally before sending the revised sequence to the reading process.

The functions of a line discipline are

- to parse input strings into lines;
- to process erase characters;
- to process a "kill" character that invalidates all characters typed so far on the current line;
- to echo (write) received characters to the terminal;
- to expand output such as tab characters to a sequence of blank spaces;
- to generate signals to processes for terminal hangups, line breaks, or in response to a user hitting the delete key;
- to allow a raw mode that does not interpret special characters such as erase, kill or carriage return.

---

4. This section will assume the use of dumb terminals, which transmit all characters typed by the user without processing them.

5. This chapter will use the generic term "carriage return" for "carriage return" and "new-line" characters.

The support of raw mode implies the use of an asynchronous terminal, because processes can *read* characters as they are typed instead of waiting until a user hits a carriage return or "enter" key.

Ritchie notes that the original terminal line disciplines used during system development in the early 1970s were in the shell and editor programs, not in the kernel (see page 1580 of [Ritchie 84]). However, because their function is needed by many programs, their proper place is in the kernel. Although the line discipline performs a function that places it logically between the terminal driver and the rest of the kernel, the kernel does not invoke the line discipline directly but only through the terminal driver. Figure 10.9 shows the logical flow of data through the terminal driver and line discipline and the corresponding flow of control through the terminal driver. Users can specify what line discipline should be used via an *ioctl* system call, but it is difficult to implement a scheme such that one device uses several line disciplines simultaneously, where each line discipline module successively calls the next module to process the data in turn.

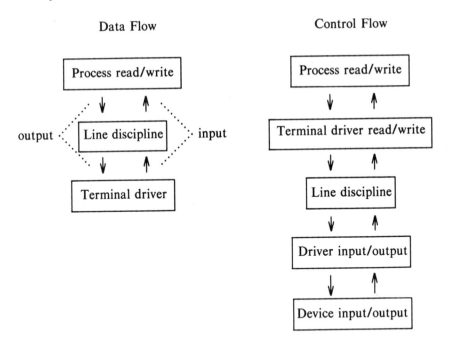

Figure 10.9. Call Sequence and Data Flow through Line Discipline

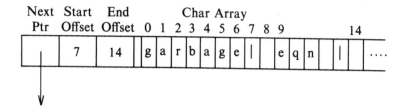

Figure 10.10. A Cblock

10.3.1 Clists

Line disciplines manipulate data on *clists*. A clist, or character list, is a variable-length linked list of *cblocks* with a count of the number of characters on the list. A cblock contains a pointer to the next cblock on the linked list, a small character array to contain data, and a set of offsets indicating the position of the valid data in the cblock (Figure 10.10). The *start* offset indicates the first location of valid data in the array, and the *end* offset indicates the first location of nonvalid data.

The kernel maintains a linked list of free cblocks and has six operations on clists and cblocks.

1. It has an operation to assign a cblock from the free list to a driver.
2. It also has an operation to return a cblock to the free list.
3. The kernel can retrieve the first character from a clist: It removes the first character from the first cblock on the clist and adjusts the clist character count and the indices into the cblock so that subsequent operations will not retrieve the same character. If a retrieval operation consumes the last character of a cblock, the kernel places the empty cblock on the free list and adjusts the clist pointers. If a clist contains no characters when a retrieval operation is done, the kernel returns the null character.
4. The kernel can place a character onto the end of a clist by finding the last cblock on the clist, putting the character onto it, and adjusting the offset values. If the cblock is full, the kernel allocates a new cblock, links it onto the end of the clist, and places the character into the new cblock.
5. The kernel can remove a group of characters from the beginning of a clist one cblock at a time, the operation being equivalent to removing all the characters in the cblock one at a time.
6. The kernel can place a cblock of characters onto the end of a clist.

Clists provide a simple buffer mechanism, useful for the small volume of data transmission typical of slow devices such as terminals. They allow manipulation of data one character at a time or in groups of cblocks. For example, Figure 10.11 depicts the removal of characters from a clist; the kernel removes one character at a time from the first cblock on the clist (Figure 10.11a—c) until there are no more clist   cblocks

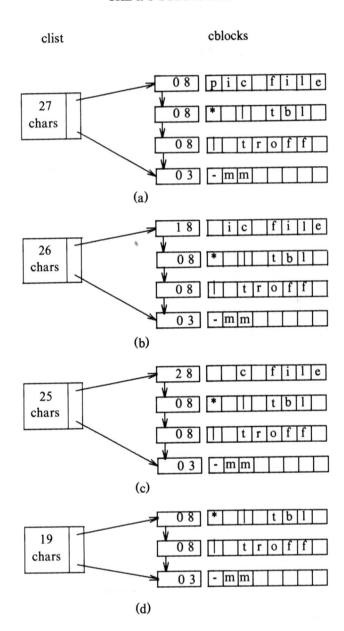

Figure 10.11. Removing Characters from a Clist

clist   cblocks

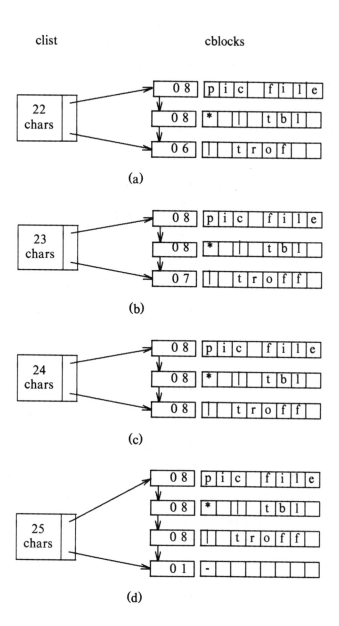

Figure 10.12. Placing a Character on a Clist

characters in the cblock (Figure 10.11d); then, it adjusts the clist pointer to point to the next cblock, which becomes the first one on the linked list. Similarly, Figure 10.12 depicts how the kernel puts characters onto a clist; assuming a cblock holds up to 8 characters, the kernel links a new cblock onto the end of the linked list (Figure 10.12d).

10.3.2 The Terminal Driver in Canonical Mode

The data structures for terminal drivers have three clists associated with them: a clist to store data for output to the terminal, a clist to store "raw" input data provided by the terminal interrupt handler as the user typed it in, and a clist to store "cooked" input data, after the line discipline converts special characters in the raw clist, such as the erase and kill characters.

```
algorithm terminal_write
{
        while (more data to be copied from user space)
        {
                if (tty flooded with output data)
                {
                        start write operation to hardware with data
                                                on output clist;
                        sleep (event: tty can accept more data);
                        continue;        /* back to while loop */
                }
                copy cblock size of data from user space to output clist:
                        line discipline converts tab characters, etc;
        }

        start write operation to hardware with data on output clist;
}
```

Figure 10.13. Algorithm for Writing Data to a Terminal

When a process writes a terminal (Figure 10.13), the terminal driver invokes the line discipline. The line discipline loops, reading output characters from user address space and placing them onto the output clist, until it exhausts the data. The line discipline processes output characters, expanding tab characters to a series of space characters, for example. If the number of characters on the output clist becomes greater than a high-water mark, the line discipline calls driver procedures to transmit the data on the output clist to the terminal and puts the writing process to sleep. When the amount of data on the output clist drops below a low-water mark, the interrupt handler awakens all processes asleep on the event the terminal can accept more data. The line discipline finishes its loop, having copied all the output data from user space to the output clist, and calls driver procedures to transmit the data to the terminal, as described earlier.

If multiple processes write to a terminal, they follow the given procedure independently. The output could be garbled; that is, data written by the processes may be interleaved on the terminal. This could happen because a process may *write* the terminal using several *write* system calls. The kernel could switch context while the process is in user mode between successive *write* system calls, and newly scheduled processes could *write* the terminal while the original process sleeps. Output data could also be garbled at a terminal because a writing process may sleep in the middle of a *write* system call while waiting for previous output data to drain from the system. The kernel could schedule other processes that *write* the terminal before the original process is rescheduled. Because of this case, the kernel does *not* guarantee that the contents of the data buffer to be output by a *write* system call appear contiguously on the terminal.

```
char form[] = "this is a sample output string from child ";
main()
{
        char output[128];
        int i;

        for (i = 0;  i < 18;  i++)
        {
                switch (fork())
                {
                case -1:        /* error --- hit max procs */
                        exit();

                default:      /* parent process */
                        break;

                case 0:             /* child process */
                        /* format output string in variable output */
                        sprintf(output, "%s%d\n%s%d\n", form, i, form, i);
                        for (;;)
                                write(1, output, sizeof(output));
                }
        }
}
```

Figure 10.14. Flooding Standard Output with Data

Consider the program in Figure 10.14. The parent process creates up to 18 children; each child process formats a string (via the library function *sprintf*) in the array *output*, which includes a message and the value of *i* at the time of the *fork* and then goes into a loop, *writ*ing the string to its standard output file during each iteration. If the standard output is the terminal, the terminal driver regulates the flow of data to the terminal. The output string is more than 64 characters long, too large to fit into a cblock (64 bytes long) in System V implementations. Hence, the terminal driver needs more than one cblock for each *write* call, and output could become garbled. For example, the following lines were part of the output produced when running the program on an AT&T 3B20 computer:

> this is a sample output string from child 1
> this is a sample outthis is a sample output string from child 0

Reading data from a terminal in canonical mode is a more complex operation. The *read* system call specifies the number of bytes the process wants to *read*, but the line discipline satisfies the *read* on receipt of a carriage return even though the character count is not satisfied. This is practical, since it is impossible for a process to predict how many characters the user will enter at the keyboard, and it does not make sense to wait for the user to type a large number of characters. For example, users type command lines to the shell and expect the shell to respond to the command on receipt of a carriage return character. It makes no difference whether the commands are simple, such as "date" or "who," or whether they are more complicated command sequences such as

> pic file* | tbl | eqn | troff —mm —Taps | apsend

The terminal driver and line discipline know nothing about shell syntax, and rightly so, because other programs that read terminals (such as editors) have different command syntax. Hence, the line discipline satisfies *read* calls on receipt of a carriage return.

Figure 10.15 shows the algorithm for reading a terminal. Assume the terminal is in canonical mode; Section 10.3.3 will cover the case of raw mode. If no data is currently on either input clist, the reading process sleeps until the arrival of a line of data. When data is entered, the terminal interrupt handler invokes the line discipline "interrupt handler," which places the data on the raw clist for input to *read*ing processes and on the output clist for echoing back to the terminal. If the input string contains a carriage return, the interrupt handler awakens all sleeping reader processes. When a reading process runs, the driver removes characters from the raw clist, does erase and kill character processing, and places the characters on the canonical clist. It then copies characters to user address space until the carriage return character or until it satisfies the count in the *read* system call, whichever number is smaller. However, a process may find that the data for which it woke up no longer exists: Other processes may *read* the terminal and remove the data from the raw clist before the first process is rescheduled. This is similar to what happens when multiple processes read data from a pipe.

Character processing in the input and output direction is asymmetric, evidenced by the two input clists and the one output clist. The line discipline outputs data from user space, processes it, and places it on the output clist. To be symmetric,

```
algorithm terminal_read
{
        if (no data on canonical clist)
        {
                while (no data on raw clist)
                {
                        if (tty opened with no delay option)
                                return;
                        if (tty in raw mode based on timer and timer not active)
                                arrange for timer wakeup (callout table);
                        sleep (event: data arrives from terminal);
                }

                /* there is data on raw clist */
                if (tty in raw mode)
                        copy all data from raw clist to canonical clist;
                else        /* tty is in canonical mode */
                {
                        while (characters on raw clist)
                        {
                                copy one character at a time from raw clist
                                        to canonical clist:
                                        do erase, kill processing;
                                if (char is carriage return or end-of-file)
                                        break;                /* out of while loop */
                        }
                }
        }

        while (characters on canonical list and read count not satisfied)
                copy from cblocks on canonical list to user address space;
}
```

Figure 10.15. Algorithm for Reading a Terminal

there should be only one input clist. However, this would require the interrupt handler to process erase and kill characters, making it more complex and time consuming, and blocking out other interrupts at a critical time. Use of two input clists means that the interrupt handler can simply dump characters onto the raw clist and wake up *read*ing processes, which properly incur the expense of processing input data. Nevertheless, the interrupt handler puts input characters immediately on the output clist, so that the user experiences minimal delay in seeing typed characters on the terminal.

Figure 10.16 shows a program where a process creates many child processes that *read* their standard input file, contending for terminal data. Terminal input is

```
char input[256];

main()
{
        register int i;

        for (i = 0;  i < 18;  i++)
        {
                switch (fork())
                {
                case -1:        /* error */
                        printf("error cannot fork\n");
                        exit();

                default:        /* parent process */
                        break;

                case 0:                 /* child process */
                        for (;;)
                        {
                                read(0, input, 256);        /* read line */
                                printf("%d read %s\n", i, input);
                        }
                }
        }
}
```

Figure 10.16. Contending for Terminal Input Data

usually too slow to satisfy all the *read*ing processes, so the processes will spend most of their time sleeping in the *terminal_read* algorithm, waiting for input data. When a user enters a line of data, the terminal interrupt handler awakens all the *read*ing processes; since they slept at the same priority level, they are eligible to run at the same priority. The user cannot predict which process runs and *read*s the line of data; the successful process prints the value of *i* at the time it was spawned. All other processes will eventually be scheduled to run, but they will probably find no input data on the input clists and go back to sleep. The entire procedure is repeated for every input line; it is impossible to guarantee that one process does not hog all the input data.

It is inherently ambiguous to allow multiple readers of a terminal, but the kernel copes with situation as best as it can. On the other hand, the kernel *must* allow multiple processes to read a terminal, otherwise processes spawned by the shell that read standard input would never work, because the shell still accesses standard input, too. In short, processes must synchronize terminal access at user level.

When the user types an "end of file" character (ASCII control-d), the line discipline satisfies terminal *read*s of the input string up to, but not including, the end of file character. It returns no data (return value 0) for the *read* system call that encounters *only* the end of file on the clists; the calling process is responsible for recognizing that it has read the end of file and that it should no longer *read* the terminal. Referring to the code examples for the shell in Chapter 7, the shell loop terminates when a user types control-d: The *read* call returns 0, and the shell *exit*s.

This section has considered the case of dumb terminal hardware, which transmits data to the machine one character at a time, precisely as the user types it. Intelligent terminals cook their input in the peripheral, freeing the CPU for other work. The structure of their terminal drivers resembles that of dumb terminal drivers, although the functions of the line discipline vary according to the capabilities of the peripherals.

10.3.3 The Terminal Driver in Raw Mode

Users set terminal parameters such as erase and kill characters and retrieve the values of current settings with the *ioctl* system call. Similarly, they control whether the terminal echoes its input, set the terminal baud rate (the rate of bit transfers), flush input and output character queues, or manually start up or stop character output. The terminal driver data structure saves various control settings (see [SVID 85] page 281), and the line discipline receives the parameters of the *ioctl* call and sets or gets the relevant fields in the terminal data structure. When a process sets terminal parameters, it does so for all processes using the terminal. The terminal settings are not automatically reset when the process that changed the settings *exit*s.

Processes can also put the terminal into *raw* mode, where the line discipline transmits characters exactly as the user typed them: No input processing is done at all. Still, the kernel must know when to satisfy user *read* calls, since the carriage return is treated as an ordinary input character. It satisfies *read* system calls after a minimum number of characters are input at the terminal, or after waiting a fixed time from the receipt of any characters from the terminal. In the latter case, the kernel times the entry of characters from the terminal by placing entries into the callout table (Chapter 8). Both criteria (minimum number of characters and fixed time) are set by an *ioctl* call. When the particular criterion is met, the line discipline interrupt handler awakens all sleeping processes. The driver moves all characters from the raw clist to the canonical clist and satisfies the process *read* request, following the same algorithm as for the canonical case. Raw mode is particularly important for screen oriented applications, such as the screen editor *vi*, which has many commands that do not terminate with a carriage return. For example, the command *dw* deletes the word at the current cursor position.

Figure 10.17 shows a program that does an *ioctl* to save the current terminal settings of file descriptor 0, the standard input file descriptor. The *ioctl* command

```
#include        <signal.h>
#include        <termio.h>
struct termio savetty;
main()
{
        extern sigcatch();
        struct termio newtty;
        int nrd;
        char buf[32];
        signal(SIGINT, sigcatch);
        if (ioctl(0, TCGETA, &savetty) == -1)
        {
                printf("ioctl failed: not a tty\n");
                exit();
        }
        newtty = savetty;
        newtty.c_lflag &= ~ICANON;      /* turn off canonical mode */
        newtty.c_lflag &= ~ECHO;        /* turn off character echo */
        newtty.c_cc[VMIN] = 5;             /* minimum 5 chars */
        newtty.c_cc[VTIME] = 100;       /* 10 sec interval */
        if (ioctl(0, TCSETAF, &newtty) == -1)
        {
                printf("cannot put tty into raw mode\n");
                exit();
        }
        for (;;)
        {
                nrd = read(0, buf, sizeof(buf));
                buf[nrd] = 0;
                printf("read %d chars '%s'\n", nrd, buf);
        }
}
sigcatch()
{
        ioctl(0, TCSETAF, &savetty);
        exit();
}
```

Figure 10.17. Raw Mode — Reading 5-Character Bursts

TCGETA instructs the driver to retrieve the settings and save them in the structure *savetty* in the user's address space. This command is commonly used to determine if a file is a terminal or not, because it does not change anything in the system: If it fails, processes assume the file is not a terminal. Here, the process does a second *ioctl* call to put the terminal into raw mode: It turns off character echo and arranges to satisfy terminal *read*s when at least 5 characters are received from the terminal or when any number of characters are received and about 10 seconds elapse since the first was received. When it receives an interrupt signal, the process resets the original terminal options and terminates.

```
#include <fcntl.h>

main()
{
        register int i, n;
        int fd;
        char buf[256];

        /* open terminal read—only with no—delay option */
        if ((fd = open("/dev/tty", O_RDONLY | O_NDELAY)) == -1)
                exit();

        n = 1;
        for (;;)        /* for ever */
        {
                for (i = 0;  i < n;  i++)
                        ;

                if (read(fd, buf, sizeof(buf)) > 0)
                {
                        printf("read at n %d\n", n);
                        n--;
                }
                else    /* no data read; returns due to no—delay */
                        n++;
        }
}
```

Figure 10.18. Polling a Terminal

10.3.4 Terminal Polling

It is sometimes convenient to poll a device, that is, to *read* it if there is data present but to continue regular processing otherwise. The program in Figure 10.18 illustrates this case: By *open*ing the terminal with the "no delay" option, subsequent *read*s will not sleep if there is no data present but will return immediately (refer to algorithm *terminal_read*, Figure 10.15). Such a method also works if a process is monitoring many devices: it can *open* each device "no delay" and poll all of them, waiting for input from any of them. However, this method wastes processing power.

The BSD system has a *select* system call that allows device polling. The syntax of the call is

select(nfds, rfds, wfds, efds, timeout)

where *nfds* gives the number of file descriptors being selected, and *rfds*, *wfds* and *efds* point to bit masks that "select" open file descriptors. That is, the bit $1 << fd$ (1 shifted left by the value of the file descriptor) is set if a user wants to select that file descriptor. *Timeout* indicates how long *select* should sleep, waiting for data to arrive, for example; if data arrives for any file descriptors and the timeout value has not expired, *select* returns, indicating in the bit masks which file descriptors were selected. For instance, if a user wished to sleep until receiving input on file descriptors 0, 1 or 2, *rfds* would point to the bit mask 7; when *select* returns, the bit mask would be overwritten with a mask indicating which file descriptors had data ready. The bit mask *wfds* does a similar function for write file descriptors, and the bit mask *efds* indicates when exceptional conditions exist for particular file descriptors, useful in networking.

10.3.5 Establishment of a Control Terminal

The control terminal is the terminal on which a user logs into the system, and it controls processes that the user initiates from the terminal. When a process *open*s a terminal, the terminal driver opens the line discipline. If the process is a process group leader as the result of a prior *setpgrp* system call and if the process does not have an associated control terminal, the line discipline makes the opened terminal the control terminal. It stores the major and minor device number of the terminal device file in the *u area*, and it stores the process group number of the opening process in the terminal driver data structure. The opening process is the control process, typically the login shell, as will be seen later.

The control terminal plays an important role in handling signals. When a user presses the delete, break, rubout, or quit keys, the interrupt handler invokes the line discipline, which sends the appropriate signal to all processes in the control process group. Similarly, if the user hangs up, the terminal interrupt handler receives a hangup indication from the hardware, and the line discipline sends a hangup signal to all processes in the process group. In this way, all processes initiated at a particular terminal receive the hangup signal; the default reaction of most processes is to *exit* on receipt of the signal; this is how stray processes are killed when a user suddenly shuts off a terminal. After sending the hangup signal, the terminal interrupt handler disassociates the terminal from the process group so that processes in the process group can no longer receive signals originating at the terminal.

10.3.6 Indirect Terminal Driver

Processes frequently have a need to read or write data directly to the control terminal, even though the standard input and output may have been redirected to other files. For example, a shell script can send urgent messages directly to the terminal, although its standard output and standard error files may have been redirected elsewhere. UNIX systems provide "indirect" terminal access via the device file "/dev/tty", which designates the control terminal for every process that has one. Users logged onto separate terminals can access "/dev/tty", but they access different terminals.

There are two common implementations for the kernel to find the control terminal from the file name "/dev/tty". First, the kernel can define a special device number for the indirect terminal file with a special entry in the character device switch table. When invoking the indirect terminal, the *driver* for the indirect terminal gets the major and minor number of the control terminal from the *u area* and invokes the real terminal driver through the character device switch table. The second implementation commonly used to find the control terminal from the name "/dev/tty" tests if the major number is that of the indirect terminal before calling the driver *open* routine. If so, it releases the inode for "/dev/tty", allocates the inode for the control terminal, resets the file table entry to point to the control terminal inode, and calls the *open* routine of the terminal driver. The file descriptor returned when opening "/dev/tty" refers directly to the control terminal and its regular driver.

10.3.7 Logging In

As described in Chapter 7, process 1, *init*, executes an infinite loop, reading the file "/etc/inittab" for instructions about what to do when entering system states such as "single user" or "multi-user." In multi-user state, a primary responsibility of init is to allow users to log into terminals (Figure 10.19). It spawns processes called *getty* (for get terminal or get "tty") and keeps track of which *getty* process opens which terminal; each *getty* process resets its process group using the *setpgrp* system call, *open*s a particular terminal line, and usually sleeps in the *open* until the machine senses a hardware connection for the terminal. When the *open* returns, *getty* *exec*s the *login* program, which requires users to identify themselves by login name and password. If the user logs in successfully, *login* finally *exec*s the shell, and the user starts working. This invocation of the shell is called the *login shell*. The shell process has the same process ID as the original *getty* process, and the login shell is therefore a process group leader. If a user does not log in successfully, *login* *exit*s after a suitable time limit, closing the opened terminal line, and *init* spawns another *getty* for the line. Init *pause*s until it receives a death of child signal. On waking up, it finds out if the zombie process had been a login shell and, if so, spawns another *getty* process to *open* the terminal in place of the one that died.

```
algorithm login                /* procedure for logging in */
{
      getty process executes:
      set process group (setpgrp system call);
      open tty line;              /* sleeps until opened */
      if (open successful)
      {
            exec login program:
            prompt for user name;
            turn off echo, prompt for password;
            if (successful)          /* matches password in /etc/passwd */
            {
                  put tty in canonical mode (ioctl);
                  exec shell;
            }
            else
                  count login attempts, try again up to a point;
      }
}
```

Figure 10.19. Algorithm for Logging In

10.4 STREAMS

The scheme for implementation of device drivers, though adequate, suffers from some drawbacks, which have become apparent over the years. Different drivers tend to duplicate functionality, particularly drivers that implement network protocols, which typically include a device-control portion and a protocol portion. Although the protocol portion should be common for all network devices, this has not been the case in practice, because the kernel did not provide adequate mechanisms for common use. For example, clists would be useful for their buffering capability, but they are expensive because of the character-by-character manipulation. Attempts to bypass this mechanism for greater performance cause the modularity of the I/O subsystem to break down. The lack of commonality at the driver level percolates up to the user command level, where several commands may accomplish common logical functions but over different media. Another drawback of the driver scheme is that network protocols require a line discipline-like capability, where each discipline implements one part of a protocol and the component parts can be combined in a flexible manner. However, it is difficult to stack conventional line disciplines together.

Ritchie has recently implemented a scheme called *streams* to provide greater modularity and flexibility for the I/O subsystem. The description here is based on his work [Ritchie 84b], although the implementation in System V differs slightly. A *stream* is a full-duplex connection between a process and a device driver. It consists of a set of linearly linked queue pairs, one member of each pair for input and the other for output. When a process *writes* data to a stream, the kernel sends the data down the output queues; when a device driver receives input data, it sends the data up the input queues to a reading process. The queues pass messages to neighboring queues according to a well-defined interface. Each queue pair is associated with an instance of a kernel module, such as a driver, line discipline, or protocol, and the modules manipulate data passed through its queues.

Each queue is a data structure that contains the following elements:

- An open procedure, called during an *open* system call
- A close procedure, called during a *close* system call
- A "put" procedure, called to pass a message into the queue
- A "service" procedure, called when a queue is scheduled to execute
- A pointer to the next queue in the stream
- A pointer to a list of messages awaiting service
- A pointer to a private data structure that maintains the state of the queue
- Flags and high- and low-water marks, used for flow control, scheduling, and maintaining the queue state

The kernel allocates queue pairs, which are adjacent in memory; hence, a queue can easily find the other member of the pair.

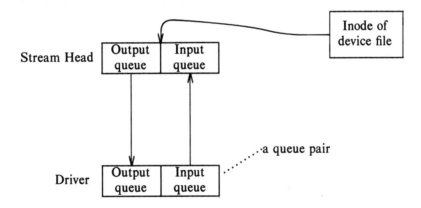

Figure 10.20. A Stream after Open

A device with a streams driver is a character device; it has a special field in the character device switch table that points to a streams initialization structure, containing the addresses of routines and high- and low-water marks mentioned above. When the kernel executes the *open* system call and discovers that the device file is character special, it examines the new field in the character device switch table. If there is no entry there, the driver is not a streams driver, and the kernel follows the usual procedure for character devices. However, for the first open of a streams driver, the kernel allocates two pairs of queues, one for the *stream-head* and the other for the driver. The stream-head module is identical for all instances of open streams: It has generic put and service procedures and is the interface to higher-level kernel modules that implement the *read*, *write*, and *ioctl* system calls. The kernel initializes the driver queue structure, assigning queue pointers and copying addresses of driver routines from a per-driver initialization structure, and invokes the driver open procedure. The driver open procedure does the usual initialization but also saves information to recall the queue with which it is associated. Finally, the kernel assigns a special pointer in the in-core inode to indicate the stream-head (Figure 10.20). When another process *open*s the device, the kernel finds the previously allocated stream via the inode pointer and invokes the open procedure of all modules on the stream.

Modules communicate by passing messages to neighboring modules on a stream. A message consists of a linked list of message block headers; each block header points to the start and end location of the block's data. There are two types of messages — control and data — identified by a type indicator in the message header. Control messages may result from *ioctl* system calls or from special conditions, such as a terminal hang-up, and data messages may result from *write* system calls or the arrival of data from a device.

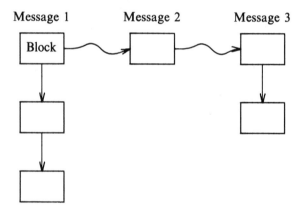

Figure 10.21. Streams Messages

When a process *write*s a stream, the kernel copies the data from user space into message blocks allocated by the stream-head. The stream-head module invokes the put procedure of the next queue module, which may process the message, pass it immediately to the next queue, or enqueue it for later processing. In the latter case, the module links the message block headers on a linked list, forming a two-way linked list (Figure 10.21). Then it sets a flag in its queue data structure to indicate that it has data to process, and schedules itself for servicing. The module places the queue on a linked list of queues requesting service and invokes a scheduling mechanism; that scheduler calls the service procedures of each queue on the list. The kernel could schedule modules by software interrupt, similar to how it invokes functions in the callout table (as described in Chapter 8); the software interrupt handler calls the individual service procedures.

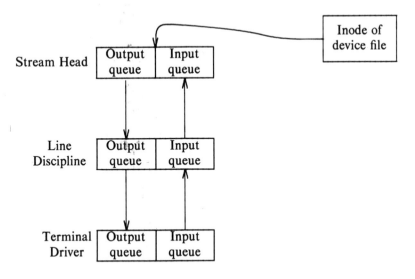

Figure 10.22. Pushing a Module onto a Stream

Processes can "push" modules onto an opened stream by issuing *ioctl* system calls. The kernel inserts the pushed module immediately below the stream head and connects the queue pointers to keep the structure of the doubly linked list. Lower modules on the stream do not care whether they are communicating with the stream head or with a pushed module: The interface is the put procedure of the next queue on the stream; the next queue belongs to the module just pushed. For example, a process can push a line discipline module onto a terminal driver stream to do erase and kill character processing (Figure 10.22); the line discipline module does not have the same interfaces as the line disciplines described in Section 10.3, but its function is the same. Without the line discipline module, the terminal driver does not process input characters, and such characters arrive unaltered at the stream-head. A code segment that *open*s a terminal and pushes a line discipline may look like this:

    fd = open("/dev/ttyxy", O_RDWR);
    ioctl(fd, PUSH, TTYLD);

where *PUSH* is the command name and *TTYLD* is a number that identifies the line discipline module. There is no restriction to how many modules can be pushed onto a stream. A process can "pop" the modules off a stream in last-in-first-out order, using another *ioctl* system call.

     ioctl(fd, POP, 0);

Given that a terminal line discipline module implements regular terminal processing
functions, the underlying device can be a network connection instead of a
connection to a single terminal device. The line discipline module works the same
way, regardless of the module below it. This example shows the greater flexibility
derived from the combination of kernel modules.

10.4.1 A More Detailed Example of Streams

Pike describes an implementation of multiplexed virtual terminals using streams
(see [Pike 84]). The user sees several virtual terminals, each occupying a separate
window on a physical terminal. Although Pike's paper describes a scheme for an
intelligent graphics terminal, it would work for dumb terminals, too; each window
would occupy the entire screen, and the user would type a control sequence to
switch between virtual windows.

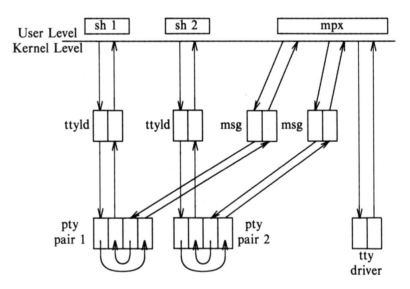

Figure 10.23. Windowing Virtual Terminals on a Physical Terminal

     Figure 10.23 shows the arrangement of processes and kernel modules. The user
invokes a process, *mpx*, to control the physical terminal. *Mpx reads* the physical
terminal line and waits for notification of control events, such as creation of a new
window, switching control to another window, deletion of a window, and so on.

```
/* assume file descriptors 0 and 1 already refer to physical tty */
for (;;)        /* loop */
{
      select(input);               /* wait for some line with input */
      read input line;
      switch (line with input data)
      {
      case physical tty:           /* input on physical tty line */
            if (control command)        /* e.g. create new window */
            {
                  open a free pseudo—tty;
                  fork a new process:
                  if (parent)
                  {
                        push a msg discipline on mpx side;
                        continue;        /* back to for loop */
                  }
                  /* child here */
                  close unnecessary file descriptors;
                  open other member of pseudo—tty pair, get
                                    stdin, stdout, stderr;
                  push tty line discipline;
                  exec shell;           /* looks like virtual tty */
            }
            /* "regular" data from tty coming up for virtual tty */
            demultiplex data read from physical tty, strip off
                        headers and write to appropriate pty;
            continue;           /* back to for loop */

      case logical tty:          /* a virtual tty is writing a window */
            encode header indicating what window data is for;
            write header and data to physical tty;
            continue;            /* back to for loop */
      }
}
```

Figure 10.24. Pseudo-code for Multiplexing Windows

When it receives notification that a user wants to create a new window, *mpx* creates a process to control the new window and communicates with it over a *pseudo-terminal* (abbreviated *pty*). A *pty* is a software device that operates in pairs: Output directed to one member of the pair is sent to the input of the other member; input is sent to the upstream module. To set up a window (Figure 10.24), *mpx* allocates a *pty* pair and *open*s one member, establishing a stream to it (the driver *open* insures that the *pty* was not previously allocated). *Mpx forks*, and the new process *opens* the other member of the *pty* pair. *Mpx* pushes a message module onto its *pty* stream to convert control messages to data messages (explained in the next paragraph), and the child process pushes a line discipline module onto its *pty* stream before *exec*ing the shell. That shell is now running on a virtual terminal; to the user, it is indistinguishable from a physical terminal.

The *mpx* process is a multiplexer, forwarding output from the virtual terminals to the physical terminal and demultiplexing input from the physical terminal to the correct virtual terminal. *Mpx* waits for the arrival of data on any line, using the *select* system call. When data arrives from the physical terminal, *mpx* decides whether it is a control message, informing it to create a new window or delete an old one, or whether it is a data message to be sent to processes reading a virtual terminal. In the latter case, the data has a header that identifies the target virtual terminal; *mpx* strips the header from the message and *writes* the data to the appropriate *pty* stream. The *pty* driver routes the data through the terminal line discipline to reading processes. The reverse procedure happens when a process *writes* the virtual terminal: *mpx* prepends a header onto the data, informing the physical terminal which window the data should be printed to.

If a process issues an *ioctl* on a virtual terminal, the terminal line discipline sets the necessary terminal settings for its virtual line; settings may differ for each virtual terminal. However, some information may have to be sent to the physical terminal, depending on the device. The message module converts the control messages that are generated by the *ioctl* into data messages suitable for reading and writing by *mpx*, and these messages are transmitted to the physical device.

10.4.2 Analysis of Streams

Ritchie mentions that he tried to implement streams only with put procedures or only with service procedures. However, the service procedure is necessary for flow control, since modules must sometimes enqueue data if neighboring modules cannot receive any more data temporarily. The put procedure interface is also necessary, because data must sometimes be delivered to a neighboring module right away. For example, a terminal line discipline must echo input data back to the terminal as quickly as possible. It would be possible for the *write* system call to invoke the put procedure of the next queue directly, which in turn would call the put procedure of the next queue, and so on, without the need for a scheduling mechanism. A process would sleep if the output queues were congested. However, modules cannot sleep on the input side, because they are invoked by an interrupt handler and an innocent process would be put to sleep. Intermodule communication would not be symmetric in the input and output directions, detracting from the elegance of the scheme.

It would also have been preferable to implement each module as a separate process, but use of a large number of modules could cause the process table to overflow. They are implemented with a special scheduling mechanism — software interrupt — independent of the normal process scheduler. Therefore, modules cannot go to sleep, because they would be putting an arbitrary process to sleep (the one that was interrupted). Modules must save their state information internally, making their code more cumbersome than it would be if sleeping were allowed.

Several anomalies exist in the implementation of streams.

- Process accounting is difficult under streams, because modules do not necessarily run in the context of the process that is using the stream. It is false to assume that all processes uniformly share execution of streams modules, because some processes may require use of complicated network protocols, whereas others may use simple terminal line disciplines.
- Users can put a terminal driver into raw mode, such that *read* calls return after a short time if no data is available (for example, if *newtty.c_cc[VMIN]* = *0;* in Figure 10.17). It is difficult to implement this feature with streams, unless special-case code is introduced at the stream-head level.
- Streams are linear connections and do not easily allow multiplexing in the kernel. For example, the window example in the previous section does the multiplexing in a user-level process.

In spite of these anomalies, streams holds great promise for improving the design of driver modules.

10.5 SUMMARY

This chapter presented an overview of device drivers on the UNIX system. Devices are either block devices or character devices; the interface between them and the rest of the kernel depends on the device type. The block device interface is the block device switch table, which consists of entry points for device open, close, and strategy procedures. The strategy procedure controls data transfer to and from the block device. The character device interface is the character device switch table, which consists of entry points for device open, close, read, write, and ioctl procedures. The *ioctl* system call uses the *ioctl* interface to character devices, which permits control information to be sent between processes and devices. The kernel calls device interrupt handlers on receipt of a device interrupt, based on information stored in the interrupt vector table and on parameters supplied by the interrupting hardware.

Disk drivers convert logical block numbers used by the file system to locations on the physical disk. The block interface allows the kernel to buffer data. The raw interface allows faster I/O to and from the disk but bypasses the buffer cache, allowing more chances for file system corruption.

Terminal drivers support the primary interface to users. The kernel associates three clists with each terminal, one for raw input from the keyboard, one for processed input to account for erase and kill characters and carriage returns, and one for output. The *ioctl* system call allows processes to control how the kernel treats input data, placing the terminal in canonical mode or setting various parameters for raw mode. The *getty* process *opens* terminal lines and waits for a connection: It sets its process group so that the login shell is eventually a process group leader, initializes terminal parameters via *ioctl*, and prompts the user through a login sequence. The control terminal thus set up sends signals to processes in the process group, in response to events such as when the user hangs up or presses the break key.

Streams are a scheme for improving the modularity of device drivers and protocols. A stream is a full-duplex connection between processes and device drivers, which may contain line disciplines and protocols to process data en route. Streams modules are characterized by well-defined interfaces and by their flexibility for use in combination with other modules. The flexibility they offer has strong benefits for network protocols and drivers.

10.6 EXERCISES

* 1. Suppose a system contains two device files that have the same major and minor number and are both character devices. If two processes wish to *open* the physical device simultaneously, show that it makes no difference whether they *open* the same device file or different device files. What happens when they *close* the device?

* 2. Recall from Chapter 5 that the *mknod* system call requires superuser permission to create a device special file. Given that device access is governed by the permission modes of a file, why must *mknod* require superuser permission?

3. Write a program that verifies that the file systems on a disk do not overlap. The program should take two arguments: a device file that represents a disk volume and a descriptor file that gives section numbers and section lengths for the disk type. The program should read the super blocks to make sure that file systems do not overlap. Will such a program always be correct?

4. The program *mkfs* initializes a file system on a disk by creating the super block, leaving space for the inode list, putting all the data blocks on a linked list, and making the root inode directory. How would you program *mkfs*? How does the program change if there is a volume table of contents? How should it initialize the volume table of contents?

5. The programs *mkfs* and *fsck* (Chapter 5) are user-level programs instead of part of the kernel. Comment.

6. Suppose a programmer wants to write a data base system to run on the UNIX system. The data base programs run at user level, not as part of the kernel. How should the system interact with the disk? Consider the following issues:
   • Use of the regular file system interface versus the raw disk,
   • Need for speed,
   • Need to know when data actually resides on disk,
   • Size of the data base: Does it fit into one file system, an entire disk volume, or several disk volumes?

7. The UNIX kernel tacitly assumes that the file system is contained on perfect disks. However, disks could contain faults that incapacitate certain sectors although the remainder of the disk is still "good." How could a disk driver (or intelligent disk controller) make allowances for small numbers of bad sectors. How would this affect performance?

8. When *mount*ing a file system, the kernel invokes the driver open procedure but later releases the inode for the device special file at the end of the *mount* call. When *umount*ing a file system, the kernel accesses the inode of the device special file, invokes the driver close procedure, and releases the inode. Compare the sequence of inode operations and driver open and close calls to the sequence when *open*ing and *clos*ing a block device. Comment.

9. Run the program in Figure 10.14 but direct the output to a file. Compare the contents of the file to the output when output goes to the terminal. You will have to interrupt the processes to stop them; let them run long enough to get a sufficient amount of output. What happens if the *write* call in the program is replaced with

    printf(output);

10. What happens when a user attempts to do text editing in the background:

    ed file &

    Why?

11. Terminal files typically have access permissions set as in

    crw−−w−−w−   2 mjb   lus   33, 11 Oct 25 20:27   tty61

    when a user is logged on. That is, read/write permission is permitted for user "mjb," but only write permission is allowed other users. Why?

12. Assuming you know the terminal device file name of a friend, write a program that allows you to write messages to your friend's terminal. What other information do you need to encode a reasonable facsimile of the usual *write* command?

13. Implement the *stty* command: with no parameters, it retrieves the values of terminal settings and reports them to the user. Otherwise, the user can set various settings interactively.

14. Encode a line discipline that writes the machine name at the beginning of each line of output.

15. In canonical mode, a user can temporarily stop output to a terminal by typing "control s" at the terminal and resume output by typing "control q." How should the standard line discipline implement this feature?

* 16. The *init* process spawns a *getty* process for each terminal line in the system. What would happen if two *getty* processes were to exist simultaneously for one terminal, waiting for a user to log in? Can the kernel prevent this?

17. Suppose the shell were coded so that it "ignored" the end of file and continued to *read* its standard input. What would happen when a user (in the login shell) hits end of file and continues typing?

* 18. Suppose a process *read*s its control terminal but ignores or catches hangup signals. What happens when the process continues to *read* the control terminal after a hangup?

19. The *getty* program is responsible for opening a terminal line, and *login* is responsible for checking login and password information. What advantages are there for doing the two functions in separate programs?

20. Consider the two methods for implementing the indirect terminal driver ("/dev/tty"), described in Section 10.3.6. What differences would a user perceive? (Hint: Think about the system calls *stat* and *fstat*.)

21. Design a method for scheduling streams modules, where the kernel contains a special process that executes module service procedures when they are scheduled to execute.

* 22. Design a scheme for virtual terminals (windows) using conventional (nonstreams) drivers.

* 23. Design a method for implementing virtual terminals using streams such that a kernel module, rather than a user process, multiplexes I/O between the virtual and physical terminals. Describe a mechanism for connecting the streams to allow fan-in and fan-out. Is it better to put a multiplexing module inside the kernel or construct it as a user process?

24. The command *ps* reports interesting information on process activity in a running system. In traditional implementations, *ps* reads the information in the process table directly from kernel memory. Such a method is unstable in a development environment where the size of process table entries changes and *ps* cannot easily find the correct fields in the process table. Encode a driver that is impervious to a changing environment.

11

INTERPROCESS COMMUNICATION

Interprocess communication mechanisms allow arbitrary processes to exchange data and synchronize execution. We have already considered several forms of interprocess communication, such as pipes, named pipes, and signals. Pipes (unnamed) suffer from the drawback that they are known only to processes which are descendants of the process that invoked the *pipe* system call: Unrelated processes cannot communicate via pipes. Although named pipes allow unrelated processes to communicate, they cannot generally be used across a network (see Chapter 13), nor do they readily lend themselves to setting up multiple communications paths for different sets of communicating processes: it is impossible to multiplex a named pipe to provide private channels for pairs of communicating processes. Arbitrary processes can also communicate by sending signals via the *kill* system call, but the "message" consists only of the signal number.

This chapter describes other forms of interprocess communication. It starts off by examining process tracing, whereby one process traces and controls the execution of another process and then explains the the System V IPC package: messages, shared memory, and semaphores. It reviews the traditional methods by which processes communicate with processes on other machines over a network and, finally, gives a user-level overview of BSD sockets. It does not discuss network-specific issues such as protocols, addressing, and name service, which are beyond the scope of this book.

11.1 PROCESS TRACING

The UNIX system provides a primitive form of interprocess communication for tracing processes, useful for debugging. A debugger process, such as *sdb*, spawns a process to be traced and controls its execution with the *ptrace* system call, setting and clearing break points, and reading and writing data in its virtual address space. Process tracing thus consists of synchronization of the debugger process and the traced process and controlling the execution of the traced process.

```
if ((pid = fork()) == 0)
{
        /* child — traced process */
        ptrace(0, 0, 0, 0);
        exec("name of traced process here");
}
/* debugger process continues here */
for (;;)
{
        wait((int *) 0);
        read(input for tracing instructions)
        ptrace(cmd, pid, ...);
        if (quitting trace)
                break;
}
```

Figure 11.1. Structure of Debugging Process

The pseudo-code in Figure 11.1 shows the typical structure of a debugger program. The debugger spawns a child process, which invokes the *ptrace* system call and, as a result, the kernel sets a trace bit in the child process table entry. The child now *exec*s the program being traced. For example, if a user is debugging the program *a.out*, the child would *exec a.out*. The kernel executes the *exec* call as usual, but at the end notes that the trace bit is set and sends the child a "trap" signal. The kernel checks for signals when returning from the *exec* system call, just as it checks for signals after any system call, finds the "trap" signal it had just sent itself, and executes code for process tracing as a special case for handling signals. Noting that the trace bit is set in its process table entry, the child awakens the parent from its sleep in the *wait* system call (as will be seen), enters a special trace state similar to the sleep state (not shown in the process state diagram in Figure 6.1), and does a context switch.

Typically, the parent (debugger) process would have meanwhile entered a user-level loop, *wait*ing to be awakened by the traced process. When the traced process awakens the debugger, the debugger returns from *wait*, *read*s user input commands, and converts them to a series of *ptrace* calls to control the child (traced) process. The syntax of the *ptrace* system call is ptrace(cmd, pid, addr, data);

where *cmd* specifies various commands such as reading data, writing data, resuming execution and so on, *pid* is the process ID of the traced process, *addr* is the virtual address to be read or written in the child process, and *data* is an integer value to be written. When executing the *ptrace* system call, the kernel verifies that the debugger has a child whose ID is *pid* and that the child is in the traced state and then uses a global trace data structure to transfer data between the two processes. It locks the trace data structure to prevent other tracing processes from overwriting it, copies *cmd*, *addr*, and *data* into the data structure, wakes up the child process and puts it into the "ready-to-run" state, then sleeps until the child responds. When the child resumes execution (in kernel mode), it does the appropriate trace command, writes its reply into the trace data structure, then awakens the debugger. Depending on the command type, the child may reenter the trace state and wait for a new command or return from handling signals and resume execution. When the debugger resumes execution, the kernel saves the "return value" supplied by the traced process, unlocks the trace data structure, and returns to the user.

If the debugger process is not sleeping in the *wait* system call when the child enters the trace state, it will not discover its traced child until it calls *wait*, at which time it returns immediately and proceeds as just described.

```
int data[32];
main()
{
        int i;
        for (i = 0;  i < 32;  i++)
                printf("data[%d] = %d\n", i, data[i]);
        printf("ptrace data addr 0x%x\n", data);
}
```

Figure 11.2. Trace — A Traced Process

Consider the two programs in Figures 11.2 and 11.3, called *trace* and *debug*, respectively. Running *trace* at the terminal, the array values for *data* will be 0; the process prints the address of *data* and *exits*. Now, running *debug* with a parameter equal to the value printed out by *trace*, *debug* saves the parameter in *addr*, creates a child process that invokes *ptrace* to make itself eligible for tracing, and *execs trace*. The kernel sends the child process (call it *trace*) a *SIGTRAP* signal at the end of *exec*, and *trace* enters the trace state, waiting for a command from *debug*. If *debug* had been sleeping in *wait*, it wakes up, finds the traced child process, and returns from *wait*. *Debug* then calls *ptrace*, writes the value of the loop variable *i* into the data space of *trace* at address *addr*, and increments *addr*; in *trace*, *addr* is an address of an entry in the array *data*. *Debug*'s last call to *ptrace* causes *trace* to run, and this time, the array *data* contains the values 0 to

```
#define TR_SETUP 0
#define TR_WRITE 5
#define TR_RESUME 7
int addr;

main(argc, argv)
      int argc;
      char *argv[];
{
      int i, pid;

      sscanf(argv[1], "%x", &addr);

      if ((pid = fork()) == 0)
      {
            ptrace(TR_SETUP, 0, 0, 0);
            execl("trace", "trace", 0);
            exit();
      }
      for (i = 0;  i < 32;  i++)
      {
            wait((int *) 0);
            /* write value of i into address addr in proc pid */
            if (ptrace(TR_WRITE, pid, addr, i) == -1)
                  exit();
            addr += sizeof(int);
      }
      /* traced process should resume execution */
      ptrace(TR_RESUME, pid, 1, 0);
}
```

Figure 11.3. Debug — A Tracing Process

31. A debugger such as *sdb* has access to the traced process's symbol table, from which it determines the addresses it uses as parameters to *ptrace* calls.

The use of *ptrace* for process tracing is primitive and suffers several drawbacks.

- The kernel must do four context switches to transfer a word of data between a debugger and a traced process: The kernel switches context in the debugger in the *ptrace* call until the traced process replies to a query, switches context to and from the traced process, and switches context back to the debugger process with the answer to the *ptrace* call. The overhead is necessary, because a debugger has no other way to gain access to the virtual address space of a traced process, but process tracing is consequently slow.

- A debugger process can trace several child processes simultaneously, although this feature is rarely used in practice. More critically, a debugger can only trace child processes: If a traced child *forks*, the debugger has no control over the grandchild, a severe handicap when debugging sophisticated programs. If a traced process *execs*, the later *exec*ed images are still being traced because of the original *ptrace*, but the debugger may not know the name of the *exec*ed image, making symbolic debugging difficult.
- A debugger cannot trace a process that is already executing if the debugged process had not called *ptrace* to let the kernel know that it consents to be traced. This is inconvenient, because a process that needs debugging must be killed and restarted in trace mode.
- It is impossible to trace *setuid* programs, because users could violate security by writing their address space via *ptrace* and doing illegal operations. For example, suppose a *setuid* program calls *exec* with file name "privatefile". A clever user could use *ptrace* to overwrite the file name with "/bin/sh", executing the shell (and all programs executed by the shell) with unauthorized permission. *Exec* ignores the *setuid* bit if the process is traced to prevent a user from overwriting the address space of a *setuid* program.

Killian [Killian 84] describes a different scheme for process tracing, based on the file system switch described in Chapter 5. An administrator mounts a file system, "/proc"; users identify processes by their PID and treat them as files in "/proc". The kernel gives permission to *open* the files according to the process user ID and group ID. Users can examine the process address space by *read*ing the file, and they can set breakpoints by *writ*ing the file. *Stat* returns various statistics about the process. This method removes three disadvantages of *ptrace*. First, it is faster, because a debugger process can transfer more data per system call than it can with *ptrace*. Second, a debugger can trace arbitrary processes, not necessarily a child process. Finally, the traced process does not have to make prior arrangement to allow tracing; a debugger can trace existing processes. As part of the regular file protection mechanism, only a superuser can debug processes that are *setuid* to root.

11.2 SYSTEM V IPC

The UNIX System V IPC package consists of three mechanisms. Messages allow processes to send formatted data streams to arbitrary processes, shared memory allows processes to share parts of their virtual address space, and semaphores allow processes to synchronize execution. Implemented as a unit, they share common properties.

- Each mechanism contains a table whose entries describe all instances of the mechanism.
- Each entry contains a numeric *key*, which is its user-chosen name.

- Each mechanism contains a "get" system call to create a new entry or to retrieve an existing one, and the parameters to the calls include a key and flags. The kernel searches the proper table for an entry named by the key. Processes can call the "get" system calls with the key IPC_PRIVATE to assure the return of an unused entry. They can set the IPC_CREAT bit in the flag field to create a new entry if one by the given key does not already exist, and they can force an error notification by setting the IPC_EXCL and IPC_CREAT flags, if an entry already exists for the key. The "get" system calls return a kernel-chosen descriptor for use in the other system calls and are thus analogous to the file system *creat* and *open* calls.

- For each IPC mechanism, the kernel uses the following formula to find the index into the table of data structures from the descriptor:

  index = descriptor modulo (number of entries in table)

For example, if the table of message structures contains 100 entries, the descriptors for entry 1 are 1, 101, 201, and so on. When a process removes an entry, the kernel increments the descriptor associated with it by the number of entries in the table: The incremented value becomes the new descriptor for the entry when it is next allocated by a "get" call. Processes that attempt to access the entry by its old descriptor fail on their access. Referring to the previous example, if the descriptor associated with message entry 1 is 201 when it is removed, the kernel assigns a new descriptor, 301, to the entry. Processes that attempt to access descriptor 201 receive an error, because it is no longer valid. The kernel eventually recycles descriptor numbers, presumably after a long time lapse.

- Each IPC entry has a permissions structure that includes the user ID and group ID of the process that created the entry, a user and group ID set by the "control" system call (below), and a set of read-write-execute permissions for user, group, and others, similar to the file permission modes.

- Each entry contains other status information, such as the process ID of the last process to update the entry (send a message, receive a message, attach shared memory, and so on), and the time of last access or update.

- Each mechanism contains a "control" system call to query status of an entry, to set status information, or to remove the entry from the system. When a process queries the status of an entry, the kernel verifies that the process has read permission and then copies data from the table entry to the user address. Similarly, to set parameters on an entry, the kernel verifies that the user ID of the process matches the user ID or the creator user ID of the entry or that the process is run by a superuser; write permission is not sufficient to set parameters. The kernel copies the user data into the table entry, setting the user ID, group ID, permission modes, and other fields dependent on the type of mechanism. The kernel does not change the creator user and group ID fields, so the user who created an entry retains control rights to it. Finally, a user can remove an entry if it is the superuser or if its process ID matches either ID field in the entry structure. The kernel increments the descriptor number so that the next instance of assigning the entry will return a different descriptor. Hence, system calls will fail if a process attempts to access an entry by an old descriptor, as explained earlier.

11.2.1 Messages

There are four system calls for messages: *msgget* returns (and possibly creates) a message descriptor that designates a message queue for use in other system calls, *msgctl* has options to set and return parameters associated with a message descriptor and an option to remove descriptors, *msgsnd* sends a message, and *msgrcv* receives a message.

The syntax of the *msgget* system call is

msgqid = msgget(key, flag);

where *msgqid* is the descriptor returned by the call, and *key* and *flag* have the semantics described above for the general "get" calls. The kernel stores messages on a linked list (queue) per descriptor, and it uses *msgqid* as an index into an array of message queue headers. In addition to the general IPC permissions field mentioned above, the queue structure contains the following fields:

- Pointers to the first and last messages on a linked list;
- The number of messages and the total number of data bytes on the linked list;
- The maximum number of bytes of data that can be on the linked list;
- The process IDs of the last processes to send and receive messages;
- Time stamps of the last *msgsnd*, *msgrcv*, and *msgctl* operations.

When a user calls *msgget* to create a new descriptor, the kernel searches the array of message queues to see if one exists with the given key. If there is no entry for the specified key, the kernel allocates a new queue structure, initializes it, and returns an identifier to the user. Otherwise, it checks permissions and returns.

A process uses the *msgsnd* system call to send a message:

msgsnd(msgqid, msg, count, flag);

where *msgqid* is the descriptor of a message queue typically returned by a *msgget* call, *msg* is a pointer to a structure consisting of a user-chosen integer type and a character array, *count* gives the size of the data array, and *flag* specifies the action the kernel should take if it runs out of internal buffer space.

The kernel checks (Figure 11.4) that the sending process has write permission for the message descriptor, that the message length does not exceed the system limit, that the message queue does not contain too many bytes, and that the message type is a positive integer. If all tests succeed, the kernel allocates space for the message from a message *map* (recall Section 9.1) and copies the data from user space. The kernel allocates a message header and puts it on the end of the linked list of message headers for the message queue. It records the message type and

```
algorithm msgsnd              /* send a message */
input:  (1) message queue descriptor
        (2) address of message structure
        (3) size of message
        (4) flags
output: number of bytes sent
{
        check legality of descriptor, permissions;
        while (not enough space to store message)
        {
                if (flags specify not to wait)
                        return;
                sleep(until event enough space is available);
        }
        get message header;
        read message text from user space to kernel;
        adjust data structures: enqueue message header,
                        message header points to data,
                        counts, time stamps, process ID;
        wakeup all processes waiting to read message from queue;
}
```

Figure 11.4. Algorithm for Msgsnd

size in the message header, sets the message header to point to the message data, and updates various statistics fields (number of messages and bytes on queue, time stamps and process ID of sender) in the queue header. The kernel then awakens processes that were asleep, waiting for messages to arrive on the queue. If the number of bytes on the queue exceeds the queue's limit, the process sleeps until other messages are removed from the queue. If the process specified not to wait (flag IPC_NOWAIT), however, it returns immediately with an error indication. Figure 11.5 depicts messages on a queue, showing queue headers, linked lists of message headers, and pointers from the message headers to a data area.

Consider the program in Figure 11.6: A process calls *msgget* to get a descriptor for *MSGKEY*. It sets up a message of length 256 bytes, although it uses only the first integer, copies its process ID into the message text, assigns the message type value 1, then calls *msgsnd* to send the message. We will return to this example later.

A process receives messages by

count = msgrcv(id, msg, maxcount, type, flag);

where *id* is the message descriptor, *msg* is the address of a user structure to contain the received message, *maxcount* is the size of the data array in *msg*, *type* specifies the message type the user wants to read, and *flag* specifies what the kernel should

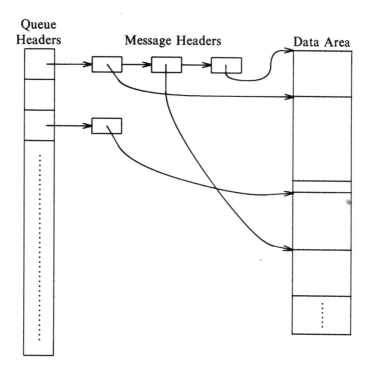

Figure 11.5. Data Structures for Messages

do if no messages are on the queue. The return value, *count*, is the number of bytes returned to the user.

The kernel checks (Figure 11.7) that the user has the necessary access rights to the message queue, as above. If the requested message *type* is 0, the kernel finds the first message on the linked list. If its size is less than or equal to the size requested by the user, the kernel copies the message data to the user data structure and adjusts its internal structures appropriately: It decrements the count of messages on the queue and the number of data bytes on the queue, sets the receive time and receiving process ID, adjusts the linked list, and frees the kernel space that had stored the message data. If processes were waiting to send messages because there was no room on the list, the kernel awakens them. If the message is bigger than *maxcount* specified by the user, the kernel returns an error for the system call and leaves the message on the queue. If the process ignores size constraints, however (bit *MSG_NOERROR* is set in *flag*), the kernel truncates the message, returns the requested number of bytes, and removes the entire message from the list.

```
#include      <sys/types.h>
#include      <sys/ipc.h>
#include      <sys/msg.h>

#define MSGKEY      75

struct msgform {
      long      mtype;
      char      mtext[256];
};

main()
{
      struct msgform msg;
      int msgid, pid, *pint;

      msgid = msgget(MSGKEY, 0777);

      pid = getpid();
      pint = (int *) msg.mtext;
      *pint = pid;        /* copy pid into message text */
      msg.mtype = 1;

      msgsnd(msgid, &msg, sizeof(int), 0);
      msgrcv(msgid, &msg, 256, pid, 0);        /* pid is used as the msg type */
      printf("client: receive from pid %d\n", *pint);
}
```

Figure 11.6. A Client Process

A process can receive messages of a particular type by setting the *type* parameter appropriately. If it is a positive integer, the kernel returns the first message of the given type. If it is negative, the kernel finds the lowest type of all messages on the queue, provided it is less than or equal to the absolute value of *type*, and returns the first message of that type. For example, if a queue contains three messages whose types are 3, 1, and 2, respectively, and a user requests a message with type -2, the kernel returns the message of type 1. In all cases, if no messages on the queue satisfy the receive request, the kernel puts the process to sleep, unless the process had specified to return immediately by setting the *IPC_NOWAIT* bit in *flag*.

Consider the programs in Figures 11.6 and 11.8. The program in Figure 11.8 shows the structure of a *server* that provides generic service to *client* processes. For instance, it may receive requests from client processes to provide information from a database; the server process is a single point of access to the database, making consistency and security easier. The server creates a message structure by setting

```
algorithm msgrcv                /* receive message */
input:  (1) message descriptor
        (2) address of data array for incoming message
        (3) size of data array
        (4) requested message type
        (5) flags
output: number of bytes in returned message
{
      check permissions;
   loop:
      check legality of message descriptor;
      /* find message to return to user */
      if (requested message type == 0)
           consider first message on queue;
      else if (requested message type > 0)
           consider first message on queue with given type;
      else     /* requested message type < 0 */
           consider first of the lowest typed messages on queue,
                such that its type is <= absolute value of
                requested type;
      if (there is a message)
      {
           adjust message size or return error if user size too small;
           copy message type, text from kernel space to user space;
           unlink message from queue;
           return;
      }
      /* no message */
      if (flags specify not to sleep)
           return with error;
      sleep (event message arrives on queue);
      goto loop;
}
```

Figure 11.7. Algorithm for Receiving a Message

the *IPC_CREAT* flag in the *msgget* call and receives all messages of type 1 —
requests from client processes. It reads the message text, finds the process ID of
the client process, and sets the return message type to the client process ID. In this
example, it sends its process ID back to the client process in the message text, and
the client process receives messages whose message type equals its process ID.
Thus, the server process receives only messages sent to it by client processes, and
client processes receive only messages sent to them by the server. The processes
cooperate to set up multiple channels on one message queue.

```
#include        <sys/types.h>
#include        <sys/ipc.h>
#include        <sys/msg.h>

#define MSGKEY        75
struct msgform
{
        long mtype;
        char mtext[256];
} msg;
int msgid;

main()
{
        int i, pid, *pint;
        extern cleanup();

        for (i = 0;  i < 20;  i++)
                signal(i, cleanup);
        msgid = msgget(MSGKEY, 0777 | IPC_CREAT);

        for (;;)
        {
                msgrcv(msgid, &msg, 256, 1, 0);
                pint = (int *) msg.mtext;
                pid = *pint;
                printf("server: receive from pid %d\n", pid);
                msg.mtype = pid;
                *pint = getpid();
                msgsnd(msgid, &msg, sizeof(int), 0);
        }
}

cleanup()
{
        msgctl(msgid, IPC_RMID, 0);
        exit();
}
```

Figure 11.8. A Server Process

Messages are formatted as type-data pairs, whereas file data is a byte stream. The *type* prefix allows processes to select messages of a particular type, if desired, a feature not readily available in the file system. Processes can thus extract messages of particular types from the message queue in the order that they arrive, and the kernel maintains the proper order. Although it is possible to implement a message passing scheme at user level with the file system, messages provide applications with a more efficient way to transfer data between processes.

A process can query the status of a message descriptor, set its status, and remove a message descriptor with the *msgctl* system call. The syntax of the call is

   msgctl(id, cmd, mstatbuf)

where *id* identifies the message descriptor, *cmd* specifies the type of command, and *mstatbuf* is the address of a user data structure that will contain control parameters or the results of a query. The implementation of the system call is straightforward; the appendix specifies the parameters in detail.

Returning to the server example in Figure 11.8, the process catches signals and calls the function *cleanup* to remove the message queue from the system. If it did not catch signals or if it receives a *SIGKILL* signal (which cannot be caught), the message queue would remain in the system even though no processes refer to it. Subsequent attempts to create (exclusively) a new message queue for the given key would fail until it was removed.

11.2.2 Shared Memory

Processes can communicate directly with each other by sharing parts of their virtual address space and then reading and writing the data stored in the *shared memory*. The system calls for manipulating shared memory are similar to the system calls for messages. The *shmget* system call creates a new region of shared memory or returns an existing one, the *shmat* system call logically attaches a region to the virtual address space of a process, the *shmdt* system call detaches a region from the virtual address space of a process, and the *shmctl* system call manipulates various parameters associated with the shared memory. Processes read and write shared memory using the same machine instructions they use to read and write regular memory. After attaching shared memory, it becomes part of the virtual address space of a process, accessible in the same way other virtual addresses are; no system calls are needed to access data in shared memory.

The syntax of the *shmget* system call is

   shmid = shmget(key, size, flag);

where *size* is the number of bytes in the region. The kernel searches the shared memory table for the given *key*: if it finds an entry and the permission modes are acceptable, it returns the descriptor for the entry. If it does not find an entry and the user had set the *IPC_CREAT* flag to create a new region, the kernel verifies that the size is between system-wide minimum and maximum values and then allocates a region data structure using algorithm *allocreg* (Section 6.5.2). The kernel saves the permission modes, size, and a pointer to the region table entry in the shared memory table (Figure 11.9) and sets a flag there to indicate that no memory is associated with the region. It allocates memory (page tables and so on) for the region only when a process attaches the region to its address space. The kernel also sets a flag on the region table entry to indicate that the region should not be freed when the last process attached to it *exits*. Thus, data in shared memory remains intact even though no processes include it as part of their virtual address space.

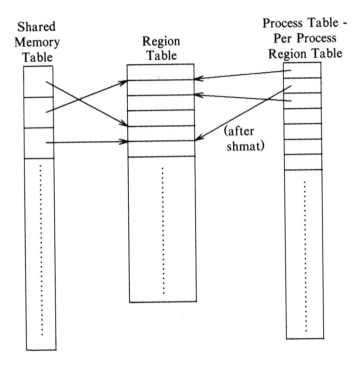

Figure 11.9. Data Structures for Shared Memory

A process attaches a shared memory region to its virtual address space with the *shmat* system call:

virtaddr = shmat(id, addr, flags);

Id, returned by a previous *shmget* system call, identifies the shared memory region, *addr* is the virtual address where the user wants to attach the shared memory, and *flags* specify whether the region is read-only and whether the kernel should round off the user-specified address. The return value, *virtaddr*, is the virtual address where the kernel attached the region, not necessarily the value requested by the process.

When executing the *shmat* system call, the kernel verifies that the process has the necessary permissions to access the region (Figure 11.10). It examines the address the user specifies: If 0, the kernel chooses a convenient virtual address.

```
algorithm shmat               /* attach shared memory */
input:  (1) shared memory descriptor
        (2) virtual address to attach memory
        (3) flags
output: virtual address where memory was attached
{
        check validity of descriptor, permissions;
        if (user specified virtual address)
        {
                round off virtual address, as specified by flags;
                check legality of virtual address, size of region;
        }
        else        /* user wants kernel to find good address */
                kernel picks virtual address: error if none available;
        attach region to process address space (algorithm attachreg);
        if (region being attached for first time)
                allocate page tables, memory for region
                                        (algorithm growreg);
        return(virtual address where attached);
}
```

Figure 11.10. Algorithm for Attaching Shared Memory

The shared memory must not overlap other regions in the process virtual address space; hence it must be chosen judiciously so that other regions do not grow into the shared memory. For instance, a process can increase the size of its data region with the *brk* system call, and the new data region is virtually contiguous with the previous data region; therefore, the kernel should not attach a shared memory region close to the data region. Similarly, it should not place shared memory close to the top of the stack so that the stack will not grow into it. For example, if the stack grows towards higher addresses, the best place for shared memory is immediately before the start of the stack region.

The kernel checks that the shared memory region fits into the process address space and attaches the region, using algorithm *attachreg*. If the calling process is the first to attach the region, the kernel allocates the necessary tables, using algorithm *growreg*, adjusts the shared memory table entry field for "last time attached," and returns the virtual address at which it attached the region.

A process detaches a shared memory region from its virtual address space by

shmdt(addr)

where *addr* is the virtual address returned by a prior *shmat* call. Although it would seem more logical to pass an identifier, the virtual address of the shared memory is used so that a process can distinguish between several instances of a shared memory region that are attached to its address space, and because the identifier may have been removed. The kernel searches for the process region attached at the indicated virtual address and detaches it from the process address space, using algorithm *detachreg* (Section 6.5.7). Because the region tables have no back pointers to the shared memory table, the kernel searches the shared memory table for the entry that points to the region and adjusts the field for the time the region was last detached.

Consider the program in Figure 11.11: A process creates a 128K-byte shared memory region and attaches it twice to its address space at different virtual addresses. It writes data in the "first" shared memory and reads it from the "second" shared memory. Figure 11.12 shows another process attaching the same region (it gets only 64K bytes, to show that each process can attach different amounts of a shared memory region); it waits until the first process writes a nonzero value in the first word of the shared memory region and then reads the shared memory. The first process *pauses* to give the second process a chance to execute; when the first process catches a signal, it removes the shared memory region.

A process uses the *shmctl* system call to query status and set parameters for the shared memory region:

shmctl(id, cmd, shmstatbuf);

Id identifies the shared memory table entry, *cmd* specifies the type of operation, and *shmstatbuf* is the address of a user-level data structure that contains the status information of the shared memory table entry when querying or setting its status. The kernel treats the commands for querying status and changing owner and permissions similar to the implementation for messages. When removing a shared memory region, the kernel frees the entry and looks at the region table entry: If no process has the region attached to its virtual address space, it frees the region table entry and all its resources, using algorithm *freereg* (Section 6.5.6). If the region is still attached to some processes (its reference count is greater than 0), the kernel just clears the flag that indicates the region should not be freed when the last process detaches the region. Processes that are using the shared memory may continue doing so, but no new processes can attach it. When all processes detach the region, the kernel frees the region. This is analogous to the case in the file system where a process can *open* a file and continue to access it after it is *unlink*ed.

11.2.3 Semaphores

The semaphore system calls allow processes to synchronize execution by doing a set of operations atomically on a set of semaphores. Before the implementation of semaphores, a process would create a lock file with the *creat* system call if it wanted to lock a resource: The *creat* fails if the file already exists, and the process would assume that another process had the resource locked. The major disadvantages of this approach are that the process does not know when to try again, and lock files may inadvertently be left behind when the system crashes or is

```
#include        <sys/types.h>
#include        <sys/ipc.h>
#include        <sys/shm.h>
#define SHMKEY        75
#define        K        1024
int shmid;

main()
{
        int i, *pint;
        char *addr1, *addr2;
        extern char *shmat();
        extern cleanup();

        for (i = 0;  i < 20;  i++)
                signal(i, cleanup);
        shmid = shmget(SHMKEY, 128 * K, 0777 | IPC_CREAT);
        addr1 = shmat(shmid, 0, 0);
        addr2 = shmat(shmid, 0, 0);
        printf("addr1 0x%x  addr2 0x%x\n", addr1, addr2);
        pint = (int *) addr1;

        for (i = 0;  i < 256;  i++)
                *pint++ = i;
        pint = (int *) addr1;
        *pint = 256;

        pint = (int *) addr2;
        for (i = 0;  i < 256;  i++)
                printf("index %d\tvalue %d\n", i, *pint++);

        pause();
}

cleanup()
{
        shmctl(shmid, IPC_RMID, 0);
        exit();
}
```

Figure 11.11. Attaching Shared Memory Twice to a Process

```
#include        <sys/types.h>
#include        <sys/ipc.h>
#include        <sys/shm.h>

#define SHMKEY 75
#define K 1024
int shmid;

main()
{
        int i, *pint;
        char *addr;
        extern char *shmat();

        shmid = shmget(SHMKEY, 64 * K, 0777);

        addr = shmat(shmid, 0, 0);
        pint = (int *) addr;

        while (*pint == 0)
                ;
        for (i = 0;  i < 256;  i++)
                printf("%d\n", *pint++);
}
```

Figure 11.12. Sharing Memory Between Processes

rebooted.

Dijkstra published the Dekker algorithm that describes an implementation of *semaphores*, integer-valued objects that have two atomic operations defined for them: P and V (see [Dijkstra 68]). The P operation decrements the value of a semaphore if its value is greater than 0, and the V operation increments its value. Because the operations are atomic, at most one P or V operation can succeed on a semaphore at any time. The semaphore system calls in System V are a generalization of Dijkstra's P and V operations, in that several operations can be done simultaneously and the increment and decrement operations can be by values greater than 1. The kernel does all the operations atomically; no other processes adjust the semaphore values until all operations are done. If the kernel cannot do *all* the operations, it does not do *any*; the process sleeps until it can do all the operations, as will be explained.

A semaphore in UNIX System V consists of the following elements:

• The value of the semaphore,
• The process ID of the last process to manipulate the semaphore,

- The number of processes waiting for the semaphore value to increase,
- The number of processes waiting for the semaphore value to equal 0.

The semaphore system calls are *semget* to create and gain access to a set of semaphores, *semctl* to do various control operations on the set, and *semop* to manipulate the values of semaphores.

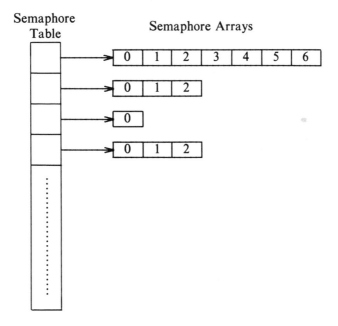

Figure 11.13. Data Structures for Semaphores

The *semget* system call creates an array of semaphores:

    id = semget(key, count, flag);

where *key*, *flag* and *id* are similar to those parameters for messages and shared memory. The kernel allocates an entry that points to an array of semaphore structures with *count* elements (Figure 11.13). The entry also specifies the number of semaphores in the array, the time of the last *semop* call, and the time of the last *semctl* call. For example, the *semget* system call in Figure 11.14 creates a semaphore with two elements.

    Processes manipulate semaphores with the *semop* system call:

    oldval = semop(id, oplist, count);

Id is the descriptor returned by *semget*, *oplist* is a pointer to an array of semaphore operations, and *count* is the size of the array. The return value, *oldval*, is the value

```
#include      <sys/types.h>
#include      <sys/ipc.h>
#include      <sys/sem.h>

#define SEMKEY      75
int semid;
unsigned int count;
/* definition of sembuf in file sys/sem.h
 * struct sembuf {
 *      unsigned shortsem_num;
 *      short sem_op;
 *      short sem_flg;
}; */
struct sembuf psembuf, vsembuf;            /* ops for P and V */

main(argc, argv)
     int argc;
     char *argv[];
{
     int i, first, second;
     short initarray[2], outarray[2];
     extern cleanup();

     if (argc == 1)
     {
          for (i = 0;  i < 20;  i++)
               signal(i, cleanup);
          semid = semget(SEMKEY, 2, 0777 | IPC_CREAT);
          initarray[0] = initarray[1] = 1;
          semctl(semid, 2, SETALL, initarray);
          semctl(semid, 2, GETALL, outarray);
          printf("sem init vals %d %d\n", outarray[0], outarray[1]);
          pause();      /* sleep until awakened by a signal */
     }

     /* continued next page */
```

Figure 11.14. Locking and Unlocking Operations

of the last semaphore operated on in the set before the operation was done. The format of each element of *oplist* is

- the semaphore number identifying the semaphore array entry being operated on,
- the operation,
- flags.

```
        else if (argv[1][0] == 'a')
        {
              first = 0;
              second = 1;
        }
        else
        {
              first = 1;
              second = 0;
        }

        semid = semget(SEMKEY, 2, 0777);
        psembuf.sem_op = -1;
        psembuf.sem_flg = SEM_UNDO;
        vsembuf.sem_op = 1;
        vsembuf.sem_flg = SEM_UNDO;

        for (count = 0;  ;  count++)
        {
              psembuf.sem_num = first;
              semop(semid, &psembuf, 1);
              psembuf.sem_num = second;
              semop(semid, &psembuf, 1);
              printf("proc %d count %d\n", getpid(), count);
              vsembuf.sem_num = second;
              semop(semid, &vsembuf, 1);
              vsembuf.sem_num = first;
              semop(semid, &vsembuf, 1);
        }
}

cleanup()
{
      semctl(semid, 2, IPC_RMID, 0);
      exit();
}
```

Figure 11.14. Locking and Unlocking Operations (continued)

The kernel reads the array of semaphore operations, *oplist*, from the user address space and verifies that the semaphore numbers are legal and that the process has the necessary permissions to read or change the semaphores (Figure 11.15). If permission is not allowed, the system call fails. If the kernel must sleep as it does the list of operations, it restores the semaphores it has already operated on to their values at the start of the system call; it sleeps until the event for which

```
algorithm semop              /* semaphore operations */
inputs: (1) semaphore descriptor
        (2) array of semaphore operations
        (3) number of elements in array
output: start value of last semaphore operated on
{
      check legality of semaphore descriptor;
start: read array of semaphore operations from user to kernel space;
      check permissions for all semaphore operations;

      for (each semaphore operation in array)
      {
            if (semaphore operation is positive)
            {
                  add "operation" to semaphore value;
                  if (UNDO flag set on semaphore operation)
                        update process undo structure;
                  wakeup all processes sleeping (event semaphore value increases);
            }
            else if (semaphore operation is negative )
            {
                  if ("operation" + semaphore value >= 0)
                  {
                        add "operation" to semaphore value;
                        if (UNDO flag set)
                              update process undo structure;
                        if (semaphore value 0)
                              /* continued next page */
```

Figure 11.15. Algorithm for Semaphore Operation

it is waiting occurs and then restarts the system call. Because the kernel saves the semaphore operations in a global array, it reads the array from user space again if it must restart the system call. Thus, operations are done atomically — either all at once or not at all.

The kernel changes the value of a semaphore according to the value of the operation. If positive, it increments the value of the semaphore and awakens all processes that are waiting for the value of the semaphore to increase. If the semaphore operation is 0, the kernel checks the semaphore value: If 0, it continues with the other operations in the array; otherwise, it increments the number of processes asleep, waiting for the semaphore value to be 0, and goes to sleep. If the semaphore operation is negative and its absolute value is less than or equal to the value of the semaphore, the kernel adds the operation value (a negative number) to the semaphore value. If the result is 0, the kernel awakens all processes asleep, waiting for the semaphore value to be 0. If the value of the semaphore is less than

```
                              wakeup all processes sleeping (event
                                  semaphore value becomes 0);
                    continue;
                }
            reverse all semaphore operations already done
                this system call (previous iterations);
            if (flags specify not to sleep)
                return with error;
            sleep (event semaphore value increases);
            goto start;        /* start loop from beginning */
        }
        else        /* semaphore operation is zero */
        {
            if (semaphore value non 0)
            {
                reverse all semaphore operations done
                    this system call;
                if (flags specify not to sleep)
                    return with error;
                sleep (event semaphore value == 0);
                goto start;        /* restart loop */
            }
        }
    } /* for loop ends here */
    /* semaphore operations all succeeded */
    update time stamps, process ID's;
    return value of last semaphore operated on before call succeeded;
}
```

Figure 11.15. Algorithm for Semaphore Operation (continued)

the absolute value of the semaphore operation, the kernel puts the process to sleep on the event that the value of the semaphore increases. Whenever a process sleeps in the middle of a semaphore operation, it sleeps at an interruptible priority; hence, it wakes up on receipt of a signal.

Consider the program in Figure 11.14, and suppose a user executes it (*a.out*) three times in the following sequence:

    a.out &
    a.out a &
    a.out b &

When run without any parameters, the process creates a semaphore set with two elements and initializes their values to 1. Then, it *pauses* and sleeps until awakened by a signal, when it removes the semaphore in *cleanup*. When executing the program with parameter 'a', the process (A) does four separate semaphore operations in the loop: It decrements the value of semaphore 0, decrements the value of semaphore 1, executes the print statement, and then increments the values of semaphores 1 and 0. A process goes to sleep if it attempts to decrement the value of a semaphore that is 0, and hence the semaphore is considered *lock*ed. Because the semaphores were initialized to 1 and no other processes are using the semaphores, process A will never sleep, and the semaphore values will oscillate between 1 and 0. When executing the program with parameter 'b', the process (B) decrements semaphores 0 and 1 in the opposite order from process A. When processes A and B run simultaneously, a situation could arise whereby process A has locked semaphore 0 and wants to lock semaphore 1, but process B has locked semaphore 1 and wants to lock semaphore 0. Both processes sleep, unable to continue. They are deadlocked and exit only on receipt of a signal.

To avoid such problems, processes can do multiple semaphore operations simultaneously. Using the following structures and code in the last example would give the desired effect.

```
struct sembuf psembuf[2];

psembuf[0].sem_num = 0;
psembuf[1].sem_num = 1;
psembuf[0].sem_op = -1;
psembuf[1].sem_op = -1;
semop(semid, psembuf, 2);
```

Psembuf is an array of semaphore operations that decrements semaphores 0 and 1 simultaneously. If either operation cannot succeed, the process sleeps until they both succeed. For instance, if the value of semaphore 0 is 1 and the value of semaphore 1 is 0, the kernel would leave the values intact until it can decrement both values.

A process can set the *IPC_NOWAIT* flag in the *semop* system call; if the kernel arrives at a situation where the process would sleep because it must wait for the semaphore value to exceed a particular value or for it to have value 0, the kernel returns from the system call with an error condition. Thus, it is possible to implement a conditional semaphore, whereby a process does not sleep if it cannot do the atomic action.

Dangerous situations could occur if a process does a semaphore operation, presumably locking some resource, and then *exit*s without resetting the semaphore value. Such situations can occur as the result of a programmer error or because of receipt of a signal that causes sudden termination of a process. If, in Figure 11.14 again, the process receives a kill signal after decrementing the semaphore values, it has no chance to reincrement them, because kill signals cannot be caught. Hence, other processes would find the semaphore locked even though the process that had locked it no longer exists. To avoid such problems, a process can set the *SEM_UNDO* flag in the *semop* call; when it *exit*s, the kernel reverses the effect of every semaphore operation the process had done. To implement this feature, the kernel maintains a table with one entry for every process in the system. Each entry

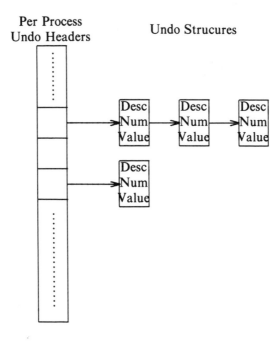

Figure 11.16. Undo Structures for Semaphores

points to a set of *undo* structures, one for each semaphore used by the process (Figure 11.16). Each undo structure is an array of triples consisting of a semaphore ID, a semaphore number in the set identified by ID, and an adjustment value.

The kernel allocates undo structures dynamically when a process executes its first *semop* system call with the *SEM_UNDO* flag set. On subsequent *semop* system calls with the *SEM_UNDO* flag set, the kernel searches the process undo structures for one with the same semaphore ID and number as the *semop* operation: If it finds one, it subtracts the value of the semaphore operation from the adjustment value. Thus, the undo structure contains a negated summation of all semaphore operations the process had done on the semaphore for which the *SEM_UNDO* flag was set. If no undo structure for the semaphore exists, the kernel creates one, sorting a list of structures by semaphore ID and number. If an adjustment value drops to 0, the kernel removes the undo structure. When a process *exits*, the kernel calls a special routine that goes through the undo structures associated with the process and does the specified action on the indicated semaphore.

Referring back to Figure 11.14, the kernel creates an undo structure every time the process decrements the semaphore value and removes the structure every time

semaphore id		semid
semaphore num		0
adjustment		1

(a) After first operation

semaphore id		semid	semid
semaphore num		0	1
adjustment		1	1

(b) After second operation

semaphore id		semid
semaphore num		0
adjustment		1

(c) After third operation

empty

(d) After fourth operation

Figure 11.17. Sequence of Undo Structures

the process increments a semaphore value, because the adjustment value of the undo structure is 0. Figure 11.17 shows the sequence when invoking the program with parameter 'a'. After the first operation, the process has one triple for *semid* with semaphore number 0 and adjustment value 1, and after the second operation, it has a second triple with semaphore number 1 and adjustment value 1. If the process were to exit suddenly now, the kernel would go through the triples and add the value 1 to each semaphore, restoring their values to 0. In the regular case, the kernel decrements the adjustment value of semaphore 1 during the third operation, corresponding to the increment of the semaphore value, and it removes the triple, because its adjustment value is 0. After the fourth operation, the process has no more triples, because the adjustment values would all be 0.

The array operations on semaphores allow processes to avoid deadlock problems, as illustrated above, but they are complicated, and most applications do not need their full power. Applications that require use of multiple semaphores should deal with deadlock conditions at user level, and the kernel should not contain such complicated system calls.

The *semctl* system call contains a myriad of control operations for semaphores:

```
semctl(id, number, cmd, arg);
```

Arg is declared as a union:

```
union semunion {
        int val;
        struct semid_ds *semstat;        /* see appendix for definition */
        unsigned short *array;
} arg;
```

The kernel interprets *arg* based on the value of *cmd*, similar to the way it interprets *ioctl* commands (Chapter 10). The expected actions take place for the *cmd*s that retrieve or set control parameters (permissions and others), set one or all semaphore values in a set, or read the semaphore values. The appendix gives the details for each command. For the remove command, *IPC_RMID*, the kernel finds all processes that have undo structures for the semaphore and removes the appropriate triples. Then, it reinitializes the semaphore data structure and wakes up all processes sleeping until the occurence of some semaphore event: When the processes resume execution, they find that the semaphore ID is no longer valid and return an error to the caller.

11.2.4 General Comments

There are several similarities between the file system and the IPC mechanisms. The "get" system calls are similar to the *creat* and *open* system calls, and the "control" system calls contain an option to remove descriptors from the system, similar to the *unlink* system call. But no operations are analogous to the file system *close* system call. Thus, the kernel has no record of which processes can access an IPC mechanism, and, indeed, processes can access an IPC mechanism if they guess the correct ID and if access permissions are suitable, even though they never did a "get" call. The kernel cannot clean up unused IPC structures automatically, because it never knows when they are no longer needed. Errant processes can thus leave unneeded and unused structures cluttering the system. Although the kernel can save state information and data in the IPC structures after the death of a process, it is better to use files for such purposes.

The IPC mechanisms introduce a new name space, keys, instead of the traditional, all-pervasive files. It is difficult to extend the semantics of keys across a network, because they may describe different objects on different machines: In short, they were designed for a single-machine environment. File names are more amenable to a distributed environment as will be seen in Chapter 13. Use of keys instead of file names also means that the IPC facilities are an entity unto themselves, useful for special-purpose applications, but lacking the tool-building capabilities inherent in pipes and files, for example. Much of their functionality can be duplicated using other system facilities, so, esthetically, they should not be in the kernel. However, they provide better performance for closely cooperating application packages than standard file system facilities (see the exercises).

11.3 NETWORK COMMUNICATIONS

Programs such as mail, remote file transfer, and remote login that wish to communicate with other machines have historically used ad hoc methods to establish connections and to exchange data. For example, standard mail programs save the text of a user's mail messages in a particular file, such as "/usr/mail/mjb" for user "mjb". When a person sends mail to another user on the same machine, the *mail* program appends the mail to the addressee's file, using lock files and temporary files to preserve consistency. When a person reads mail, the *mail* program *opens* the person's mail file and *reads* the messages. To send mail to a user on another machine, the *mail* program must ultimately find the appropriate mail file on the other machine. Since it cannot manipulate files there directly, a process on the other machine must act as an agent for the local mail process; hence the local process needs a way to communicate with its remote agent across machine boundaries. The local process is called the *client* of the remote *server* process.

Because the UNIX system creates new processes via the *fork* system call, the server process must exist before the client process attempts to establish a connection. It would be inconsistent with the design of the system if the remote kernel were to create a new process when a connection request comes across the network. Instead, some process, usually *init*, creates a *server* process that *reads* a communications channel until it receives a request for service and then follows some protocol to complete the setup of the connection. Client and server programs typically choose the network media and protocols according to information in application data bases, or the data may be hard-coded into the programs.

For example, the *uucp* program allows file transfer across a network and remote execution of commands (see [Nowitz 80]). A client process queries a data base for address and routing information (such as a telephone number), *opens* an auto-dialer device, *writes* or *ioctls* the information on the open file descriptor, and calls up the remote machine. The remote machine may have special lines dedicated for use by *uucp*; its *init* process spawns *getty* processes — the servers — to monitor the lines and wait for connection notification. After the hardware connection is established, the client process logs in, following the usual login protocol: *getty execs* a special command interpreter, *uucico*, specified in the "/etc/passwd" file, and the client process *writes* command sequences to the remote machine, causing the remote machine to execute processes on behalf of the local machine.

Network communications have posed a problem for UNIX systems, because messages must frequently include data and control portions. The control portion may contain addressing information to specify the destination of a message. Addressing information is structured according to the type of network and protocol being used. Hence, processes need to know what type of network they are talking to, going against the principle that users do not have to be aware of a file type, because all devices look like files. Traditional methods for implementing network communications consequently rely heavily on the *ioctl* system call to specify control information, but usage is not uniform across network types. This has the unfortunate side effect that programs designed for one network may not be able to work for other networks.

There has been considerable effort to improve network interfaces for UNIX systems. The streams implementation in the latest releases of System V provides an elegant mechanism for network support, because protocol modules can be combined flexibly by pushing them onto open streams and their use is consistent at user level. The next section briefly describes sockets, the BSD solution to the problem.

11.4 SOCKETS

The previous section showed how processes on different machines can communicate, but the methods by which they establish communications are likely to differ, depending on protocols and media. Furthermore, the methods may not allow processes to communicate with other processes on the same machine, because they assume the existence of a server process that sleeps in a driver *open* or *read* system call. To provide common methods for interprocess communication and to allow use of sophisticated network protocols, the BSD system provides a mechanism known as *sockets* (see [Berkeley 83]). This section briefly describes some user-level aspects of sockets.

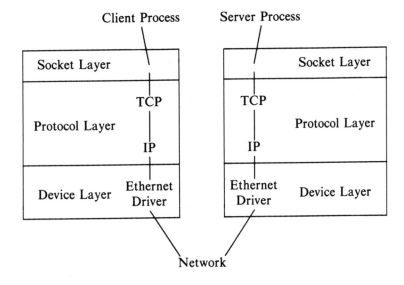

Figure 11.18. Sockets Model

The kernel structure consists of three parts: the socket layer, the protocol layer, and the device layer (Figure 11.18). The socket layer provides the interface between the system calls and the lower layers, the protocol layer contains the protocol modules used for communication (TCP and IP in the figure), and the device layer contains the device drivers that control the network devices. Legal combinations of protocols and drivers are specified when configuring the system, a method that is not as flexible as pushing streams modules. Processes communicate using the client-server model: a server process listens to a *socket*, one end point of a two-way communications path, and client processes communicate to the server process over another socket, the other end point of the communications path, which may be on another machine. The kernel maintains internal connections and routes data from client to server.

Sockets that share common communications properties, such as naming conventions and protocol address formats, are grouped into *domains*. The 4.2 BSD system supports the "UNIX system domain" for processes communicating on one machine and the "Internet domain" for processes communicating across a network using the DARPA (Defense Advanced Research Project Agency) communications protocols (see [Postel 80] and [Postel 81]). Each socket has a type — a *virtual circuit* (*stream* socket in the Berkeley terminology) or *datagram*. A virtual circuit allows sequenced, reliable delivery of data. Datagrams do not guarantee sequenced, reliable, or unduplicated delivery, but they are less expensive than virtual circuits, because they do not require expensive setup operations; hence, they are useful for some types of communication. The system contains a default protocol for every legal domain-socket type combination. For example, the Transport Connect Protocol (TCP) provides virtual circuit service and the User Datagram Protocol (UDP) provides datagram service in the Internet domain.

The socket mechanism contains several system calls. The *socket* system call establishes the end point of a communications link.

    sd = socket(format, type, protocol);

Format specifies the communications domain (the UNIX system domain or the Internet domain), *type* indicates the type of communication over the socket (virtual circuit or datagram), and *protocol* indicates a particular protocol to control the communication. Processes use the socket descriptor *sd* in other system calls. The *close* system call closes sockets.

The *bind* system call associates a name with the socket descriptor:

    bind(sd, address, length);

Sd is the socket descriptor, and *address* points to a structure that specifies an identifier specific to the communications domain and protocol specified in the *socket* system call. *Length* is the length of the *address* structure; without this parameter, the kernel would not know how long the address is because it can vary across domains and protocols. For example, an address in the UNIX system domain is a file name. Server processes *bind* addresses to sockets and "advertise" their names to identify themselves to client processes.

The *connect* system call requests that the kernel make a connection to an existing socket:

    connect(sd, address, length);

The semantics of the parameters are the same as for *bind*, but *address* is the address of the target socket that will form the other end of the communications line. Both sockets must use the same communications domain and protocol, and the kernel arranges that the communications links are set up correctly. If the *type* of the socket is a datagram, the *connect* call informs the kernel of the address to be used on subsequent *send* calls over the socket; no connections are made at the time of the call.

When a server process arranges to accept connections over a virtual circuit, the kernel must queue incoming requests until it can service them. The *listen* system call specifies the maximum queue length:

    listen(sd, qlength)

where *sd* is the socket descriptor and *qlength* is the maximum number of outstanding requests.

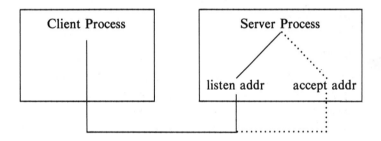

Figure 11.19. A Server Accepting a Call

The *accept* call receives incoming requests for a connection to a server process:

    nsd = accept(sd, address, addrlen);

where *sd* is the socket descriptor, *address* points to a user data array that the kernel fills with the return address of the connecting client, and *addrlen* indicates the size of the user array. When *accept* returns, the kernel overwrites the contents of *addrlen* with a number that indicates the amount of space taken up by the address. *Accept* returns a new socket descriptor *nsd*, different from the socket descriptor *sd*. A server can continue listening to the advertised socket while communicating with a client process over a separate communications channel (Figure 11.19).

The *send* and *recv* system calls transmit data over a connected socket:

count = send(sd, msg, length, flags);

where *sd* is the socket descriptor, *msg* is a pointer to the data being sent, *length* is its length, and *count* is the number of bytes actually sent. The *flags* parameter may be set to the value *SOF_OOB* to send data "out-of-band," meaning that data being sent is not considered part of the regular sequence of data exchange between the communicating processes. A "remote login" program, for instance, may send an "out of band" message to simulate a user hitting the delete key at a terminal. The syntax of the *recv* system calls is

count = recv(sd, buf, length, flags);

where *buf* is the data array for incoming data, *length* is the expected length, and *count* is the number of bytes copied to the user program. *Flags* can be set to "peek" at an incoming message and examine its contents without removing it from the queue, or to receive "out of band" data. The datagram versions of these system calls, *sendto* and *recvfrom*, have additional parameters for addresses. Processes can use *read* and *write* system calls on stream sockets instead of *send* and *recv* after the connection is set up. Thus, servers can take care of network-specific protocol negotiation and spawn processes that use *read* and *write* calls only, as if they are using regular files.

The *shutdown* system call closes a socket connection:

shutdown(sd, mode)

where *mode* indicates whether the sending side, the receiving side, or both sides no longer allow data transmission. It informs the underlying protocols to close down the network communications, but the socket descriptors are still intact. The *close* system call frees the socket descriptor.

The *getsockname* system call gets the name of a socket bound by a previous *bind* call:

getsockname(sd, name, length);

The *getsockopt* and *setsockopt* calls retrieve and set various options associated with the socket, according to the communications domain and protocol of the socket.

Consider the server program in Figure 11.20. The process creates a stream socket in the "UNIX system domain" and *bind*s the name *sockname* to it. Then it invokes the *listen* system call to specify the internal queue length for incoming messages and enters a loop, waiting for incoming requests. The *accept* call sleeps until the underlying protocol notices that a connection request is directed toward the socket with the bound name; then, *accept* returns a new descriptor for the incoming request. The server process *fork*s a process to communicate with the client process: parent and child processes *close* their respective descriptors so that they do not interfere with communications traffic of the other process. The child process carries on its conversation with the client process, terminating, in this

```
#include <sys/types.h>
#include <sys/socket.h>

main()
{
    int sd, ns;
    char buf[256];
    struct sockaddr sockaddr;
    int fromlen;

    sd = socket(AF_UNIX, SOCK_STREAM, 0);

    /* bind name — don't include null char in the name */
    bind(sd, "sockname", sizeof("sockname") — 1);
    listen(sd, 1);

    for (;;)
    {
        ns = accept(sd, &sockaddr, &fromlen);
        if (fork() == 0)
        {
            /* child */
            close(sd);
            read(ns, buf, sizeof(buf));
            printf("server read '%s'\n", buf);
            exit();
        }
        close(ns);
    }
}
```

Figure 11.20. A Server Process in the UNIX System Domain

example, after return from the *read* system call. The server process loops and waits for another connection request in the *accept* call.

Figure 11.21 shows the client process that corresponds to the server process. The client creates a socket in the same domain as the server and issues a *connect* request for the name *sockname*, bound to some socket by a server process. When the *connect* returns, the client process has a virtual circuit to a server process. In this example, it *writes* a single message and *exits*.

If the server process were to serve processes on a network, its system calls may specify that the socket is in the "Internet domain" by

socket(AF_INET, SOCK_STREAM, 0);

```
#include <sys/types.h>
#include <sys/socket.h>

main()
{
    int sd, ns;
    char buf[256];
    struct sockaddr sockaddr;
    int fromlen;

    sd = socket(AF_UNIX, SOCK_STREAM, 0);

    /* connect to name — null char is not part of name */
    if (connect(sd, "sockname", sizeof("sockname") — 1) == —1)
        exit();

    write(sd, "hi guy", 6);
}
```

Figure 11.21. A Client Process in the UNIX System Domain

and *bind* a network address obtained from a name server. The BSD system has library calls that do these functions. Similarly, the second parameter to the client's *connect* would contain the addressing information needed to identify the machine on the network (or routing addresses to send messages to the destination machine via intermediate machines) and additional information to identify the particular socket on the destination machine. If the server wanted to listen to network and local processes, it would use two sockets and the *select* call to determine which client is making a connection.

11.5 SUMMARY

This chapter has presented several forms of interprocess communication. It considered process tracing, where two processes cooperate to provide a useful facility for program debugging. However, process tracing via *ptrace* is expensive and primitive, because a limited amount of data can be transferred during each call, many context switches occur, communication is restricted to parent-child processes, and processes must agree to be traced before execution. UNIX System V provides an IPC package that includes messages, semaphores, and shared memory. Unfortunately, they are special purpose, do not mesh well with other operating system primitives, and are not extensible over a network. However, they are useful to many applications and afford better performance compared to other schemes.

UNIX systems support a wide variety of networks. Traditional methods for implementing protocol negotiation rely heavily on the *ioctl* system call but their usage is not uniform across network types. The BSD system has introduced the socket system calls to provide a more general framework for network communications. In the future, System V will use the streams mechanism described in Chapter 10 to handle network configurations uniformly.

11.6 EXERCISES

1. What happens if the *wait* call is omitted by *debug* (Figure 11.3)? (Hint: There are two possibilities.)
2. A debugger using *ptrace* reads one word of data from a traced process per call. What modifications should be made in the kernel to read many words with one call? What modifications would be necessary for *ptrace*?
3. Extend the *ptrace* call such that *pid* need not be the child process of the caller. Consider the security issues: Under what circumstances should a process be allowed to read the address space of another, arbitrary process? Under what circumstances should it be able to write the address space of another process?
4. Implement the set of message system calls as a user-level library, using regular files, named pipes, and locking primitives. When creating a message queue, create a control file that records status of the queue; the file should be protected with file locks or other convenient mechanisms. When sending a message of a given type, create a named pipe for all messages of that type if such a file does not already exist, and write the data (with a prepended byte count) to the named pipe. The control file should correlate the type number with the name of the named pipe. When reading messages, the control file directs the process to the correct named pipe. Compare this scheme to the implementation described in the chapter for performance, code complexity, functionality.
5. What is the program in Figure 11.22 trying to do?
* 6. Write a program that attaches shared memory too close to the end of its stack, and let the stack grow into the shared memory region. When does it incur a memory fault?
7. Rewrite the program in Figure 11.14 and use the *IPC_NOWAIT* flag, so that the semaphore operations are conditional. Demonstrate how this avoids deadlocks.
8. Show how Dijkstra's *P* and *V* semaphore operations could be implemented with named pipes. How would you implement a conditional *P* operation?
9. Write programs that lock resources, using (a) named pipes, (b) the *creat* and *unlink* system calls, and (c) the message system calls. Compare their performance.
10. Write programs to compare the performance of the message system calls to *read* and *write* on named pipes.
11. Write programs to compare the data-transfer speed using shared memory and messages. The programs for shared memory should include semaphores to synchronize completion of reads and writes.

```
#include        <sys/types.h>
#include        <sys/ipc.h>
#include        <sys/msg.h>
#define ALLTYPES 0

main()
{
    struct msgform
    {
        long mtype;
        char mtext[1024];
    } msg;
    register unsigned int id;

    for (id = 0;  ;  id++)
        while (msgrcv(id, &msg, 1024, ALLTYPES, IPC_NOWAIT) > 0)
            ;
}
```

Figure 11.22. An Eavesdropping Program

12

MULTIPROCESSOR SYSTEMS

The classic design of the UNIX system assumes the use of a uniprocessor architecture, consisting of one CPU, memory, and peripherals. A multiprocessor architecture contains two or more CPUs that share common memory and peripherals (Figure 12.1), potentially providing greater system throughput, because processes can run concurrently on different processors. Each CPU executes independently, but all of them execute one copy of the kernel. Processes behave exactly as they would on a uniprocessor system — the semantics of each system call remain the same — but they can migrate between processors transparently. Unfortunately, a process does not consume less CPU time. Some multiprocessor systems are called attached processor systems, because the peripherals may not be accessible to all processors. This chapter will not distinguish between attached processor systems and general multiprocessor systems, unless explicitly stated.

Allowing several processors to execute simultaneously in kernel mode on behalf of different processes causes integrity problems unless protection mechanisms are used. This chapter explains why the original design of the UNIX system cannot run unchanged on multiprocessor systems and considers two designs for running on a multiprocessor.

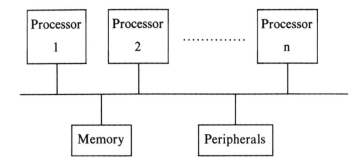

Figure 12.1. Multiprocessor Configuration

12.1 PROBLEM OF MULTIPROCESSOR SYSTEMS

Recall from Chapter 2 that the design of the UNIX system protects the integrity of kernel data structures by two policies: The kernel cannot preempt a process and switch context to another process while executing in kernel mode, and it masks out interrupts when executing a critical region of code if an interrupt handler could corrupt kernel data structures. On a multiprocessor, however, if two or more processes execute simultaneously in the kernel on separate processors, the kernel could become corrupt in spite of the protective measures that suffice for uniprocessor systems.

```
struct queue {

} *bp, *bp1;
bp1->forp = bp->forp;
bp1->backp = bp;
bp->forp = bp1;
/* consider possible context switch here */
bp1->forp->backp = bp1;
```

Figure 12.2. Placing a Buffer on a Doubly Linked List

For example, reconsider the fragment of code from Chapter 2 (Figure 12.2) that places a data structure (pointer *bp1*) after an existing structure (pointer *bp*). Suppose two processes execute the code simultaneously on different processors, such that processor A wants to place structure *bpA* after *bp* and processor B wants to place structure *bpB* after *bp*. No assumptions can be made about the relative processor execution speed: the worst case is possible, where processor B could execute the four C statements before processor A can execute another statement.

For example, handling an interrupt can delay execution of a code sequence on processor A. Corruption could occur as was illustrated in Chapter 2, even though interrupts were blocked.

The kernel must make sure that such corruption can never occur. If it were to leave a window open in which a corrupt situation could arise, no matter how rare, the kernel would be unsafe and its behavior unpredictable. There are three methods for preventing such corruption (see [Holley 79]):

1. Execute all critical activity on one processor, relying on standard uniprocessor methods for preventing corruption;
2. Serialize access to critical regions of code with locking primitives;
3. Redesign algorithms to avoid contention for data structures.

This chapter describes the first two methods to protect the kernel from corruption, and an exercise explores the third.

12.2 SOLUTION WITH MASTER AND SLAVE PROCESSORS

Goble implemented a system on a pair of modified VAX 11/780 machines where one processor, called the *master*, can execute in kernel mode and the other processor, called the *slave*, executes only in user mode (see [Goble 81]). Although Goble's implementation contained two machines, the technique extends to systems with one master and several slaves. The master processor is responsible for handling all system calls and interrupts. Slave processors execute processes in user mode and inform the master processor when a process makes a system call.

The scheduler algorithm decides which processor should execute a process (Figure 12.3). A new field in the process table designates the processor ID that a process must run on; for simplicity, assume it indicates either master or slave. When a process on a slave processor executes a system call, the slave kernel sets the processor ID field in the process table, indicating that the process should run only on the master processor, and does a context switch to schedule other processes (Figure 12.4). The master kernel schedules the process of highest priority that must run on the master processor and executes it. When it finishes the system call, it sets the processor ID field of the process to slave, allowing the process to run on slave processors again.

If processes must run on the master processor, it is preferable that the master processor run them right away and not keep them waiting. This is similar to the rationale for allowing process preemption on a uniprocessor system when returning from a system call, so that more urgent processing gets done sooner. If the master processor were executing a process in user mode when a slave processor requested service for a system call, the master process would continue executing until the next context switch according to this scheme. The master processor could respond more quickly if the slave processor set a global flag that the master processor checked in the clock interrupt handler; the master processor would do a context switch in at most one clock tick. Alternatively, the slave processor could interrupt the master

```
algorithm schedule_process (modified)
input:   none
output: none
{
        while (no process picked to execute)
        {
                if (running on master processor)
                        for (every process on run queue)
                                pick highest priority process
                                that is loaded in memory;
                else          /* running on a slave processor */
                        for (every process on run queue that need not run on master)
                                pick highest priority process that is loaded in memory;
                if (no process eligible to execute)
                        idle the machine;
                        /* interrupt takes machine out of idle state */
        }
        remove chosen process from run queue;
        switch context to that of chosen process, resume its execution;
}
```

Figure 12.3. Scheduler Algorithm

```
algorithm syscall        /* revised algorithm for invocation of system call */
input:   system call number
output: result of system call
{
        if (executing on slave processor)
        {
                set processor ID field in process table entry;
                do context switch;
        }
        do regular algorithm for system call here;
        reset processor ID field to "any" (slave);
        if (other processes must run on master processor)
                do context switch;
}
```

Figure 12.4. Algorithm for System Call Handler

processor and force it to do a context switch immediately, but this assumes special hardware capability.

The clock interrupt handler on a slave processor makes sure that processes are periodically rescheduled so that no one process monopolizes the processor. Aside from that, the clock handler "wakes up" a slave processor from an idle state once a second. The slave processor schedules the highest priority process that need not run on the master processor.

The only chance for corruption of kernel data structures comes in the scheduler algorithm, because it does not protect against having a process selected for execution on two processors. For instance, if a configuration consists of a master processor and two slaves, it is possible that the two slave processors find one process in user mode ready for execution. If both processors were to schedule the process simultaneously, they would read, write and corrupt its address space.

The system can avoid this problem in two ways. First, the master can specify the slave processor on which the process should execute, permitting more than one process to be assigned to a processor. Issues of load balancing then arise: One processor may have lots of processes assigned to it, whereas others are idle. The master kernel would have to distribute the process load between the processors. Second, the kernel can allow only one processor to execute the scheduling loop at a time, using mechanisms such as *semaphores*, described in the next section.

12.3 SOLUTION WITH SEMAPHORES

Another method for supporting UNIX systems on multiprocessor configurations is to partition the kernel into critical regions such that at most one processor can execute code in a critical region at a time. Such multiprocessor systems were designed for use on the AT&T 3B20A computer and IBM 370, using semaphores to partition the kernel into critical regions (see [Bach 84]). The description here will follow those implementations. There are two issues: How to implement semaphores and where to define critical regions.

As pointed out in Chapter 2, various algorithms in uniprocessor UNIX systems use a sleep-lock to keep other processes out of a critical region in case the first process later goes to sleep inside the critical region. The mechanism for setting the lock is

    while (lock is set)   /* test operation */
        sleep(condition until lock is free);
    set lock;

and the mechanism for unlocking the lock is

    free lock;
    wake up all processes sleeping on condition lock set;

Sleep-locks delineate some critical regions, but they do not work on multiprocessor systems, as illustrated in Figure 12.5. Suppose a lock is free and two processes on

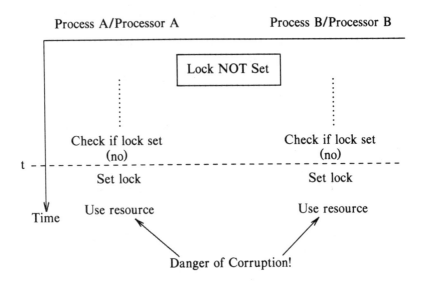

Figure 12.5. Race Conditions in Sleep-Locks on Multiprocessors

two processors simultaneously attempt to test and set it. They find that the lock is free at time t, set it, enter the critical region, and may corrupt kernel data structures. There is leeway in the requirement for simultaneity: the sleep-lock fails if neither process executes the lock operation before the other process executes the test operation. For example, if processor A handles an interrupt after finding that the lock is free and, while handling the interrupt, processor B checks the lock and sets it, processor A will return from the interrupt and set the lock. To prevent this situation, the locking primitive must be atomic: The actions of testing the status of the lock and setting the lock must be done as a single, indivisible operation, such that only one process can manipulate the lock at a time.

12.3.1 Definition of Semaphores

A semaphore is an integer valued object manipulated by the kernel that has the following atomic operations defined for it:

- Initialization of the semaphore to a nonnegative value;
- A P operation that decrements the value of the semaphore. If the value of the semaphore is less than 0 after decrementing its value, the process that did the P goes to sleep;
- A V operation that increments the value of the semaphore. If the value of the semaphore becomes greater than or equal to 0 as a result, *one* process that had been sleeping as the result of a P operation wakes up;

- A *conditional P* operation, abbreviated *CP*, that decrements the value of the semaphore and returns an indication of true, if its value is greater than 0. If the value of the semaphore is less than or equal to 0, the value of the semaphore is unchanged and the return value is false.

The semaphores defined here are, of course, independent from the user-level semaphores described in Chapter 11.

12.3.2 Implementation of Semaphores

Dijkstra [Dijkstra 65] shows that it is possible to implement semaphores without special machine instructions. Figure 12.6 presents C functions to implement semaphores. The function *Pprim* locks the semaphore by checking the values of the array *val*; each processor in the system controls one entry in the array. When a processor locks a semaphore, it checks to see if other processors already locked the semaphore (their entry in *val* would be 2), or if processors with a lower ID are currently trying to lock it (their entry in *val* would be 1). If either condition is true, the processor resets its entry in *val* to 1 and tries again. *Pprim* starts the outer loop with the loop variable equal to the processor ID one greater than the one that most recently used the resource, insuring that no one processor can monopolize the resource (refer to [Dijkstra 65] or [Coffman 73] for a proof). The function *Vprim* frees the semaphore and allows other processors to gain exclusive access to the resource by clearing the entry of the executing processor in *val* and resetting *lastid*. The following code sequence would protect a resource.

Pprim(semaphore);
use resource here;
Vprim(semaphore);

Most machines have a set of indivisible instructions that do the equivalent locking operation more cheaply, because the loops in *Pprim* are slow and would drain performance. For instance, the IBM 370 series supports an atomic *compare and swap* instruction, and the AT&T 3B20 computer supports an atomic *read and clear* instruction. When executing the *read and clear* instruction, for example, the machine reads the value of a memory location, clears its value (sets it to 0), and sets the condition code according to whether or not the original value was zero. If another processor uses the *read and clear* instruction simultaneously on the same memory location, one processor is guaranteed to read the original value and the other process reads the value 0: The hardware insures atomicity. Thus, the function *Pprim* can be implemented more simply with the *read and clear* instruction (Figure 12.7). A process loops using the *read and clear* instruction, until it reads a nonzero value. The semaphore lock component must be initialized to 1.

This semaphore primitive cannot be used in the kernel as is, because a process executing it keeps on looping until it succeeds: If the semaphore is being used to

```
struct semaphore
{
     int val[NUMPROCS];        /* lock———1 entry for each processor */
     int lastid;               /* ID of last processor to get semaphore */
};
int procid;                    /* processor ID, unique per processor */
int lastid;                    /* ID of last proc to get the semaphore */

INIT(semaphore)
     struct semaphore semaphore;
{
     int i;
     for (i = 0;  i < NUMPROCS;  i++)
          semaphore.val[i] = 0;
}
Pprim(semaphore)
     struct semaphore semaphore;
{
     int i, first;

 loop:
     first = lastid;
     semaphore.val[procid] = 1;
     /* continued next page */
```

Figure 12.6. Implementation of Semaphore Locking in C

lock a data structure, a process should sleep if it finds the semaphore locked, so that the kernel can switch context to another process and do useful work. Given *Pprim* and *Vprim*, it is possible to construct a more sophisticated set of kernel semaphore operations, *P* and *V*, that conform to the definitions in Section 12.3.1.

First, let us define a semaphore to be a structure that consists of a lock field to control access to the semaphore, the value of the semaphore, and a queue of processes sleeping on the semaphore. The lock field controls access to the semaphore, allowing only one process to manipulate the other fields of the structure during *P* and *V* operations. It is reset when the *P* or *V* operation completes. The value field determines whether a process should have access to the critical region protected by the semaphore. At the beginning of the *P* algorithm (Figure 12.8), the kernel does a *Pprim* operation to ensure exclusive access to the semaphore and then decrements the semaphore value. If the semaphore value is nonnegative, the executing process has access to the critical region: It resets the semaphore lock with the *Vprim* operation so that other processes can access the semaphore and returns an indication of success. If, as a result of decrementing its value, the semaphore value is negative, the kernel puts the process to sleep, following

```
forloop:
    for (i = first;  i < NUMPROCS;  i++)
    {
        if (i == procid)
        {
            semaphore.val[i] = 2;
            for (i = 1;  i < NUMPROCS;  i++)
                if (i != procid && semaphore.val[i] == 2)
                    goto loop;
            lastid = procid;
            return;              /* success! now use resource */
        }
        else if (semaphore.val[i])
            goto loop;
    }
    first = 1;
    goto forloop;
}
Vprim(semaphore)
    struct semaphore semaphore;
{
    lastid = (procid+1) % NUMPROCS;      /* reset to next processor */
    semaphore.val[procid] = 0;
}
```

Figure 12.6. Implementation of Semaphore Locking (continued)

semantics similar to those of the regular sleep algorithm (Chapter 6): It checks for signals according to the priority value, enqueues the executing process on a first-in-first-out list of sleeping processes, and does a context switch. The *V* function (Figure 12.9) gains exclusive access to the semaphore via the *Pprim* primitive and increments the semaphore value. If any processes were on the semaphore sleep queue, the kernel removes the first one and changes its state to "ready to run."

The *P* and *V* functions are similar to the sleep and wakeup functions: The major difference in implementation is that a semaphore is a data structure, whereas the address used for sleep and wakeup is just a convenient number. A process will always sleep when doing a *P* operation on a semaphore if the initial value of the semaphore is 0, so *P* can replace the sleep function. However, the *V* operation wakes up only one process, whereas the uniprocessor wakeup function wakes up all processes asleep on an event address.

Semantically, use of the wakeup function indicates that a given system condition is no longer true, hence all processes that were asleep on the condition must wake up. For example, when a buffer is no longer in use, it is incorrect for processes to sleep on the event the buffer is busy, so the kernel awakens all processes that were

```
struct semaphore {
      int lock;
};

Init(semaphore)
      struct semaphore semaphore;
{
      semaphore.lock = 1;
}

Pprim(semaphore)
      struct semaphore semaphore;
{
      while (read_and_clear(semaphore.lock))
            ;
}

Vprim(semaphore)
      struct semaphore semaphore;
{
      semaphore.lock = 1;
}
```

Figure 12.7. Semaphore Operations Using Read and Clear Instruction

asleep on the event. As a second example, if multiple processes *write* data to a terminal, the terminal driver may put them to sleep because it cannot handle the high volume of data. Later, when the driver decides it can accept more data for output, it wakes up all processes that were asleep, waiting to output data. Use of the *P* and *V* operations is more applicable for locking operations where processes gain access to a resource one by one and other processes are granted access in the order they requested the resource. This is usually more efficient than the uniprocessor sleep-lock, because if all processes wake up on occurrence of an event, most may find the lock still set and return to sleep immediately. On the other hand, it is more difficult to use *P* and *V* for cases where all processes should be awakened at once.

Given a primitive that returns the value of a semaphore, would the following operation be the equivalent of the wakeup function?

    while (value(semaphore) < 0)
          V(semaphore);

Assuming no interference from other processors, the kernel executes the loop until the value of the semaphore is greater than or equal to 0, meaning that no processes are asleep on the semaphore. However, it is possible for process A on processor A

```
algorithm P                /* P semaphore operation */
input:   (1) semaphore
         (2) priority
output: 0 for normal return
         −1 for abnormal wakeup due to signals catching in kernel
         long jumps for signals not catching in kernel
{
        Pprim(semaphore.lock);
        decrement (semaphore.value);
        if (semaphore.value >= 0)
        {
                Vprim(semaphore.lock);
                return(0);
        }
        /* must go to sleep */
        if (checking signals)
        {
                if (there is a signal that interrupts sleep)
                {
                        increment (semaphore.value);
                        if (catching signal in kernel)
                        {
                                Vprim(semaphore.lock);
                                return(−1);
                        }
                        else
                        {
                                Vprim(semaphore.lock);
                                longjmp;
                        }
                }
        }
        enqueue process at end of sleep list of semaphore;
        Vprim(semaphore.lock);
        do context switch;
        check signals, as above;
        return(0);
}
```

Figure 12.8. Algorithm for Implementation of P

to test the semaphore and find its value equal to 0 and for process B on processor B to do a *P*, decrementing the value of the semaphore to −1 (Figure 12.10) just after the test on A. Process A would continue executing, assuming that it had awakened every sleeping process on the semaphore. Hence, the loop does not insure that every sleeping process wakes up, because it is not atomic.

```
algorithm V              /* V semaphore operation */
input:   address of semaphore
output: none
{
     Pprim(semaphore.lock);
     increment (semaphore.value);
     if (semaphore.value <= 0)
     {
          remove first process from semaphore sleep list;
          make it ready to run (wake it up);
     }
     Vprim(semaphore.lock);
}
```

Figure 12.9. Algorithm for Implementation of V

Consider another phenomenon in the use of semaphores on a uniprocessor system. Suppose two processes, A and B, contend for a semaphore: Process A finds the semaphore free and process B sleeps; the value of the semaphore is −1. When process A releases the semaphore with a V, it wakes up process B and increments the semaphore value to 0. Now suppose process A, still executing in kernel mode, tries to lock the semaphore again: It will sleep in the P function, because the value of the semaphore is 0, even though the resource is still free! The system will incur the expense of an extra context switch. On the other hand, if the lock were implemented by a sleep-lock, process A would gain immediate reuse of the resource, because no other process could lock it in the meantime. In this case, the sleep-lock would be more efficient than a semaphore.

When locking several semaphores, the locking order must be consistent to avoid deadlock. For instance, consider two semaphores, A and B, and consider two kernel algorithms that must have both semaphores simultaneously locked. If the two algorithms were to lock the semaphores in reverse order, a deadlock could arise, as shown in Figure 12.11; process A on processor A locks semaphore SA while process B on processor B locks semaphore SB. Process A attempts to lock semaphore SB, but the P operation causes process A to go to sleep, since the value of SB is at most 0. Similarly, process B attempts to lock semaphore SA, but its P puts process B to sleep. Neither process can proceed.

Deadlocks can be avoided by implementing deadlock detection algorithms that determine if a deadlock exists and, if so, break the deadlock condition. However, implementation of deadlock detection algorithms would complicate the kernel code. Since there are only a finite number of places in the kernel where a process must simultaneously lock several semaphores, it is easier to implement the kernel algorithms to avoid deadlock conditions before they occur. For instance, if particular sets of semaphores were always locked in the same order, the deadlock condition could never arise. But if it is impossible to avoid locking semaphores in

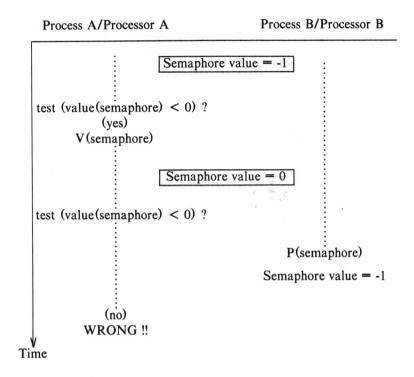

Figure 12.10.   Failed Simulation of Wakeup with V

reversed order, the *CP* operation prevents the deadlock, as shown in Figure 12.12: If the *CP* fails, process B releases its resources to avoid the deadlock and reenters the algorithm at a later time, presumably when process A completes use of the resource.

An interrupt handler may have to lock a semaphore to prevent processes from using a resource simultaneously, but it cannot go to sleep, as explained in Chapter 6, and therefore cannot use a *P* operation. Instead, it can execute a *spin lock* to avoid going to sleep as in the following:

    while (! CP(semaphore)) ;

The operation loops as long as the semaphore value is less than or equal to 0; the handler does not sleep, and the loop terminates only when the semaphore value becomes positive, at which time *CP* decrements the semaphore value.

To avoid a deadlock, the kernel must block out interrupts that execute a spin lock. Otherwise, a process could lock a semaphore and be interrupted before it unlocks the semaphore; if the interrupt handler attempts to lock the same semaphore using a spin lock, the kernel deadlocks itself. In Figure 12.13, for

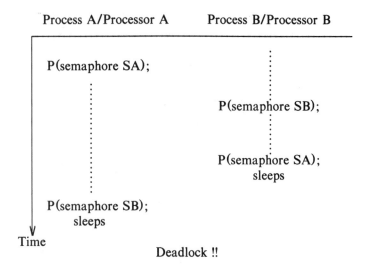

Figure 12.11. Deadlock because of Reversed Order of Locking

example, the value of the semaphore is at most 0 when the interrupt occurs, so the *CP* in the interrupt handler will always be false. The situation is avoided by blocking out interrupts while the process has the semaphore locked.

12.3.3 Some Algorithms

This section reviews four kernel algorithms as implemented with semaphores. The buffer allocation algorithm illustrates a complicated locking scenario, the *wait* algorithm illustrates process synchronization, a driver-locking scheme illustrates an elegant approach for locking device drivers, and finally, the method for processor idling shows how an algorithm was changed to avoid contention.

12.3.3.1 Buffer Allocation

Recall the algorithm *getblk* for buffer allocation in Chapter 3. The three major data structures for buffer allocation are the buffer header, the hash queue of buffers, and the free list of buffers. The kernel associates a semaphore with each instance of every data structure. In other words, if the kernel contains 200 buffers, each buffer header contains a semaphore for locking the buffer; when a process does a *P* on the buffer header semaphore, other processes that do a *P* sleep until the first process does a *V*. Each hash queue of buffers also has a semaphore that locks access to the hash queue. The uniprocessor system did not require a lock for the

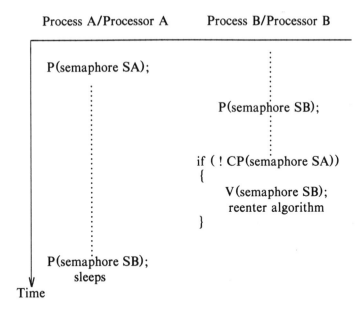

Figure 12.12. Use of Conditional P to Avoid Deadlock

hash queue, because a process would never go to sleep and leave the hash queue in an inconsistent state. In a multiprocessor system, however, two processes could manipulate the linked list of the hash queue; the semaphore for the hash queue permits only one process at a time to manipulate the linked list. Similarly, the free list requires a semaphore because several processes could otherwise corrupt it.

Figure 12.14 depicts the first part of the *getblk* algorithm as implemented with semaphores on a multiprocessor system (recall Figure 3.4). To search the buffer cache for a given block, the kernel locks the hash queue semaphore with a *P* operation. If another process had already done a *P* operation on the semaphore, the executing process sleeps until the original process does a *V*. When it gains exclusive control of the hash queue, it searches for the appropriate buffer. Assume that the buffer is on the hash queue. The kernel (process A) attempts to lock the buffer, but if it were to use a *P* operation and if the buffer was already locked, it would sleep with the hash queue locked, preventing other processes from accessing the hash queue, even though they were searching for other buffers. Instead, process A attempts to lock the buffer using the *CP* operation; if the *CP* succeeds, it can use the buffer. Process A locks the free list semaphore using *CP* in a spin loop, because the expected time the lock is held is short, and hence, it does not pay to sleep with a *P* operation. The kernel then removes the buffer from the free list, unlocks the free list, unlocks the hash queue, and returns the locked buffer.

P(semaphore);
(Semaphore value now 0)

Interrupt

CP(semaphore) fails---
semaphore locked.

Semaphore not unlocked until return from interrupt.

Cannot return from interrupt, without servicing it.

Deadlocked

Time

Figure 12.13. Deadlock in Interrupt Handler

Suppose the *CP* operation on the buffer fails because another process had locked the buffer semaphore. Process A releases the hash queue semaphore and then sleeps on the buffer semaphore with a *P* operation. The *P* operates on the semaphore that just caused the *CP* to fail! It does not matter whether process A sleeps on the semaphore: After completion of the *P* operation, process A controls the buffer. Because the rest of the algorithm assumes that the buffer and the hash queue are locked, process A now attempts to lock the hash queue.[1] Because the locking order here (buffer semaphore, then hash queue semaphore) is the opposite of the locking order explained above (hash queue semaphore, then buffer semaphore), the *CP* semaphore operation is used. The obvious processing happens if the lock fails. But if the lock succeeds, the kernel cannot be sure that it has the correct buffer, because another process may have found the buffer on the free list and changed the contents to those of another block before relinquishing control of the buffer semaphore. Process A, waiting for the semaphore to become free, had no idea that the buffer it was waiting for was no longer the one in which it was interested and must therefore check that the buffer is still valid; if not, it restarts the algorithm. If the buffer contains valid data, process A completes the algorithm.

---

1. The algorithm could avoid locking the hash queue here by setting a flag and testing it before the *V* later on, but this method illustrates the technique for locking semaphores in reversed order.

```
algorithm getblk        /* multiprocessor version */
input:   file system number
         block number
output: locked buffer that can now be used for block
{
      while (buffer not found)
      {
            P(hash queue semaphore);
            if (block in hash queue)
            {
                  if (CP(buffer semaphore) fails)          /* buffer busy */
                  {
                        V(hash queue semaphore);
                        P(buffer semaphore);          /* sleep until free */
                        if (CP(hash queue semaphore) fails)
                        {
                              V(buffer semaphore);
                              continue;          /* to while loop */
                        }
                        else if (dev or block num changed)
                        {
                              V(buffer semaphore);
                              V(hash queue semaphore);
                        }
                  }
                  while (CP(free list semaphore) fails)
                        ;          /* spin loop */
                  mark buffer busy;
                  remove buffer from free list;
                  V(free list semaphore);
                  V(hash queue semaphore);
                  return buffer;
            }
            else        /* buffer not in hash queue */
            /* remainder of algorithm continues here */
      }
}
```

Figure 12.14. Buffer Allocation with Semaphores

```
multiprocessor algorithm wait
{
        for (;;)        /* loop */
        {
                search all child processes:
                if (status of child is zombie)
                        return;
                P(zombie_semaphore);        /* initialized to 0 */
        }
}
```

Figure 12.15. Multiprocessor Algorithm for Wait/Exit

The remainder of the algorithm is left as an exercise.

12.3.3.2 Wait

Recall from Chapter 7 that a process sleeps in the *wait* system call until a child *exits*. The problem on a multiprocessor system is to make sure that a parent does not miss a zombie child as it executes the *wait* algorithm; for example, if a child *exits* on one processor as the parent executes *wait* on another processor, the parent must not sleep waiting for a second child to *exit*. Each process table entry contains a semaphore *zombie_semaphore*, initialized to 0, where a process sleeps in *wait* until a child *exits* (Figure 12.15). When a process *exits*, it does a V on the parent semaphore, awakening the parent if it was sleeping in *wait*. If the child process *exits* before the parent executes *wait*, the parent finds the child in the zombie state and returns. If the two processes execute *exit* and *wait* simultaneously but the child *exits* after the parent already checked its status, the child V will prevent the parent from sleeping. At worst, the parent will make an extra iteration through the loop.

12.3.3.3 Drivers

The multiprocessor implementation for the AT&T 3B20A computer avoided inserting semaphores into driver code by doing P and V operations at the driver entry points (see [Bach 84]). Recall from Chapter 10 that the interface to device drivers is well defined with only a few entry points (about 20, in practice). Drivers are protected by bracketing the entry points, as in:

```
P(driver_semaphore);
open(driver);
V(driver_semaphore);
```

By using the same semaphore for all entry points to a driver and using different semaphores for each driver, at most one process can execute critical code in the driver at a time. The semaphores can be configured per device unit or for classes of devices. For example, a semaphore may be associated with each physical terminal, or one semaphore may be associated with all terminals. The former case is potentially faster, because processes accessing one terminal do not lock the semaphore for other terminals, as in the latter case. However, some device drivers interact internally with other device drivers; in such cases, specifying one semaphore for a class of devices is easier to understand. Alternatively, the 3B20A implementation allows particular devices to be configured such that the driver code runs on specified processors.

Problems could occur when a device interrupts the system when its semaphore is locked: the interrupt handler cannot be invoked, because otherwise there would be danger of corruption. On the other hand, the kernel must make sure that it does not lose an interrupt. The 3B20A queues interrupts until the semaphore is unlocked and it is safe to execute the interrupt handler, and it calls the interrupt handler from the code that unlocks drivers, if necessary.

12.3.3.4 Dummy Processes

When the kernel does a context switch on a uniprocessor, it executes in the context of the process relinquishing control, as explained in Chapter 6. If no processes are ready to run, the kernel idles in the context of the process that last ran. When interrupted by the clock or by other peripherals, it handles the interrupt in the context of the process it had been idling in.

In a multiprocessor system, the kernel cannot idle in the context of the process executed most recently on the processor. For if a process goes to sleep on processor A, consider what happens when the process wakes up: It is ready to run, but it does not execute immediately even though its context is already available on processor A. If processor B now chooses the process for execution, it would do a context switch and resume execution. When processor A emerges from its idle loop as the result of another interrupt, it executes in the context of process A again until it switches context. Thus, for a short period of time, the two processors could be writing the identical address space, particularly, the kernel stack.

The solution to this problem is to create a dummy process per processor; when a processor has no work to do, the kernel does a context switch to the dummy process and the processor idles in the context of its dummy process. The dummy process consists of a kernel stack only; it cannot be scheduled. Since only one processor can idle in its dummy process, processors cannot corrupt each other.

12.4 THE TUNIS SYSTEM

The Tunis system has a user interface that is compatible to that of the UNIX system, but its *nucleus*, written in the language Concurrent Euclid, consists of kernel processes that control each part of the system. The Tunis system solves the mutual exclusion problem because only one instance of a kernel process can run at a time, and because kernel processes do not manipulate the data structures of other processes. Kernel processes are activated by queuing messages for input, and Concurrent Euclid implements *monitors* to prevent corruption of the queues. A monitor is a procedure that enforces mutual exclusion by allowing only one process at a time to execute the body of the procedure. They differ from semaphores because they force modularity (the P and V are at the entry and exit points of the monitor routine) and because the compiler generates the synchronization primitives. Holt notes that such systems are easier to construct using a language that supports the notion of concurrency and monitors (see page 190 of [Holt 83]). However, the internal structure of the Tunis system differs radically from traditional implementations of the UNIX system.

12.5 PERFORMANCE LIMITATIONS

This chapter has presented two methods that have been used to implement multiprocessor UNIX systems: the master-slave configuration, where only one processor can execute in kernel mode, and a semaphore method that allows all processors to execute in kernel mode simultaneously. The implementations of multiprocessor UNIX systems described in this chapter generalize to any number of processors, but system throughput will not increase at a linear rate with the number of processors. First, there is degradation because of increased memory contention in the hardware, meaning that memory accesses takes longer. Second, in the semaphore scheme, there is increased contention for semaphores; processes find semaphores locked more frequently, more processes queue waiting for semaphores to become free, and therefore processes have to wait a longer period of time to gain access to the semaphore. Similarly, in the master-slave scheme, the master processor becomes a system bottleneck as the number of processors in the system grows, because it is the only processor that can execute kernel code. Although careful hardware design can reduce contention and provide nearly linear increase in system throughput with additional processors for some loads (see [Beck 85], for example), all multiprocessor systems built with current technology reach a limit beyond which the addition of more processors does not increase system throughput.

12.6 EXERCISES

1. Implement a solution to the multiprocessor problem such that any processor in a multiprocessor configuration can execute the kernel but only one processor can do so at

a time. This differs from the first solution discussed in the text, where one processor is designated the master to handle all kernel services. How could such a system make sure that only one processor is in the kernel? What is a reasonable strategy for handling interrupts and still make sure that only one processor is in the kernel?

2. Use the shared memory system calls to test the C code for implementation of semaphores, shown in Figure 12.6. Several independent processes should execute P-V sequences on a semaphore. How would you demonstrate a bug in the code?

3. Design an algorithm for CP (conditional P) along the lines of the algorithm for P.

4. Explain why the algorithms for P and V in Figure 12.8 and 12.9 must block interrupts. At what points should they be blocked?

5. If a semaphore is used in a spin-lock, as in

   while (! CP(semaphore));

   why can the kernel *never* use an unconditional P operation on it? (Hint: If a process sleeps on the P operation, what happens in the spin-lock?)

6. Refer to the algorithm *getblk* in Chapter 3 and describe a multiprocessor implementation for the case that the block is not in the buffer cache.

* 7. In the buffer allocation algorithm, suppose there is too much contention for the buffer free list semaphore. Implement a scheme to cut down the contention by partitioning the free list into two free lists.

* 8. Suppose a terminal driver has a semaphore, initialized to 0, where processes sleep if they flood the terminal with output. When the terminal can accept more data, it wakes up every process sleeping on the semaphore. Design a scheme to wake up all processes using P and V. Define other flags and driver locking semaphores, as necessary. If the wakeup results from an interrupt and a processor cannot block interrupts on other processors, how safe can the scheme be?

* 9. When protecting driver entry points with semaphores, provision must be made to release the semaphore when a process sleeps in the driver. Describe an implementation. Similarly, how should the driver handle interrupts that occur when the driver semaphore is locked?

10. Recall the system calls in Chapter 8 for setting and accessing system time. A system cannot assume identical clock rates for different multiprocessors. How should the time system calls work?

13

DISTRIBUTED UNIX SYSTEMS

The previous chapter examined tightly coupled multiprocessor systems that share common memory and kernel data structures and schedule processes from a common pool. However, it is frequently desirable to pool computers to allow resource sharing such that each computer retains autonomy over its environment. For example, a user of a personal computer wants to access files that are stored on a larger machine but wants to retain control of the personal computer. Although several programs such as *uucp* allow file transfer and other applications across a network, their use is not transparent because the user is aware of the network. Furthermore, programs such as text editors do not work on remote files as they do for local files. Users would like to do the normal set of UNIX system calls and, except for a possible degradation in performance, not be aware that they cross a machine boundary. Specifically, system calls such as *open* and *read* should work for files on remote machines just as they do for files on local systems.

Figure 13.1 shows the architecture of a distributed system. Each computer, shown in a circle, is an autonomous unit, consisting of a CPU, memory and peripherals. A computer can fit the model even though it does not have local file storage: It must have peripherals to communicate with other machines, but all its regular files can be on another machine. Most critically, the physical memory available to each machine is independent of activity on other machines. This feature distinguishes distributed systems from the tightly coupled multiprocessor systems described in the last chapter. Consequently, the kernels on each machine

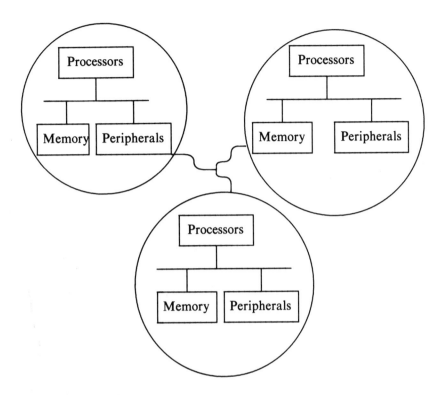

Figure 13.1. Model of Distributed Architectures

are independent, subject to the external constraints of running in a distributed environment.

Many implementations of distributed systems have been described in the literature, falling into the following categories.

- *Satellite* systems are tightly clustered groups of machines that center on one (usually larger) machine. The satellite processors share the process load with the central processor and refer all system calls to it. The purpose of a satellite svstem is to increase system throughput and, possibly, to allow dedicated use of a processor for one process in a UNIX system environment. The system runs as a unit; unlike other models of distributed systems, satellites do not have real autonomy except, sometimes, in process scheduling and in local memory allocation.

- "Newcastle" distributed systems allow access to remote systems by recognizing names of remote files in the C library. (The name comes from a paper entitled "The Newcastle Connection" — see [Brownbridge 82].) The remote files are designated by special characters embedded in the path name or by special path component sequences that precede the file system root. This method can be implemented without making changes to the kernel and is therefore easier to implement than the other implementations described in this chapter, but it is less flexible.

- Fully transparent distributed systems allow standard path names to refer to files on other machines; the kernel recognizes that they are remote. Path names cross machine boundaries at mount points, much as they cross file system mount points on disks.

This chapter examines the architecture of each model; the descriptions here are *not* based on particular implementations but on information published in various technical papers. They assume that low-level protocol modules and device drivers take care of addressing, routing, flow control, and error detection and correction and, thus, assume that each model is independent of the underlying network. The system call examples given in the next section for the satellite processor systems work in similar fashion for the Newcastle and transparent models presented in later sections; hence, they will be explained in detail once, and the sections on the other models will concentrate on particular features that most distinguish them.

13.1 SATELLITE PROCESSORS

Figure 13.2 shows the architecture for a satellite processor configuration. The purpose of such a configuration is to improve system throughput by offloading processes from the central processor and executing them on the satellite processors. Each satellite processor has no local peripherals except for those it needs to communicate with the central processor: The file system and all devices are on the central processor. Without loss of generality, assume that all user processes run on a satellite processor and that processes do not migrate between satellite processors; once a process is assigned to a processor, it stays there until it *exits*. The satellite processor contains a simplified operating system to handle local system calls, interrupts, memory management, network protocols, and a driver for the device it uses to communicate with the central processor.

When the system is initialized, the kernel on the central processor downloads a local operating system into each satellite processor, which continues to run there until the system is taken down. Each process on a satellite processor has an associated *stub* process on the central processor (see [Birrell 84]); when a process on a satellite processor makes a system call that requires services provided only by the central processor, the satellite process communicates with its stub on the central processor to satisfy the request. The stub executes the system call and sends the results back to the satellite processor. The satellite process and its stub enjoy a client-server relationship similar to those described in Chapter 11: The satellite is the client of the stub, which provides file system services. The term *stub* emphasizes that the remote server process serves only one client process. Section 13.4 considers server processes that serve several client processes. For convenience,

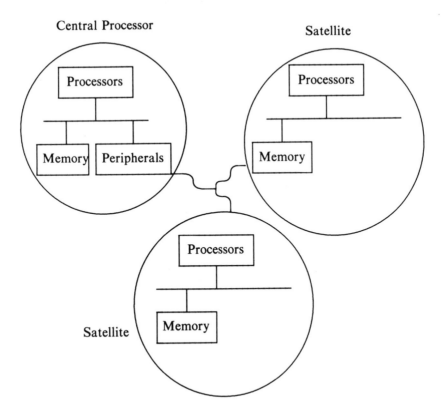

Figure 13.2. Satellite Processor Configuration

the term *satellite process* will refer to a process running on a satellite processor.

When a satellite process makes a system call that can be handled locally, the kernel does not have to send a request to the stub process. For example, it can execute the *sbrk* system call locally to obtain more memory for a process. But if it needs to obtain service from the central processor, such as when *open*ing a file, it encodes the parameters of the system call and the process environment into a message that it sends to the stub process (Figure 13.3). The message consists of a token that specifies the system call the stub should make on behalf of the client, parameters to the system call, and environmental data such as user ID and group ID, which may vary per system call. The remainder of the message contains variable length data, such as a file path name or data for a *write* system call.

The stub waits for requests from the satellite process; when it receives a request, it decodes the message, determines what system call it should invoke, executes the system call, and encodes the results of the system call into a response for the satellite process. The response contains the return values to be returned to the

Message Format

Token for Syscall	Syscall Parameters	Environment Data	Path Name or Data Stream
			....

Response

Syscall Return Values	Error Code	Signal Number	.... Data Stream ....

Figure 13.3. Message Formats

calling process as the result of the system call, an error code to report errors in the stub, a signal number, and a variable length data array to contain data read from a file, for example. The satellite process sleeps in the system call until it receives the response, decodes it, and returns the results to the user. This is the general scheme for handling system calls; the remainder of this section examines particular system calls in greater detail.

To explain how the satellite system works, consider the following system calls: *getppid*, *open*, *write*, *fork*, *exit* and *signal*. The *getppid* system call is simple, because it requires a simple request and response between the satellite and central processors. The kernel on the satellite processor forms a message with a token that indicates that the system call was *getppid*, and sends the request to the central processor. The stub on the central processor *read*s the message from the satellite processor, decodes the system call type, executes the *getppid* system call, and finds its parent process ID. It then forms a response and *write*s it to the satellite process, which had been waiting, *read*ing the communication link. When the satellite receives the answer from the stub, it returns the result to the process that had originally invoked the *getppid* system call. Alternatively, if the satellite process retains data such as the parent process ID locally, it need not communicate with its stub at all.

For the *open* system call, the satellite process sends an *open* message to the stub process, including the file name and other parameters. Assuming the stub does the *open* call successfully, it allocates an inode and file table entry on the central processor, assigns an entry in the user file descriptor table in its *u area*, and returns the file descriptor to the satellite process. Meanwhile, the satellite process had been *read*ing the communications link, waiting for the response from the stub process. The satellite process has no kernel data structures that record information about

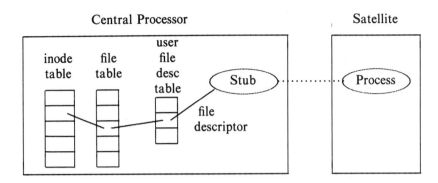

Figure 13.4. Open Call from a Satellite Process

the *open* file; the file descriptor returned by the *open* is the index into the user file descriptor table of the stub process. Figure 13.4 depicts the results of an *open* system call.

For the *write* system call, the satellite processor formulates a message, containing a *write* token, file descriptor and data count. Afterwards, it copies the data from the satellite process user space and *writes* it to the communications link. The stub process decodes the *write* message, *reads* the data from the communications link, and *writes* it to the appropriate file, following the file descriptor to the file table entry and inode, all on the central processor. When done, the stub *writes* an acknowledgment message to the satellite process, including the number of bytes successfully written. The *read* call is similar: The stub informs the satellite process if it does not return the requested number of bytes, such as when *read*ing a terminal or a pipe. Both *read* and *write* may require the transmission of multiple data messages across the network, depending on the amount of data and network packet sizes.

The only system call that needs internal modification on the central processor is the *fork* system call. When a process on the central processor executes the *fork* system call, the kernel selects a satellite to execute the process and sends a message to a special server process on the satellite, informing it that it is about to download a process. Assuming the server accepts the *fork* request, it does a *fork* to create a new satellite process, initializing a process table entry and a *u area*. The central processor downloads a copy of the *fork*ing process to the satellite processor, overwriting the address space of the process just created there, *fork*s a local stub process to communicate with the new satellite process, and sends a message to the satellite processor to initialize the program counter of the new process. The stub process (on the central processor) is the child of the *fork*ing process; the satellite process is technically a child of the server process, but it is logically a child of the process that *fork*ed. The server has no logical relationship with the child process after the *fork* completes; the only purpose of the server process is to assist in

Central Processor   Satellite

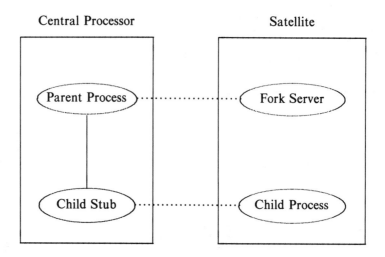

Figure 13.5. Fork on the Central Processor

downloading the child. Because of the tight coupling of the system (the satellite processors have no autonomy), the satellite and stub processes have the same process ID. Figure 13.5 illustrates the relationship between the processes: the solid line shows parent-child relationships and dotted lines depict peer-to-peer communication lines, either parent process to satellite server or child process to its stub.

When a process on a satellite processor *fork*s, it sends a message to its stub on the central processor, which then goes through a similar sequence of operations. The stub finds a new satellite processor and arranges to download the old process image: It sends a message to the parent satellite process requesting to read the process image, and the satellite responds by *writing* its process image to the communications link. The stub *reads* the process image and *writes* it to the child satellite. When the satellite is completely downloaded, the stub *forks*, creating a child stub on the central processor, and *writes* the program counter to the child satellite so that it knows where to start execution. Obvious optimizations can occur if the child process is assigned to the same satellite as its parent, but this design allows processes to run on other satellite processors besides the one on which they were *fork*ed. Figure 13.6 depicts the process relationships after the *fork*. When a satellite process *exits*, it sends an *exit* message to the stub, and the stub *exits*. The stub cannot initiate an *exit* sequence.

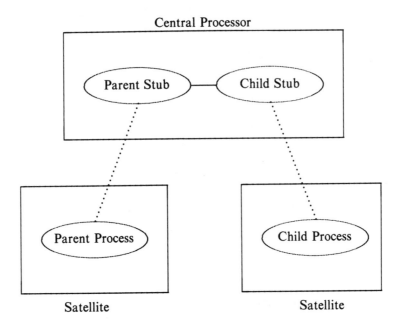

Figure 13.6. Fork on a Satellite Processor

A process must react to signals in the same way that it would react on a uniprocessor: Either it finishes the system call before it checks for the signal or it awakens immediately from its sleep and abruptly terminates the system call, depending on the priority at which it sleeps. Because a stub process handles system calls for a satellite, it must react to signals in concert with the satellite process. If a signal causes a process on a uniprocessor to finish a system call abnormally, the stub process should behave the same way. Similarly, if a signal causes a process to *exit*, the satellite *exits* and sends an *exit* message to the stub process, which *exits* naturally.

When a satellite process executes the *signal* system call, it stores the usual information in local tables and sends a message to the stub process, informing it whether it should ignore the particular signal or not. As will be seen, it makes no difference to the stub whether a process catches a signal or does the default operation. A process reacts to signals based on the combination of three factors (see Figure 13.7): whether the signal occurs when the process is in the middle of a system call, whether the process had called the *signal* system call to ignore the signal, or whether the signal originates on the satellite processor or on another processor. Let us consider the various possibilities.

Suppose a satellite process is asleep as the stub process executes a system call on its behalf. If a signal originates on another processor, the stub sees the signal

```
algorithm sighandle              /* algorithm for handling signals */
input:  none
output: none
{
        if (clone process)
        {
                if (ignoring signal)
                        return;
                if (in middle of system call)
                        set signal against clone process;
                else
                        send signal message to satellite process;
        }
        else      /* satellite process */
        {
                /* whether in middle of system call or not */
                send signal to clone process;
        }
}

algorithm satellite_end_of_syscall      /* satellite end of system call */
input:      none
output:     none
{
        if (system call interrupted)
                send message to satellite telling about interrupt, signal;
        else      /* system call not interrupted */
                send system call reply:  include flag indicating arrival
                                        of signal;
}
```

Figure 13.7. Handling Signals on Satellite System

before the satellite process. There are three cases.

1. If the stub does not sleep on an event where it would wake up on occurrence of a signal, it completes the system call, sends the appropriate results in a message to the satellite process, and indicates which signal it had received.

2. If the process was ignoring the signal, the stub continues the system call algorithm without doing a *longjmp* out of an interruptible sleep — the usual behavior for ignored signals. When the stub replies to the satellite process, it does not indicate that it had received a signal.

3. If the stub process had done a *longjmp* out of the system call because of receipt of a signal, it informs the satellite process that the system call was interrupted and indicates the signal number.

The satellite process checks the response to see if signals have occurred and, if they have, handles them in the usual fashion before returning from the system call. Thus, a process behaves exactly as it would on a uniprocessor: It *exits* without returning from the kernel, or it calls a user signal handling function, or it ignores the signal and returns from the system call.

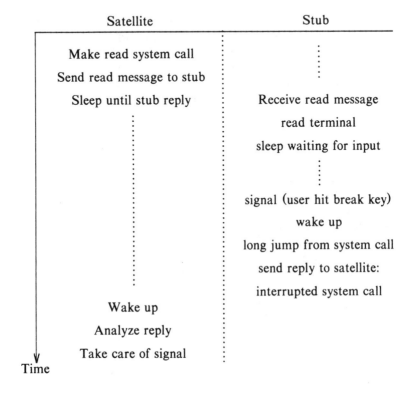

Figure 13.8. Interrupt in Middle of a System Call

For example, suppose a satellite process *read*s a terminal, which is connected to the central processor, and sleeps while the stub process executes the system call (Figure 13.8). If a user hits the break key, the stub kernel sends an interrupt signal to the stub process. If the stub was sleeping, waiting for input, it immediately wakes up and terminates the *read* call. In its response to the satellite process, the stub sets an error code (interrupted from the system call) and the signal number for interrupt. The satellite process examines the response and, because the message shows that an interrupt signal was sent, posts the signal to itself. Before returning from the *read* call, the satellite kernel checks for signals, finds the interrupt signal returned by the stub process, and handles it in the usual way. If the satellite process *exits* as a result of the interrupt signal, the *exit* system call takes care of killing the stub process. If it is catching interrupt signals, it calls the user signal catcher function and later returns from the *read* call, giving the user an error return. On the other hand, if the stub process was executing a *stat* system call on behalf of the satellite process, it does not terminate the system call on receipt of a signal (*stat* is guaranteed to wake up from all sleeps because it never has to wait indefinitely for a resource). The stub completes the system call and returns the signal number to the satellite process. The satellite process posts the signal to itself and discovers the signal when it returns from the system call.

If the process had been in the middle of a system call and a signal originates on the satellite processor, the satellite process has no idea whether the stub will return soon or sleep indefinitely. The satellite process sends a special message to the stub, informing it of the occurrence of the signal. The kernel on the central processor reads the message and sends the signal to the stub, which now reacts as described in the previous paragraphs: Either it interrupts the system call or it completes it. The satellite process cannot send the message to the stub directly, because the stub is in the middle of a system call and is not *read*ing the communications line. The central processor kernel recognizes the special message and posts the signal to the appropriate stub.

Repeating the *read* example explained above, the satellite process has no idea whether the stub process is waiting for input from a terminal or whether it is doing other processing. It sends the stub process a signal message: If the stub was asleep at an interruptible priority, it wakes up immediately and terminates the system call; otherwise, it completes the system call normally.

Finally, consider the cases where a signal arrives when a process is not in the middle of a system call. If the signal originates on another processor, the stub receives the signal first and sends a special signal message to the satellite process, regardless of how the satellite process wishes to dispose of the signal. The satellite kernel deciphers the message and sends the signal to the process, which reacts to it in the usual manner. If the signal had originated on the satellite processor, the satellite process does the usual processing and does not require special communication to the stub process.

When a satellite process sends a signal to other processes, it encodes a message for the *kill* system call and sends it to the stub, which executes the *kill* system call locally. If some processes that should receive the signal are on other satellite processors, their stubs receive the signal and react as described above.

13.2 THE NEWCASTLE CONNECTION

The previous section explored a tightly coupled system configuration where all file subsystem calls on a satellite processor are trapped and forwarded to a remote (central) processor. This view extends to more loosely coupled systems, where each machine wants to access files on the other machines. In a network of personal computers and work stations, for example, users may want to access files stored on a mainframe. The next two sections consider system configurations where local systems execute all system calls but where calls to the file subsystem may access files on other machines.

These systems use one of two ways to identify remote files. Some systems insert a special character into the path name: The component name preceding the special character identifies a machine, and the remainder of the path name identifies a file on that machine. For example, the path name

"sftig!/fs1/mjb/rje"

identifies the file "/fs1/mjb/rje" on the machine "sftig". This file naming scheme follows the convention established by the *uucp* program for transferring files between UNIX systems. Other naming schemes identify remote files by prepending a special prefix such as

/../sftig/fs1/mjb/rje

where the "/.." informs the parser that the file reference is remote, and the second component name gives the remote machine name. The latter naming scheme uses the syntax of conventional file names on the UNIX system, so user software need not be converted to cope with "irregularly constructed names" as in the former scheme (see [Pike 85]).

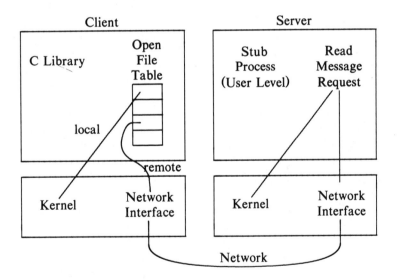

Figure 13.9. Formulation of File Service Requests

The remainder of this section describes a system modeled after the Newcastle connection, where the kernel does not participate in determining that a file is remote; instead, the C library functions that provide the kernel interface detect that a file access is remote and take the appropriate action. For both naming conventions, the C library parses the first components of a path name to determine that a file is remote. This departs from usual implementations where the library does not parse path names. Figure 13.9 depicts how requests for file service are formulated. If a file name is local, the local kernel handles the request in the usual way. But consider execution of the system call

open("/../sftig/fs1/mjb/rje/file", O_RDONLY);

The C library routine for *open* parses the first two components of the path name and recognizes that the file should be on the remote machine "sftig". It maintains a data structure to keep track of whether the process had previously established communication to machine "sftig" and, if not, establishes a communications link to a file server process on the remote machine. When a process makes its first remote request, the remote server validates the request, mapping user and group ID fields as necessary, and creates a stub process to act as the agent for the client process.

The stub, executing requests for the client process, should have the same access rights to files that the client user would have on the remote machine. That is, user "mjb" should access remote files according to the same permissions that govern access to local files. Unfortunately, the client user ID for "mjb" may be that of a different user on the remote machine. Either the system administrators of the various machines must assign unique identifiers to all users across the network, or they must assign a transformation of user IDs at the time of request for network service. Failing the above, the stub process should execute with "other" permissions on the remote machine.

Allowing superuser access permission on remote files is a more ticklish situation. On the one hand, a client superuser should not have superuser rights on the remote system, because a user could thereby circumvent security measures on the remote system. On the other hand, various programs would not work without remote superuser capabilities. For instance, recall from Chapter 7 that the program *mkdir*, which creates a new directory, runs as a *setuid* program with superuser permissions. The remote system would not allow a client to create a new directory, because it would not recognize remote superuser permissions. The problem of creating a remote directory provides a strong rationale for implementing a *mkdir* system call, which would automatically establish all necessary directory links. Nevertheless, execution of *setuid* programs that access remote files as superuser is still a general problem that must be dealt with. Perhaps this problem could best be solved by providing files with a separate set of access permissions for remote superuser access; unfortunately, this would require changes to the structure of the disk inode to save the new permission fields and would thus cause too much turmoil in existing systems.

When an *open* call returns successfully, the local library makes an appropriate notation in a user-level library data structure, including a network address, stub process ID, stub file descriptor, and other appropriate information. The library routines for the *read* and *write* system calls examine the file descriptor to see if the original file reference was remote and, if it was, send a message to the stub. The client process communicates with its stub for all system calls that need service on that machine. If a process accesses two files on a remote machine, it uses one stub, but if it accesses files on two remote machines, it uses two stubs: one on each machine. Similarly, if two processes access a file on a remote machine, they use two stubs. When executing a system call via a stub, the process formulates a message including the system call number, path name, and other relevant information, similar to the type of message described for satellite processors.

Manipulation of the current directory is more complicated. When a process changes directory to a remote directory, the library sends a message to the stub, which changes its current directory, and the library remembers that the current directory is remote. For all path names not beginning with a slash character, the library sends the path name to the remote machine, where the stub process resolves the path name from the current directory. If the current directory is local, the library simply passes the path name to the local kernel. Handling a *chroot* system call to a remote directory is similar, but the local kernel does not find out that the process had done a *chroot*; strictly speaking, a process can ignore a *chroot* to a remote directory, because only the library has a record of it. Exercise 13.9 considers the case of ".." over a mount point.

When a process *fork*s, the *fork* library routine sends each stub a *fork* message. The stub processes *fork* and send their child process IDs to the client parent process. The client process then invokes the (kernel) *fork* system call, and on its return to the child process, the library routine stores the appropriate address information about the child stub process; the local child process carries on its dialogue with the remote child stub. This treatment of the *fork* system call makes it easy for the stubs to keep track of open files and current directories. When a process with remote files *exit*s, the library routine sends a message to the remote stubs, which *exit* in response. The exercises explore the *exec* system call and the *exit* system call in greater detail.

The advantage of the Newcastle design is that processes can access remote files transparently, and no changes need be made to the kernel. However, there are several disadvantages with this design. System performance may be degraded. Because of the larger C library, each process takes up more memory even though it makes no remote references; the library duplicates kernel functions and takes up more space. Larger processes take longer to start up in *exec* and may cause greater contention for memory, inducing a higher degree of paging and swapping on a system. Local requests may execute more slowly because they take longer to get into the kernel, and remote requests may also be slow because they have to do more processing at user level to send requests across a network. The extra user-level processing provides more opportunities for context switches, paging, and swapping. Finally, programs must be recompiled with the new libraries to access remote files; old programs and vender supplied object modules do not work for remote files unless recompiled. The scheme described in the next section does not have these disadvantages.

13.3 TRANSPARENT DISTRIBUTED FILE SYSTEMS

The term *transparent distribution* means that users on one machine can access files on another machine without realizing that they cross a machine boundary, similar to crossing a mount point from one file system to another on one machine. Path names that access files on the remote machine look like path names that access local files: They contain no distinguishing symbols. Figure 13.10 shows a configuration where directory "/usr/src" on machine B is *mount*ed on the directory "/usr/src" on machine A. This configuration is convenient for systems that wish to share one copy of system source code, conventionally found in "/usr/src". Users on machine A can access files on machine B with the regular file name syntax, such as "/usr/src/cmd/login.c", and the kernel decides internally whether a file is remote or local. Users on machine B access local files without being aware that users on machine A can access them, too, but they cannot access files on machine A. Of course, other scenarios are possible where all remote systems are mounted at root of the local system, giving users access to all files on all systems.

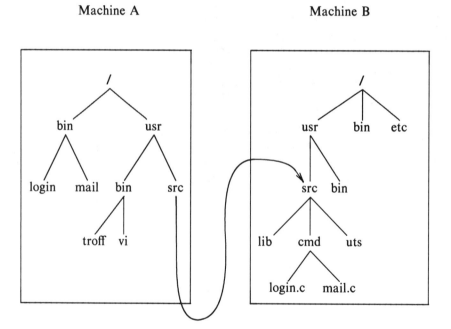

Figure 13.10. File Systems after Remote Mount

Because of the analogy between *mount*ing local file systems and providing access to remote file systems, the *mount* system call is adapted for remote file systems. The kernel contains an expanded mount table: When executing a remote *mount* system call, the kernel establishes a network connection to the remote machine and stores the connection information in the mount table.

An interesting problem arises for path names that include ".." (dot-dot): If a process changes directory to a remote file system, subsequent use of ".." should return the process to the local file system rather than allow it to access files above the remotely mounted directory. Referring to Figure 13.10 again, if a process on machine A, whose current directory is in the (remote) directory "/usr/src/cmd", executes

cd ../../..

its new current directory should be root on machine A, not root on machine B. Algorithm *namei* in the remote kernel therefore checks all ".." sequences to see if the calling process is an agent for a client process, and if so, checks the current working directory to see if that client treats the directory as the root of a remotely mounted file system.

Communication with a remote machine takes on one of two forms: remote procedure call or remote system call. In a remote procedure call design, each kernel procedure that deals with inodes recognizes whether a particular inode refers to a remote file and, if it does, sends a message to the remote machine to perform a specific inode operation. This scheme fits in naturally to the abstract file system types presented at the end of Chapter 5. Thus, a system call that accesses a remote file may cause several messages across the network, depending on how many internal inode operations are involved, with correspondingly higher response time due to network latency. Carried to an extreme, the remote operations include manipulation of the inode lock, reference count, and so on. Various optimizations to the pure model have been implemented to combine several logical inode operations into a single message and to cache important data (see [Sandberg 85]).

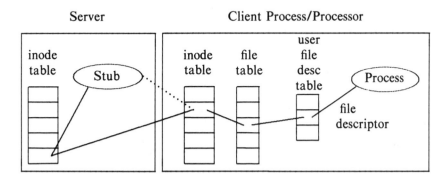

Figure 13.11. Opening a Remote File

Consider a process that *open*s the remote file "/usr/src/cmd/login.c", where "src" is the mount point. As the kernel parses the path name in *namei-iget*, it detects that the file is remote and sends a request to the remote machine to return a locked inode. On receipt of a successful response, the local kernel allocates an in-core inode that corresponds to the remote file. It then checks file modes for necessary permissions (permission to read, for instance), by sending another message to the remote machine. It continues executing the *open* algorithm as presented in Chapter 5, sending messages to the remote machine when necessary, until it completes the algorithm and unlocks the inode. Figure 13.11 illustrates the relationship of the kernel data structures at conclusion of the *open*.

For a *read* system call, the client kernel locks the local inode, sends a message to lock the remote inode, sends a message to read data, copies the data into local memory, sends a message to unlock the remote inode, and unlocks the remote inode. This scheme conforms to the semantics of existing, uniprocessor kernel code, but the frequency of network use (potentially several times per system call) hurts performance. Several operations can be combined into one message to reduce network traffic, however. In the *read* example, the client can send one "read" message to the server, which knows that it has to lock and unlock its inode while doing the read operation. Implementation of remote caches can further reduce network traffic, as mentioned above, but care must be taken to maintain the semantics of file system calls.

In a remote system call design, the local kernel recognizes that a system call refers to a remote file, as above, and sends the parameters of the system call to the remote system, which executes the *system call* and returns the results to the client. The client machine receives the results of the remote system call and *longjmp*s out of the system call. Most system calls can be executed with only one network message, resulting in reasonably good system response, but several kernel operations do not fit the model. For instance, the kernel creates a "core" file for a process on receipt of various signals (Chapter 7). Creation of a core file does not correspond to one system call but entails several inode operations, such as creation of a file, checking access permissions, and doing several write operations.

For an *open* system call, the remote system call message consists of the remainder of the path name (the path name string after the component where the remote path name was detected) and the various flags. Repeating the earlier example for a process that *open*s the file "usr/src/cmd/login.c", the kernel sends the path name "cmd/login.c" to the remote machine. The message also contains identifying information, such as user ID and group ID, needed to determine file access capabilities on the remote machine. When the remote machine responds that the *open* call succeeded, the local kernel allocates a free, local, in-core inode, marks it "remote," saves the information needed to identify the remote machine and the remote inode, and allocates a new file table entry in the usual manner. The inode on the local machine is a dummy for the real inode on the remote machine, resulting in the same configuration as the remote procedure call model (Figure 13.11). When a process issues a system call that accesses a remote file by its file descriptor, the local kernel recognizes that the file is remote by examining its (local) inode, formulates a message encapsulating the system call, and sends the message to the remote machine. The message contains the remote inode index so that the stub can identify the remote file.

For all system calls, the local kernel may execute special code to take care of the response and may eventually *longjmp* out of the system call, because subsequent local processing, designed for a uniprocessor system, may be irrelevant. Therefore, the semantics of kernel algorithms may change to support a remote system call model. However, network traffic is kept to a minimum, allowing system response to be as fast as possible.

13.4 A TRANSPARENT DISTRIBUTED MODEL WITHOUT STUB PROCESSES

Use of stub processes in the transparent distributed system model makes it easy for the remote system to keep track of remote files, but the process table on the remote system becomes cluttered with stubs that are idle most of the time. Other schemes use special server processes on the remote machine to handle remote requests (see [Sandberg 85] and [Cole 85]). The remote system has a pool of server processes and assigns them temporarily to handle each remote request as it arrives. After handling a request, the server process reenters the pool and is available for reassignment to other requests: The server does not remember the user context (such as user ID) between system calls, because it may handle system calls for several processes. Consequently, each message from a client process must include data about its environment, such as UIDs, current directory, disposition of signals, and so on. Stub processes acquire this data at setup time or during the normal course of system call execution.

When a process *open*s a remote file, the remote kernel allocates an inode for later reference to the file. The local machine has the usual entries in the user file descriptor table, file table, and inode table, and the inode entry identifies the remote machine and inode. For system calls that use a file descriptor, like *read*, the kernel sends a message that identifies the previously allocated remote inode and passes over process-specific information, such as the user ID, the maximum allowed file size, and so on. When the remote machine dispatches a server, communication with the client process is similar to what was described previously, but the connection between the client and server exists only for the duration of the system call.

Handling flow control, signals, and remote devices is more difficult using server processes instead of stubs. If a remote machine is flooded with requests from many machines, it must queue the requests if it does not have enough server processes. This requires a higher-level protocol than the one already provided with the underlying network. In the stub model, on the other hand, a stub cannot be flooded with requests, because all transactions with a client are synchronous: A client can have at most one outstanding request.

Handling signals that interrupt a system call is also more complicated with server processes, because the remote machine must find the correct server process that is executing the system call. It is even possible that the system call request is still waiting for service if all server processes were busy. Similarly, race conditions are possible if the server returns the result of the system call to the calling process, and the response passes the signal message en route through the network. Each message must be tagged so that the remote system can locate it and interrupt server processes, if necessary. Using stub processes, the process servicing the client system call is automatically identified, and it is easy to determine if it already finished handling a system call when a signal arrives.

Finally, if a process issues a system call that causes the server process to sleep indefinitely (reading a remote terminal, for example), the server process cannot handle other requests, effectively removing it from the server process pool. If many processes access remote devices and if there is an upper bound on the number of server processes, this can be a severe bottleneck. This cannot happen when using stub processes, because the stubs are allocated per client process. Exercise 13.14 explores another problem in using server processes for remote devices.

In spite of the advantages for using process stubs, the need for process table slots is so critical in practice that most schemes use a pool of service processes to handle remote requests.

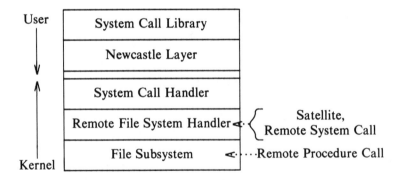

Figure 13.12. Conceptual Kernel Layer for Remote File Access

13.5 SUMMARY

This chapter has described three schemes for allowing processes to access files stored on remote machines, treating the remote file systems as an extension of the local file system. Figure 13.12 illustrates the architectural difference between them. These systems are distinguished from the multiprocessor systems described in the previous chapter, because processors do not share physical memory. The satellite processor scheme consists of a tightly coupled set of processors that share the file resources of a central processor. The Newcastle connection gives the appearance of transparent, remote file access, but remote access is provided by a special implementation of the C library, not by the kernel. Consequently, programs must be recompiled to use the Newcastle connection, sometimes a serious drawback. Remote files are designated by special character sequences that identify the machine that stores the file, another factor that can limit portability.

A transparent distributed system uses a variation of the *mount* system call to give access to a remote file system, much as the usual *mount* system call extends the local file system to newly mounted disk units. Inodes on the local system indicate that they refer to remote files, and the local kernel sends messages to the remote kernel, describing the kernel algorithm (system call), its parameters, and the remote inode. Two designs support the remote transparent, distributed operations: a remote procedure call model, where the messages instruct the remote machine to execute inode operations, and a remote system call model, where the messages instruct the remote machine to execute system calls. Finally, the chapter examined the issues involved with serving remote requests with stub processes or with server processes from a general pool.

13.6 EXERCISES

* 1. Describe an implementation of the *exit* system call on a satellite processor system. How is this different from the case where a process *exit*s as a result of receipt of an uncaught signal? How should the kernel dump the "core" file?
  2. Processes cannot ignore the *SIGKILL* signal; describe what happens on a satellite system when a process receives this signal.
* 3. Describe an implementation of the *exec* system call on a satellite processor system.
* 4. How should a central processor assign processes to satellite processors to balance the execution load?
* 5. What happens if a satellite processor does not contain enough memory for the processes downloaded to it? How should it handle swapping or paging across a network?
  6. Consider a system that allows access to remote file server machines by recognizing path names by special prefaces. Suppose a process executes

    execl("/../sftig/bin/sh", "sh", 0);

    The executable image is on the remote machine but should execute on the local machine. Describe how the local system brings the remote executable file to the local system to do the *exec*.
  7. If an administrator wishes to add new machines to a Newcastle system, what is the best way to inform the C library modules?
* 8. The kernel overwrites the address space of a process during *exec*, including the library tables used by a Newcastle-style implementation to keep track of remote file references. The process must still be able to access these files by their old file descriptors after the *exec*. Describe an implementation.

* 9. As described in Section 13.2, execution of the *exit* system call on Newcastle systems results in a message being sent to the stub process that causes it to *exit*. This is done at the library level. What happens if the local process receives a signal that causes it to *exit* from the kernel?

* 10. In a Newcastle-style system, where remote files are designated by special prefaces, how should the system allow a user to use the ".." (parent directory) component to back up over a remote mount point?

11. Recall from Chapter 7 that various signals cause a process to dump a core file in its current directory. What should happen if the current directory is in a remote file system? What happens on a Newcastle system?

* 12. If someone on a remote processor kills all stub or server processes, how should the local processes hear the good news?

* 13. In the transparent distribution system, discuss implementations of *link*, which has two possibly remote path names, and *exec*, which has several internal read operations. Consider the two designs: remote procedure call and remote system call.

* 14. When a (nonstub) server process accesses a device, it may have to sleep until the device driver wakes it up. Given a fixed number of servers, it is conceivable that a system would be unable to satisfy any more requests from a local machine, because all servers are sleeping in a device driver. Devise a scheme that is safe, in that not all servers can sleep, waiting for device I/O. A system call should not fail because all servers are currently busy.

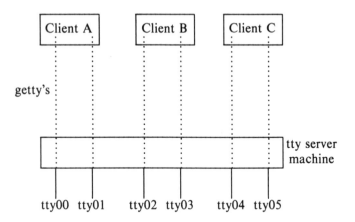

Figure 13.13. A Terminal Server Configuration

* 15. When a user logs into a system, the terminal line discipline saves information that the terminal is a control terminal, noting the process group. In this way, processes receive interrupt signals when a user hits the break key at the terminal. Consider a system configuration where all terminals are physically connected to one machine, but users log in logically on other machines (Figure 13.13). Specifically, a system spawns a *getty* process for a remote terminal. If a pool of server processes handle remote system calls, a server sleeps in the driver open procedure, waiting for a connection. When the server completes the *open* system call, it goes back into the process pool, severing its

connection to the terminal. If a user hits the break key, how is the interrupt signal sent to processes in the process group executing on the client machine?

* 16. The shared memory feature is inherently a local-machine operation. Logically, it would be possible for processes on different machines to access a common piece of physical memory, whether the memory is local or remote. Describe an implementation.

* 17. The demand paging and swapping algorithms examined in Chapter 9 assume the use of a local swap device. What modifications must be made to these algorithms to support remote swap devices?

* 18. Suppose a remote machine crashes (or the network goes down) and the local network protocol can recognize this fact. Design recovery schemes for a local system that makes requests of a remote, server system. Conversely, design recovery schemes for a server system that loses its connection with client machines.

* 19. When a process accesses a remote file, the path name may stretch across several machines until it is completely resolved. Following the path name "/usr/src/uts/3b2/os" for example, "/usr" may be on machine A, the root of machine B may be mounted on "/usr/src", and the root of machine C may be mounted on "/usr/src/uts/3b2". Moving through several machines to get to the final destination is called *multihop*. If a direct network connection exists between A and C, however, it is inefficient to transfer data between the machines via machine B. Describe a design for multi-hop in the Newcastle and transparent distribution models.

APPENDIX —
SYSTEM CALLS

This appendix contains a brief synopsis of the UNIX system calls. Refer to the UNIX System V User Programmer's Manual for a complete specification of these calls. The specification here is sufficient for reference when reading the various program examples in the book.

The specified file names are null terminated character strings, whose individual components are separated by slash characters. All system calls return −1 on error, and the external variable errno indicates the specific error. Unless specified otherwise, system calls return 0 on success. Some system calls are the entry point for several functions: this means that the assembly language interface for the functions is the same. The list here follows the usual conventions for UNIX system manuals, but the programmer should not care whether a system call entry point handles one or many system calls.

access   F

    access(filename, mode)
    char *filename;
    int mode;

Access checks if the calling process has read, write, or execute permission for the file, according to the value of *mode*. The value of *mode* is a combination of the bit patterns 4 (for read), 2 (for write), and 1 (for execute). The real-user ID is checked instead of the effective user ID.

acct

    acct(filename)
    char *filename;

Acct enables system accounting if *filename* is non-null, and disables it otherwise.

alarm   F

    unsigned alarm(seconds)
    unsigned seconds;

Alarm schedules the occurrence of an alarm signal for the calling process in the indicated number of *seconds*. It returns the amount of time remaining until the alarm signal at the time of the call.

brk

    int brk(end_data_seg)
    char *end_data_seg;

Brk sets the highest address of a process's data region to *end_data_seg*. Another function, *sbrk*, uses this system call entry point and changes the highest address of a process's data region according to a specified increment.

chdir   F

    chdir(filename)
    char *filename;

Chdir changes the current directory of the calling process to *filename*.

chmod   F

    chmod(filename, mode)
    char *filename;

Chmod changes the access permissions of the indicated file to the specified *mode*, which is a combination of the following bits (in octal):

            04000   setuid bit
            02000   set group ID bit

01000	sticky bit
00400	read for owner
00200	write for owner
00100	execute for owner
00040	read for group
00020	write for group
00010	execute for group
00004	read for others
00002	write for others
00001	execute for others

chown

```
chown(filename, owner, group)
char *filename;
int owner, group;
```

Chown changes the owner and group of the indicated file to the specified *owner* and *group* IDs.

chroot

```
chroot(filename)
char *filename;
```

Chroot sets the private, changed-root of the calling process to *filename*.

close

```
close(fildes)
int fildes;
```

Close closes a file descriptor obtained from a prior *open*, *creat*, *dup*, *pipe*, or *fcntl* system call, or a file descriptor inherited from a *fork* call.

creat

```
creat(filename, mode)
char *filename;
int mode;
```

Creat creates a new file with the indicated file name and access permission modes. *Mode* is as specified in *access*, except that the sticky-bit is cleared and bits set via *umask* are cleared. If the file already exists, *creat* truncates the file. *Creat* returns a file descriptor for use in other system calls.

dup

    dup(fildes)
    int fildes;

Dup duplicates the specified file descriptor, returning the lowest available file descriptor. The old and new file descriptors use the same file pointer and share other attributes.

exec

    execve(filename, argv, envp)
    char *filename;
    char *argv[];
    char *envp[];

Execve executes the program file *filename*, overlaying the address space of the executing process. *Argv* is an array of character strings parameters to the *exec*ed program, and *envp* is an array of character strings that are the environment of the new process.

exit   F

    exit(status)
    int status;

Exit causes the calling process to terminate, reporting the 8 low-order bits of status to its waiting parent. The kernel may call exit internally, in response to certain signals.

fcntl

    fcntl(fildes, cmd, arg)
    int fildes, cmd, arg;

Fcntl supports a set of miscellaneous operations for open files, identified via the file descriptor *fildes*. The interpretation of *cmd* and *arg* is as follows (manifest constants are defined in file "/usr/include/fcntl.h"):

F_DUPFD	return lowest numbered file descriptor >= arg
F_SETFD	set close-on-exec flag to low order bit of arg
	(if 1, file is closed in exec)
F_GETFD	return value of close-on-exec flag
F_SETFL	set file status flags (O_NDELAY do not sleep for I/O and

                          O_APPEND append written data to end of file)
        F_GETFL   get file status flags

struct flock
        short l_type;   /* F_RDLCK for read lock, F_WRLCK for write lock,
                              F_UNLCK for unlock operations */
        short l_whence; /* lock offset is from beginning of file (0), current position of file
                              pointer (1), or end of file (2) */
        long l_start;   /* byte offset, interpreted according to l_whence */
        long l_len;   /* number of bytes to lock. If 0, lock from l_start to end of file */
        long l_pid;   /* ID of process that locked file */
        long l_sysid;   /* sys ID of process that locked file */

        F_GETLK   get first lock that would prevent application of the lock specified by *arg*
                    and overwrite *arg*. If no such lock exists, change l_type in *arg* to
                    F_UNLCK
        F_SETLK   lock or unlock the file as specified by *arg*. Return -1 if unable to lock.
        F_SETLKW   lock or unlock data in a file as specified by *arg*. Sleep if unable to lock.

Several read locks can overlap in a file. No locks can overlap a write lock.

fork   F

  fork()

Fork creates a new process. The child process is a logical copy of the parent
process, except that the parent's return value from the *fork* is the process ID of the
child, and the child's return value is 0.

getpid   F

  getpid()

Getpid returns the process ID of the calling process. Other calls that use this entry
point are *getpgrp*, which returns the process group of the calling process, and
getppid, which returns the parent process ID of the calling process.

getuid   F

  getuid()

Getuid returns the real user ID of the calling process. Other calls that use this
system call entry point are *geteuid*, which returns the effective user ID, *getgid*,
which returns the group ID, and *getegid*, which returns the effective group ID of
the calling process.

ioctl

> ioctl(fildes, cmd, arg)
> int fildes, cmd;

Ioctl does device-specific operations on the open device whose file descriptor is *fildes*. *Cmd* specifies the command to be done on the device, and *arg* is a parameter whose type depends on the command.

kill   ⌐

> kill(pid, sig)
> int pid, sig;

Kill sends the signal sig to the processes identified by *pid*.

pid positive	send signal to process whose PID is pid.
pid 0	send signal to processes whose process group ID is PID of sender.
pid −1	if effective UID of sender is super user, send signal to all processes otherwise, send signal to all processes whose real UID equals effective UID of sender.
pid < −1	send signal to processes whose process group ID is pid.

The effective UID of the sender must be superuser, or the sender's real or effective UID must equal the real or effective UID of the receiving processes.

link   F

> link(filename1, filename2)
> char *filename1, *filename2;

Link gives another name, *filename2*, to the file *filename1*. The file becomes accessible through either name.

lseek   F

> lseek(fildes, offset, origin)
> int fildes, origin;
> long offset;

Lseek changes the position of the read-write pointer for the file descriptor *fildes* and returns the new value. The value of the pointer depends on *origin*:

0	set the pointer to offset bytes from the beginning of the file.
1	increment the current value of the pointer by offset.
2	set the pointer to the size of the file plus offset bytes.

mknod

```
mknod(filename, modes, dev)
char *filename;
int mode, dev;
```

Mknod creates a special file, directory, or FIFO according to the type of *modes*:

010000	FIFO (named pipe)
020000	character special device file
040000	directory
060000	block special device file

The 12 low order bits of *modes* have the same meaning as described above for *chmod*. If the file is block special or character special, *dev* gives the major and minor numbers of the device.

mount

```
mount(specialfile, dir, rwflag)
char *specialfile, *dir;
int rwflag;
```

Mount mounts the file system specified by *specialfile* onto the directory *dir*. If the low-order bit of *rwflag* is 1, the file system is mounted read-only.

msgctl

```
#include <sys/types.h>
#include <sys/ipc.h>
#include <sys/msg.h>

msgctl(id, cmd, buf)
int id, cmd;
struct msqid_ds *buf;
```

Msgctl allows processes to set or query the status of the message queue id, or to remove the queue, according to the value of *cmd*. The structure *msqid_ds* is defined as follows:

```
struct ipc_perm {
    ushort      uid;        /* current user id */
    ushort      gid;        /* current group id */
    ushort      cuid;       /* creator user id */
    ushort      cgid;       /* creator group id */
    ushort      mode;       /* access modes */
    short       pad1;       /* used by system */
    long        pad2;       /* used by system */
};
```

```
struct msqid_ds {
    struct ipc_perm    msg_perm;        /* permission struct */
    short              pad1[7];         /* used by system */
    ushort             msg_qnum;        /* number of messages on q */
    ushort             msg_qbytes;      /* max number of bytes on q */
    ushort             msg_lspid;       /* pid of last msgsnd operation */
    ushort             msg_lrpid;       /* pid of last msgrcv operation */
    time_t             msg_stime;       /* last msgsnd time */
    time_t             msg_rtime;       /* last msgrcv time */
    time_t             msg_ctime;       /* last change time */
};
```

The commands and their meaning are as follows:

IPC_STAT   Read the message queue header associated with id into buf.
IPC_SET   Set the values of msg_perm.uid, msg_perm.gid, msg_perm.mode (9
             low-order bits), and msg_qbytes from the corresponding values in buf.
IPC_RMID   Remove the message queue for id.

msgget

```
#include  <sys/types.h>
#include  <sys/ipc.h>
#include  <sys/msg.h>

msgget(key, flag)
key_t key;
int flag;
```

Msgget returns an identifier to a message queue whose name is *key*. *Key* can specify that the returned queue identifier should refer to a private queue (*IPC_PRIVATE*), in which case a new message queue is created. *Flag* specifies if the queue should be created (*IPC_CREAT*), and if creation of the queue should be exclusive (*IPC_EXCL*). In the latter case, *msgget* fails if the queue already exists.

msgsnd and msgrcv

```
#include  <sys/types.h>
#include  <sys/ipc.h>
#include  <sys/msg.h>

msgsnd(id, msgp, size, flag)
int id, size, flag;
struct msgbuf *msgp;
```

```
msgrcv(id, msgp, size, type, flag)
int id, size, type, flag;
struct msgbuf *msgmp;
```

Msgsnd sends a message of size bytes in the buffer *msgp* to the message queue *id*. *Msgbuf* is defined as

```
struct msgbuf
        long mtype;
        char mtext[];
};
```

If the *IPC_NOWAIT* bit is off in *flag*, *msgsnd* sleeps if the number of bytes on the message queue exceeds the maximum, or if the number of messages system-wide exceeds a maximum value. If *IPC_NOWAIT* is set, *msgsnd* returns immediately in these cases.

Msgrcv receives messages from the queue identified by *id*. If *type* is 0, the first message on the queue is received; if positive, the first message of that type is received; if negative, the first message of the lowest type less than or equal to type is received. *Size* indicates the maximum size of message text the user wants to receive. If *MSG_NOERROR* is set in *flag*, the kernel truncates the received message if its size is larger than *size*. Otherwise it returns an error. If *IPC_NOWAIT* is not set in *flag*, *msgrcv* sleeps until a message that satisfies *type* is sent. If *IPC_NOWAIT* is set, it returns immediately. *Msgrcv* returns the number of bytes in the message text.

nice

```
nice(increment)
int increment;
```

Nice adds *increment* to the process nice value. A higher nice value gives the process lower scheduling priorities.

open

```
#include  <fcntl.h>

open(filename, flag, mode)
char *filename;
int flag, mode;
```

Open opens the specified file according to the value of *flag*. The value of *flag* is a combination of the following bits (exactly one of the first three bits must be used).

O_RDONLY   open for reading only.

O_WRONLY   open for writing only.

O_RDWR   open for reading and writing.

O_NDELAY   For special devices, open returns without waiting for carrier.
            if set. For named pipes, open will return immediately (with an
            error if O_WRONLY set), instead of waiting for another process to
            open the named pipe.

O_APPEND   causes all writes to append data to the end of the file.

O_CREAT   create the file if it does not exist. Mode specifies permissions
            as in creat system call. The flag has no meaning if the file
            already exists.

O_TRUNC   Truncate length of file to 0.

O_EXCL   Fail the open call if this bit and O_CREAT are set and file exists.
            This is a so-called exclusive open.

Open returns a file descriptor for use in other system calls.

pause

pause()

Pause suspends the execution of the calling process until it receives a signal.

pipe

pipe(fildes)
int fildes[2];

Pipe returns a read and write file descriptor (*fildes[0]* and *fildes[1]*, respectively).
Data is transmitted through a pipe in first-in-first-out order; data cannot be read
twice.

plock

#include <sys/lock.h>

plock(op)
int op;

Plock locks and unlocks process regions in memory according to the value of *op*:

PROCLOCK	lock text and data regions in memory.
TXTLOCK	lock text region in memory.
DATLOCK	lock data region in memory.
UNLOCK	remove locks for all regions.

profil

>   profil(buf, size, offset, scale)
>   char *buf;
>   int size, offset, scale;

Profil requests that the kernel give an execution profile of the process. *Buf* is an array in the process that accumulates frequency counts of execution in different addresses of the process. *Size* is the size of the buf array, *offset* is the starting address in the process that should be profiled, and *scale* is a scaling factor.

ptrace

>   ptrace(cmd, pid, addr, data)
>   int cmd, pid, addr, data;

Ptrace allows a process to trace the execution of another process, *pid*, according to the value of *cmd*.

0	enable child for tracing (called by child).
1,2	return word at location addr in traced process pid.
3	return word from offset addr in traced process u area.
4,5	write value of data into location addr in traced process.
6	write value of data into offset addr in u area.
7	cause traced process to resume execution.
8	cause traced process to exit.
9	machine dependent — set bit in PSW for single-stepping execution.

read

>   read(fildes, buf, size)
>   int fildes,
>   char *buf;
>   int size;

Read reads up to size bytes from the file *fildes* into the user buffer *buf*. *Read* returns the number of bytes it read. For special devices and pipes, *read* returns immediately if *O_NDELAY* was set in open and no data is available for return.

semctl

>   #include <sys/types.h>
>   #include <sys/ipc.h>
>   #include <sys/sem.h>

```
semctl(id, num, cmd, arg)
int id, num, cmd;
union semun {
        int val;
        struct semid_ds *buf;
        ushort *array;
} arg;
```

Semctl does the specified *cmd* on the semaphore queue indicated by *id*.

GETVAL	return the value of the semaphore whose index is num.
SETVAL	set the value of the semaphore whose index is num to arg.val.
GETPID	return value of last PID that did a semop on the semaphore whose index is num.
GETNCNT	return number of processes waiting for semaphore value to become positive.
GETZCNT	return number of processes waiting for semaphore value to become 0.
GETALL	return values of all semaphores into array arg.array.
SETALL	set values of all semaphores according to array arg.array.
IPC_STAT	read structure of semaphore header for id into arg.buf.
IPC_SET	set sem_perm.uid, sem_per.gid, and sem_perm.mode (low-order 9 bits) according to arg.buf.
IPC_RMID	remove the semaphores associated with id.

Num gives the number of semaphores in the set to be processed. The structure *semid_ds* is defined by:

```
struct semid_ds {
        struct ipc_perm    sem_perm;      /* permission struct */
        int *              pad;           /* used by system */
        ushort             sem_nsems;     /* number of semaphores in set */
        time_t             sem_otime;     /* last semop operation time */
        time_t             sem_ctime;     /* last change time */
};
```

The structure *ipc_perm* is the same as defined in *msgctl*.

semget

```
#include  <sys/types.h>
#include  <sys/ipc.h>
#include  <sys/sem.h>

semget(key, nsems, flag)
key_t key;
int nsems, flag;
```

Semget creates an array of semaphores, corresponding to *key*. *Key* and *flag* take on the same meaning as they do in *msgget*.

semop

```
semop(id, ops, num)
int id, num;
struct sembuf **ops;
```

Semop does the set of semaphore operations in the array of structures *ops*, to the set of semaphores identified by *id*. *Num* is the number of entries in *ops*. The structure of *sembuf* is:

```
struct sembuf {
        short       sem_num;    /* semaphore number */
        short       sem_op;     /* semaphore operation */
        short       sem_flg;    /* flag */
};
```

Sem_num specifies the index in the semaphore array for the particular operation, and *sem_flg* specifies flags for the operation. The operations *sem_op* for semaphores are:

negative   if sum of semaphore value and sem_op >= 0, add sem_op to
            to semaphore value. Otherwise, sleep, as per flag.
positive   add sem_op to semaphore value.
zero   continue, if semaphore value is 0. Otherwise, sleep as per flag.

If *IPC_NOWAIT* is set in *sem_flg* for a particular operation, *semop* returns immediately for those occasions it would have slept. If the *SEM_UNDO* flag is set, the operation is subtracted from a running sum of such values. When the process exits, this sum is added to the value of the semaphore. *Semop* returns the value of the last semaphore operation in *ops* at the time of the call.

setpgrp

```
setpgrp()
```

Setpgrp sets the process group ID of the calling process to its process ID and returns the new value.

setuid

```
setuid(uid)
int uid;
```

```
setgid(gid)
int gid;
```

Setuid sets the real and effective user ID of the calling process. If the effective user ID of the caller is superuser, *setuid* resets the real and effective user IDs. Otherwise, if its real user ID equals *uid*, *setuid* resets the effective user ID to *uid*. Finally, if its saved user ID (set by executing a setuid program in *exec*) equals *uid*, *setuid* resets the effective user ID to *uid*. *Setgid* works the same way for real and effective group IDs.

shmctl

```
#include  <sys/types.h>
#include  <sys/ipc.h>
#include  <sys/shm.h>

shmctl(id, cmd, buf)
int id, cmd;
struct shmid_ds *buf;
```

Shmctl does various control operations on the shared memory region identified by *id*. The structure *shmid_ds* is defined by:

```
struct shmid_ds {
        struct ipc_perm   shm_perm;      /* permission struct */
        int               shm_segsz;     /* size of segment */
        int *             pad1;          /* used by system */
        ushort            shm_lpid;      /* pid of last operation */
        ushort            shm_cpid;      /* pid of creator */
        ushort            shm_nattch;    /* number currently attached */
        short             pad2;          /* used by system */
        time_t            shm_atime;     /* last attach time */
        time_t            shm_dtime;     /* last detach time */
        time_t            shm_ctime;     /* last change time */
};
```

The operations are:

```
IPC_STAT     read values of shared memory header for id into buf.
IPC_SET      set shm_perm.uid, shm_perm.gid, and shm_perm.mode (9 low-order
             bits) in shared memory header according to values in buf.
IPC_RMID     remove shared memory region for id.
```

shmget

```
#include  <sys/types.h>
#include  <sys/ipc.h>
#include  <sys/shm.h>
```

```
shmget(key, size, flag)
key_t key;
int size, flag;
```

Shmget accesses or creates a shared memory region of *size* bytes. The parameters *key* and *flag* have the same meaning as they do for *msgget*.

shmop

```
#include  <sys/types.h>
#include  <sys/ipc.h>
#include  <sys/shm.h>

shmat(id, addr, flag)
int id, flag;
char *addr;

shmdt(addr)
char *addr;
```

Shmat attaches the shared memory region identified by *id* to the address space of a process. If *addr* is 0, the kernel chooses an appropriate address to attach the region. Otherwise, it attempts to attach the region at the specified address. If the *SHM_RND* bit is on in *flag*, the kernel rounds off the address, if necessary. *Shmat* returns the address where the region is attached.

Shmdt detaches the shared memory region previously attached at *addr*.

signal ⊦

```
#include  <signal.h>

signal(sig, function)
int sig;
void (*func)();
```

Signal allows the calling process to control signal processing. The values of *sig* are:

SIGHUP	hangup
SIGINT	interrupt
SIGQUIT	quit
SIGILL	illegal instruction
SIGTRAP	trace trap
SIGIOT	IOT instruction
SIGEMT	EMT instruction
SIGFPE	floating point exception
SIGKILL	kill

SIGBUS	bus error
SIGSEGV	segmentation violation
SIGSYS	bad argument in system call
SIGPIPE	write on a pipe with no reader
SIGALRM	alarm
SIGTERM	software termination
SIGUSR1	user-defined signal
SIGUSR2	second user-defined signal
SIGCLD	death of child
SIGPWR	power failure

The interpretation of *function* is as follows:

SIG_DFL   default operation. For all signals except SIGPWR and SIGCLD, process terminates. It creates a core image for signals SIGQUIT, SIGILL, SIGTRAP, SIGIOT, SIGEMT, SIGFPE, SIGBUS, SIGSEGV, and SIGSYS.

SIG_IGN   ignore the occurrence of the signal.

function   an address of a procedure in the process. The kernel arranges to call the function with the signal number as argument when it returns to user mode. The kernel automatically resets the value of the signal handler to SIG_DFL for all signals except SIGILL, SIGTRAP, and SIGPWR. A process cannot catch SIGKILL signals.

stat

```
stat(filename, statbuf)
char *filename;
struct stat *statbuf;

fstat(fd, statbuf)
int fd;
struct stat *statbuf;
```

Stat returns status information about the specified file. *Fstat* does the same for the open file whose descriptor is *fd*. The structure of *statbuf* is:

```
struct stat {
        dev_t    st_dev;     /* device number for dev containing file */
        ino_t    st_ino;     /* inode number */
        ushort   st_mode;    /* file type (see mknod) and perms (see chmod) */
        short    st_nlink;   /* number of links for file */
        ushort   st_uid;     /* user ID of file's owner */
        ushort   st_gid;     /* group ID of file's group */
        dev_t    st_rdev;    /* major and minor device numbers */
        off_t    st_size;    /* size in bytes */
```

```
    time_t    st_atime;    /* time of last access */
    time_t    st_mtime;    /* time of last modification */
    time_t    st_ctime;    /* time of last status change */
};
```

stime

```
    stime(tptr)
    long *tptr;
```

Stime sets the system time and date, according to the value pointed to by *tptr*. Times are specified in seconds since 00:00:00 January, 1, 1970, GMT.

sync

```
    sync()
```

Sync flushes file system data in system buffers onto disk.

time ⊏

```
    time(tloc)
    long *tloc;
```

Time returns the number of seconds since 00:00:00 January 1, 1970, GMT. If *tloc* is not 0, it will contain the return value, too.

times

```
    #include  <sys/types.h>
    #include  <sys/times.h>

    times(tbuf)
    struct tms *tbuf;
```

Times returns the elapsed real time in clock ticks from an arbitrary fixed time in the recent past, and fills *tbuf* with accounting information:

```
    struct tms {
        time_t    tms_utime;     /* CPU time spent in user mode */
        time_t    tms_stime;     /* CPU time spent in kernel mode */
        time_t    tms_cutime;    /* Sum of tms_utime and tms_cutime of children */
        time_t    tms_sutime;    /* Sum of tms_stime and tms_sutime of children */
    };
```

ulimit

> ulimit(cmd, limit)
> int cmd;
> long limit;

Ulimit allows a process to set various limits according to the value of *cmd*:

1   return maximum file size (in 512 byte blocks) the process can write
2   set maximum file size to limit.
3   return maximum possible break value (highest possible address in data region).

umask

> umask(mask)
> int mask;

Set the file mode creation *mask* and return the old value. When creating a file, permissions are turned off if the corresponding bits in *mask* are set.

umount

> umount(specialfile)
> *char *specialfile;

Unmount the file system in the block special device *specialfile*.

uname

> #include <sys/utsname.h>
>
> uname(name)
> struct utsname *name;

Uname returns system-specific information according to the following structure:

```
struct utsname {
     char      sysname[9];     /* name */
     char      nodename[9];    /* network node name */
     char      release[9];     /* system version information */
     char      version[9];     /* more version information */
     char      machine[9];     /* hardware */
};
```

unlink

    unlink(filename)
    char *filename;

Remove the directory entry for the indicated file.

ustat

    #include <sys/types.h>
    #include <ustat.h>

    ustat(dev, ubuf)
    int dev;
    struct ustat *ubuf;

Ustat returns statistics about the file system identified by *dev* (the major and minor number). The structure *ustat* is defined by:

               struct ustat {
                     daddr_t   f_tfree;   /* number of free blocks */
                     ino_t   f_tinode;   /* number of free inodes */
                     char   f_fname[6];   /* filsys name */
                     char   f_fpack[6];   /* filsys pack name */
               };

utime

    #include <sys/types.h>

    utime(filename, times)
    char *filename;
    struct utimbuf *times;

Utime sets the access and modification times of the specified file according to the value of *times*. If 0, the current time is used. Otherwise, *times* points to the following structure:

               struct utimbuf {
                     time_t   axtime;   /* access time */
                     time_t   modtime;   /* modification time */
               };

All times are measured from 00:00:00 January 1, 1970 GMT.

wait   ☞

> wait(wait_stat)
> int *wait_stat;

Wait causes the process to sleep until it discovers a child process that had exited or a process asleep in trace mode. If *wait_stat* is not 0, it points to an address that contains status information on return from the call. Only the 16 low order bits are written. If wait returns because it found a child process that had exited, the low order 8 bits are 0, and the high order 8 bits contain the low order 8 bits the child process had passed as a parameter to *exit*. If the child exited because of a signal, the high order 8 bits are 0, and the low order 8 bits contain the signal number. In addition, bit 0200 is set if core was dumped. If *wait* returns because it found a traced process, the high order 8 bits (of the 16 bits) contain the signal number that caused it to stop, and the low order 8 bits contain octal 0177.

write

> write(fd, buf, count)
> int fd, count;
> char *buf;

Write writes *count* bytes of data from user address *buf* to the file whose descriptor is *fd*.

BIBLIOGRAPHY

[Babaoglu 81] Babaoglu, O., and W. Joy, "Converting a Swap-Based System to do Paging in an Architecture Lacking Page-Referenced Bits," *Proceedings of the 8th Symposium on Operating Systems Principles, ACM Operating Systems Review*, Vol. 15(5), Dec. 1981, pp. 78-86.

[Bach 84] Bach, M. J., and S. J. Buroff, "Multiprocessor UNIX Systems," *AT&T Bell Laboratories Technical Journal*, Oct. 1984, Vol 63, No. 8, Part 2, pp. 1733-1750.

[Barak 80] Barak, A. B. and A. Shapir, "UNIX with Satellite Processors," *Software - Practice and Experience*, Vol. 10, 1980, pp. 383-392.

[Beck 85] Beck, B. and B. Kasten, "VLSI Assist in Building a Multiprocessor UNIX System," *Proceedings of the USENIX Association Summer Conference*, June 1985, pp. 255-275.

[Berkeley 83] *UNIX Programmer's Manual, 4.2 Berkeley Software Distribution, Virtual VAX-11 Version*, Computer Science Division, Department of Electrical Engineering and Computer Science, University of California at Berkeley, August 1983.

[Birrell 84] Birrell, A.D. and B.J. Nelson, "Implementing Remote Procedure Calls," *ACM Transactions on Computer Systems*, Vol. 2, No. 1, Feb. 1984, pp. 39-59.

[Bodenstab 84] Bodenstab, D. E., T. F. Houghton, K. A. Kelleman, G. Ronkin, and E. P. Schan, "UNIX Operating System Porting Experiences," *AT&T Bell Laboratories Technical Journal*, Vol. 63, No. 8, Oct. 1984, pp. 1769-1790.

[Bourne 78] Bourne, S. R., "The UNIX Shell," *The Bell System Technical Journal*, July-August 1978, Vol. 57, No. 6, Part 2, pp. 1971-1990.

[Bourne 83] Bourne, S.R., *The UNIX System*, Addison-Wesley, Reading, MA, 1983.

[Brownbridge 82] Brownbridge, D. R., L. F. Marshall, and B. Randell, "The Newcastle Connection or UNIXes of the World Unite!" in *Software - Practice and Experience*, Vol. 12, 1982, pp. 1147-1162.

[Bunt 76] Bunt, R.B., "Scheduling Techniques for Operating Systems," *Computer*, Oct. 1976, pp. 10-17.

[Christian 83] Christian, K., *The UNIX Operating System*, John Wiley & Sons Inc., New York, NY, 1983.

[Coffman 73] Coffman, E.G., and P.J. Denning, *Operating Systems Theory*, Prentice-Hall Inc., Englewood Cliffs, NJ, 1973.

[Cole 85] Cole, C.T., P.B. Flinn, and A.B. Atlas, "An Implementation of an Extended File System for UNIX," *Proceedings of the USENIX Conference*, Summer 1985, pp. 131-149.

[Denning 68] Denning, P.J., "The Working Set Model for Program Behavior, *Communications of the ACM*, Volume 11, No. 5, May 1968, pp. 323-333.

[Dijkstra 65] Dijkstra, E.W., "Solution of a Problem in Concurrent Program Control," *CACM*, Vol. 8, No. 9, Sept. 1965, p. 569.

[Dijkstra 68] Dijkstra, E.W., "Cooperating Sequential Processes," in *Programming Languages*, ed. F. Genuys, Academic Press, New York, NY, 1968.

[Felton 84] Felton, W. A., G. L. Miller, and J. M. Milner, "A UNIX Implementation for System/370," *AT&T Bell Laboratories Technical Journal*, Vol. 63, No. 8, Oct. 1984, pp. 1751-1767.

[Goble 81] Goble, G.H. and M.H. Marsh, "A Dual Processor VAX 11/780," *Purdue University Technical Report*, TR-EE 81-31, Sept. 1981.

[Henry 84] Henry, G. J., "The Fair Share Scheduler," *AT&T Bell Laboratories Technical Journal*, Oct. 1984, Vol 63, No. 8, Part 2, pp. 1845-1858.

[Holley 79] Holley, L.H., R.P. Parmelee, C.A. Salisbury, and D.N. Saul, "VM/370 Asymmetric Multiprocessing," *IBM Systems Journal*, Vol. 18, No. 1, 1979, pp. 47-70.

[Holt 83] Holt, R.C., *Concurrent Euclid, the UNIX System, and Tunis*, Addison-Wesley, Reading, MA, 1983.

[Horning 73] Horning, J. J., and B. Randell, "Process Structuring," *Computing Surveys*, Vol. 5, No. 1, March 1973, pp. 5-30.

[Hunter 84] Hunter, C.B. and E. Farquhar, "Introduction to the NS16000 Architecture," *IEEE Micro*, April 1984, pp. 26-47.

[Johnson 78] Johnson, S. C. and D. M. Ritchie, "Portability of C Programs and the UNIX System," *The Bell System Technical Journal*, Vol. 57, No. 6, Part 2, July-August, 1978, pp. 2021-2048.

[Kavaler 83] Kavaler, P. and A. Greenspan, "Extending UNIX to Local-Area Networks," *Mini-Micro Systems*, Sept. 1983, pp. 197-202.

[Kernighan 78] Kernighan, B. W., and D. M. Ritchie, *The C Programming Language*, Prentice-Hall, Englewood Cliffs, NJ, 1978.

[Kernighan 84] Kernighan, B.W., and R. Pike, *The UNIX Programming Environment*, Prentice-Hall, Englewood Cliffs, NJ, 1984.

[Killian 84] Killian, T.J., "Processes as Files," *Proceedings of the USENIX Conference, Summer 1984*, pp. 203-207.

[Levy 80] Levy, H.M., and R.H. Eckhouse, *Computer Programming and Architecture: The VAX-11*, Digital Press, Bedford, MA, 1980.

[Levy 82] Levy, H.M., and P.H. Lipman, "Virtual Memory Management in the VAX/VMS Operating System," *Computer*, Vol. 15, No. 3, March 1982, pp. 35-41.

[Lu 83] Lu, P.M., W. A. Dietrich, et. al., "Architecture of a VLSI MAP for BELLMAC-32 Microprocessor," *Proc. of IEEE Spring Compcon*, Feb. 28, 1983, pp. 213-217.

[Luderer 81] Luderer, G.W.R., H. Che, J.P. Haggerty, P.A. Kirslis, and W.T. Marshall, "A Distributed UNIX System Based on a Virtual Circuit Switch," *Proceedings of the Eighth Symposium on Operating Systems Principles*, Asilomar, California, December 14-16, 1981.

[Lycklama 78a] Lycklama, H. and D. L. Bayer, "The MERT Operating System," *The Bell System Technical Journal*, Vol. 57, No. 6, Part 2, July-August 1978, pp. 2049-2086.

[Lycklama 78b] Lycklama, H. and C. Christensen, "A Minicomputer Satellite Processor System," *The Bell System Technical Journal*, Vol. 57, No. 6, Part 2, July-August 1978, pp. 2103-2114.

[McKusick 84] McKusick, M.K., W.N. Joy, S.J. Leffler, and R.S. Fabry, "A Fast File System for UNIX," *ACM Transactions on Computer Systems*, Vol. 2(3), August 1984, pp. 181-197.

[Mullender 84] Mullender, S.J. and A.S. Tanenbaum, "Immediate Files," *Software - Practice and Experience*, Vol. 14(4), April 1984, pp. 365-368.

[Nowitz 80] Nowitz, D.A. and M.E. Lesk, "Implementation of a Dial-Up Network of UNIX Systems," *IEEE Proceedings of Fall 1980 COMPCON*, Washington, D.C., pp. 483-486.

[Organick 72] Organick, E.J., *The Multics System: An Examination of Its Structure*, The MIT Press, Cambridge, MA, 1972.

[Peachey 84] Peachey, D.R., R.B. Bunt, C.L. Williamson, and T.B. Brecht, "An Experimental Investigation of Scheduling Strategies for UNIX," *Performance Evaluation Review, 1984 SIGMETRICS Conference on Measurement and Evaluation of Computer Systems*, Vol. 12(3), August 1984, pp. 158-166.

[Peterson 83] Peterson, James L. and A. Silberschatz, *Operating System Concepts*, Addison-Wesley, Reading, MA, 1983.

[Pike 84] Pike, R., "The Blit: A Multiplexed Graphics Terminal," *AT&T Bell Laboratories Technical Journal*, Oct. 1984, Vol 63, No. 8, Part 2, pp. 1607-1632.

[Pike 85] Pike, R., and P. Weinberger, "The Hideous Name," *Proceedings of the USENIX Conference, Summer 1985*, pp. 563-568.

[Postel 80] Postel, J. (ed.), "DOD Standard Transmission Control Protocol," *ACM Computer Communication Review*, Vol. 10, No. 4, Oct. 1980, pp. 52-132.

[Postel 81] Postel, J., C.A. Sunshine, and D. Cohen, "The ARPA Internet Protocol," *Computer Networks*, Vol. 5, No. 4, July 1981, pp. 261-271.

[Raleigh 76] Raleigh, T.M., "Introduction to Scheduling and Switching under UNIX," *Proceedings of the Digital Equipment Computer Users Society*, Atlanta, Ga., May 1976, pp. 867-877.

[Richards 69] Richards, M., "BCPL: A Tool for Compiler Writing and Systems Programming," *Proc. AFIPS SJCC 34*, 1969, pp. 557-566.

[Ritchie 78a] Ritchie, D. M. and K. Thompson, "The UNIX Time-Sharing System," *The Bell System Technical Journal*, July-August 1978, Vol. 57, No. 6, Part 2, pp. 1905-1930.

[Ritchie 78b] Ritchie, D. M., "A Retrospective," *The Bell System Technical Journal*, July-August 1978, Vol. 57, No. 6, Part 2, pp. 1947-1970.

[Ritchie 81] Ritchie, D.M. and K. Thompson, "Some Further Aspects of the UNIX Time-Sharing System," *Mini-Micro Software*, Vol. 6, No. 3, 1981, pp. 9-12.

[Ritchie 84a] Ritchie, D. M., "The Evolution of the UNIX Time-sharing System," *AT&T Bell Laboratories Technical Journal*, Oct. 1984, Vol 63, No. 8, Part 2, pp. 1577-1594.

[Ritchie 84b] Ritchie, D. M., "A Stream Input Output System," *AT&T Bell Laboratories Technical Journal*, Oct. 1984, Vol 63, No. 8, Part 2, pp. 1897-1910.

[Rochkind 85] Rochkind, M.J., *Advanced UNIX Programming*, Prentice-Hall, 1985.

[Saltzer 66] Saltzer, J. H., *Traffic Control in a Multiplexed Computer System*, Ph.D. Thesis, MIT, 1966.

[Sandberg 85] Sandberg, R., D. Goldberg, S. Kleiman, D. Walsh, and B. Lyon, "Design and Implementation of the Sun Network Filesystem" *Proceedings of the USENIX Conference*, Summer 1985, pp. 119-131.

[SVID 85] *System V Interface Definition*, Spring 1985, Issue 1, AT&T Customer Information Center, Indianapolis, IN.

[SystemV 84a] *UNIX System V User Reference Manual*.

[SystemV 84b] *UNIX System V Administrator's Manual*.

[Thompson 74] Thompson, K. and D.M. Ritchie, "The UNIX Time-Sharing System," *Communications of the ACM*, Vol. 17, No. 7, July, 1974, pp. 365-375 (revised and reprinted in [Ritchie 78a]).

[Thompson 78] Thompson, K., "UNIX Implementation," *The Bell System Technical Journal*, Vol. 57, No. 6, Part 2, July-August, 1978, pp. 1931-1946.

[Weinberger 84] Weinberger, P.J., "Cheap Dynamic Instruction Counting," *The AT&T Bell Laboratories Technical Journal*, Vol. 63, No. 6, Part 2, October 1984, pp. 1815-1826.

A

Abortive return, 170
Accept system call, 385
Ada, 4
Address space, 171, 277
Address translation, 18, 151, 154-157, 160, 181, 189
Administration, 34, 41, 276, 295, 314, 325, 328
Age bit, 287, 288
Alarm signal, 150, 201, 260
Alarm system call, 258, 260, 261, 270
    algorithm, 84-86
    use of, 92, 101
Allocreg algorithm, 172, 173, 224
    use of, 178, 179, 220, 223, 367
Architecture, 5, 19
Asynchronous execution, 11, 233, 235
Asynchronous I/O, 46, 54
Asynchronous write, 48, 55
AT&T 3B2 computer, 189
AT&T 3B20 computer, 223, 230, 267, 336, 397
AT&T 3B20A computer, 395, 408, 409
AT&T, 1, 3, 256
Atomic operation, 134, 142, 370, 378, 397, 401
Attachreg algorithm, 173, 174
    use of, 178, 194, 220, 223, 369

B

B language, 2
Bach, 395, 408
Background execution, 12, 37, 233, 353
Basic, 4
BCPL, 2
Beck, 410
Bell Laboratories, 1, 3
Berkeley, University of California at, 3,
    See also BSD
Bind system call, 384
Birrell, 414

Block device, 21, 23, 122, 134, 139, 313, 314
    buffer cache and, 323
    close procedure, 320
    interface to disk, 326, 327
Block device special file, 88, 108
Block device switch table, 314-317, 327
Block number, 39, 41-43, 289, 325
Bmap algorithm, 68-70, 89
    use of, 75, 97, 102
Bodenstab, 4
Boot block, 24, 119, 235, 326
Boot system, 24, 109, 134, 156, 235, 236, 268
Bootstrap, 24, 235
Bourne, Steve, 12, 13
Bread algorithm, 54, 60
    strategy procedure and, 322
    use of, 65, 75, 83, 98
Breada algorithm, 54, 55
    use of, 60, 98, 100
Break key, 201, 204, 210, 245, 342
Brelse algorithm, 46
    use of, 48, 54, 55, 56, 75
Brk system call, 21, 229
    algorithm, 229-231
    shared memory and, 369
    swap and, 276, 279
    use of, 243
Brownbridge, 413
BSD, 3, 72, 141, 209, 240, 271, 291, 292, 309, 342, 383, 384, 388
Bss, 25, 220, 293
Buffer, 21, 39, 41, 42, 46
    alignment, 56
    allocation, 44-52, 92, *See also* getblk
    allocation in multiprocessor, 404
    comparison to inode, 65
    busy, 40, 43, 46, 48, 51
    no reference count, 63
Buffer cache, 38-57
    advantages and disadvantages 56, 57
    analogous to page cache, 289
    disk interface, 328

driver close procedure, 320
not used in swapping, 276
umount and, 127
used for block device, 314
Buffer header, 39, 40, 48
driver strategy procedure and, 322
Buffer queue, 41-43, 48
Building block primitives, 13
Built-in command, 232
Bwrite algorithm, 56
strategy procedure and, 322
use of, 107
Byte offset, 68, 325
Byte stream, 4, 7

C

C, 2, 4
C library, 165, 167
in Newcastle connection, 413, 423-425,
430, 431
Callout table, 263, 264
Canonical mode, 329, 334, 336
Catch signal, *See* Signal, catch
Cblock, 331-334
Central processor, in satellite system, 414
Change directory, *See* chdir system call,
109
Change mode, *See* chmod system call, 110
Change owner, *See* chown system call, 110
Change root, *See* chroot system call, 109
Changed root, 213
Changing (execution) mode, 157
Character device, 21, 313, 352, *See also*
Raw device
close procedure, 320
Character device special file, 88, 108
Character device switch table, 314-317,
327
Chdir system call, 109, 144
use of, 123
Checking signals, 202
Child process, 25, 192
Chmod command, 89, 243
Chmod system call, 21, 110
devices and, 323
read-only file system and, 144

sticky bit and, 225, 226
Chown system call, 21, 110
read-only file system and, 144
Chroot system call, 74, 109, 110, 143
fork and, 194
in Newcastle connection, 425
Client process, 382, 388, 424
Clist, 331-334, 344
Clock, 260, 265-268
restarting, 262
Clock handler, 251, 254, 262, 269, 280
in multiprocessor, 395
Clock interrupt, 247, 251, 253, 265
Clock tick, 247, 268
Close system call, 21, 103-105
driver interface, 314, 318-320
dup and, 119
inode and, 65
pipe and, 115
relation to inode lock, 100
sockets, 386
use of, 198, 234
Cobol, 4
Coffman, 397
Cole, 429
Command, 11
Command line, 11, 234
Compare and swap instruction, 397
Computing Science Research Center, 2
Concurrent Euclid, 410
Conditional P semaphore operation, *See* CP
semaphore operation
Conditional semaphore, IPC, 378
Configuration, 41, 57, 313, 314
Connect system call, 385
Consent Decree, 3
Consistency
file data, 101
file system, 133, 139
kernel, 168
link and, 129
Context, 16, 29, 156, 160, 161, 195
definition, 159
exec and, 220
fork and, 196
saving, 162
Context layer, 160-165, 168, 169, 183, 195,
207

Context switch, 29, 31, 33, 160, 168-170, 189, 190, 248, 254
  sleep and, 186
  tracing and, 358
Contiguous file, 67
Contiguous swap space, 272
Control q character, 353
Control s character, 353
Control terminal, 150, 213, 342, 343, 353
  standard input and, 96
Cooked input, 334
Copy on write bit, 287, 290, 303-306, 309
Core dump, 204, 205, 239
  in distributed system, 428
Corruption, 134, 392, 393
CP semaphore operation, 397, 403, 405, 411
Crash, 57, 133, 134, 139, 140, 370
Creat system call, 105-107, 143, 144
  and directory, 74
  locks and, 370
  read-only file system and, 144
  use of, 8, 13, 22, 234
Critical region of code, 30, 32, 33, 393
Current directory, 7, 12, 29, 74, 213, 245
  fork and, 194
  in Newcastle connection, 425
  initial, 109, 235
Current root, 29

D

Daemon process, 238
DARPA, 384
Data region, 25, 229
Data section, 24, 151
Datagram, 384, 386
Deadlock, 142, 169, 242, 380, 403
  in multiprocessor, 402, 404, 406
  link and, 130, 131
  swap and, 285
Death of child signal, 200, 201, 203, 209, 210, 213-217, 239, 241
DEC, 325
Defense Advanced Research Project Agency, *See* DARPA
Dekker, 372

Delayed write, 39, 40, 43, 48, 49, 55-60, 102
  umount and, 126
Delete key, 201, 204, 210, 245, 329, 342
Demand fill, 288, 293, 300, 303
Demand paging, 21, 152, 189, 190, 271, 272, 285-307
  in distributed system, 433
  on less sophisticated hardware, 306
Demand paging policy, 310
Demand paging system, defintion, 15
Demand zero, 289, 293, 300, 303
Denning, 286
Detachreg algorithm, 180, 181
  use of, 213, 220, 223, 370
Device, 4, 8, 15, 312
  in distributed system, 429, 432
  open procedure, 122
Device driver, 21, 312-324
  interface, 313, 315
  multiprocessor, 408
Device file, *See* Device special file
Device interrupt, 315, 324
Device number, 23, 39, 43, 63, 64, 120, 123, 289, 322, 325
  parameter to getblk, 44
Device special file, 6, 10, 60, 313, 315
  See also Character device special file
  and block device special file
Dijkstra, 372, 389, 397
Direct block, *See* Inode, direct block
Directory, 6,7, 23, 60, 75, 76, 90, 108, 109, 133
  access permission, 74
  creat system call and, 74, 107
  creation of, 107
  linear search, 75, 76, 90
  link system call and, 74, 129
  mknod system call and, 74
  structure, 73, 74, 89
  unlink system call and, 74
Directory hierarchy, 73, 137
Disk, 52-56
  configuration, 326
  raw interface, 352
Disk block
  allocation, 84, 86, 85, 87, 102

buffer and, 42
   free, 132
Disk block descriptor, 286, 288-290, 293,
   298-301
Disk driver, 52-54, 325
Disk section and file system, 121
Distributed systems, 412, 413
DMA, 289, 322
Domain, 384
Dot, 10, 73, 108, 142, 241
   link and, 132
Dot-dot, 73, 108, 142, 241
   in distributed system, 427
   in Newcastle connection, 432
   mount point and, 126
Double fault, 302
Driver, *See* Device driver
Dummy process, 409
Dup system call, 117-119
   comparison to fork, 194
   reference count and, 104
   shared pointer and, 96
   use of, 198, 199, 234
Dup2 system call, 144
Dupreg, 182
   use of, 194
DZ11 Controller, 321

E

Echo, 329, 340
Effective user ID, 150, 211, 227, 228
End-of-file, 100, 213, 339, 353
Erase character, 334, 337
Erase key, 329
Event, *See* Sleep event
Exception condition, 16, 156, 200
   context and, 162
Exec environment, 217, 218
Exec system call, 21, 25, 200, 217
   algorithm, 218-225, 242
   disk block descriptor and, 288
   in paging system, 290, 293
   in satellite system, 431
   of setuid program, 229
   signals and, 200
   use of, 10, 233, 234

Execl, 217
Execle, 217
Execlp, 245
Executable file
   layout, 218, 219
   page from, 293
Execv, 217
Execve, 217
Execvp, 245
Exit system call, 21, 147, 212, 216, 225,
   242
   algorithm 212, 213
   context switch and, 168, 169, 254
   current directory and, 109
   receipt of signal and, 203
   in muliprocessor, 408
   in satellite system, 419, 431
   use of, 8, 10
Expansion swap, 279

F

Fair share scheduler, 255, 257, 269
Fault handler, 307
Fclose, 140
Fcntl system call, 142, 313
Feedback, 248
Felton, 4
Fflush, 57
FIFO, 88
File, 21, 68
   access permission, 8, 22, 60, 61, 65, 67,
      93, 108, 151, 227
   access permission and chdir, 109
   access time, 61, 67
   group, 8, 61, 74, 110
   link count, 129
   links, 62, 65
   offset and pipe, 113
   owner, 8, 60, 61, 65, 67, 74, 110, 227
   size, 60, 62, 65, 151
   structure, 60, 69
   type, 61, 65, 83, 86
File descriptor, 8, 23, 29, 92-98, 101, 103,
   104, 107, 117, 118, 135, 200, 316,
   318
   in satellite system, 417

File locking, 100, 103, 135, 142
File subsystem, 19, 21, 22
File system, 15, 23, 43, 84, 91, 119-122
   address, 325
   disk section and, 352
   hierarchy, *See* File system tree
   initialization, 73
   link and, 128
   maintenance, 122, 134, 139, 140
   root 6, 109, 110
   structure, 24, 92
   tree, 4, 6, 121, 92, 120, 139
   user perspective 6-10
File system abstraction, 138, 145
File system calls, 92
File system type, 138, 139
File table, 22, 93-98, 101, 104, 105, 107,
     112, 117, 118, 194, 316, 318, 323
   analogous to pregion, 152
   driver close procedure, 319
   in satellite system, 416
   offset, 93, 97-99, 101, 103
First-fit, 272
First-in-first-out buffer replacement, 57, 58
Flow control, 320, 350, 429
Fopen, 140
Fork system call, 21, 25, 147, 192
   algorithm, 193-198
   copy on write and, 303
   current directory and, 109
   in Newcastle connection, 425
   in paging system, 289, 290, 291, 297,
     309
   in satellite system, 417-419
   reference count and, 104
   shared pointer and, 96
   swap and, 276, 278, 279
   use of, 10, 199, 233, 234
   usually followed by exec, 226
Fortran, 2, 4
Fragmentation, 67, 68, 72, 141, 142, 272,
   297
Fread, 140
Free algorithm, 85
   use of, 92, 107, 132
Free library routine, 243
Free list

buffer, 41, 43, 46, 48, 56, 60
disk block, 139
inode, 63, 64, 67
page, 300
Freereg algorithm, 179-181, 225, 370
Fsck command, 134, 139, 326, 328, 352
Fstat system call, 110, 111
Fubyte, 171
Fwrite, 140

G

GECOS, 2
General Electric 1
General-purpose registers, 159
Getblk algorithm, 43, 44
   comparison to iget, 64
   in multiprocessor, 40-407, 411
   use of, 46-56, 122
Geteuid system call, 227
Getpgrp system call, 211
Getpid system call, 211
Getppid in satellite system, 416
Getsockname system call, 386
Getsockopt system call, 386
Getty, 212, 238, 246, 318, 343, 353, 382
Getuid system call, 227
Goble, 393
Growreg algorithm, 174-176, 177
   use of, 174, 178, 179, 220, 229
Gtty system call, 323

H

Handling signals, *See* Signal handler
Hangup signal, 213, 353
Hash function, 41, 42, 58
Henry, 256
History, 1
Holley, 393
Holt, 410
Honeywell 635, 2
Hybrid system, 307

I

I/O parameters, 29

I/O Subsystem, 312
Ialloc algorithm, 77-84, 122
 use of, 92, 107, 112
IBM System/370, 4, 322, 395, 397
IBM 7900, 25
Ifree algorithm, 80
 use of, 92, 132
Iget algorithm, 64-66, 89 123, 124
 comparison to getblk, 64
 mount point and, 122-124
 use of, 75, 76, 82, 109, 132, 223
Inconsistency, 100, 139
Indirect block, *See* Inode, indirect block
Indirect terminal driver, 343, 353
Init, 25, 212, 213, 216, 235-237, 245, 246,
 343, 353, 382
Inittab, 236, 237
Inode, 22, 23, 24, 38, 60, 62, 65, 68-71,
 74-76, 81, 88, 93-96, 100, 102, 105,
 107-109, 118, 121, 123, 126, 139,
 225, 316, 318
 accessing, 64
 assignment of, 77-86
 close system call and, 65
 comparison to region, 152
 definition of, 61
 direct block, 68-71, 74, 102, 114, 132
 exec system call and, 220
 file system type and, 138
 in distributed system, 428, 429
 in region, 173
 in satellite system, 416
 indirect block,, 68-71, 74, 100-102, 132
 link count, 129-135, 139
 lock, 63
 mount system call and, 353
 open system call and, 65
 pipe system call and, 114
 reference count, 63, 65-67, 104, 109,
  112, 121, 126, 129, 130, 132, 135,
  145, 192, 194, 223-225, 316
 releasing, 67
Inode cache, 66, 67
Inode list, 24, 65, 76, 77, 80, 119
Inode number, 63, 73, 77, 79-81, 89, 107,
 108, 132, 139
Integrity, 135

buffer cache, 46
file system, 57
kernel, 168
Intelligent terminal, 339
Interactive Systems Corporation, 3
Internet domain, 384, 387
Interprocess communication, 21, 22, 355,
 359-381 general comments, 381
Interrupt, 16, 22, 29, 30, 46, 190, 314
 disk, 54, 56
Interrupt handler, 31-33, 163, 164, 324
 context and, 160, 162
 context switch and, 168, 169
 disk, 56
 in multiprocessor, 403, 406
 terminal, 337
Interrupt level, 161
Interrupt stack, 163
Interrupt vector, 162, 163, 315, 324
Interruptible priority, 201, 209, 215, 252,
 377
Ioctl system call, 313, 314, 323, 330
 networks, 382
 streams, 347, 348, 350
 terminal, 339, 340
IPC, *See* Interprocess communication
Iput algorithm, 66, 89
 use of, 75, 76, 109, 110, 126, 129, 132,
  179, 221, 223
Issig algorithm, 201, 203
 in wait, 214

K

Kernel, 4
 introduction to, 19
 data structures, 34
 layout, 156
Kernel mode, 15, 16, 26, 30, 31, 147, 157
Kernel priority, 249, 250, 252
Kernel process, 238
Kernel profiler, 312
Kernel running state, 30, 147-150, 182
Kernel stack, 26, 27, 160-163, 168, 189,
 195, 220
 swap and, 278
Kernighan, Brian, 2

Key, IPC, 359, 360, 381
Kill character, 329, 334, 337
Kill system call, 200, 201, 210, 211, 239
   comparison to IPC, 355
   effective user ID and, 227
   use of, 207
Killian, 138, 359

L

Least-frequently-used buffer replacement,
   57, 58
Least-recently-used, 40, 41
Levy, 306, 307, 321
Library, 20, 26, 165, 168
Library interface, 19
Line break, 329
Line discipline, 329-334, 336, 339, 342,
   347, 350, 353
Link count, *See* File link count
Link system call, 22, 128-131, 135
   across file systems, 120
   directory, 74
   read-only file system and, 144
   use of, 241
Lisp, 4
Listen system call, 385
Loadreg algorithm, 176-178
   use of, 179, 220, 223
Locality principle, 286
Lock, 33
   buffer, 40, 46, 50, 53, 54
   inode, 64-66, 97, 100, 316
   region, 172
   sleep, 395
   super block, 77, 84
Lock file, 370
Logging in, 343, 344
Logical block, 23, 24
Logical block number, 100
Logical device number, *See* Device number
Logical device, 23
Logical disk block, 39
Login, 229, 238, 353
   algorithm, 344
Login shell, 343
   process group and, 210

Login terminal, 150, 204 *See also* Control
   terminal
Longjmp algorithm, 170, 171, 240
   use of, 188, 209, 318, 420
Lseek system call, 71, 103, 104
   adjusts file offset, 98
   devices and, 323
   pipe and, 113
   signals and, 200
Lycklama, 3, 4

M

Major number, 88, 108, 121, 218, 219,
   316, 322, 352
Malloc algorithm, 273
Malloc library routine, 243
Mandatory file lock, 142
Map, 272, 273, 277, 308
   messages, 361
Massachusetts Institute of Technology, 1
Master processor, 393, 410
MC 68451 memory management unit, 189
McKusick, 72
Memory contention, 410
Memory fault, 231
Memory management, 21, 17, 154
Memory management policy, 152, 271
Memory management register triple, 155-
   158, 174
Memory management subsystem, 151
Memory mapped I/O, 321
MERT, 3,4
Message, 22, *See also* Streams message
   descriptor, 361, 362, 367
   header, 362
   in distributed system, 415, 416
   IPC, 359, 361-366, 389
   queue, 361
   type, 361-366
Mfree algorithm, 308
Minor number, 88, 108, 121, 316, 322, 352
Mkdir command, 145, 229, 241, 424
   link and, 129
Mkdir system call, 129, 424
Mkfs command, 73, 84, 326, 352
Mknod command, 314

Mknod system call, 10, 107, 108, 143, 314, 352, 353
  directory, 74
  use of, 241
Modify bit, 287, 288, 296, 303, 305, 306
Monitor, 410
Motorola 68000, 166, 167, 189
Mount command, 123
Mount point, 63, 120-127, 144
  crossing, 122, 123
Mount system call, 24, 119-123, 145, 235
  buffers and, 52
  device and, 314
  disk sections and, 325
  in distributed system, 426, 427
Mount table, 120-123, 126
Msgctl system call, 361, 367
Msgget system call, 361
  use of, 365
Msgrcv system call, 361
  algorithm, 365
  use of, 390
Msgsnd system call, 361
  algorithm, 362
Mullender, 72
Multics, 2, 190
Multihop, 433
Multilevel feedback, 248
Multiplexing, 348-350
Multiprocessor systems, 391, 392, 395
  performance, 410
Mutual exclusion, 30, 77, 410

N

Named pipe, 111-117, 144
  creation of, 107
Namei algorithm, 74, 75, 90, 125, 126
  chroot and, 110
  in distributed system, 427
  mount point and, 122-126
  unlink and, 135
  use of, 92, 93, 106, 129, 221, 223
Network communications, 23, 382, 383
  IPC and, 381
Newcastle connection, 413, 414, 422-425, 430-432

Nice command, 269
Nice system call, 254
  use of, 207, 208
Nice value, 255, 282
  fork and, 194
  swap and, 280, 285
No delay
  driver open procedure, 318
  named pipe and, 115
  terminal, 341
Non-preemption, 30
Nowitz, 382
NSC Series 32000, 189
Nucleus, 410

O

Open system call, 21, 22, 92-96
  comparison to chdir, 109
  comparison to creat, 106
  comparison to shared memory, 370
  driver interface, 314, 316-318
  in distributed system, 427, 428
  in Newcastle connection, 424
  in satellite system, 416
  inode and, 63, 65
  multiple calls, 101
  named pipe and, 111, 113, 115
  sticky bit and, 226
  terminal, 343
  unlink and, 135, 137
  use of, 8
Operating system services, 14
Operating system trap, 165, 166
Organick, 2

P

P semaphore operation, 372, 389, 396-402, 408, 411
Page, 152-154, 230, 272, 286, 289, 300
  aging, 295, 296
  cache, 289
  fault, 190, 293, 298
Page frame data table, *See* Pfdata
Page stealer, 238, 294-297, 300, 307, 309, 310

Page table, 153-160, 175-177, 189, 193,
        277, 286, 288, 290, 291, 296, 301,
        302, 305, 308
Paging, *See* Demand paging
Parent process, 25, 192
Pascal 4
Password, 242
Path name, 6, 7, 60, 73-76, 134
    conversion to inode, 74, 75
    in distributed system, 423
    unlink and, 137
PATH, 245
Pause system call, 211, 270
PDP, 223, 271
PDP 11/23, 284
PDP 11/70, 219
PDP 7, 2
Peachey, 282, 284
Per process region table, *See* Pregion
Pfault algorithm, *See* Protection fault
        handler
Pfdata, 286, 289, 291, 297, 301-303, 305,
        309
Physical memory, 151, 278
PID, 25, 150, 192-194, 214
Pike, 348, 423
Pipe, 13, 60, 88, 108, 111, 116, 117, 144,
        226, 239, 245
    consistency and, 139
    delayed write and, 102
    signal and, 200
Pipe system call, 112, 143
    comparison to IPC, 355
    standard input and, 96
    use of, 198, 199, 234
Pipe device, 112
Pipeline, 245
Plock system call, 310
Pop streams module, 347
Postel, 384
Preempt state, 147-150, 248
Preemption, 100, 254, 392
Pregion, 26, 28, 152, 155, 161, 173, 177,
        179, 181, 291
    context and, 160
    shared memory, 368
Prepaging, 309

Primary header, 218, 219
Priority queue, 252
Priority, 21, 169, 187, 194, 247, 249, 250,
        252, 253, 255, 268, 269, 282, 305
Prober instruction, 171
Process
    creation, 192
    definition, 10
    environment, 10
    overview, 24
    scheduling, 14, 21, 33
    structure, 146
    synchronization, 21
Process accounting, 213, 260, 267
    streams and, 351
Process control subsystem, 19, 21
Process group, 210, 213, 241
Process ID, *See* PID
Process state, 30, 147-149
    Process state diagram, *See* State
            transition diagram
    Process state transition, *See* State
            transition
Process table, 26, 28, 29, 150, 192, 246
    context and, 160
    definition, 149
    ps and, 354
    shared memory and, 368
Process tree, pipes and, 111
Process *0*, 25, 74, 109, 147, 212, 235, 238,
        280, *See also* Swapper
Process *1*, 25, 212, 235, 343, *See also* Init
Processor execution level, 17, 32, 33, 46,
        58, 89, 162, 186, 190
Processor priority, *See* Processor execution
        level
Processor status register, 159
Profil system call, 265, 266
Profile driver, 264
Profiling, 260, 264, 265
Program counter, 159
Program, 10
Programmed I/O, 322
Programmed interrupt, 162, 264
Prolog, 4
Protection bits, 286, 305, 310
Protection fault, 223, 298, 303-305

Protection fault handler, 303
    algorithm, 304
    interaction with validity fault handler,
      306
Ps command, 312, 354
PS register, 159, 166, 167
Pseudo-terminal, 349
Ptrace system call, 356-359, 389
Push streams module, 347
Put procedure, 345, 350

Q

Quit key, 342
Quit signal, 205

R

Race condition, 77
    assignment of inodes, 82-84
    buffer, 51, 53
    in distributed system, 430
    in multiprocessor, 396
    link and, 135
    signals and, 207-209
    umount, 144
    unlink, 134, 136
Raw device interface, 327, *See also*
    Character device
Raw disk interface, 134, 139, 326, 328,
    329, 352
Raw I/O, 322
Raw mode, *See* Terminal, raw mode
Read ahead, 54-56, 98-100, 141
Read and clear instruction, 397, 400
Read system call, 21, 96-101, 140
    disk interface, 327, 328
    driver interface, 314, 320, 328
    fork and, 197
    in distributed system, 428
    page fault and, 293
    pipe and, 113-115, 143
    terminal, 187, 188, 336-341
    terminal and satellite system, 421, 422
    use of, 8, 233
Read-only file system, 119, 122, 144
Ready to run state, 33, 147-150, 182, 183,
    190, 195, 248, 254, 279, 281, 307,
    399

Real user ID, 150, 227, 228
Real-time processing, 257, 258
Record Locking, 100, 103, 135, 142
Recovery of distributed system, 433
Recv system call, 386
Recvfrom system call, 386
Redirect I/O, 13, 234
Reference bit, 286-288, 294, 295, 306
    software, 307
Reference count, *See* Inode reference count
Reference count, *See* Region reference
    count
Region, 25, 26, 28, 153-157, 174, 181, 213,
    222, 276, 291
    allocation, 172
    attaching, 173, 175
    context and, 160
    definition, 152, 172
    detaching, 181
    duplication, 181
    exec, 28
    exit, 28
    fork, 28, 194
    freeing, 179
    inode pointer, 172
    loading, 176
    reference count, 172, 179, 181, 192,
      225, 290
    shared, 223, 225
    shared memory, 367-369
    size, 174
    type, 172
Register context, 159, 162-165, 168, 195,
    205, 207, 220
Regular file, 6, 7, 23, 60, 74
    delayed write and, 102
    reading, 96
    structure, 62-71
    writing, 101
Remote file system, 23, 138
Remote procedure call, 427-430
Remote system call, 427-430
Response time, 57, 249
Restartable instruction, 285
Richards, 2
Ritchie, Dennis, 2-4, 103, 142, 201, 209,
    226, 330, 344, 350

Rmdir command, 134
Root directory, 73, 74
Root inode, 24, 76, 120, 122, 123, 127, 145
Root inode number, 73, 123
Round robin, 248, 251, 255
RP07 disk, 325, 326
Rubout key, 342

S

Sandberg, 427, 429
Satellite process, 415
Satellite system, 413-422
Saved user ID, 227, 229
Sbrk system call, 174
Scheduler, 21, 150, 169, 186, 187, 190,
    247-249, 253, 255, 257, 272
  algorithm, 248
  clock and, 260
  in multiprocessor, 393, 394
Sdb, 356, 358
Section header, 218, 219
Security, 135, 243
Select system call, 342
  use of, 388
Semaphore
  contention, 410
  IPC, 359, 370-381
  multiprocessor, 395-397, 402
  primitives coded in C, 398-400
Semctl system call, 373, 380
Semget system call, 373
Semop system call, 373, 376-379
SEM-UNDO flag, 378
Send system call, 386
Sendto system call, 386
Server process, 382, 387, 429-432
Service procedure, 345, 347, 350
Setjmp, algorithm, 170, 171
  use of, 188, 318
Setpgrp system call, 210, 211
  terminal, 342
  use of, 343
Setuid program, 227-229, 243, 424
  tracing and, 359
Setuid system call, 227-229
Seventh Edition, 269

Shared memory, 151, 189, 359, 367-370,
    372, 389
  attaching, 371
  in distributed system, 433
  region, 181
Shared memory table, 368
Shell, 11, 12, 15, 336, 343, 353
  dup and, 119
  exec and, 226
  implementation, 232-235, 244, 245
Shell pipeline, dup and, 118
Shmat system call, 367-369
Shmctl system call, 367, 370
Shmdt system call, 367, 369
Shmget system call, 367, 368
Shutdown system call, 386
Signal, 21, 22, 130, 150, 187, 200-210,
    239-241, 245, 249
  catching, 205-209, 220
  checking, 305
  driver open procedure, 318
  fault causes, 300
  handler, 202-205, 210, 240
  ignoring, 203
  in distributed system, 429, 430
  in satellite system, 419-422, 431
  pipe and, 200
  recognition, 203
  sleep and, 188
  from terminal, 329, 342
Signal system call, 200-210, 240
  in satellite system, 419
Sixth Edition, 269
(Slash) /proc, 359
Slave processor, 393, 410
Sleep, 30, 31, 33, 37, 201, 249
  address, 183, 184
  algorithm, 150, 182-190, 209
  comparison to P operation, 399
  context switch and, 169, 254
  event, 28, 33, 34, 37, 150, 183, 184,
    187
  in wait, 214
  lock, 395, 396
  priority, 187, 188
  streams and, 351
  swap and, 280

Sleep library routine, 270

Sleep state, 28, 30, 150, 147, 148, 182, 183

Socket system call, 384
    use of, 387

Sockets, 383-387

Software device, 312

Software interrupt, 162, 264, 347

Space Travel, 2

Special file, 88, 108
    creation of, 107
    See also Character device special file
        and Block device special file

Spin lock, 403

Stack, 24

Stack frame, 25

Stack pointer, 25, 159, 168

Stack region, 25

Stack section, 151

Standard error, 13, 96, 200

Standard I/O Library, 20, 57, 99, 140

Standard input, 13, 96, 198, 200, 226, 234, 353

Standard output, 13, 96, 119, 198, 200, 226, 234

Starvation, 52

Stat system call, 21, 110, 111
    devices and, 323

State transition, 30, 147

State transition diagram, 30, 147, 148, 202

Sticky bit, 181, 225, 226, 242

Stime system call, 258, 268

Strategy interface, 314-316, 322, 325, 328

Stream socket, 384

Stream-head, 345-347

Streams, 344-351
    analysis, 350
    message, 346
    module, 346, 347
    multiplexer, 351, 354
    queue, 345, 347
    scheduling, 347, 350, 353

Stty command, 353

Stty system call, 323

Stub process, 414-425, 429-432

Super block, 24, 38, 60, 76, 84, 90, 119-126, 139
    free block list, 84-87

free inode list, 77-83
    lock, 80, 84

Superuser, 36, 61, 110, 194, 211, 227, 229, 242, 245, 254, 310, 352, 360
    in Newcastle connection, 424
    link and, 128
    mount and, 121

SVID, 170, 339

Swap device, 15, 271, 272, 275-277, 289, 297, 300
    exec and, 220, 226

Swap map, 274, 275

Swap space, 272, 274, 275
    allocation in paging system, 298

Swap-use table, 286, 289, 290, 297

Swapped state, 147-149, 307, 280

Swapper process, 21, 25, 147, 212, 238, 280, 310
    algorithm, 281, 282
    clock and, 260

Swapping, 21, 152, 189, 271-285, 307, 309
    in distributed system, 433
    signal and, 300
    strategy procedure and, 322

Swapping system, definition, 15

Symbolic link, 145

Sync system call, buffers and, 60

System call, 5
    buffers and, 51
    context and, 160, 164
    context switch and, 168
    for devices, 313
    interface, 19, 165-168
    interrupt in satellite system, 421, 422
    multiprocesser interface, 394

System III, 3

System memory layout, 151

System V, 1, 3, 6, 12, 25, 68, 73, 89, 90, 103, 120, 138, 142, 152, 200, 221, 240, 251, 252, 272, 275, 286, 290-292, 307, 325, 326, 336, 344, 359, 372, 383

System-level context, 159-161

T

Tab character, 329

Tannenbaum, 72
TCP, 384
Terminal, 238, 353
    driver, 329-342, 351
    hangup, 329
    in distributed system, 430, 432
    open procedure, 317, 318
    raw mode, 263, 329, 330, 339, 340, 351
    signals and, 201
    virtual, 354
Text, 24
Text region, 25, 222-226
Text section, 151
Text table, 223
Thompson, Ken, 2, 3, 96, 103, 226, 251
Threshold priority, 250
Throughput, 57, 60, 250, 307
Time, 258, 260, 268
    in multiprocessor, 411
Time quantum, 14, 21, 247, 248, 251
Time sharing, 14, 30, 247
Time slice, 190, 247
Time system call, 258, 268
Timeout, 263
Times system call, 258
Times, use of, 259, 260
Tracing, 356, 359
Transparent distribution, 414, 426
Transport Connect Protocol, *See* TCP
Trap instruction, 26, 356, 357
Tunis system, 410

U

U area, 26, 28, 29, 93
    chroot and, 110
    context and, 160, 161
    current directory and, 74, 109, 150
    current root, 150
    definition, 150
    directory offset and creat, 107
    exec and, 220
    fork and, 194, 195
    I/O parameters, 97-100, 115, 150, 178, 325, 328
    process accounting and, 267
    signal handler and, 205

    signals and, 203
    swap and, 278, 308
    system call parameters, 166
    virtual address, 156-158
UDP, 384
UID, 28, 150
Umount system call, 119, 126, 127, 144, 145, 353
    buffers and, 52, 60
    device and, 314
    sticky bit and, 226
Undo structure, 378-380
UNIVAC 1100 Series, 4
UNIX system domain, 384, 386-388
Unlink system call, 132-137, 143, 145
    comparison to shared memory, 370
    consistency and, 139, 140
    directory, 74
    named pipe and, 113
    read-only file system and, 144
    region and, 173
    sticky bit and, 226
User Datagram Protocol, *See* UDP
User file descriptor table, 22, 23, 93-95, 104-107, 117, 118, 150
User ID, 28, 74, 150, 227
User mode, 15, 16, 30, 51, 147, 149, 157, 165
User priority, 249, 250, 252, 254
User running state, 147-150
User stack, 26, 27, 174, 189, 230, 231
    signals and, 205, 207, 209
    swap and, 276
User-level context, 159, 161
Uucp, 382, 423

V

V semaphore operation, 372, 389, 396-403, 408, 411
Valid bit, 287, 296-298, 301, 303, 304, 306, 307, 310
    software, 306, 307
Valid page, 294
Validity fault, 286, 296, 298, 300, 301, 304
Validity fault handler, 293, 298, 299, 301, 305, 309

interaction with protection fault
handler, 306
VAX, 171, 189, 205, 206, 306, 307, 310,
321, 393
Version 6, 282
Version 7, 144
Vfault, algorithm, *See* Validity fault
handler
Vfork, 291, 292, 309
Vhand, *See* Page stealer
Virtual address, 18, 158, 189, 278, 298
Virtual address space, 15, 151, 152, 156,
159
Virtual address translation, *See* Address
translation
Virtual circuit, 384
Virtual terminal, 348, 349
VMS, 307
Volume table of contents, 326, 352

W

Wait system call, 21, 213, 216
algorithm, 214, 215, 242
in multiprocessor, 408
time and, 269

tracing and, 356, 357
use of, 233
Wakeup, 33, 34, 37, 184
algorithm, 150, 182, 186, 187, 190
comparison to V operation, 399, 403
Weinberger, 138, 265
Window of terminal, 348, 349, 354
Window of working set, 286
Working set, 286, 287, 307, 310
Write system call, 21, 71, 100-102
disk interface, 328
driver interface, 314, 320, 328
fork and, 197
pipe and, 113-115, 143
read-only file system and, 144
streams interface, 346
terminal interface, 334, 335
Write-append mode, 93, 140

X

Xalloc, algorithm, 223, 224

Z

Zombie, 147, 149, 213-217, 258, 280